Essays in honor of Nelson Glueck

NEAR EASTERN ARCHAEOLOGY
IN THE TWENTIETH CENTURY

"This is for a celebration . . ."

(From the subscription to Qumran Psalm 145:
Discoveries in the Judaean Desert, IV, p. 38)

NELSON GLUECK

Essays in Honor of Nelson Glueck

Near Eastern Archaeology in the Twentieth Century

Edited by
James A. Sanders

GARDEN CITY, NEW YORK
Doubleday & Company, Inc.

Library of Congress Catalog Card Number 75-103773
Copyright © 1970 by Hebrew Union College–Jewish Institute of Religion
All Rights Reserved
Printed in the United States of America

CONTENTS

I. INTRODUCTION

II. THE BRONZE AGE

III. THE IRON AGE

LIST OF PHOTOGRAPHS

ABBREVIATIONS

(See the footnotes of the several articles for other abbreviations
special to each)

AAA	*Annals of Archaeology and Anthropology*
AASOR	*Annual of the American Schools of Oriental Research*
ADAJ	*Annual of the Department of Antiquities of Jordan*
AfO	*Archiv für Orientforschung*
AJA	*American Journal of Archaeology*
AJSL	*American Journal of Semitic Languages and Literatures*
ANEP	*The Ancient Near East in Pictures*, ed. by J. B. Pritchard
ANET	*Ancient Near Eastern Texts Relating to the Old Testament*, ed. by J. B. Pritchard
AnOr	*Analecta Orientalia*
AnSt	*Anatolian Studies*
Ant	*Antiquity*
AOS	*American Oriental Society*
AOTS	*Archaeology and Old Testament Study*, ed. by D. Winton Thomas
APN	*Amorite Personal Names*, by H. B. Huffmon
Arch	*Archaeology*
ARM	*Archives Royales de Mari*, ed. by A. Parrot and G. Dossin
ArOr	*Archiv Orientální*
ASAE	*Annales du Service des Antiquités de l'Egypte*
AWBL	*The Art of Warfare in Biblical Lands*, by Y. Yadin
BA	*Biblical Archaeologist*
BANE	*The Bible and the Ancient Near East*, ed. by G. E. Wright
BASOR	*Bulletin of the American Schools of Oriental Research*
BBB	*Bonner Biblische Beiträge*
Bib	*Biblica*
BibOrPont	*Biblica et Orientalia* of the Pontifical Biblical Institute
BIES	*Bulletin of the Israel Exploration Society*
BInstArch	*Bulletin of the Institute of Archaeology, University of London*
BiTerS	*Bible et Terre Sainte*
BJPES	*Bulletin of the Jewish Palestine Exploration Society*
BZAW	*Beiheft zur Zeitschrift für die alttestamentliche Wissenschaft*
CAD	*Chicago Assyrian Dictionary*
CAH²	*Cambridge Ancient History* (revised edition)
CBQ	*Catholic Biblical Quarterly*

CIS	*Corpus Inscriptionum Semiticarum*
ClassW	*Classical Weekly*
COWA²	*Chronologies in Old World Archaeology*, ed. by R. W. Ehrich (1965)
CRAI	*Comptes Rendus de l'Académie des Inscriptions et Belles Lettres*
CTM	*Concordia Theological Monthly*
Exped	*Expedition*
HDB	*Harvard Divinity School Bulletin*
HTR	*Harvard Theological Review*
HTS	*Harvard Theological Studies*
IEJ	*Israel Exploration Journal*
ILN	*Illustrated London News*
IrAnt	*Iranica Antiqua*
JAOS	*Journal of the American Oriental Society*
JARCE	*Journal of the American Research Center in Egypt*
JBL	*Journal of Biblical Literature*
JCS	*Journal of Cuneiform Studies*
JE	*Jewish Encyclopedia*
JESHO	*Journal of Economic and Social History of the Orient*
JHS	*Journal of Hellenic Studies*
JNES	*Journal of Near Eastern Studies*
JPOS	*Journal of the Palestine Oriental Society*
LB	*The Land of the Bible*, by Y. Aharoni
MDOG	*Mitteilungen der Deutschen Orientgesellschaft*
MiOr	*Mitteilungen des Instituts für Orientforschung*
NedTTs	*Nederlands Theologisch Tijdschrift*
NumChron	*Numismatic Chronicle and Journal*
OIC	*Oriental Institute Communications*
OIP	*Oriental Institute Publications*
OLZ	*Orientalistische Literaturzeitung*
Or	*Orientalia*
OrAnt	*Oriens Antiquus*
PEFA	*Palestine Exploration Fund Annual*
PEFQS	*Palestine Exploration Fund Quarterly Statement*
PEQ	*Palestine Exploration Quarterly*
PJB	*Palästinajahrbuch*
QDAP	*Quarterly of the Department of Antiquities in Palestine*
RA	*Revue d'Assyriologie et d'Archéologie Orientale*
RB	*Revue Biblique*
RHPR	*Revue d'Histoire et de Philosophie Religieuses*
RHR	*Revue de l'Histoire des Religions*
RSO	*Rivista degli Studi Orientali*
Sem	*Semitica*

SDB	*Supplément au Dictionnaire de la Bible*
Syr	*Syria*
TB	Babylonian Talmud
TJ	Palestinian Talmud
VT	*Vetus Testamentum*
Yediot	*Yedi'ot baHaqirat Eretz-Israel ve'Atiqoteha* (Hebrew)
YGC	*Yahweh and the gods of Canaan*, by W. F. Albright
ZAW	*Zeitschrift für die Alttestamentliche Wissenschaft*
ZDMG	*Zeitschrift der Deutschen Morgenländischen Gesellschaft*
ZDPV	*Zeitschrift des Deutschen Palästina-Vereins*
ZfA	*Zeitschrift für Assyriologie*
ZfN	*Zeitschrift für Numismatik*
ZTK	*Zeitschrift für Theologie und Kirche*

CONTRIBUTORS

Yohanan Aharoni, Professor of Archaeology, Tel-Aviv University, Israel

W. F. Albright, Professor Emeritus of Near Eastern Studies, Johns Hopkins University

Ruth Amiran, Field Archaeologist, The Israel Museum, Jerusalem

N. Avigad, Professor of Archaeology, Hebrew University, Jerusalem

Fritz Bamberger, Professor of Intellectual History, Hebrew Union College–Jewish Institute of Religion, New York

R. D. Barnett, Keeper, Department of Western Asiatic Antiquities, The British Museum

Frank M. Cross, Jr., Hancock Professor of Hebrew and Oriental Languages and Literatures, Harvard University

William G. Dever, Resident Director, Hebrew Union College Biblical and Archaeological School, Jerusalem

George M. A. Hanfmann, Professor of Fine Arts, Fogg Art Museum, Harvard University

Kathleen M. Kenyon, Principal, St. Hugh's College, Oxford University

Paul W. Lapp, Professor of Old Testament and Archaeology, Pittsburgh Theological Seminary

Abraham Malamat, Professor of Bible and Ancient Jewish History, Hebrew University, Jerusalem

Joseph Naveh, Jerusalem District Archaeologist, Department of Antiquities, and Research Fellow, Institute of Archaeology, Hebrew University, Jerusalem

Jacob Neusner, Professor of Religious Studies, Brown University

Peter J. Parr, Lecturer in the Archaeology of the Levant, Institute of Archaeology, University of London

Marvin H. Pope, Professor of Northwest Semitic Languages and Literature, Yale University

James B. Pritchard, Curator of Biblical Archaeology, The University Museum, University of Pennsylvania

Jonathan Z. Smith, Assistant Professor of History of Religions, University of Chicago Divinity School

Roland de Vaux, Professor of History and Archaeology, Ecole biblique et archéologique française, Jerusalem

Eleanor K. Vogel, Archaeological Assistant, Hebrew Union College–Jewish Institute of Religion, Cincinnati

Jane C. Waldbaum, Research Fellow in Classical Art and Archaeology, Fogg
Art Museum, Harvard University

John A. Wilson, Professor of Egyptology, The Oriental Institute, The University of Chicago

G. Ernest Wright, Parkman Professor of Divinity and Curator of the Semitic
Museum, Harvard University

Yigael Yadin, Professor of Archaeology, Institute of Archaeology, Hebrew
University, Jerusalem

FOREWORD

"THIS IS FOR A CELEBRATION . . ."

James A. Sanders

IT IS a distinct honor for me to be associated in this manner with my teacher, Nelson Glueck. When I was first approached about editing this volume, my reactions were two—distinct, unmixed, but quite simultaneous: not being a field archaeologist and having no pretensions to that discipline, I knew I was unqualified for the assignment; but being a student of Nelson Glueck, I could not refuse an opportunity to honor him. It has been two years since contributions were invited. The minor difficulties I understand to be normally associated with editing a Festschrift have not been lacking, but those, too, I dedicate to Nelson Glueck. But no one (and I sought the advice of experienced scholars) had even hinted at the moments of intense joy experienced by the editor of a Festschrift as the volume takes shape. It has been a pleasure to receive these twenty-one papers and, with the help of others (see below), to make of them a gift that the contributors and I hope is worthy of the occasion, Nelson Glueck's seventieth birthday.

Nelson Glueck, born June 4, 1900, is a child of the twentieth century and, with it, has attained three score years and ten. As a boy growing up in Cincinnati, Glueck developed a love for his Jewish heritage that emerged less from a mediating orthodox tradition than from the young student's boundless curiosity about history and nature. Glueck's "emotional loyalty" to "the miracle of nascent Judaism" (as he put it to Fritz Bamberger) was inherited from his parents. That was the given. But as a true son of liberal Judaism, Glueck could not merely accept from the past the "genius of this people." He had to make it his own; he had literally "to dig for it": so he searched the ground for a background. Thus Glueck's past came alive for him, in the true sense of the ancient Hebrew cultic word *zikkaron* (celebration). The more rigorously scientific his search and research, the more he considered them a proper *kavvanah* (devotion). Neither the orthodox nor the secularist fully appreciates the genuine religious liberal like Glueck, who feels that objective investigation is the greatest *mitzvah* (duty) he can perform.

Our volume is intended as a *zikkaron:* a celebration of the lifelong labor of Nelson Glueck, who has made the background of the Bible a reality for himself and for others by the most rigorous scientific methods; and a lively exercise in the meaning of a professional career, a reflection of it and a promise of its meaning. *Zo't lezikkaron:* "This is for a celebration," says the subscription to Psalm 145 in the Cave 11 Psalter from Qumran.

The structure of the book is due to the early planning of George Ernest Wright of Harvard University. Without his original vision and his constant encouragement and advice to the editor, the volume might never have been done. Part I shows the growth of Near Eastern archaeology in the twentieth century and Nelson Glueck's influence upon its development. We have made no attempt to cover the field in all its aspects. The intention has been to appraise some of the major developments in archaeology, to offer an honest critique of what has happened in this field, and to identify its problems. Such openness and honesty best reflect the spirit and the work of the man we honor. Part II probes some of the most important problems encountered by students of the Bronze Age: synchronology, nomenclature, periodization and the origins of man's social organization, institutions and symbols. Part III touches on a few of the most important recent developments in Iron Age research, especially as they relate to problems arising out of biblical study. In Part III, as in all four sections, there are papers based mainly on archaeological fieldwork and others based principally on textual study. Here, and in the first paper in Part IV, three important studies in the area of semitic epigraphy are presented; as in other important areas of scholarly difficulty, more than one point of view is expressed. (It is perhaps the pluralistic and dialogical nature of the volume that most pleases the editor.) Part IV deals mainly with ancient Near Eastern art and archaeology in the later periods.

Since the editor is not also a contributor, he may justifiably express some pride in the value of the volume. It opens with strength and builds to a brilliant climax in the scoop report on ceramic chronology in the 1958–64 excavations at Petra, a site long associated with the name of Nelson Glueck. And if the editor may venture a prediction outside his field, a number of the papers are destined to become milliaria in their areas. No editor could have had a more reliable or luminous roster of scholars with whom to correspond. Each contributor added to the book his own considerable strength, so that editing has been largely an effort to coordinate scholarly references.

There are six people, other than Professors Wright and Bamberger, to whom I am grateful for assistance. Mrs. Margaret Apgar, executive assistant at Union Theological Seminary, did the early stenographic and clerical work connected with the volume; Miss Thelma Pyle, secretary to the dean of students, took Mrs. Apgar's place as we approached final manuscript. Two graduate students at Union assumed some of the editorial work: M. Eric de Wasseige, of Liège, made the first-draft translation of Père Roland de Vaux's article; and Mr. Merrill Miller checked the translation of Yigael Yadin's article against the Hebrew original, then set his exceptionally scrupulous eye upon the footnotes of each article. But my deepest thanks are reserved for Judith Dollenmayer and Sallie Waterman of Doubleday; no author or editor could wish for more from a publisher than to work with house editors like them.

Another type of assistance came from Mrs. Sanders. My wife has known Nelson Glueck as long as I have, and is as devoted to him in her own way as any student could be. We were at the Hebrew Union College from 1951–54, when Nelson Glueck was expanding and developing the College, giving more and more of himself to its administration as well as to the critical advances then taking place within the Reform Jewish Movement.

Glueck did very little formal teaching in those days. But his secretary, Mrs. Dunsker, would let us know in advance when he planned to meet his course on archaeology, so Mrs. Sanders was able to attend almost as many sessions as I. Often we would linger after class to speak with Nelson Glueck. The talk ranged considerably beyond archaeology, and to us he became a sort of pastor-counselor. Everyone knows Nelson Glueck as a man of extraordinary dedication and drive; my wife and I came to know him as a man of deep wisdom and a warm heart. In those informal talks, Nelson Glueck was a more effective teacher than most others in more formal settings. He has given us much, and will perhaps forgive me now if I close the foreword to this *zikkaron* with a personal message of affection from us both.

J.A.S.
Auburn Professor of Biblical Studies
Union Theological Seminary, New York

PREFACE

THE MIND OF NELSON GLUECK

Fritz Bamberger

This volume is addressed to Nelson Glueck, the archaeologist. His contributions to the archaeology of the Bible lands, and his methods and position as an archaeologist, are described in essays provided by his archaeological confrères. But to this writer, who is not an archaeologist, it appears (as it must have to many readers of Glueck's books and many listeners at his lectures) that the mind of this scholar cannot be understood fully or adequately if one views him strictly within the confines of his archaeological work.[1]

In interesting juxtaposition with that work, motivating it as well as taking off from it (yet conscientiously never interfering with it) are convictions, vistas and visions that do not stem from archaeological research; they form a basic world-view in the mind of Nelson Glueck and reveal deep-seated, ever-present incentives and stimuli that one must try to understand in order to comprehend Glueck's intellectuality.

These concerns are rooted in his student days. At Hebrew Union College in Cincinnati Glueck studied Bible under Julian Morgenstern, who in 1922 became president of the College and whom Glueck was to succeed in the college presidency twenty-five years later. Morgenstern's main interest was biblical exegesis, strongly influenced by the Wellhausen school, though differing from that school's radical linguistic approach by the application of cultural and theological differences as criteria for separating the layers that appear in the biblical text as we have it. Glueck confirms Morgenstern's influence upon him. While he did not adopt his teacher's methods of biblical criticism, he was stirred by the complexities of the Bible that they revealed. He was intrigued by the inner dynamics of the Bible's history, the ideas that motivated its writing and constant rewriting, editing and reediting.

In 1923, after his ordination as rabbi, Glueck went to Germany for graduate study and found two teachers, Hugo Gressmann in Berlin and

Willi Staerk in Jena, whose emphasis on the ideational background of biblical writings attracted him. Gressmann recognized the importance of textual, *literarkritische,* biblical research, but the stronger, novel facets of scholarship that established his fame lay elsewhere: namely, in *Traditionsanalyse* (analysis of tradition) as employed in his *Moses und seine Zeit,* and in biblical archaeology conceived as part of *Palaestinawissenschaft* (research on the historical, cultural and civilizational aspects of Palestine).

The result of Glueck's studies in Germany was a book on a biblical idea, his doctoral thesis, *Das Wort Ḥesed im alttestamentlichen Sprachgebrauche als menschliche und göttliche gemeinschaftgemässe Verhaltungsweise.*[2]

This study was planned as the first chapter of a systematic *Ideengeschichte* of the Bible. It shows that the *Ḥesed* idea[3] did not spring into existence full-blown, with its definitive meaning precisely shaped. Rather, Glueck follows the idea's logical, dynamic development as it parallels the biblical writer's growing insight into the divinely based relationships of man to man and man to God. The whole gamut of biblical concepts was to be included in such a "history of ideas," tracing the changes in the great ideational concepts of the Bible from their initial appearance to ultimate maturity, with meticulous attention to every nuance of their progress.

This project was never completed. Instead of becoming a historian of biblical ideas, Glueck became a biblical archaeologist, joining William F. Albright, then director of the American Schools of Oriental Research in Jerusalem, and taking Albright as his master.

One's first impression might place an hiatus between Glueck's scholarly beginnings and his life's work. What happened to his interest in the great ideas of the Bible? Archaeologists do not excavate ideas. "I am interested in archaeology," says Glueck, "because it is a branch of history" or, "Archaeology is the servant of history because it makes the ground reveal the secrets of buried civilizations." It is "the handmaiden, one of the tools of history."

Oliver Wendell Holmes hailed archaeology in this way: "I believe in the spade. It has fed the tribes of mankind. It has furnished them water, coal, iron and gold. And now it is giving them truth—historic truth—the mines of which have never been opened till our time." Certainly, the historic truth of which Holmes spoke does not relate to ideas, although it would be patently unfair to archaeology to state its limits, as at least one writer did, by gloomily quoting John Donne: "The ashes of an oak in the chimney are no epitaph of that oak, to tell me how high or large it was. The dust of great persons' graves is speechless too; it says nothing, it distinguishes nothing." Excavations do speak, most eloquently, revealing the beauty, grandeur and dignity—or, for that matter, the decay—of past civilizations. What does biblical archaeology, as Glueck conceives it, principally reveal?

Glueck is firmly aware of what biblical archaeology cannot provide. "The full value of biblical archaeology can be achieved. . . only when it is pursued for the objective historical information that it almost always so richly yields when scientifically undertaken." However, "the depth and authority of the spiritual insights cannot be affected positively or negatively by whether or not an archaeological discovery confirms or possibly confounds one or more of its historical statements."

Throughout his career, Glueck has distinctly separated the historical data furnished by archaeological research from religious truth, which is unaffected by it. He frowns on using archaeology as an instrument to prove the Bible.[4] "The truths of the Bible—expressed in commandments and prophecy, in legend and law, in history and myth, in unvarnished biographical sketches and compressed genealogical tables, and some of them repeated in different versions, not only in different books but in the same chapters—can be neither buttressed nor invalidated archaeologically. New discovery may perhaps modify or fill out or make clear a particular account in the biblical annals, but it can never replace or refute or corroborate its religious worth."

In this sense, no direct or essential relationship exists between archaeological discoveries in Bible lands and the Bible itself, between the finds of biblical archaeology and the teachings of biblical religion. To Glueck the scholar, the entire Bible is open to critical inquiry. He knows that the historical, topographical and geographical data which the biblical writers put in the Bible were sometimes incorporated through purposive editing and that "the criterion for inclusion derived from their usefulness in underscoring or defining religious principles." But Glueck, the religious man, believes that "the moral and spiritual values of the teachings or tradition of the Bible transcend the changes of time or tide" and "are inseparably connected with belief in God Eternal who established the changing universe in accordance with changeless natural [sic] law. . ." Glueck states that the authors of the Bible recognized God in the forces of history. But he knows too that the recognition of Sacred Writ—a recognition possible also for the non-fundamentalist *homo religiosus*—does not compel the scholar to accept the idea of Sacred History. The Bible is not history; it was not compiled for historical purposes. In it, however, appears a strong and extensive "historical memory" that has proved so continuously correct that from it the archaeological scholar draws a large measure of challenge and guidance. Archaeological research can well provide additional, and more detailed, information than the Bible itself furnishes about the "historical situations" in which (and often in contradistinction to which) the great and novel religious ideas of biblical religion grew.

By way of this relationship between "historical situation" and "idea," which clearly is not a causal one, Glueck sees the continuity of his scholarly motivation running from his early *ideengeschichtliche* research to, and through, his lifework as an archaeologist. He says he entered archaeology to learn the "background" of the biblical ideas; and "in the final analysis, after utilizing all the extant material, the only way to get there was to dig for it."

More than once, Glueck has emphatically stated that his deepest personal involvement is not with the archaeological facts as such. He did an impressive amount of archaeological research in Middle Bronze I and identified this period as the Age of Abraham (*circa* 2100–1900 BC). His research has greatly aided scholars in reconstructing the civilization and milieu of that period. Glueck is fully cognizant that the faith of Abraham (for example, Abraham's belief in the sanctity of human life, which in Jewish tradition made him one of the fathers of the Jewish religion) is not explicable by milieu; the greatness of Abraham did not flow from the civilization that surrounded him and of which he was a part. Yet the awareness that his research carried him to the "background" of a great biblical idea provides Glueck with a great deal of personal and emotional satisfaction.

Glueck's archaeological research filled out our scant knowledge of the Edomites, Moabites and Ammonites. They spoke, Glueck says, the same language as the Judeans, perhaps with a slightly different accent; they used the same kind of script; they built the same kind of buildings; they wore the same kind of clothes; and they fashioned the same kind of pottery. Yet, he emphasizes, they disappeared, while the Jewish people, physical and spiritual descendants of their Judean contemporaries, lived on to transmit the perennial tradition of Jewish religion. As a matter of fact, the early transmitters of Jewish tradition were a tiny minority. Nearly every excavation of sites from periods before the Babylonian Exile shows that the majority of the Judeans practiced idolatry. All the more gloriously, to Glueck, shines the greatness and the genius of the few who in the exile and thereafter "perceived the ways and words of God, who were able to infuse into the special tissue and substance of an entire people the acceptance of the authority of the God of Abraham, Isaac and Jacob" and who started the unbroken chain of an "ideational history" (Glueck's term) that carried the ideas of Judaism to our time.

The manner in which Glueck is able to combine archaeology with a set of beliefs and sentiments drawn from religious sources, yet never to confuse the two, is greatly revealing. He is, he says, immensely and endlessly fascinated by "the straight chain of ideas which result from Abraham to Moses to the Essenes to Akiba to Judah Halevi to Maimonides to the present." The object of this life-long fascination, the origin and development of the great, formative ideas of Judaism, remains outside the realm of scholarship Glueck chose. The pursuit of scientific archaeological work is not allowed to be affected by it. Writings of Glueck such as his *Explorations in Eastern Palestine* and his articles in the *Bulletin of the American Schools of Oriental Research* are straight archaeological research. But in those books directed toward larger audiences, *The River Jordan* and *Rivers in the Desert,* and particularly in his popular lectures, emotional and religious elements of distinct structure and color appear, adding new perspective to the archaeological picture.

"I have never traveled through this part of the world," wrote Glueck, "without being seized by a sense of excitement. I have never wandered about across its spaces, knowing that I was treading ground where the Patriarchs and the Prophets had lived, without wondering what new view of the miraculous [sic] might possibly be unrolled before me. I have never explored the Negev or Sinai without realizing that in those lands God's will was revealed to mortal men, giving them the possibility of a status little lower than the angels. I have never paced up and down the banks of the Jordan without in my mind's eye seeing the people of Israel cross over into the Promised Land and wondering what the spiritual equivalent of the Promised Land might be in our time."

Glueck explains the addition of this element of personal identification ("treading ground where the Patriarchs and the Prophets had lived") to the strictly historical or archaeological account: "The emotional loyalty of the Jew to his past seizes hold of me. I am not aiming for it, I am not trying for it; it just comes through." It reflects, Glueck explains, the wonder and awe arising from the thought that, far back in time, his Jewish ancestors had arrived at a concept of divinity that enabled them to perform an "ideational break-through" that marked the transition from paganism to a great religion whose ideas became the heritage of all mankind.

Glueck elaborates little upon this feeling. It is elemental rather than theological, immediate rather than developed from theoretical or systematic reflection. It is Glueck's personal, emotional reaction to the sublimity and enduring power of the religious ideas emanating from the Palestine of ancient times, his wonder at the absolutely new element that entered the world to endure to the present. The incessant question is, why in that corner of the world the great ideas of Judaism, which are among the enduring ideas of mankind, were born. Biblical archaeology gives no answer to this question. Progress in archaeology merely increases our knowledge of the people and the civilization in which the ideas were born; but even this adds to what Glueck calls the "miracle" of the ideational genesis.

One of Glueck's archaeological and literary accomplishments is his rediscovery and comprehensive account of the Nabataean civilization. For a long time, the Nabataeans had been considered merely a caravaning folk whose base was Petra. Glueck's researches have helped to reconstruct the entire lifespan of the brilliant Nabataean civilization. The Nabataeans spoke Aramaic; they also spoke Greek and Latin and traveled all over the civilized world. They worshiped a whole pantheon of astrodeities. They could not have failed to talk with the Essenes, the people of Qumran. What particularly intrigued Glueck in his effort to elucidate the civilization of these people was the task of establishing the essential differences between their religion and the religion of the Jews of that period. For Glueck, there is something miraculous in those inexplicable differences and it adds to the miracle of nascent Judaism.

Why were the foundations of Judaism laid in Palestine and nowhere else? Why were Judeans, and no one else, the originators and transmitters of the great biblical perceptions? While he was aware that such questions are "essentially irrational," Glueck nevertheless, and all the more insistently, pursued his search for "rational factors for further elucidation."

Views held by the proponents of "geopolitics," an interdisciplinary attempt by a number of geographical and historical scholars to explain recurring historical and political constellations by means of geographic constants, seemed to provide assistance. Some of these men maintained that there exists a physical heartland of the world, a physical centrality, created by geographic location and physical features, the physical control of which insures control of vast neighboring areas. In fact, at a time when modern means of global communication and transportation did not exist, possession of this heartland meant control of the civilized world. This heartland is Palestine and her neighboring areas. Whoever held this land commanded access to Europe, Africa and Asia. For this reason, as the geopoliticians have pointed out, the peoples of the world have from time immemorial converged toward this centrality. The Egyptians and the Mesopotamians fought to the death for control of this area; so did the Persians and the Greeks, the Parthians and the Romans. The power struggle has continued through the centuries—today Russia and America are the major contestants. During World War II, when Glueck was an OSS agent in the Near East, the political and strategic information he was privy to validated his conviction that Palestine was the geopolitical center of the world.

Glueck, whose geopolitical convictions had been shaped particularly by the ideas of Halford John McKinder, went further. To his way of thinking, "physical factors have an influence upon the human being. This very physical centrality, I believe, has necessarily had an effect upon the human being who has for one reason or another come into contact with it or lived in this part of the world. I simply cannot divorce the accident of location completely from the cultural development of the people who live in that part of the world." This means that Glueck does not entirely separate the pivotal quality of the geographic location of Palestine from the religious insights to which Israel gave birth.

It is an interesting and surprisingly naturalistic hypothesis, not unknown in classical Jewish thought. Judah Halevi, the medieval Jewish philosopher (1085–1140), asserted that the Holy Land, because of its favorable climate, was especially predisposed to the development of Israel's religion, and that, for the same reason, biblical prophecy could have taken place only there.

To Glueck, the consideration of such a physico-theological theory is one more attempt to find "rational facts" to explain and to illuminate the origin of the great ideas of his religion. He well realizes the insufficiency of the theory. Other peoples lived in the same pivotal location; yet the religions they produced bore a different stamp and did not carry the spiritual energy—the religionist would say truth—that has carried the great perceptions of the Bible through time. Yet Glueck's attachment to this theory is strong enough for him to press another unanswerable question: would Israel's religious concepts, had they developed in an entirely different location—for example, in Africa—have had the same effect on mankind?

All of Glueck's attempts to find rational facts and specific background to throw light on the mystery of the ideational genesis are variations on Glueck's leitmotif. It led him into archaeology and has stayed with him although, as Glueck himself has often insisted, archaeology would lose its scientific character if it were forced to respond to it. One might think that the inherent disability of scientific archaeology to give ultimate answers to his questions would have disappointed Glueck. Not so. The inability of archaeology, or for that matter any other scholarly discipline, to clarify or rationally solve the miracle of the birth of a great religion has not silenced Glueck's inquiry. Characteristic of his intellectual drive, the quest itself became part of his religiosity.

Nowhere does this become more apparent than in his popular essays and in his lectures before laymen. There one finds another approach to the origin of the great concepts of biblical religion coupled with his archaeological findings. Peculiar to one people, the Judeans, these great concepts are ascribed to the "genius of this people," arising out of the distant past and moving through time in unbroken identity from their first classic manifestations to later ones. Each stage in their development represents an organic unfolding of that "genius." Holding this view, Glueck approaches the theories of the "Historical School" that was grounded in the thought of late-eighteenth-century writers such as Johann Gottfried Herder, who spoke of *Volksgeist* (folk spirit) to explain the specific creations of a people and their organic growth. During the Romantic period it was given more elaborate definition. It is an interesting sidelight that the founders of *Wissenschaft des Judentums,* the discipline of the scientific investigation of Jewish history and literature, also adopted this organic philosophy of history from the Historical School.

Glueck's approaches to questions of the past are varied and multilinear. But Glueck has a remarkable, artful ability to interweave them. In the process of doing so his imaginative talent succeeds in removing from the past the mark of remoteness, in making it live in human terms, and in bringing the distant near while restoring its color and topicality, as well as its mysteries. Through empathetic understanding, Glueck finds in ancient times a source in which the present is foreseen, illuminated by its beginnings. The remote event becomes a convincing parallel to the contemporary one. Perennial ideas and perceptions move through the ages without losing their validity: historical constellations and experiences obey the same laws, then as now.

FOOTNOTES

1. Part of the quotes in this essay are from the following papers and articles by Nelson Glueck: "Archaeology in Israel," *Israel—Life and Letters* (Oct.–Nov. 1953); "The Bible and Archaeology," in *Five Essays on the Bible. Papers read at the 1960 Annual Meeting of the American Council of Learned Societies* (1960); "Biblical Archaeology and Reform Judaism," in *The Time of Harvest: Essays in Honor of Abba Hillel Silver* (1963); and "Why I am a Biblical Archaeologist," *Cincinnati* (June 1968). Other quotes are taken from a lengthy taped interview with Glueck.

2. *BZAW*, 47 (1927; second edition 1961); English translation, *Ḥesed in the Bible*, translated by Alfred Gottschalk with an introduction by Gerald A. Larue (1967).

3. According to Glueck, *ḥesed* in the Bible expresses the "mutual relationship of rights and duties" among humans in normal social intercourse and the qualities of loyalty and love that obtained in the covenant relationship between God and Israel.

4. See G. Ernest Wright, "Is Glueck's Aim to Prove that the Bible is True?" *BA*, 22 (1959), pp. 101–8.

I
Introduction

THE PHENOMENON OF AMERICAN
ARCHAEOLOGY IN THE NEAR EAST

G. Ernest Wright

I

DURING most of the nineteenth century America was apparently in-different to the archaeological recovery of the ancient Near East be-ginning at the time. While Europe was being dazzled by the British and French archaeological discoveries in Mesopotamia and Egypt, not to mention Schliemann's proof of the meaning of a tell at Troy, nor the prehistoric discoveries of Jacques Boucher de Perthes in the Somme Valley near Abbeville, France, this country produced but one great scholar who was our sole claim to early international fame in the ancient field. He was Edward Robinson of Union Theological Seminary (1794–1863), the first American scholar whose main work was published simultaneously in English and German.[1] Though frequently mentioned, there is no adequate biography of this giant in American scholarly history. Praising Robinson's *Biblical Researches* in Palestine and Sinai, the great German topographical historian, Albrecht Alt, wrote in 1938 that "in Robinson's footnotes are forever buried the errors of many generations."[2]

Preceding Robinson there had been, of course, a long tradition of study of the classics and the Bible in this country. Students at Harvard College from the very beginning had to study Hebrew, "Chaldee" (Ara-maic), Syriac and Greek. To be sure, there were objections. Professor Michael Wigglesworth complained as early as 1653 that his students came to him with a petition to drop the study of Hebrew: "I withstood it with all the reason that I could, yet all will not satisfy them. Thus am I requited for my love; and thus little fruit of all my prayers and tears for their good."[3] The first Hebrew grammar in this country was printed by Jacob Monis in 1735, with great difficulty because of defective Hebrew type imported from England. The Puritans especially kept to their ideals of the educated professional, based on British and European models, but in general they could not be said to be innovative scholars. Following the Revolutionary War, the breach of normal intercourse with England, the growth of rationalism and the Boston Unitarian movement combined to lessen interest in the serious study of the Old Testament. However, there were exceptions among Boston and Cambridge Unitarians. A few among them turned to Germany and became absorbed in the new philological and exegetical studies there, but this interest was short-lived because the Unitarians generally turned to other concerns.[4]

Edward Robinson was born in a spacious and beautiful white clapboard home, still standing in Southington, Connecticut. His father was a well-known clergyman, student of Timothy Dwight of Yale, and those who knew him well thought he could have become one of the theological giants of his time. Spurning all offers of advancement, he stayed at Southington until his death. Instead of advancing his career as a churchman, he advanced in material prosperity with his farm and a large variety of business dealings until he became a wealthy man, as the description of his home suggests.[5]

Edward Robinson was the second son of Elizabeth Norton, the fourth wife of his thrice widowed father. He grew up without a strong constitution, and his father did not consider him a suitable candidate for farming. He early showed considerable mechanical ingenuity and became an expert weaver. In his fifteenth year, while studying under a neighboring minister, he was also at work on "kine pox" as an antidote for small pox and successfully inoculated his whole family against the dread disease. While he was fond of books, his family did not consider him a particularly bright scholar. Instead of sending him to college, his father apprenticed him to a Southington store with special responsibility for the drug department. The usually mild and kindly youth soon rebelled at this decision, and left home to live with his maternal uncle, Professor Seth Norton, in Clinton, New York. In the fall of 1812, he entered Hamilton college as a freshman; this new college was beginning its career on the central New York frontier, a center of Puritan emigration with its chief city, Oneida.

In college he showed the same amazing capacities as much later would characterize the college years of W. F. Albright. While leading his class in every subject studied, he was especially gifted as linguist and mathematician. Graduating from Hamilton in 1816, he was soon called back to the college as tutor in mathematics and Greek. In 1818 he married Eliza Kirkland, whose father founded the academy from which Hamilton College grew, and whose brother, John Thornton Kirkland, was president of Harvard College at the time.[6] She died in less than a year, leaving him heir to her father's large and handsome farm. He continued his studies while maintaining the farm until 1821. In that year he journeyed to Andover, Massachusetts, to publish his first book, a critical edition of the *Iliad,* with a Latin introduction and notes.

The trip to Andover in his twenty-eighth year was the turning point of his career, for there he came under the influence of the magnetic personality of Moses Stuart. For background we must pause and turn back a few years.

While a new era of fresh biblical work had dawned on the continent of Europe, America might not have been touched by it had it not been for the sectarian theological seminaries established by the more orthodox groups. Chief and first among these was Andover Theological Seminary, founded by the Congregationalists in 1808, where Moses Stuart was called as professor of Old Testament in 1810. Stuart may perhaps be called the father of modern biblical study in America. As the thirty-year-old Congregational pastor of the Center Church on the Green in New Haven, he began his work, as he says, "with little more than a knowledge of the Hebrew alphabet . . . I had not, and never have had, the aid of any teacher in my biblical studies. Alas! for our country at that time (AD 1810); there was scarcely a man in it, unless by accident someone who had been educated abroad, that had such a knowledge of Hebrew as was requisite in order to be an instructor."[7] There was only one other institution in the country, he says, where Hebrew was taught, and that was Dr. Mason's Divinity School in New York, later united with the theological seminary established by the Presbyterians at Princeton.

Stuart not only taught himself Hebrew but soon discovered that he must learn German as well. This he did, though he was roundly criticized because, to many, German and Boston liberalism were synonymous. It was perhaps twenty or thirty years before his fight for the recognition of German scholarly work can be said to have triumphed. Before his death in 1852 he had published some forty monographs and books, including a translation of the Gesenius-Rödiger *Hebrew Grammar* (1846) and a number of elaborate commentaries in which he showed how German scholarship had revolutionized the field of biblical studies. Among the 1500 ministers whom he taught were some seventy men who became professors and presidents of colleges; and after his time it was no longer unusual for an enterprising young scholar to go to Germany for graduate study.

Under Stuart's tutelage, Robinson stayed in Andover and rapidly learned Hebrew. In the fall of 1823, the Seminary appointed him instructor in Hebrew, though he had been helping Stuart to correct proof on the second edition of Stuart's *Hebrew Grammar,* which appeared in the same year. This began a collaboration that lasted throughout their lives, planning together even when working separately. Their great aim was to publish their own revisions and translations of the best German grammars and dictionaries of both Hebrew and Greek, and keep them up-to-date by constant revision and new editions. In 1831 Robinson founded the *Biblical Repository,* appearing as volumes of biblical studies as the material was ready, the first scholarly series of tracts and essays on biblical and theological topics to appear in this country; and in 1843 he began in New York another series of essays in volumes, named *The Biblioteca Sacra,* which ultimately became a journal, united in 1851 with *The Repository.* In 1832 he edited and greatly improved a translation of Calmet's *Dictionary of the Bible.* In 1833 he began the series of editions, kept up-to-date with Stuart's assistance, of Buttmann's *Greek Grammar.* In 1834 he produced a revised edition of Newcome's *Greek Harmony of the Gospels,* and in 1845 replaced it with a Greek harmony of his own, which was soon issued in London and also used as basis for a French harmony. In 1836 Robinson translated Gesenius' Hebrew-Latin Lexicon, which appeared in 1833, revised editions appearing regularly in 1842, 1849, 1850 and 1854. This lexicon was basic to serious American Old Testament study throughout the nineteenth century, being revised by Brown, Driver and Briggs at the turn of the century. It is said that "if Stuart was the more brilliant, adventurous, and electric, firing his pupils with enthusiasm, Robinson was looked upon as the more careful, exact, and thorough . . . , a most indefatigable student. There seemed to be no end to his endurance of mental toil."[8]

Of great advantage to Robinson's scholarly career was his independent income from his father's and his first wife's estates. This enabled him to spend four years in Germany between 1826 and 1830, to teach without fixed salary at Andover Seminary as Professor Extraordinary, 1830–33, to work in Boston 1834–37, to make his Palestinian trips and return to Germany to complete the two volumes of his *Biblical Researches* (1838–40), the volumes being published simultaneously here and in Germany in 1841, and, because of eye trouble, to return to Germany for treatment and rest in 1862, shortly before his death.

For years he had hoped to make a scholar's tour of Palestine and neighboring lands, and had thoroughly prepared himself for the work, with the journeys of Burckhardt and others serving as model. He also profited from the advice and counsel of the great German geographer, Karl Ritter, with whom he was especially intimate.

His opportunity came in 1838. In 1836 he was called to a chair at New York University, which he declined. But in 1837, soon after the first edition of his Hebrew Lexicon was published, he accepted a professorship of Biblical Literature at the newly formed Union Theological Seminary in New York, on condition that he be granted a leave of absence for three or four years to complete his Palestinian trip. During the spring and summer of 1852 the directors of Union Seminary granted him a second leave, enabling him to cover parts of northern Palestine and lower Syria which he had not traversed in 1838. This trip resulted in a third volume, named *Later Biblical Researches,* which appeared in 1856.

According to Albright, it was Robinson who "showed how ancient topography should be reconstructed."[9] Indeed, without his work, who would have been the first to cut through the maze of mistaken traditions obscuring what we now consider basic to the very ABCs of biblical learning? To this very day no tourist can trust uncritically what a professional guide says about ancient places and events of biblical times, least of all around Jerusalem. The late F.-M. Abel, O.P., writes that "if we compare the poverty and inexactness of the information of Seetzen in 1806 for the environs of Jerusalem with the researches of Robinson, *which are for the most part definitive,*[10] we may judge the progress realized by the latter" in releasing truth from the stranglehold of the myth and lore of the pilgrim literature and popular tradition.[11] On May 4–5, 1836, for example, he was the first to discover the locations of Anathoth, Geba, Rimmon, Ramah and Michmash by simply recognizing their names preserved in the names of modern Arabic villages: 'Anâta, Jeba', Rammûn, er-Râm and Mukhmâs. Similarly, on May 10 he discovered the Judean sites Maon, Carmel, Ziph, Juttah, Jattir, Socoh, Anab, and Eshtemoa in Arabic names changed but little from the original Hebrew.

Before beginning his trips Robinson secured the assistance of a traveling companion, a former student, excellent Arabist and missionary in Lebanon, Eli Smith. With precision and exactness in compiling Arabic placenames and in consulting Arab elders about traditions of ancient places and ruins, Robinson was astonished at the amount of important information retained by local tradition. Yet another secret of his success was his thorough and critical self-instruction in biblical data and in later written records from classical antiquity until modern times.

Alt summarizes this aspect of Robinson's work in the following perceptive words:

> . . . he recognized with his sober vision that this endless literature in general rather obscured Biblical reality than illumined it. Precisely the tradition that in his own time claimed to be authoritative, seemed to him least worthy of credence, for comparison with older testimony taught him that the original foundation of fact was buried under a number of still-distinguishable layers of arbitrary misinterpretation. The former, he saw, could only be reached after the mass of later opinions and mistakes had been resolutely cleared away. Robinson seems to have been the first to understand this situation, and he was certainly the first scholar who analyzed it with the methods of historical criticism, instead of treating it with unfruitful skepticism. We may justly suppose that this was the first decisive methodical advance which he made in his study of the literature. Without the critical use of sources, according to the methods he first recognized as necessary, no scientific Palestinology was thenceforth possible; he himself worked along this line with so much energy and with such great success that he was able definitely to disprove a large part of what his predecessors had thought and had written."[12]

The great aim of Robinson's topographical work was a *Biblical Geography*. He began to write it on June 3, 1859, and by June 3, 1861, he had completed only the first part of the first volume, *Physical Geography*,[13] when eye trouble and blindness made it impossible for him to finish. Roswell Hitchcock ends his story of this volume with these words, in an address written within less than two months of Robinson's death. "There lives no man to finish it; and when one shall be born to do it, God only knows."

II

Hitchcock's lament and question could be answered by no one in the nineteenth century. When one considers the other great explorers of that century, Robinson stands alone. Perhaps the German scholar Eric Tobler is a candidate for next place. Certainly the French scholar Charles Clermont-Ganneau is to be mentioned, even though his pages are few in comparison with Tobler's.

For countries other than Palestine in the ancient Near East the work was also of a pioneering nature, but languages had to be deciphered, grammars and dictionaries prepared. The great work of Mariette and

Lepsius in Egypt, of Layard, Rawlinson and Rassam among others in Mesopotamia, released material of whole civilizations which had to be studied and assimilated so that new histories of the "cradle of civilization" could be written, and that only in our century, after assimilation of the material was sufficiently advanced. None of these countries had resource material available in the received literature, which when critically understood could be used to interpret traditions and actual ruins in a meaningful way. The literature had to be dug from the soil or copied from temple walls (Egypt).

In Palestinian exploration the greatest achievement of the second half of the nineteenth century was the work of the British Palestine Exploration Fund, directly influenced by Robinson's work. The Fund was organized in 1865, and under C. R. Conder and H. H. Kitchener conducted the great survey of Western Palestine between 1871 and 1878, producing an excellent map in twenty-six sheets at a scale of one inch to a mile, and covering an area of about six thousand square miles. This was the first and for many decades the only detailed map, including all recognized ruins, which existed for any Near Eastern country. The maps currently available for Palestine in the scale of 1:20,000 and 1:100,000 were completed by the authorities of the British Mandate at the beginning of the Second World War, and have been updated periodically, especially by Israeli scholars. For Jordan archaeology, a series of three maps, in whose preparation G. Lancaster Harding played a specially important role, is an almost unique attempt to provide dates of occupation for all ruins. The British Mandate's new map was a contour map and thus a great improvement on the work of Conder and Kitchener, but for archaeological study it by no means superseded their excellent work. It is still necessary to refer to the old maps for details not included in the work of the 1930s, just as it is necessary to use the latter for details not observed in the 1870s.

In addition, the several volumes of *Memoirs of Western Palestine,* which give detailed commentary on the map of the 1870s, have no modern equivalent. It should be noted, however, that this work is purely a geographical collection of observed phenomena. The historical topographer finds the maps an indispensable tool, but they cannot replace his own work in either study or field. Egyptologists have today an incomparably valuable bibliographical tool in B. Porter, R. L. B. Moss and E. W. Burney, *Topographical Bibliography of Egyptian Hieroglyphic Texts, Reliefs, and Paintings.*[14] This is the envy of archaeologists in every other country. Except for occasional localities, however, with regard to detailed archaeological survey of ancient ruins of all periods, most of the ancient Near East is at best only superficially known. This fact makes the new *Atlas of Israel*[15] almost a unique scholarly document, since it attempts to put into one large folio volume all that has come to be known of the geography, geology and historical topography of the land west of the Jordan.

As for American efforts, only one piece of topographical research, besides the work of Robinson, needs to be mentioned. This is the exploration of the Dead Sea in 1848 by Lieutenant W. F. Lynch of the United States Navy. Floating two metal boats down the Jordan from the Sea of Galilee, his party spent three weeks on the Dead Sea. Perhaps the most important observation was the actual depth of the Jordan Valley-Dead Sea rift below the level of the Mediterranean Sea.[16] Two attempts to found an "American Exploration Society" were made in the 1870s. The second even hoped to make a map of Palestine, but its only accomplishment was to employ the Rev. Selah Merrill as explorer for two years, a man without scholarly training, whose name was soon to appear prominently in connection with the most famous forgery in Near Eastern history. This was the complete manuscript of the book of Deuteronomy, which the British Museum almost purchased for a huge sum before Clermont-Ganneau made many faces red with embarrassment by proving it a forgery, inspired by the ancient Hebrew script newly found on the royal stele of King Mesha of Moab, which celebrated Moab's freedom and reconquest of territory from ancient Israel in the 840s BC.

III

The impetus for this country's first entry into actual excavation in the Near East came from Philadelphia. At the 1884 meeting of the American Oriental Society in New Haven, the dominant mood was that the time had come for this country to join England and France in the great work they had been doing.[17] A small expedition set out for Babylonia, headed by W. H. Ward, and for eight weeks in early 1885 it explored and recorded a great many tells south of Babylon.[18] Dr. John P. Peters, Professor of Hebrew at the Episcopal Divinity School in Philadelphia in 1884, and two years later called to a similar chair at the University of Pennsylvania, was also stimulated by the AOS meeting in 1884. With the interest of a group of people who were loyal friends of the university and of its administration, two expeditions were dispatched to ancient

Nippur under his direction in the period 1888–90, and a third for a longer period, 1893–96, under the direction of Peters' assistant, J. H. Haynes; Haynes had been an instructor at Robert College, Constantinople, before joining Ward's expedition and later serving as U. S. Consul in Baghdad.

It must be remembered that it was impossible to secure training as a field archaeologist at that time. The success or failure of an expedition was directly due to the practical common sense of the director, to his scholarly training and vision, and to his ability to set forth clear goals and methods for achieving them. During the first campaign, R. F. Harper, then of Yale, and H. V. Hilprecht accompanied the expedition as Assyriologists, but Peters seemed hampered by them. Thus, on his second expedition and during the third campaign of three years' duration under Haynes' direction, there was no architect, no photographer (Haynes being fully occupied in the field), and no one trained in Akkadian studies who could read and understand the significance of the thousands of cuneiform tablets being turned up in each campaign. Added to this were the primitive conditions of the area, the tell being the center of the once wealthy and well-irrigated Babylonian plain, but now surrounded by swamps (and still so, seventy years later), and the natives consisting often of tribes hostile to one another, only nominally controlled by Ottoman Turkish authority. It would have been disturbing to any director to have two hundred laborers peaceably at work at one moment, and at the next dropping their tools to split up into two or more groups noisily engaged in war dances!

As an excavation it was saved from disaster only by the wealth of the site and by the fact that the orderly and well-stocked mind of Hilprecht gradually assumed increasing influence, until he himself became director during the final campaigns, 1898–1900. Peters, followed by Haynes, was so desperate to obtain objects quickly in order to make money-raising easier that he directed not an excavation proper but a treasure hunt, trenching and tunneling in every direction without respect to architecture. As soon as he had the authority, Hilprecht stopped this proceeding for a more orderly investigation of the city's history and architecture, and in 1898–1900 insisted that two architects be present to record at least such architecture as was possible at that late date.[19] Between 1893 and 1896, Haynes worked alone with no staff at all, like Macalister at Gezer, except for one period of six months when a student of architecture at the Massachusetts Institute of Technology, Joseph A. Meyer, on a traveling fellowship in Baghdad from India, stopped to work at Nippur until he sickened from dysentery and malaria, and died because he had not sought proper medical assistance in time.

Nippur, the greatest city of third millennium Babylonia, was not so much a political as a religious city. We now know it to be the center of a group of independent city-states that comprised the area of ancient Sumer.[20] Its ziggurat and temple of Enlil, the divine chief executive of the Sumerian universe, were the central features of the site. On a neighboring hill, Hilprecht surmised, should be the scribal school and library. This proved to be correct, and there emerged one of the great literary finds of archaeological history. The latest group of items in the library date from *circa* the eighteenth century BC in the 1st Dynasty of Babylon, when Sumerian was still studied as the classical language of cultural Nippur. Hence grammatical and lexical texts found there have proved invaluable in the recovery of the language, enabling the great German scholar, F. Delitzsch, to produce his Sumerian grammar in 1914, following his Assyrian grammar of 1889 and Assyrian dictionary of 1896. Of special importance in the Nippur library, however, has been the long-lost literature of the Sumerians. The publication of this material has been the work chiefly of Samuel Noel Kramer of our time,[21] a distinguished pupil of E. A. Speiser, both men deriving from the scholarly impact and impetus of H. V. Hilprecht, and subsequently from the same department in the University of Pennsylvania headed by J. Alan Montgomery.

IV

While America's first great archaeological venture was underway at Nippur, a far different project began in Egypt under the direction of Harvard-trained George A. Reisner.[22] An archaeological contemporary and genius as great as England's Sir Flinders Petrie, and just as much "a lone wolf," he taught those who worked in Western Asia how to dig so that a minimum of historical evidence is destroyed by disturbance and removal of the earth at antiquity sites.

Reisner graduated from Harvard College *summa cum laude* in 1889, and in 1893 received his Ph.D. degree after completing a dissertation on an Accadian subject: "A Review of the Grammatical Development of the Noun Endings in Assyro-Babylonian." From 1893 to 1896 he held a traveling fellowship for research in cuneiform and studied Egyptian under Kurt Sethe in Berlin. Returning to Harvard as an Instructor in Semitic Languages, he taught the first course in Egyptian to be given at Harvard during the year 1896–97. In 1899 he organized the Egyptian

Expedition of the University of California (1899–1905), supported entirely by Mrs. Phoebe Apperson Hearst. In 1905 this expedition became the Joint Egyptian Expedition of Harvard University and the Boston Museum of Fine Arts, of which Reisner remained director until his death in 1942. He returned to Harvard to give Egyptological courses as Professor of Egyptology only in occasional semesters. During a period of over forty years of field work he trained a number of excellent assistants and left a distinguished record of accomplishments. This includes particularly the history of the royal family of Dynasty IV, the development of arts and crafts during the Pyramid Age, and the history of Lower Nubia and of Ethiopia from *circa* 4000 BC to AD 350. The Egyptological collections of the Boston Museum of Fine Arts as well as many items in the Cairo Museum are a visual monument to his work.

Reisner once wrote that among the outstanding features of the Harvard-Boston Egyptian Expedition were:

> "Development and improvement of methods of excavation and recording with the idea of making archaeological field-work a scientific method of historical research.
> The creation of a working organization carrying out as a matter of habit the principles laid down for efficient work."[23]

It is to be noted that method and skilled staff-development were keystones of Reisner's approach to field archaeology. Furthermore, field archaeologist and linguist-philologian were not to be separated. Where they could not be the same person in a given case, at least the aim could be realized in the staff as a whole. In more recent times, the history of the Oriental Institute of the University of Chicago has suffered when separation of linguist and field archaeologist became too great, and when the field archaeologist lacked the necessary breadth to be maintained on the Institute's *academic* staff.

In any event, with regard to archaeological method, it may safely be claimed that modern archaeology has few examples equal in excellence to Reisner's excavation of the tomb of Queen Hetep-heres, wife of Sneferu, first king of the Fourth Dynasty, and mother of Cheops, builder of the great pyramid. He and his staff spent a total of 321 days during two years (1925–27) meticulously taking apart the deposit, with complete record by notes (1701 pages), plans and sketches made in the tomb, supplemented by 1057 photographs also taken in the tomb.[24]

Reisner served as director of the Harvard Excavations at Samaria during 1909–10, with C. S. Fisher assisting as architect. The latter had begun his archaeological field work as an architect with the final campaign of the University of Pennsylvania's Nippur Expedition (1888–1900). Reisner's excavation in Palestine was simply a brief interlude during his work in Egypt, and he brought a number of his experienced Egyptian workmen to assist him, particularly, as trained foremen, photographic experts and camp managers. These men had been with Reisner for many years in Egypt—indeed, were his trusted team. From the untrained local labor the Egyptians created a well-disciplined force who by the second year "could distinguish different kinds of debris, recognize and clean a floor, or clear a wall, as well as could be desired."[25] The areas to be attacked were divided into sections,[26] and the workers were divided into "gangs," one "gang" for each digging sector, the number of workmen in a "gang" varying according to the work requirements in a given section. Each working unit had three to five pickmen, five to eight hoemen, and twelve to twenty-five basket-carriers. One Egyptian was assigned to oversee three to five workers. In other words, the Egyptians served both as foremen and as what today we call "technical" men. Presumably, they were responsible for discovering floors, cleaning them as well as associated walls, and distinguishing layers of debris while making sure that all objects were labeled, not only according to the sections ("strips" for Reisner) where found but also by debris layers in given areas (what today we call "loci").

Between 1906 and 1908, faced by delays and harassment from Turkish authorities, Reisner was forced to leave Palestine for his work in Egypt. When digging at intervals was finally possible for short periods in 1908, the German scholar, Dr. Gottlieb Schumacher, acted as director. After consultation with Reisner, work began in a trench laid out on the highest part of the mound's summit in order to discover any large building which Reisner felt ought to be encountered at this point. Reisner's reactions to Schumacher's work are illuminating. He says that "the stratification could not be made out clearly, although there were walls at various levels. On the other hand, a large building had been found and identified as the temple built by Herod and dedicated to Augustus . . . three trenches had been driven southward . . . From an examination of Dr. Schumacher's notes and plans, and of the trenches themselves, I could learn little more than that a temple had stood on the summit . . . In short, the whole problem of the history of the site remained to be worked out."[27] This is a succinct statement applicable to all excavations before World War I, except Samaria and Jericho, and even to certain excavations in the post-war period until this day.

After solving the vexing problem created by Schumacher's debris dumps and planning the disposition of his own debris, Reisner began work. He did not think that the "strip" system was as ideal as excavating the site as a whole. The disadvantages were minimized "by leaving the walls on the edge of each strip exposed until connected with the walls in the adjoining strip, by very careful records, including plans, sections, and photographs, and by making the strips as wide as possible."

At first the attempt was made to remove the debris layer by layer; but this was quickly found to be impossible, for as soon as the cultivation stratum had been removed there were no regular horizontal strata. The *debris of decay* of each period had been considerably disturbed during the construction of the buildings of the next period, in the search for building material and in the effort to place the new foundations on rock. As a result, foundations of all periods rested on the rock, and stood side by side. *Amid this apparent confusion, however, the successive deposition and disturbance of strata proved easily traceable, at least over certain areas.*[28]

In a mound where the depth of debris is not great and where Hellenistic and Roman builders liked to put their buildings on bedrock, the chaos of stratification can be imagined. Yet Reisner makes the astonishing statement that for the most part the strata were "easily traceable." How many excavations since then would have profited by Reisner's secret?

What was the secret which simplified Reisner's task? It was the attention given to the study of debris which is "indispensable to the understanding of the history of the site." Hence in describing his method Reisner goes into detail over "the different forms of debris and the various activities which modified them."

In other words, Reisner approached the problem of an Asiatic tell as a geologist approaches the problem of rock and soil stratification. The archaeological debris section showed not only walls but also the soil layer(s) into which foundation trenches were cut to erect them, and the layers and floors contemporary with their use, as well as those covering them as fill to level for a new building. This method was independently developed in England and independently reintroduced to Palestine by Kathleen M. Kenyon in her work at Samaria in the 1930s, and at Jericho and Jerusalem between 1952 and 1968.[29] Developed with the method were also precise methods of recording: daily field diaries, carefully prepared maps and plans, a numbered register of objects and a full photographic record. The aim is to be able to reconstruct on paper what has been excavated and to place each object within the proper soil layer where it was originally found. As field archaeologist, Reisner was the greatest to work in Western Asia up to his time. Without detracting from the vast importance of Sir Flinders Petrie's work, it must be said that Reisner was far more meticulous in method and in detail.

As for Samaria itself, here were found the first spectacular Israelite ruins erected by the Dynasty of Omri, in the ninth century BC, a dynasty already known outside the Bible from records found in Assyrian palaces. Its destruction during the winter of 722–721 BC is also eloquently described as a great event by the annals of Sargon II (cf. II Kings 17). Here also are the first carefully excavated Hellenistic and Roman ruins of Palestine, including those of the great temple erected by Herod the Great in honor of Caesar Augustus, directly over the ruins of the palace of the Israelite kings.

v

The other great American Egyptological giant, a contemporary of Reisner, was James Henry Breasted. For details of his life and work see John Wilson's summary below, pages 41–56. Without repeating what is said there, certain points may be emphasized which were of primary significance for American archaeology in Western Asia.

Immediately after World War I, it was Breasted more than any other who persuaded the American academic community that archaeology is an academic discipline which is a necessary part of the study of man. Because man had lived for so long without adequate knowledge of his past, Breasted termed our new knowledge of antiquity as the discovery of "the new past," and he made an eloquent case for its importance in current life. Furthermore, he convinced many people of the short-sightedness of most American colleges and universities at that time, which began the teaching of western history with the Greeks and Romans, completely omitting the achievement of "the Cradle of Civilization," "the Fertile Crescent," without which the Greco-Roman civilizations would not have existed. The story of civilization began with Sumer and with Egypt, and Breasted in his *Ancient Times*[30] provided the best textbook of ancient history ever written in this country for secondary schools, to show how the subject should be taught.

It remained a logical necessity for the next generation to add a survey of prehistory to this educational vision. That has come about mostly with a revolution in the field of anthropology since World War II, which has shifted its primary, though not exclusive, interest in those few examples of modern Stone Age people still existing, to a cultural and historical responsibility for man's prehistory as archaeology is making it known. The expeditions of the University of Chicago among the northern and eastern hilly flanks of Iraq, directed by a team of scientists headed by Robert J. Braidwood, has been of primary influence at this point. Braidwood, a product of Breasted's Syrian Expedition, has focused attention upon "the Neolithic Revolution," which between *circa* 10,000 and 5000 BC in the Near East led men to forego their "savage ways" and hunting economy for villages, domestication of animals and agriculture.

Another of Breasted's great accomplishments was to secure the interest of John D. Rockefeller, Jr., in founding an American institute for a massive effort in the recovery of our "new past." The Oriental Institute, liberally supplied with Rockefeller money, ushered in this country's greatest archaeological era in the Near East. During the 1920s and 1930s, major expeditions of the Oriental Institute worked in every Near Eastern country: Alishar Hüyük in Turkey, the Syrian 'Amûq plain behind Antioch on the Orontes, the Diyala basin northeast of Baghdad and the Assyrian royal palace-fort of Khorsabad in Iraq, the marvelous Persian capital, Persepolis, in southwestern Iran, and a typical tell, ancient Megiddo, in Palestine.

Except for a prehistoric survey, for Breasted the most important thing to be done in Egypt was not excavation, but the careful recording and interpretation of the hieroglyths on the ruins of temples and monuments still standing above ground. For this reason Chicago House was established at Luxor, the capital of ancient Egypt well up the Nile. Here a small staff has constantly been maintained which has only recently completed the recording of the temple of Rameses III at Medinet Habu, and is now beginning another project in the ancient capital. With regard to the cuneiform in Mesopotamia and Asia, Breasted was rightly persuaded that the most important single task was the examination of the huge quantity of written material already published, and the critical compilation of results in a definitive Akkadian dictionary (see below, p. 48). It is a matter of considerable satisfaction that the volumes of this great project have begun to appear during the last decade.

The death of Breasted early in 1935 was a great and irreplaceable loss to the world of archaeology. His great dream has faded. The Rockefeller support has never been matched by any other major source of financial backing in this country. Problems of staff selection, money, and World War II made it difficult to keep staffs together and publications of excavations completed.[31] Definitive works of the highest quality of scholarship proved impossible to produce in all cases, particularly with regard to the excavations of Alishar and Megiddo. Yet what has been accomplished is a great monument to archaeological scholarship, and it all took place at the best of all possible periods from the archaeologist's point of view—the time of mandates, when the countries in question welcomed western work and control was maintained by western directed departments of antiquities. Today that period is past and will not again return, at least in our time.

VI

Meanwhile, as the American Oriental Society had been the impetus behind the Nippur excavation, so the Society of Biblical Literature and Exegesis was responsible for establishing a permanent organization to facilitate the study and training of American scholars in the Near East. In a presidential address to the Society in December, 1895, Professor James Henry Thayer of Harvard University suggested that the time had come to establish a center for continued American research in Jerusalem. A committee was promptly formed which organized the American School of Oriental Research in Jerusalem. Its academic sponsors were: the Society of Biblical Literature and Exegesis, the American Oriental Society, and the Archaeological Institute of America. In addition to the home-based officers of the organization, each year in Jerusalem there would be, if possible, a director, an annual professor and at least one fellow.

It was expected that academic institutions would individually become members of the School's corporation, paying $100 a year each as a membership fee. The charter members of the corporation were:

Andover Theological Seminary
Auburn Theological Seminary
Boston University
Brown University
Bryn Mawr College
Colgate University
Columbia University
Cornell University
Episcopal School of Cambridge
Episcopal School of Philadelphia
General Theological Seminary of
    New York
Harvard University
Hebrew Union College
Johns Hopkins University
New York University
Pennsylvania University
Princeton University
Princeton Theological Seminary
Trinity College, Hartford
Union Theological Seminary,
    New York
Yale University

By 1940 the number had grown to sixty-four, and thirty years later to approximately one hundred and fifty, with virtually no special solicitation. In addition to this income, the Archaeological Institute of America, under whose aegis the School was placed, very generously provided a yearly stipend, contributing a total of some $30,000 during the early years of the School's existence.

The first director, Charles C. Torrey of Yale, went to Jerusalem in 1900 and subsequently published a group of stone sarcophagi from Sidon, which he studied while in the area.[32] Each year a variety of studies were made by the various scholars in residence,[33] until in 1919 dreams of something more elaborate seized the minds of the officers. The organization was incorporated under a new name: The American Schools of Oriental Research: Jerusalem and Baghdad. The wide interests of the officers[34] and others of the organization led to a desire to expand the institution's services for its members to other areas of the Near East. Baghdad was chosen because of the Nippur precedent, the hegemony of Breasted in Egyptology, and the special interests of the men involved, particularly those of the Schools' first sizable donor, the Rev. Dr. James B. Nies. Dr. Nies left a sizable estate in his will for the Baghdad School, the full income from which was to support the School after certain relatives had passed away. This income was released to the Schools in the early 1940s, twenty years later, after a considerable amount in legal fees had to be spent on the ASOR's part. During those two decades, unfortunate investments by the bank handling the funds caused the total sum to dwindle to only a fraction of what Dr. Nies had led the Schools to believe was available.[35] Unfortunately, the sum has never been added to. However, the Nies generosity also made it possible to erect a handsome and substantial building for the School in Jerusalem in the mid-1920s, the special house for the director not being completed until 1931 with assistance from the Rockefeller Foundation. During the 1930s, the Rockefeller Foundation offered the ASOR $250,000, plus a set sum for a short period for administrative costs. By 1940 the last of this money was received, providing the institution with $350,000 of endowment which had grown to over three-quarters of a million dollars in 1969. Encouraged by new prospects, two publications were begun: a *Bulletin* and an *Annual*.

The very small income available to the Baghdad School made it impossible to maintain a resident director in Iraq, although every effort was made for there to be an annual professor. In 1925 Dr. Edward Chiera of the Oriental Institute, as annual professor, began excavating a moderate sized town, whose ruins are called Yorgan Tepe, near Kirkuk, south-east of ancient Nineveh. A prosperous patrician's house was excavated, containing approximately a thousand cuneiform tablets which were records of business transactions during the fifteenth century BC. These records give the ancient name of the town as Nuzi. Though the tablets were written in the Assyrian language, the people of the town were not Semites, and the art of their cylinder seals was also something new. This led Chiera to prepare his report under the title, "A New Factor in the History of the Ancient Near East."[36]

Professor Robert H. Pfeiffer was so interested in the discovery that he organized four seasons of excavation at Nuzi between 1927–31, under the sponsorship of Harvard University and the Baghdad School. Chiera and Pfeiffer directed the first two seasons, and Richard F. S. Starr the last two. While all three were amateurs in field archaeology, the excavation of the fifteenth-century Hurrian town yielded a rich horde of information about the daily life and customs of a fifteenth-century town of the empire of Mitanni, which had a history of no more than two centuries before being crushed by the Hittites, *circa* 1370 BC. Yet the expedition produced the now well-known archive of Nuzi tablets which have thrown so much light on biblical Patriarchal customs, the meaning of which had been forgotten even by the Israelites themselves. The discovery also gave great impetus to Hurrian research, resulting in E. A. Speiser's *Hurrian Grammar* of 1941.[37] The resources of this archive, however, have scarcely been touched, even though it would be difficult to spend a more entertaining evening than by reading "One Hundred Selected Nuzi Texts" by Pfeiffer and Speiser![38] A small team on a new excavation and a fresh study of the tablets, art and artifacts, could give us the first and most complete picture of the life of a Western Asiatic town that is possible.

While Annual Professor of the Baghdad School in 1927–28, Professor Leroy Waterman of the University of Michigan began the excavation of the Iraqi Tell Umar, which he continued for several years under the auspices of his university and the Toledo Museum of Art. It was the site of Seleucia of the Hellenistic period, under the control of first the Seleucid and then Partian kingdoms, and it was in these levels that Waterman concentrated, though earlier remains below, back to Sumerian times, exist.

In the same year, 1927, the brilliant young scholar, E. A. Speiser, having obtained his doctorate from the University of Pennsylvania, was also an annual professor of the Baghdad School, and became its director between 1934 and 1947. After a survey of the area that was once southeastern Assyria, Speiser decided to excavate two mounds, a half dozen miles from one another, the history of which seemed to complement each other. The latter, Tell Billah, produced an Assyrian royal palace of King Asshurnazirpal II (884–860 BC) and stratification back to the Hurrian period, contemporary with Nuzi.

Tepe Gawra, on the other hand, proved to have a stratification extending from the fifth millennium BC to *circa* 2000 BC, when the top of the tell became too small for further occupation. The most spectacular discoveries were those of the Obeid period of the fourth millennium BC. Here were found the first large public buildings discovered up to that time. They were temples which, one after the other in succeeding strata, the sacred compound becoming larger as time went on, were the main feature of the site. They were not subsidiary to a royal palace, and represent that stage in Mesopotamian history reconstructed from Sumerian mythology by Thorkild Jacobsen in a brilliant piece of deduction.[39] The chief deity of the city, whose palace was the temple, was conceived to own the town and all its lands, so that the people were servants or serfs of the divine lord. A subsidiary series of deities, each of whom had a human counterpart, took care of all the various functions of the great manor house and the needs of the divine lord and his family. By the end of the fourth millennium, the commercial life of such temples had become so complex that the earliest known writing was invented (cuneiform Sumerian) to make the accounts easier to handle.

Meanwhile, in Jerusalem conditions ideal for excavation existed under the British Mandate following World War I. Clarence Stanley Fisher returned from Egypt, where he had worked for Near East Relief during World War I, and took up permanent abode in Palestine, serving as Professor of Archaeology in the Jerusalem School from 1925 until his death in 1941. As the only trained field archaeologist of note available, he was to exert a decisive and positive influence on all excavations of the 1920s and 1930s. He insisted on Reisner's great care in recording architectural, artifactual and photographic data. As an architect, however, the walls and buildings in the mound were his primary concern. Gone was what was crucial to Reisner, the close recording of debris layers in association to walls. Fisher's sections showed only wall elevations in relation to one another with the debris layers omitted.[40]

Nevertheless, he was the initial director or advisor of nearly all American excavations of the time, with the result that field technique was vastly improved over pre-war standards. First in the field was the University of Pennsylvania at Beth-shan (1921–33), which produced the first known series of Cannaanite temples, dating between 1400 and 1000 BC. Fisher set up the project and was its initial director, as he was also for the

Oriental Institute's great Megiddo Expedition, which began in 1925, and for a number of smaller projects initiated by small American institutions under the aegis of the American Schools of Oriental Research.[41]

A sizable project, initially directed by Fisher, was the excavation of Jerash (ancient Gerasa) beginning in 1931 by Yale University and the ASOR. This site is the most spectacular and best-preserved Roman and Byzantine town of the Palestine area, with forum, central north-south colonnaded street, two theaters, temples and later churches, triumphal arch, fortification and gates, all in a remarkable state of preservation considering the years since the site was abandoned. Petra, in its hidden valley surrounded by mountains, is more spectacular, but it is a quite different type of site from the small Roman town placed across a central trading route.

Other very important and well-known American projects can only be mentioned here. Princeton University initially sponsored the important surveys of classical monuments and churches in the Levant by Howard Crosby Butler during the first decade of this century; it followed this by excavations begun in the 1930s in Antioch, Syria, where Fisher assisted its director, George W. Elderkin, and by the excavation of the mound of ancient Tarsus, under the direction of Hetty Goldman. Most exciting, however, have been the excavations of Yale University at Dura Europus on the middle Euphrates River. The highly decorated and unique synagogue of the city has been re-erected in the Damascus Museum. The Christian church, a house-church with baptistry, is still the earliest to have been excavated. These excavations mark a substantial beginning on the classical periods of the Near East. They are only a beginning, however, for most of the American effort in the area has been on older ruins.

VII

When Breasted came to national prominence as the author of *Ancient Times* and the founder of the Oriental Institute, William Foxwell Albright emerged with his Ph.D. from Johns Hopkins University with a dozen articles already published. He did not expect to find a permanent position, but he did hope to discover sufficient fellowships and research grants to permit him to continue his studies. Like Breasted, he was born to parents of very humble means (see below, p. 54). But there the resemblance ends. If ever there were circumstances to block the development of a great scholar, Albright had them in twofold abundance. Born in a missionary compound in Chile of Methodist missionary parents, because of their low income he was brought up with only the necessities of life and no luxuries. After his parents returned to this country in 1903, his father was pastor of one small Methodist church after another in the midwest and six children were reared on an income never in excess of $400 per year. In Chile he was a *gringo* and a *canuto* (American and Protestant), and by the age of seven his parents had to spank him to force him to run errands outside the compound, where he faced insults and even stones. He belonged to a minority in a hostile environment, and from then to this day his emotional tendency has been to identify with the poor and the unloved, and to be intensely interested in minorities wherever found.

He was born so near-sighted that to read or, even now, to examine closely something that interests him, he must bring the book or object to within one or two inches of his eyes. Though tall and very strong physically, he has always felt his eyes to be his weakest point. Sure that one day he would go blind, he even taught himself Braille. Another childhood misfortune was an accident which caused his left hand to be virtually useless. Thus deprived of the ordinary life of a child, the give and take of play or normal association with his peers, his world was created largely within himself and in his father's library. That library consisted mostly of history and theology. His play was solitary and mental, in which he constructed ever larger and more complex historical worlds, peopled by imaginary heroes and non-heroes—an activity to which he credits his adult success in historical synthesis.

He does not tell us what it was in his eighth year (1899) that turned his interest to archaeology, and especially biblical archaeology. In any event, by saving pennies earned from running errands for his parents, he was able to accumulate five dollars by his tenth year, with which he bought the newly published *History of Babylonia and Assyria* by R. W. Rogers of Drew University, the best work on its subject to appear in English up to its time. Albright read and reread it until he had it memorized. As a teen-ager he taught himself Hebrew by the use of Harper's inductive introduction.

In 1907, at the age of sixteen, he entered the preparatory school of Upper Iowa University, where his father had graduated with his B.A. degree twenty-two years earlier. In 1912 he graduated with his own B.A., having worked hard in college in the two fields where the teaching was excellent, classics and mathematics. The poverty of his family forced him to make his own way through school, working regularly as a farm hand during the summer and even developing his crippled left hand to the point where he could milk cows. He lived so frugally and worked so hard at manual labor that he claims to have lost his fear of poverty and what we would now call marginal existence. Those who have ever worked under him on an excavation can certainly agree with him that this was excellent training for an archaeologist! He possessed a will and a constitution of iron. Fortunately, he was able to earn enough to go straight through college without interruption, though he was plagued continually by a guilty conscience. His family needed every extra dollar he could earn. Nevertheless he continued to buy books, mostly from Germany, and these he would read and study surreptitiously on Sundays![42]

After serving as principal of a South Dakota high school in a German speaking community for one year, he applied to Paul Haupt, head of the Oriental Seminary of The Johns Hopkins University, for admittance and a scholarship. Fortunately, he was able to send with his application the proof sheets of an Accadian article, "Dallalu," shortly to appear in *Orientalistische Literaturzeitung* (Vol. 16 [1913], p. 213). Evidently Haupt was sufficiently impressed, for Albright was admitted. When he arrived he brought with him speaking fluency in Spanish and German, in addition to English. He had had considerable training and self-instruction in the classics, including Greek and Latin; and he also says that "he possessed a fair elementary knowledge of Hebrew and Assyrian, together with a considerable reading knowledge of ancient history and related subjects"—typical understatements to which his students are accustomed![43]

Much of his work at Hopkins was in Akkadian, and in 1916 he was awarded his doctorate; his dissertation, never published, was "The Assyrian Deluge Epic." For three years, 1916–19, he continued to hold research fellowships, except for a short period of "limited service"—meaning labor battalions—at the end of World War I. During this time he broadened his scope into other Near Eastern fields. His flow of articles continued each year, some of them pointing into increasingly subjective fields in comparative religion and mythology. Examples, which he now would prefer did not exist, are "Historical and Mythical Elements in the Story of Joseph," *JBL,* 37 (1919), pp. 111–43; "Gilgamesh and Engidu, Mesopotamian Genii of Fecundity," *JAOS,* 40 (1920), pp. 307–35; and "The Goddess of Life and Wisdom," *American Journal of Semitic Languages,* 36 (1920), pp. 258–94.

In 1919, he was awarded the Thayer Fellowship of the American School of Oriental Research in Jerusalem, and toward the end of that year he arrived in Palestine, a country which he worried about as a boy because he feared that all the tells would have been excavated by the time he was grown! In 1920–21 he became acting director, and in the following year, director, a post which he retained until 1936; there was an interruption in 1929–33, because in 1929 he began as Paul Haupt's successor at Hopkins, where he served as W. W. Spence Professor of Semitic Languages until his retirement in 1958.

A study of his bibliography,[44] and especially of the content of the ASOR's *Bulletin,* illustrates the prompt shift in his focus of interest. After acquiring a speaking ability in Arabic and modern Hebrew, he began a serious study, over many years, of problems in ancient historical and archaeological topography; but never, of course, to the complete neglect of any other topic that came along to elicit his interest, such as: "The Amorite form of the Name Hammurabi," revisions in Hebrew, early Assyrian and Middle Babylonian chronology, "The Location of the Garden of Eden," "The Date and Personality of the Chronicler," "The Principles of Egyptian Phonological Development," "The Etymology of Egyptian *ḥmt,* 'woman,'" "Some Observations Favoring the Palestinian Origin of the Gospel of John," etc. No subject lay outside his interest, and, if it interested him enough, he could and usually did write a brilliant article on it, whether or not he had had specific academic training in the particular subject.

Yet here we must confine ourselves to archaeology. In Albright we encounter the first giant who interested himself in the same problems as those of Edward Robinson. Nearly sixty years after Hitchcock's lament (see above, p. 8), Robinson's successor as a critical scholar in Palestinology was at work, every trip a scholarly adventure. A series of articles on his results began to appear, indeed to become the main scholarly content of ASOR's *Bulletin,* while more lengthy contributions were published in the *Annual.* In 1922, after identifying Tell el-Fûl, four miles north of Jerusalem, with Israel's first capital—Gibeah of Saul—he remarks with joy that not one of Israel's main cities had yet been excavated, and he proceeded to a small work at the site; his results, with full topographical survey of the area, became the content of *Annual IV* (1924). Albright returned to the site for an extra campaign in 1933. His most publicized result was the identification and reconstruction of Saul's palace-fortress. Paul W. Lapp's excavation in 1964, to check Albright's results for a final time before King Hussein erected his own palace on the ruins, confirmed Albright's chronology and main conclusions. The only difficult question is whether the Philistines built the fort for a garrison, or whether Saul himself erected it, instead of taking it over from those whom he defeated.

Albright had now learned to use a new tool which Robinson had lacked. Robinson was intensely interested in ruins, but could not date them. Albright's great peer in topographical history was the German scholar, Albrecht Alt, whose work with his students during the German Evangelical Institute's yearly study-trip to Palestine formed the most important content of the yearly *Palästinajahrbuch*. Alt's sole major weakness was that he could not date the ruins either. The tool was pottery chronology. Quickly learning all that the great masters of the time, Père L. H. Vincent and Clarence Fisher, could teach him, Albright went far beyond them by closely observing the types of pottery found on the surface of various mounds and using such chronological precision as could be provided by a thorough knowledge of an area's history and dislocations by war. With this tool he could tell by examining the sherds collected on a mound whether its occupation would allow it to be identified with an ancient site.

Without going into great detail, one can judge the value of the new tool by studying his excavation of a small mound, scarcely half the size of Megiddo, southwest of Hebron in the foothills. Its name is Tell Beit Mirsim, which Albright identified with biblical Debir. His work there covered four seasons, 1926, 1928, 1930 and 1932. He had very little money; and the dig was possible only because it was a cooperative enterprise between ASOR and a member institution, Xenia Theological Seminary (subsequently, Pittsburgh-Xenia, and now Pittsburgh Theological Seminary). The representative of that school, M. G. Kyle, a well-known conservative and a man of impeccable taste and manner, was made Administrative Director, with Albright in charge of all archaeological and scientific matters. Their cooperation on this and also on a Dead Sea exploration was excellent. Pittsburgh-Xenia was surely an "underdog" in the scholarly world, and Albright delighted in a cooperation which could be so meaningful, even though the available funds for the excavation of Tell Beit Mirsim in four campaigns totaled little more than $30,000.

Albright first published the pottery of the site's ten strata in *Annual XII* (1932), and a correction and revision of the Bronze Age Strata following the fourth campaign in *Annual XIII* (1933). These were followed by the Bronze Age excavations described in detail (*Annual XVII*, 1938) and by the Iron Age (*Annual XXI–XXII*, 1943). This work established Palestinian archaeology as a science for the first time, something more than simply a digging in which the details are more or less well-described in an indifferent chronological framework which is as general as possible and often wildly wrong. Note, for example, Alan

Rowe's two volumes, *The Topography and History of Beth-shan* (Philadelphia, 1930) and *The Four Canaanite Temples of Beth-shan* (Philadelphia, 1940), in which everything is misdated in the worst possible way because the author refused to believe Albright's complete chronological reworking of the site's history from evidence made necessary by the finds. In contrast, Lamon and Shipton, *Megiddo* I (Chicago, 1939) and Loud, *Megiddo* II (Chicago, 1949), while failing to recognize at least one stratum, and at almost every point, especially in Vol. II, making mistakes of judgment and attribution, nevertheless had an accurate overall chronological framework because they used Albright's results at Tell Beit Mirsim as an established model.

Before 1932 there was no way one could learn pottery chronology, unless the rudiments were obtained on an excavation or with some instruction, especially from Père Vincent. As for Fisher, Albright quickly learned all he knew and from that time on it was Albright who dated Fisher's pottery; the latter was working on a *Corpus* he could never complete because Albright had so accelerated the pace of learning that his work could not be adapted quickly enough. If, as Alt has stated, in Robinson's footnotes lie buried the errors of many generations, so it is with Albright's basic work on Palestinian ceramic chronology. He took the discipline out of the mists of oral tradition, and with actual material from a well-stratified site, dated it with every comparative and historical tool available. To this day, if a Harvard student desires to learn Palestinian pottery chronology as the indispensable tool for dealing critically with excavation reports, this writer starts him on Albright's *Annuals XII* and *XIII,* asking him to prepare a detailed notebook with drawings and characteristics of each period given, before supplementation and updating is provided from other sites.

The wise student will study the pottery volumes and the excavation reports of Tell Beit Mirsim carefully, because for the first time virtually the whole of Palestinian archaeological discovery up to the time they were written—plus frequent forays into other countries, wherever the evidence can be seen to lead—comes under critical review. Thus it must be said that Albright created the discipline of Palestinian archaeology as we know it.[45] Furthermore, he has tried to articulate the methods of scholarship employed: archaeology, he maintains, uses in interrelation the principles of typology and stratigraphy. Comparable objects can only be successfully dealt with if they can be separated into types which possess an evolving history. It is stratigraphy which enables one to trace that history. Seldom can one tell, otherwise, in which direction the evolution of a type is proceeding. In the idealism of the last century it was commonly assumed that evolution proceeded in only one direction, upward toward the more pure and complex. Yet archaeology shows evolving types and cultures proceeding up or down, not to speak of other directions, and the direction cannot be plotted in advance by a fixed theory.

Finally, Albright's extraordinary role in extending the service of the ASOR has come about not only with his teaching and influence through personal involvement with countless scholars, but through his involvement with ASOR's *Bulletin*. During the 1920s with James A. Montgomery as editor, Albright's incredible ability to write a large number of articles and critical reviews rapidly each year meant that the *Bulletin's* main scholarly content came from Jerusalem. In 1931 he became the journal's editor, and continued as such for thirty-seven years until his resignation, because of eye problems, in the fall of 1968.

His own contributions and his editing of others brought the whole of the ancient Near East under critical survey. The constant reader of the *Bulletin* felt himself to be on the forefront of scholarly discovery and discussion. Scarcely an issue appeared for which Albright had not written something fresh and original. The *Bulletin* was an extension of his far-ranging scholarly activity, of his vast learning and of his enthusiastic participation in nearly every new development or new discovery. As he now retires from editing the journal that has been so much his own, an exciting chapter in American scholarship comes to a close. His students and disciples do their best, but no combination of these can add up to one of him. His real greatness as scholar and teacher has come, not so much from his mastery and new discovery in any one field, but rather from the fact that in whatever he touched a whole range of disciplines came neatly together in his mind, ready to be used as needed. He was brilliant to be sure, and had a remarkable memory. Yet his intensive preparation had started as a boy in his father's library, with Roger's *History of Babylonia and Assyria,* Harper's inductive Hebrew grammar, and the easy fluency of the practical linguist, which so easily became structured by grammar and theory.

VIII

In the area of archaeological topography and exploration, the next man of our time to be ranked after Edward Robinson is Nelson Glueck.[46] Following what has been said in this volume's Preface, at this point only an evaluation of his contribution to our subject is necessary. Born

and reared in Cincinnati, a graduate of the University of Cincinnati
and of the Hebrew Union College, he went to Germany for a doctorate
in biblical studies. There was something within him pushing for self-ex-
pression and special achievement. His dissertation, *Das Word ḥesed im
alttestamentlichen Sprachgebrauche,* brought with it a Ph.D. from the
University of Jena and the promise of becoming a great biblical scholar.
Before returning home, however, he made a study trip to Palestine, and
the summer of 1928 found him a member of Albright's second expedition to Tell Beit Mirsim.

These two men rapidly developed a warm affection for each other, and
Albright's influence led Glueck to shift his career goals to Palestinian
archaeology, the first and only American Jew to have done so before
about 1965. As a student of Albright's at the American School in Jerusalem, he became Albright's first serious student of ceramic chronology on
excavation and on field trips. Once Albright discovered a student's particular interest or aptitude in the field, he was an excellent empirical
trainer, continually testing the student's knowledge and always keeping
him on the run, as it were, with the bait of an expert's knowledge dan-
gling just beyond, but not too far beyond, his grasp. Glueck, judging from
firsthand testimony, was a very apt pupil in what was still a most esoteric
subject. Having learned Albright's lesson well, his field trips suddenly
brought him a vision of a vast job to be done, one which would take years
of hard effort: exploring Transjordan. When completed, the job would be
a living monument that would be its own reward as a vast exploration into
the unknown. Beginning in 1932 Glueck went to work on the project year
after year, with only two real breaks as far as this writer is aware, one in
1940–41, and the other 1948–51.[47]

When one lifts his eyes to the horizon from Palestine with his back
to the Mediterranean, at almost any point along the central ridge he sees
to the east the higher hills of Transjordan. Journeying south, one notices
how small the tells become at about the eight-inch rainfall area at Beersheba. Beyond that they cease entirely, except for an occasional oasis.
Surrounding the familiar land was wilderness with a few miles of sedentary
life, traversed many times but poorly recorded and gradually sloping
away into desert. This land to east and south, on the borderline between
the sown and the unsown—this is the terrain of bedouin or, in antiquity,
of the semi-nomadic peoples. How have the occupation patterns differed
in antiquity from what they are today? Here was a major challenge to an
explorer.

Glueck was not the first man by any means who had searched these lands, but he was the first to do as complete a survey as possible with a small budget and few helpers, and he was the first to use the pottery-dating tool as a basic scientific aid. Between 1932 and 1947, he spent nearly all his exploration time in Transjordan and in the Jordan-Dead Sea rift as far south as the Gulf of Aqabah. Between 1952 and 1964 he used his vacations to complete the explorations by a survey of the Negeb, or southland below Beersheba. Unless one has visited these lonely deserts, it would be difficult to imagine the fortitude, the will and physical endurance necessary for such exploration. Without the knowledge or strength to survive in the wilderness, one is always on exceedingly dangerous ground, as is proved by the recent death there of the American Bishop James Pike. Most of Glueck's work in Transjordan had to be on foot or on horseback. Refusing elaborate equipment, the explorer lived for days at a time as a Bedu, drinking what water was available from any source, living as a guest of the bedouin, and so well known and trusted that he was always protected, needed no foreign guards, and was never harmed.

The technical reports of the Transjordan survey are published in *Explorations in Eastern Palestine* I–IV, to be found in ASOR *Annuals* XIV (1934), XV (1935), XVIII–XIX (1939), and XXV–XXVIII (1951). Less technical surveys appear in two books, *The Other Side of the Jordan* (1940; 2d ed., 1970)[48] and *The River Jordan* (1946; 2d ed., 1968).[49] The results of the Negeb survey have not yet been published except in preliminary articles and in a popular vein in *Rivers in the Desert: A History of the Negeb* (1959; 2d ed., 1968).

The story Glueck has pieced together is a very unusual one. Here and there throughout the area occasional prehistoric settlements are to be found. Curiously, in Middle Bronze I (*circa* twenty-second to twentieth centuries BC) there is a period when semi-nomads began to become sedentary in the whole area, a movement spreading also to Western Palestine, though always in unfortified villages. With the reintroduction of walled cities and the city-state system during the nineteenth century in Western Palestine and northern Transjordan, central and southern Transjordan reverted to the non-sedentary life. This was replaced by organized states between the thirteenth and sixth centuries—in the Negeb for the most part between the tenth and sixth centuries. Another gap appears between the sixth and second to first centuries BC, when the amazing Nabateans mastered their environment by vast irrigation and water conservation methods. These enabled them to feed themselves in their sedentary base, with their capital at Petra, while they took vigorous control of the South Arabic trade with north and west. Their civilization continued, even though increasingly Romanized, after their conquest by the Romans in the second century AD.

Certain sites appear to fill in these peculiar gaps in sedentary life, but in the main Glueck's conclusions hold true because they are based on a wide sampling from so many hundreds of hitherto unknown sites. Various skeptics still exist, but thus far the evidence adduced has failed to change the overall picture materially. The major question which cannot be answered is "Why?" Albright and Glueck have both strongly insisted that the reasons must be social and political, because since the end of the last advancing glacier in the northern hemisphere—*circa* 9000 or 8000 BC—there has been no marked climatic change in the Near East. This is certainly true, though the effect of slight variations in rainfall cannot be completely ruled out as an *additional* factor, since they do occur periodically and their effects and regularities have not been studied over a sufficiently long period of time in marginal lands.

During the late 1930s Glueck carried out two excavations to give a depth dimension to his surface exploration. Khirbet et-Tannur was the ruin of a Nabatean temple. Its publication in *Deities and Dolphins* (1965–66) revealed for the first time in some detail the nature of Nabatean art and religion in its often almost flamboyant mixture of oriental and occidental motifs.

Tell el-Kheleifeh on the Gulf of Aqabah was long considered to be a copper refinery, a unique installation of its kind in the Near East. After the publication of Tannur, Glueck turned to the Kheleifeh material again to begin its study for publication. Now he saw that what he had earlier taken for flues were simply holes in the brick walls where wooden beams had rotted away. Yet when his plans and material are finally published, this writer believes we will see the first fine example yet found of a Solomonic fort erected to control an area. Its history and frequent rebuilding represent part of the struggle between the Judeans and Edomites over control of the vital Arabian trade route, until the fortress was destroyed forever with the Arab destruction of the Kingdom of Edom.[50] Glueck's continued record of original publication, despite his life as a very busy administrator, is one that few scholars in similar position have ever achieved.[51]

IX

World War II and the period of stabilization which followed meant that over a decade went by before American archaeologists were in the Near

East again. Of great significance has been the work of the Oriental Institute in Iraq, Iran and Turkey, in which the Baghdad School of the ASOR participated to the limit of its small resources. A new expedition to Nippur has been in the field several seasons, its main project being to uncover the successive rebuildings of another temple, this one the manor house of the goddess of fertility. Alternating with Nippur have been the great expeditions of Robert F. Braidwood in the hilly borderlands of Iraq with Iran and Turkey. The transition from food-gathering to food-producing economy, Braidwood theorizes, must have taken place naturally in areas where the grains and animals domesticated were already present in their wild state. The significance of these explorations and many test excavations for the fields of anthropology, paleobotany and paleozoology, among others, has already been alluded to.

Not well known is the Iraq Government's request that the Oriental Institute undertake a survey of the ancient canal systems in Iraq, to learn how to rebuild the country's ancient irrigation system for a growing economy today. A team under Thorkild Jacobsen began work in 1953 in the Diyala River area northeast of Baghdad, where under the overall direction of Henri Frankfort of the same institution so much had been accomplished in the late 1920s and 1930s. The first product of that expedition is the book by its present Director, Robert McCormick Adams, *Land Behind Baghdad* (Chicago, 1965). This volume reveals a new type of exploration which, using various types of scientific expertise, makes available to the historian knowledge of what the country was once like and to the modern agronomist knowledge of what must be done to restore it. There are problems here which are evidently most difficult to solve, particularly the high degree of soil salinity in earth left unirrigated for so long a time. In 1968–69 Professor Adams completed the second stage of the survey in the Nippur area under ASOR auspices, while Thorkild Jacobsen, as an annual professor of the Baghdad School, began work in the area of el-Hiba within the same region, a site which in 1953 he had identified with the Sumerian ancient Lagash. There New York University and the Metropolitan Museum had completed a first campaign of excavations under the direction of Donald Hansen and Vaughn Crawford during the same winter.

Another major story, yet to be assembled in detail, is the mad scramble by most Egyptologists of the western world to rescue as much information as possible from antiquity sites to be covered by the waters behind Upper Egypt's High Dam. The publicity released huge sums of money from western sources, so that under a liberal governmental policy in Egypt a vast amount of digging was accomplished, often in unfavorable scientific circumstances. A generation will be required before scholars "dig out from under" their results.

In Turkey, the Cornell-Harvard-ASOR Expedition to Sardis began in 1958 and still continues, with major efforts now being given over to architects to reconstruct and consolidate certain monuments, including an unexpected and truly monumental synagogue. Of special significance also has been the expedition at Gordion headed since 1951 by Rodney Young of the University of Pennsylvania, which has been responsible for resurrecting the Phrygian civilization, and the remarkable underwater discoveries of George Bass and staff, also of the University of Pennsylvania, off the southwest coast of Turkey. Machteld Mellink of Bryn Mawr College began in 1967 the excavation of the Early Bronze site of Karataş. Most excavations along the western area of Turkey have had a classical (Graeco-Roman) inspiration behind them. Two classical sites are currently being excavated by American institutions: Aphrodisias by Kenan Erim of New York University (the site was a center of sculpture in western Asia Minor in the Roman period) and Knidos by Iris Love of Long Island University.

Most significant also has been the work on Arab archaeology by Oleg Grabar, formerly of the University of Michigan and now of Harvard. In the spring of 1969, he completed his third campaign at the medieval Islamic desert town, Qasr el-Hayr, in Syria.

In the Palestinian area the great post-war story has been, of course, that of the Dead Sea scrolls, ever since the manuscripts of Cave I were brought to the Jerusalem School for identification in February, 1948. Even now there are rumors each year of new scrolls, and forgeries are available for the unwary. The Bedouin, and many who would like to act as their agents, do not seem to realize that such manuscripts are not simple antiquities which, if smuggled into a western antiquities market, can be easily sold. Before paying a huge sum the manuscript must be examined by an expert whom no forger can fool. Such experts are few in number, and when a document is certified as genuine, it becomes a political liability to own unless returned to the governments of Jordan or Israel.

Beginning in 1951, Directors Winnett, Reed, Tushingham, and Morton of the Jerusalem School carried out a series of campaigns at Dhiban, ancient Dibon and the capital of Moab, as we know from the stele of its King Mesha, which was erected in Dibon to celebrate his victory over Israel in the 840s BC. Andrews University, with Siegfried Horn as director, carried out the first campaign in 1968 at Heshbon, another of Mesha's cities. The University of Pennsylvania's James B. Pritchard completed his excavation at Gibeon, eight miles northeast of Jerusalem, with its great tunnels for water within the city, and was in the process of even more exciting discoveries at Tell es-Sa'idiyeh (ancient Zarethan) in the Jordan Valley when the 1967 war stopped all archaeology in the valley, including the College of Wooster's first season at the magnificent site of Pella, directed by Robert H. Smith.

Yet the central fact about American archaeology in Jordan and Israel, following the 1948 war and the long directorships of Albright and Glueck, is this: we on this side of the Atlantic did not have a supply of highly trained archaeologists to replace them and to man our Jerusalem School. With this weighing heavily upon us, Dr. Bernhard W. Anderson, then Dean of Drew Theological Seminary, and the writer began in 1956 the Drew-McCormick excavations of Shechem, Tell Balâṭah on the eastern outskirts of Nablus. It was, like several of the finest mounds dug earlier before the sufficient development of archaeological method, in very bad shape. There were great ruins, but their story could not be told! We made it our objective to develop a training program around the most difficult of archaeological objectives: the re-excavation of ruins already dug, with great emphasis being laid on working method, so that by self-criticism a working team could improve steadily in quality of achievement and also in teaching. By 1960 Lawrence E. Toombs had become associate director in charge of field operations, and during the fifth through seventh campaigns (1964, 1966, 1968), Edward F. Campbell, Jr., replaced the writer as archaeological director.

The expedition grew into a joint enterprise of a number of institutions, Garrett and Austin Seminaries joining Drew and McCormick as full sponsors. Not only did we succeed in wresting one exciting story after another from the mound and its environs,[52] but we were able to inspire a series of young men to do something comparable. First was the work of Paul W. Lapp at several sites while he was director and then professor of ancient Near Eastern history and archaeology at the Jerusalem School. Especially important has been the Concordia Expedition at ancient Ta-anach which he directed. Secondly, Joseph A. Callaway has returned to the great ruin, Ai in Hebrew, et-Tell in Arabic, primarily a third-millennium site with an Israelite occupation during the twelfth to eleventh centuries.[53] His success as teacher and stratigrapher has been amply demonstrated by the great success he has had with both site and staff.

Finally, while the writer was the archaeological director of the new Hebrew Union College branch in Jerusalem during 1964–65, he was able to begin a long cherished project with the support of Nelson Glueck and the College. That was the excavation of the great site of Gezer, half-way between Jerusalem and Tel Aviv. With the aid of two Harvard graduate students and student volunteers in Israel, we began to trench down the slope to date the fortifications, beside the last trench dug by Macalister on the tell's southwest side. Since then the expedition has continued every summer, with former students William G. Dever as director and H. Darrell Lance as associate director, and with the Hebrew Union College as sponsor. This expedition has particularly emphasized training in field method, as well as in archaeological history, and its results in excellence of workmanship, as well as in discovery, have been important for the future of American work.

X

This review of American involvement in the archaeology of the ancient Near East has been necessarily sketchy, with much material omitted in order to focus on certain dominant personalities.[54] One would like to leave the impression that this hemisphere, though late to start concentrated work in the Near East, is now ready and poised for its greatest era in the history of American archaeological scholarship, and for world archaeological leadership in many respects as well.

Unfortunately, this optimism may not be solidly based. The major inhibiting factor is the Near Eastern Iron Curtain, the attempt to polarize even the non-political, and the growing nationalism in the countries of the region, which are increasingly suspicious of western scholars and their motives. This is to be expected in a people's development, it would seem, and Americans, as well as others, will have to work where and as they may. At the moment, Iranian archaeology is obtaining a much-needed thrust into the limelight because westerners are still welcome there, and the country's history is so poorly known, except for certain periods. Also, at the present time Jerusalem and Beirut provide two foci for different kinds of scholarly interest. The archaeological investigation of the ancient Phoenicians has barely begun, though they played such an important role as bearers of ancient culture into the Mediterranean lands. Phoenicia, like modern Lebanon, was commercially and culturally oriented in two directions at once. Thus from Beirut a scholar would have a wide horizon before him. If he is prevented from moving eastward into Asia, he can certainly move westward, following Phoenician trade routes and exploring their trading colonies. Thus a major gap in ancient history might be filled. At the same time biblical archaeology, so closely tied to Canaanite culture both by acceptance and rejection, could not be more enriched by needed knowledge.

FOOTNOTES

1. W. F. Albright, *Dictionary of American Biography*, ed. by Dumas Malone (1935), pp. 39–40; also Hitchcock, see below, note 5, pp. 70–71.

2. Alt, *JBL*, 58 (1939), p. 374.

3. Quoted by George Foot Moore, "Alttestamentliche Studien in Amerika," *ZAW*, Achter Jahrgang (1888), p. 6.

4. See C. Conrad Wright, *Three Prophets of Religious Liberalism: Channing, Emerson, Parker*. (1961), pp. 13–17.

5. For details of Robinson's life, see Albright, *op. cit.* (n. 1), and especially the detailed essay of Roswell D. Hitchcock in Smith and Hitchcock, *The Life, Writings and Character of Edward Robinson, D.D., LL.D.* (1863), pp. 18–100.

6. He was President of Harvard from 1810 to 1828.

7. *The Christian Review*, 6 (1841), p. 448.

8. Hitchcock, *op. cit.*, pp. 46–47.

9. W. F. Albright, *From the Stone Age to Christianity* (1940), p. 2.

10. Italics are by this writer.

11. *JBL*, 58 (1939), p. 366.

12. *Ibid.*, p. 374.

13. *Op. cit.*, p. 79.

14. Oxford University Press, 1951.

15. According to recent announcement at the time of writing, this great work, now available only in Hebrew, is shortly to be published also in English.

16. See Lynch's *Official Report of the United States Expedition to Explore the Dead Sea and the River Jordan* (1852).

17. So reported by H. V. Hilprecht, ed., *Explorations in Bible Lands during the 19th Century* (1903), p. 290.

18. See Ward's "Report of the Wolfe Expedition to Babylonia," published in *Papers of the Archaeological Institute of America* (1886).

19. One of these architects was Clarence S. Fisher, a young man "borrowed" from the Department of Agriculture of the University of Pennsylvania.

20. See Thorkild Jacobsen, "Early Political Development in Mesopotamia," *ZfA*, N.F. 18 (1957), pp. 104–6; and William Hallo, "Sumerian Amphictyony," *JCS*, 14 (1960), pp. 88–114. For the results of the expedition, see J. P. Peters, *Nippur* (1897), the series of volumes published by the University of Pennsylvania under the series title *The Babylonian Expedition of the University of Pennsylvania*, ed. by H. V. Hilprecht, and the latter's connected account of the whole expedition, written in a lively and interesting vein, *Explorations in Bible Lands during the 19th Century*, pp. 289–568.

21. For a collection of some of Kramer's widely spread publications of the Nippur literary library, see his *History Begins at Sumer* (Doubleday Anchor Books, 1959), *Sumerian Literary Texts from Nippur in the Museum of the Ancient Orient at Istanbul* (*Annual of the American Schools of Oriental Research*, XXIII, 1944); "Sumerian Literature, a General Survey," *BANE* (Doubleday, 1961 [Anchor Books ed., 1965, pp. 249–66], pp. 267–78). The most penetrating religious analysis is that of Thorkild Jacobsen in widely scattered articles: see his "Formative Tendencies in Sumerian Religion," *ibid.* (*BANE*), pp. 267–78; his chapters on Mesopotamian

religion in H. and H. A. Frankfort, *The Intellectual Adventure of Ancient Man* (1946; later in Penguin Books, *Before Philosophy*); and the forthcoming collection of his articles to be published by Harvard University Press, ed. by W. L. Moran.

22. The following section is abstracted from the writer's article "Archaeological Method in Palestine—an American Interpretation," *Eretz Israel,* Vol. 9 (Jerusalem, 1960—The W. F. Albright Volume), pp. 120–33.

23. See the first work, below, in note 24, p. 247.

24. See Reisner's personal account in "Egyptology, 1896–1928," which is Chapter XIV in *The Development of Harvard University since the Inauguration of President Eliot 1869–1929,* ed. by Samuel Eliot Morison (1930). Reisner's bibliography is too massive to be repeated here. Cf. his *Mycerinus: The Temples of the Third Pyramid at Giza* (1931); *A History of the Giza Necropolis* I (1942); and (with W. S. Smith) *A History of the Giza Necropolis* II. *The Tomb of Hetepheres* (1955). Brief but regular yearly reports of his work are to be found in the successive *Bulletins* of the Museum of Fine Arts in Boston.

25. Reisner, Fisher and Lyon, *Harvard Excavations at Samaria* I (1924), p. 33.

26. The digging areas are said to vary from fifty to one hundred meters in extent: i.e. from seven to ten meters on a side if square, only slightly larger than our current five-meter squares (though even this latter figure may occasionally vary from smaller to larger, depending upon the type of digging situation being faced).

27. *Op. cit.,* p. 35.

28. *Ibid.,* p. 36. Italics are this author's.

29. For her description of the method, see *Beginning in Archaeology* (1952).

30. *Ancient Times* was first published in 1916 by Ginn and Co. and has been kept in print. With more lavish illustration, the same volume was issued under the title *The Conquest of Civilization* by the Literary Guild of America in 1938.

31. Most serious is the failure to publish the results of the Syrian Expedition, particularly the important ceramic, artifactual and architectural discoveries belonging to the second and first millennia BC. Robert and Linda Braidwood's first volume of the series, the only one published in addition to the description of the initial survey, *Excavations in the Plain of Antioch,* Vol. I. *The Early Assemblages, Phases A–J* (1960), is a model of its kind. Dr. Gus Swift's unpublished University of Chicago dissertation on the ceramic groups in question is sufficient to verify the vast importance of the material, but much too schematic and poorly illustrated to be of real use. Asia Minor and Egypt can be connected only through Palestine, Lebanon and Syria. Byblos, the only major site in Lebanon excavated, has been dug in such a peculiar fashion as to make it virtually useless for the purpose. Other sites, especially Hama, Alalakh and Ugarit, are helpful, but the wealth of stratified material unearthed by the Syrian Expedition could be much greater if critically handled in the light of present knowledge. Political conditions in the Near East are such that a new assessment by the advancing field techniques of contemporary archaeology will probably be impossible for a long time to come in the critically important areas of the Orontes Valley and the area of Aleppo.

32. "A Phoenician Necropolis at Sidon," *AASOR,* I (1920), pp. 1–27.

33. For some of these, see *ibid.,* II–III (1923).

34. In 1919 the "fathers" of the organization as represented by the Executive Committee were:

James A. Montgomery, Chairman	Morris Jastrow, Jr.
George A. Barton, Secretary—	James B. Nies
Acting Treasurer	J. H. Ropes
Cyrus Adler	C. C. Torrey
A. T. Clay	
J. C. Egbert, *ex-officio,* Pres. of AIA	

35. Dr. Nies did not think scholars could be trusted with the wise handling of funds. Consequently, a trust fund was set up separately in a certain major bank in New York City, the Trustees to be designated by that bank. The income was turned over to the ASOR, only after its amount was too small to support work in Iraq. Over the years the growth rate of the Schools' regular financial portfolio has been at an excellent rate, as have the private Baghdad funds since about 1950. With the exception of one major lapse, ASOR funds have been invested only with the very best expert advice in New York.

36. *AASOR*, VI (1926), pp. 75–92.

37. *Ibid.*, XX.

38. *Ibid.*, XVI (1937). Professor Ernest Lacheman of Wellesley College has spent his life publishing the several volumes of these texts in careful transcription without translation. The last volume, completing the project, should be ready shortly for press.

39. See the works of Jacobsen cited in notes 20 and 21, and also his "Primitive Democracy in Ancient Mesopotamia," *JNES*, 2 (1943), pp. 159–72.

40. This analysis need not be repeated in detail here. See the writer's article on "Archaeological Method in Palestine," cited in note 22 above. The best description of Fisher's teaching is given by William F. Badè, *A Manual of Excavation in the Near East* (Berkeley, Pacific School of Religion, 1934), which should be compared with Reisner's own description in *Harvard Excavations at Samaria*, Vol. I, and with Kenyon's *Beginning in Archaeology* (1952).

41. The greatest service of the ASOR has been in its publications and its assistance of scholars with small budgets from smaller American academic institutions. Large institutions with large budgets, like the University of Pennsylvania and the Oriental Institute, do not need the ASOR, though they have always remained loyal members.

42. The detailed information in this section comes from conversation with Albright and from his autobiography in Louis Finkelstein, ed., *American Spiritual Biographies* (1948), pp. 156–81.

43. *Ibid.*, p. 164.

44. Published as Appendix II in *BANE* (ed. by G. E. Wright, 1961). This was his first main *Festschrift*, presented to him in ceremony by the editor at Hebrew Union College in Cincinnati on May 24, 1961, his seventieth birthday. His second main *Festschrift* was Vol. 9 of *Eretz Israel*, presented to him by Israeli scholars at a special ceremony in the President's Mansion in Israel on March 13, 1969, for his seventy-eighth birthday.

45. This is not true of all sorts of advances in method and knowledge; that would not be expected. The question of how Albright made Fisher's method work as an excellent vehicle for his scholarship puzzled the writer for a decade, but the purpose of his article on "Archaeological Method in Palestine," cited in note 22 above, was precisely to work out how this was accomplished. This had to be said, it seemed to the writer, at a time when British archaeologists in particular were losing perspective completely about Albright's achievements, and confusing the discipline with the method used in pursuing it. A genius at any time in history has been able to rise above his time with the tools available, however simple; that is what defines the term.

46. Though the work of the British scholar George Adam Smith, *Historical Geography of Palestine*, first published in 1894 and still in print as a paperback, has been an excellent best-selling geography, so beautifully written, so dramatic in its descriptions, it has never fulfilled Edward Robinson's dream of what such a geography should be. Much closer to it has been Père F.-M. Abel, *Géographie de la Palestine*, I (1933), II (1938), from Jerusalem's Dominican École Biblique. Y.

Aharoni, *The Land of the Bible. A Historical Geography* (tr. by A. F. Rainey, 1967) is more up to date but does not replace Abel.

47. Glueck was Albright's successor as director of the Jerusalem School of ASOR 1936–40, 1942–47. Most of the academic year 1939 was spent in a major coast-to-coast ASOR lecture tour, mainly among the Corporate Members, following the steps of Albright's grand tour in 1927. The third such major lecture tour of an ASOR archaeologist was that of Paul W. Lapp in 1966. Even though he had to be on leave much of the time, Glueck was made a member of the faculty of the Hebrew Union College in 1928, given tenure as professor in 1936 and made President in 1947. His most obvious accomplishment as President has been the great expansion of the School's activities. A union with the Jewish Institute of Religion in New York was brought about during 1949–50, another branch begun in Los Angeles at approximately the same time, and the Hebrew Union College Biblical and Archaeological School in Jerusalem opened in 1963.

48. To be reissued in a revised edition by ASOR in 1970.

49. Republished in a revised edition by McGraw-Hill in 1968.

50. The beautiful plans of these two excavations represent the last major work of Clarence S. Fisher before his death in 1941. His tomb in the Mt. "Zion" Protestant cemetery—one must go through the arch and grounds of the Institute for Holy Land Studies (the former Bp. Gobat's School) to reach it—is near those of Petrie, Mrs. Bliss and many other notables of the First War and Mandate eras.

51. Special mention should also be made of his very energetic research assistant, Eleanor K. Vogel, who has compiled Nelson Glueck's bibliography for this volume, pp. 382–94.

52. See, for example, the writer's *Shechem: The Biography of a Biblical City* (1965).

53. For this writer's support of his teacher, Albright, in the interpretation of the sacred character of the city during the third millennium BC, see his article "The Significance of Ai in the Third Millennium B.C.," forthcoming in the Kurt Galling *Festschrift* in Germany.

54. A list of American projects omitted from mention is too great to include here, though for Palestinian archaeology one excavation will be of especial importance. That is the current investigation at Ashdod, begun by David Noel Freedman and continued by James Swauger of the Carnegie Museum, with Moshe Dothan of the Israeli Department of Antiquities as archaeological director.

JAMES HENRY BREASTED—
THE IDEA OF AN
ORIENTAL INSTITUTE

John A. Wilson

JAMES HENRY BREASTED of the University of Chicago became both a legend and a myth. With his fellow Egyptologists he was a legend for producing sound and useful translations and the most lucid history of ancient Egypt. For a large segment of the public he was *the* historian of ancient times, because of a high school textbook of great acceptance. Within academic circles he became a myth as a promoter who could raise financial support for studies seeming remote in time and space. Both the myth and the legend had a large content of truth, but truth which needs to be seen in context.

The framework of his career may be set down briefly.[1] Born at Rockford, Illinois, on August 27, 1865, he studied at Northwestern College, Chicago Theological Seminary, and Yale University, and received his Ph.D. from the University of Berlin in 1894. At the University of Chicago he held the first chair in Egyptology in the United States. From 1905 to 1907 he led an epigraphic survey of Nubia and the Sudan, which emphasized his interest in copying rather than excavating. In 1919, with financial aid from John D. Rockefeller, Jr., and later from the Rockefeller boards, he established at the University of Chicago the Oriental Institute, which became a leading agency for the study of the ancient Near East. He died in New York City on December 2, 1935.

By the age of forty Breasted had translated all of the historical records of ancient Egypt down to the Persian period—*Ancient Records of Egypt* (5 vols., 1906). Upon these translations he based his *History of Egypt* (1905), a lucid work of appealing style. The latter work was translated into German, French, and Arabic, and set into Braille. His *Development of Religion and Thought in Ancient Egypt* (1912), was a sound introduction to Egyptian religion, based, like the *History,* on fresh translations. It was the basis for his more popularly written *Dawn of Conscience* (1933). The high school textbook *Ancient Times* (1916), was widely used and went through various transformations of edition and title. His translation and commentary, *The Edwin Smith Surgical Papyrus* (2 vols., 1930), was a typical piece, since it combined translation of exemplary strength with a commentary of persuasive appeal. All of these writings show a responsible craftsman and a visionary motivated by deep faith.

Breasted was born to middle class parents, who suffered financial difficulties when he was a child. The setting of his youth was one of restricted circumstances in a small Midwest city, and he wavered between becoming a prescription druggist or a preacher. When a generous friend of the family aided his education, he decided to prepare for the ministry and enrolled in the Chicago Theological Seminary. There two forces shaped his direction. He discovered in himself an extraordinary gift for languages —he had perfect marks in a written and an oral examination in Hebrew— and he fell under the spell of a teacher of Old Testament, Samuel Ives Curtiss, who had broken with the cloistered tradition. Curtiss believed in field work along the lines of Edward Robinson or of Robertson Smith, and he was to write a book entitled *Primitive Semitic Religion Today.* These influences turned young Breasted away from theology toward philology. Curtiss sent him to Yale, to study under that young genius, William Rainey Harper.

In 1890–91 Harper was forming an outline of the mid-western institution which would become the University of Chicago. It would have strong biblical studies departments, but to be shielded from fundamentalist attacks, they were to be in the university proper, rather than in the Divinity School, and were to be bulwarked by studies of other ancient cultures. Harper's own brother could teach Assyriology, and an Arabist might be found, but there was no one in the United States to teach Egyptology. Harper suggested that Breasted, as a young language prodigy, go abroad to study Egyptian, with the goal of an assured position in the university. There was no difficulty in deciding among England, France, or Germany: the American academic tradition of the 1890s was oriented toward a German Ph.D. Breasted went to Berlin, to study under the gifted Adolf Erman.

Erman was a remarkable person. He was of the methodical German school, collecting, carding, codifying, and classifying, but an individual of warm human sympathy, as close to his students as the German university permitted. He must have encouraged in young Breasted two characteristics already present: the laying of a solid and careful foundation, and the erection of an imaginative structure upon that foundation. The doctoral dissertation (in Latin) dealt with the "monotheistic" hymns directed by the Pharaoh Akh-en-Aton to the sun-god. The future teaching of the young man was foreshadowed by the argument, "unius cultus dei ab Amenophide IV instauratus maximum momentum attulit ad cultum solis posteris temporibus propagandum."[2] There is an unbroken line from that claim of continuing Egyptian influence to his writings of forty years later.

The Ph.D. in Berlin was followed by marriage and a honeymoon in Egypt, where another strong psychological element entered. The sight of so many Egyptian monuments exposed and deteriorating, before they had been adequately copied, sharpened his idea of field work in Egypt. Feeling that there should be little more excavation until the extant monuments had been thoroughly studied and copied, he turned down an opportunity to collaborate with Sir Flinders Petrie in excavation; epigraphy was his first line of responsibility (see above, p. 17).

The position at the University of Chicago turned out to be less than blissful. His salary of $800 a year was small even for that day; and students in Egyptology failed to appear. Breasted also began one of those academic feuds which would cast some cloud over his career, in this case standing up to the Assyriologist of his department for his just share of things. Three factors rescued him from stultifying lethargy: the writing to which he had set himself, a barnstorming campaign of public lectures to relieve the family budget, and an invitation from Germany to collate Egyptian inscriptions in European museums for the benefit of a forthcoming dictionary of hieroglyphic. The European forays increased his strong predilection for epigraphy and gave him personal copies of Egyptian inscriptions for his own books. The five volumes of translations went apace, and public lecturing shaped the young scholar's style and lucidity. He had a rather dashing presence, a fine head, and a willingness to reach oratorical heights. He believed in himself and his work, and his conviction was communicable to his listeners. He became a fine lecturer, and this in turn lightened his writing.

But he was restless, and the opportunity came in 1905–06 and 1906–07 to spend seasons along the Nile copying inscriptions. He began in the Sudan and Nubia, but he hoped this would be the beginning of a copying enterprise encompassing all of Egypt. Toward that end he devised a rapid system of collation, setting the copyist's observations directly in ink upon an enlarged photograph. This ultimately was to become the "Chicago method," adapted for the copying work at Luxor. These two winter seasons along the Nile were arduous and rigorous; the product was all the more creditable. Unhappily the death of President Harper in Chicago brought the expedition to an end, without publication and without continuation of the copying into Egypt proper.[3]

That was discouraging, but the publication of the *Ancient Records* and the *History* made Breasted an international figure and the best known American Egyptologist. When he reluctantly consented to write a high school textbook, *Ancient Times*—he thought that he had no gift for popularization—and when that book went into exceptional demand, he became a figure on a wider stage. There is no doubt that the success of *Ancient Times* was a reason for the establishment of the Oriental Institute. A man who could make himself persuasively clear to a large reading public might be entrusted to direct a research organization.

Disappointments within the University of Chicago and the coming of World War I had temporarily dulled the Breasted exuberance. His student days in Berlin had been so stimulating an experience that he was a devoted admirer of the German intellectual world. The shock of the war and the anti-American attitude of such Germans as his former teacher, Eduard Meyer, were sobering forces. But Breasted still dreamed of "a laboratory for the study of the rise and development of civilization," and three months after the Armistice, in February 1919, he sent a letter to John D. Rockefeller, Jr., proposing an Oriental Institute at the University of Chicago. "It could be set going for about $10,000 a year." Mr. Rockefeller accepted this proposal, with support at the indicated rate for a period of five years. Although the appeal had been couched in Breasted's most eloquent language, Rockefeller later made it clear that he had been supporting a man and not a branch of study. "A well-trained man," Rockefeller wrote, "with high purpose and fine spirit" was "the most important factor in the advancement of the well-being of Mankind."[4] This was typical of Breasted's experience: time and again he tried to sell an idea or a project; when he succeeded he had sold himself, rather than the program.

Thus in 1919 the Oriental Institute was established at the University of Chicago, with Breasted the director. He immediately led a daring reconnaissance trip through Near Eastern countries which were still unsettled after the war. The nature of the Oriental Institute had been stated. "Summarized briefly, the purpose of this organization will be to trace as fully as possible the rise of man from Stone Age savagery through successive stages of advance, the emergence of civilization, the history of the earliest great civilized states, and the transmission to Europe of the fundamentals of civilization which we have since inherited."[5] The field reconnaissance through Egypt, Iraq, Syria, Lebanon, and Palestine sharpened up the possible points of attack.

While Mr. Rockefeller had provided the start and continued his annual subvention for several years, he was not interested in the indefinite support of an institution. Over the years his contributions to the Oriental Institute's formal budget were relatively slight. He did give generously to individual projects in which Breasted was interested, such as the production of the Berlin Dictionary of Egyptian and the publicaion of Mrs. Davies' copies of Egyptian tomb paintings, but the support which enabled the Oriental Institute to send more than a dozen expeditions to the field came from the Rockefeller Foundation, the International Education Board, and the General Education Board. The 1920s were the decade of expansive prosperity, of an outreach from America to other cultures, and of an interest in archaeology illustrated by the excitement over the Tomb of Tut-ankh-Amon. The current world was not as insistent as it became in the 1930s and 1940s. Thus it was possible for the Rockefeller boards and a few individuals like Julius Rosenwald, John Nicholas Brown, and others to support archaeology handsomely. Before the Depression forced a sharp curtailment in the operations of the Institute, its annual budget approached two-thirds of a million dollars, with field expeditions in Egypt, Palestine, Syria, Turkey, Iraq, and Iran, and an ambitious home program of research and publications.

The Oriental Institute had growing pains. Breasted was too trusting to be a good judge of men, and a rapid expansion of home and field staff brought in some difficult personalities. Moreover, with nine expeditions simultaneously in the field it was difficult to comprehend the results; Breasted felt that archaeology in the Near East had just about ten years leeway before restrictive nationalism limited the scope of operations. In the late 1920s that was a prescient remark. As it turned out, both nationalism and the Depression shortened the viable time to somewhat less than ten years.

At the time of his death in 1935, Breasted was proposing a solid basis for the Oriental Institute through massive endowment grants. He did not live to learn that the financial times and the trends in philanthropy were both against any such firm continuance. He has a very substantial memorial in Oriental Institute publications, which number about 175.

What were Breasted's essential ideas? Some of them can be seen in the purposes he laid down for the Oriental Institute, others in his various writings. How did a prairie boy become an internationally accepted figure, member of seven different foreign academies, recipient of an honorary degree from Oxford University, and a man whose books were translated into eight languages?

In a perceptive obituary notice, W. F. Albright called Breasted's philosophy "an essentially individualistic meliorism, in which 'character is man's destiny.' "[6] There is no doubt that he was a humanist, believing in the ultimate perfectibility of man. And his meliorism appears constantly in such terms as "the rise of man," "the upward course of human civilization," and the "unconquerable buoyancy of the human soul." Apart from some reverent references to Jesus, conventional religion did not appear to concern him. His interest was in man as a being of expansive capacity.

We have already seen that his 1894 Ph.D. dissertation posited the argument that the monotheistic cult of Amen-hotep IV about 1375 BC was a force leading to the cults of later times. Stated in crudest terms, Breasted saw a culturally genetic line coming down from ancient Egypt to our times. In 1905 he wrote: "It is to Egypt that we must look as the dominant power in the Mediterranean basin, whether by force of arms or by sheer weight of superior civilizations. . . . To us who are in civilization the children of early Europe, it is of vital interest to raise the curtain and peer beyond into the ages which bequeathed our forefathers so precious a legacy."[7] In 1933 he wrote: "The sources of our inheritance of moral teaching extend far beyond the borders of Palestine, and include the whole ancient Near East, especially Egypt, where the earliest transcendental vision of social idealism arose."[8] Consistently he saw man inventing forms for human betterment, these forms inherited by later ages, with the whole coming down in a great flood to our time. Here and there he admits that some expression had eroded or dropped out of currency within the culture of the inventor, yet he believed that it must have been cherished somewhere, to bring about its revival elsewhere.[9] It is as if human betterment were additive, with technical skill appearing here, scientific attitude there, and social justice elsewhere, and each of these being added to a current which would become a flood in modern times. The line, in simplified form, seemed to be Egypt, Greece and Rome, western Europe, and thus to us today.

It must be emphasized that criticism of such ideas comes from the standpoint of the skeptical 1960s. It is not simply that it is more difficult to share the abundant faith of the 1900s in our more emaciated days. It is not simply that the picture as painted now is complicated, with many variant approaches to higher culture, rather than the simple line of

Egypt to western Europe and the United States. It is also that the dying away of the classical tradition, with its focus on heroes, and the invasion of the social sciences, with their analysis of process without regard to value, have made us shy of such concepts as "the rise of man." The confusion of process and progress is still constant in our thinking, but there is a recognition that material abundance and high complexity do not in themselves constitute advance. So we confusedly debate the idea of "rise" or "progress." One may enviously offer Breasted a tribute for the vigor of his faith in man and man's upward climb.

Breasted was consistent throughout his writings. In 1905 he characterized Akh-en-Aton (Amen-hotep IV) as a "man, who in an age so remote and under conditions so adverse, became the world's first idealist and the world's first *individual*."[10] Although H. R. Hall sourly commented that others had a claim to the title of "first individual," and "Certainly Akhenaten was the first doctrinaire in history, and, what is much the same thing, the first prig,"[11] Breasted stuck to his guns—or shifted them only slightly. By 1933 he could accommodate another Egyptian hero: "With the possible exception of Imhotep," Akh-en-Aton "was the first individual in history."[12] Breasted's appealing showmanship was not a manufactured act; it bubbled up out of deep belief.[13]

Certainly no one had written about ancient Egypt so attractively. If his *Dawn of Conscience* does not carry the conviction of his earlier *Development of Religion and Thought,* that is because the *Development* was a pioneering treatment of Egyptian religious texts. Like the *History,* which rested upon the *Ancient Records,* the *Development* seemed to speak with an Egyptian voice because it was founded upon a fresh translation of the Pyramid Texts. Some twenty years later the *Dawn of Conscience* did not so obviously rest upon ancient inscriptions, and it therefore seemed a piece of special pleading for Egypt's priority in man's moral and ethical history. In any case, as critics pointed out, it is difficult to deny conscience to man in stages of history prior to the twenty-second century BC in the Nile Valley.

The *Ancient Records,* the *History,* and the *Development of Religion and Thought* lie two generations back, and they are out of date, both in specific content and in attitude. Yet they are still in demand, having recently been reissued and apparently selling well. Nobody else gave Egypt that high appeal. Breasted was able to stretch the imagination of the reader and make him aware of a long and dignified past.

If an institution is the lengthened shadow of man, that is true of the Oriental Institute and Breasted, even though the shadow may show a few deviations of its own. "The Institute is essentially an organized endeavor to *recover the lost story of the rise of man* by salvaging the surviving evidence on a more comprehensive scale than has hitherto been possible and then by analysis and synthesis building up an account of human development on a broader basis of evidence than has heretofore been available."[14] Certainly the Oriental Institute has contributed in a major way to the study of the cultures in the ancient Near East and their continuation into medieval times. But individual projects and individual persons have addressed themselves in different ways to the concept of "the rise of man," and the "analysis" has of necessity been stronger than the "synthesis." An institution which has attracted men of highly individual genius may find that the whole is less than the sum of its parts, that the sons of the prophets speak with a variety of tongues, rather than with a single voice. This is not a major failure: if the individual scholars have pursued their highly individual ways, they have been encouraged to express their own genius, which is better than the coercion to submit a single and unified product. And the common goal of better understanding of ancient oriental history has produced a good amount of joint activity and joint product.

We shall review some of the Institute's field expeditions below. At home, a gigantic enterprise seemed to be bogged down by its own weight for a generation until the Assyrian Dictionary in 1956 began the publication of its analysis of Akkadian cuneiform. This activity in itself brought to Chicago scholars of world fame and young scholars in training, making the Oriental Institute a focal center for Assyriological studies.

The point is that the Oriental Institute has developed basically along the lines which Breasted conceived, but has not been slavishly held to a few specified lines. He himself was enthusiastic about new approaches, and might have appreciated some of the deviations from the classical pattern. The major change of direction from the middle 1920s is that at that time the priorities were to set up a sound project and then find the men to staff it; whereas today the Institute has a coterie of scholars of established ability, so that the priorities are to tailor any new activities to fit the staff.

What were Breasted's ideas about archaeology? They focused entirely upon the Near East, even though he made respectful bows to work in Europe or in Central America. His concept of the beginnings of civilized life in the ancient Near East and the line of inheritance from those beginnings to our day was so imperative that he offered no suggestions about work outside of the Nile Valley, the Fertile Crescent, and its hinterland.[15] His ideas were quite consistent between 1902, when he submitted proposals to the elder John D. Rockefeller,[16] and the more complex interests of the 1920s.

First of all, archaeology would recover a story which was *our story*. The logic was different from the argument of the 1880s: it was no longer our story because Near Eastern archaeology would prove the accuracy of the biblical account; it was our story because our secular beginnings were in that ancient world. The origins of our modern living were back there in the Nile Valley and the Fertile Crescent: economy, household life, government, education, even our "conscience." Breasted never attacked or defended the specific validity of the Bible statements. His *History of Egypt* has a few passing allusions to elements in the Joseph story, none at all on Abraham or Moses; there is a rather indifferent reference to the Exodus (pp. 446 f.) in that 1905 text. Breasted's interests were the ancient Egyptians for themselves. He made much less use of Herodotus, Diodorus, or Josephus than his predecessors; the *History* is based upon the translations of Egyptian texts in the *Ancient Records*. The Egyptians were the most important people in antiquity to him, important because they began that state of affairs which we have inherited as civilization. The Babylonians and the Hebrews and the other ancient peoples merited honor, because they too belonged to that great tradition.

The second factor was that the story which began in prehistoric times in the Near East and came down to our day was a single story, so that the approach to it should be coordinated. There should not be several separate institutions working at discrete pieces of that story, isolated from each other in purpose and program and results. Under some auspices it would be necessary to have a concerted attack on the archaeology of the ancient world, and later a coordinated analysis and synthesis of the results for publication. Ideally of course, this would be organized under a single agency, an Oriental Institute. But cooperative action could be secured in the same way as there is group activity under the American Schools of Oriental Research. In April 1919, while awaiting an answer to his appeal to Mr. Rockefeller, Breasted proposed to the American Oriental Society an American Institute in the Near East, maintained by a small group of universities, with one headquarters in Asia and one in Egypt.[17] The School in Jerusalem would be a partner in this enterprise, which was otherwise not defined in its relations to the Archaeological Institute of America or the American Oriental Society.

Shortly after Breasted made this suggestion, the support came through for an Oriental Institute at the University of Chicago so that his organized and coordinated attack developed under one roof. It was never clear just how the unified program would be achieved, apart from a single administration. If—let us say—there was to be an epigraphic expedition in Egypt, an excavation in Palestine, an excavation in southern Iraq, and a prehistoric reconnaissance in Iran, there was no statement about the coordinated activities of the field directors or the field staffs of these enterprises. Presumably the overall common program would bring the field researchers together, or the synthesis would be achieved by the director of the entire program; this is about what happened at the Oriental Institute. With the exception of a period of two or three years around 1940, when Henri Frankfort conducted a seminar at Chicago on comparative stratigraphy of the Near East, attended by a dozen of the young field workers from different areas, the coordination was up to the director of the Oriental Institute. Frankfort and his coworkers did much to compare results from different enterprises, but their efforts arose out of the stimulating personality of Henri Frankfort, rather than out of any organizational planning. One has to say that the idea of a group of scholars, highly skilled in their individual metiers, working in and from a single headquarters, will not normally produce a single connected account. They will do best in their own specialties.[18]

A third conviction held by Breasted was that archaeological sites should be tackled on a long-range basis, just as the Germans in our times have approached Warka and Boghaz Keui, and the French Byblos and Ugarit. An important mound could be identified and excavated season after season, instead of the haphazard process of undertaking a new site each season or of leaving a number of fallow years between seasons of excavating the same mound. For the treatment of a mound under such a perennial attack, Breasted advocated the onion peel stripping, rather than the cheese wedge sampling. Thus, his proposal for Megiddo in Palestine was to peel off layer by layer, season after season, until one finally came down to bedrock. This ideal was never carried out in any one case. Some mounds did not justify more than a sampling by step trench. In other cases funds and the experienced staff ran out before the peeling process was well advanced, so that there had to be a final test pit down to bedrock before the site was abandoned. However, the wisdom of picking a site which would be returned to season after season seems justified.

Despite the twenty-five lean years preceding the sixteen years of plenty, Breasted formulated his proposals in terms of the scientific ends, not tailoring them to the limited funds available. Thus his proposition to undertake mounds on a long-range basis was made before there was enough money to envisage one season on a small dig. His optimistic belief was that the work in which he was interested was so good that supporting funds must ultimately come. That was a state of mind which provided a broad channel for philanthropy, and this proved very successful.

The requirements of perennial field projects and adequate funds were professional and salaried researchers. If the same place is visited every year, the same field staff must come along. Workers would no longer be picked up from the student body or amateur volunteers, serving for three months and then gone off to other interests. They would be put on an annual salary, returning to the expedition each season and working during the off-season on the preparation of publication. By the 1920s the field directors of most excavations were experienced professionals, and their assistants were becoming specialists—in architecture, pottery, lapidary arts, photography, and so on. The efficiency of an expedition was greatly increased without having to train inexperienced volunteers, who might reach some stage of usefulness just about the time their service ended.

Another requirement of continuing at the same site was good field quarters, which might range from refurbished local houses to specially built and equipped complexes. They were not hovels, tents, or caves; but had sanitation and usually refrigeration, and a modest field library. The complex included living quarters, a common room, working rooms, and storage stage. Older archaeologists who had been obliged to put every penny into the work and to skimp on food and room scoffed at Breasted's "lordly bathrooms," but perhaps the proof of the wisdom of adequate quarters lay in the excellent health record of the Oriental Institute expeditions. Illness was not common or severe. For the most part the staff members were happy to return to such quarters year after year.

The optimum conditions of a continuing staff and of comfortable field accommodations came to an end in the latter 1930s. The chief cause for retrenchment was the Depression, but another factor lay in the more rigid conditions for field work imposed by rising nationalism. Between 1936 and 1939 the number of Oriental Institute field operations went down from an annual normal of nine to three. World War II completed the retreat.

There were other lights and shadows in the Breasted program. His emphasis on the origins of civilization led to an interest in prehistory, in the hope that the search might some day provide an unbroken line of evidence from the palaeolithic artifacts known to him on terraces above the Nile Valley down to man—settled in villages along the edge of the river. The Prehistoric Survey which he launched in Egypt should later have been moved to Mesopotamia, "where such researches are still as entirely unknown as they were in the Nile Valley when the Oriental Institute organized this work."[19] In the specific sense that dream was not achieved; but the Institute did participate in other ways in exploring the prehistory of the Fertile Crescent.

For southwest Asia Breasted wanted excavations; for Egypt he wanted copying. This might have seemed inconsistent, since storage rooms in Europe and the United States contained thousands of cuneiform tablets still to be studied and one might have asked for a moratorium on digging in Mesopotamia until the collections at home had been handled; but it was not quite that. Much more was it the deterioration of the stone structures in Egypt that oppressed his conscience. From that first visit in 1894 Breasted had been alarmed at the destruction of temples and tombs in the Nile Valley. For centuries they had been sheathed in a protecting depth of sand and debris; with excavation they were exposed to the erosive forces of wind, water, driven sand, and, above all, human superstition and greed. What was above the ground should be copied and studied before anything more was exposed. Breasted saw the situation as quite different in southwest Asia.

The only exceptions in Egypt were clearances, like the "architectural survey" of the temples of Medinet Habu. If those temples were to be understood completely, the work of copying had to be supplemented by digging out the entire complex of stone and brick structures. Certainly the visible erosion of monuments in the Nile Valley has justified Breasted's priority there, even though the old interest in finding new things by excavation affects everybody, including the Institute staff. In recent years they have cleared a Theban tomb and participated in the Nubian emergency campaign.

The final tenet of the Breasted doctrine was that publication should be an integral part of field activity, that an excavation was not completed until it had appeared in its final and definitive publication. Part of this dogma was served by the permanent field staffs, who were supposed to work at the preparation of written reports during their off-seasons. There was thus no excuse to let the writing go because of the pressure of other obligations. Further, the Oriental Institute set up an editorial office, which assisted authors on manuscripts and gave the final product a rigorous examination for accuracy and consistency. Nevertheless, there was still the cost of printing, engraving, and binding. That expense was met at first by a grant from one of the Rockefeller boards, but Breasted had a rather ingenuous optimism that the sale of Oriental Institute volumes would create a revolving fund which would finance the production of later volumes. This expectation never came anywhere near being realized, so covering publication costs has remained a problem. The belief that preparing manuscripts and the actual production of books should be an integral part of field expedition costs is certainly correct, but financing that belief has been difficult for all private scholarship.

The success and the significance of the archaeology initiated by Breasted were uneven, as would have been inevitable under varying conditions and different field directors. Excavations at Khorsabad and Persepolis were in the classical mold, with monumental expectations and monumental results. The pioneering activity of the Prehistoric Survey in the Nile Valley, of the Syrian expedition in the Amuq Plain, and of the Anatolian expedition made definite and valuable contributions to areas where there had been little knowledge. Later operations by others made extensive alterations in the findings of the Prehistoric Survey and the Anatolian expedition. The Megiddo expedition in Palestine had been conceived with roseate expectations, and while the mound produced very important evidence, it did not in itself become the prototype stratigraphic site for Palestinian archaeology, and some shifting of the levels assigned by the successive excavators has been demanded. The ideal of the Prehistoric Survey for western Asia was to be approached by others in other ways. For example, Braidwood reached backward from the earliest evidence of sedentation and the "pottery horizon," rather than attempt to come forward from the palaeolithic and mesolithic.

The two most successful enterprises were the Epigraphic Survey at Thebes in Egypt and the excavation of a constellation of mounds northeast of Baghdad: Tell Asmar, Khafaje, Ishchali, and Tell Agrab. The Epigraphic Survey has maintained over forty years a standard of accurate copying quite unparalleled for the Near East. The carefully organized work in Iraq was under the direction of Henri Frankfort, and was of great use in clarifying the predynastic and early dynastic periods in Mesopotamia. If the name of Frankfort has again appeared within an aura of success, it may illustrate the point that an archaeological program may be developed in admirable clarity, but the achievement of striking and persuasive results often depends upon superior personalities.

How did the Midwest a century ago produce James Henry Breasted? How did he come to be a world scholar instead of druggist in Downers

Grove, Illinois, or preacher in some rural Congregational church? One can only speculate about the answer to those questions.

His genius for languages is inexplicable. No experience in the western prairie could have equipped a boy with that feeling for Semitic and Egyptian. While he did enjoy music, and thus may have had an ear for sounds, that does not lead one into the syntactical structure of a different family of languages. Here he was simply a prodigy.

The fervor with which he embraced his chosen field of ancient Egypt and his belief in the ultimate perfectibility of mankind can perhaps be explained. A generation before the birth of Breasted, the United States had been shaken by religious fervors of various sorts. There had been vatic outpourings and eschatological expectations, and experiments in perfect social communities. Except for the Mormon movement, none of these tremendous convulsions quite came off. The earth did not come to an end, and the perfect societies became imperfect. Conventional religion reasserted its authority, but the hope for the great miracle was still in the air, particularly in the "Bible belt" of the American Midwest. Surely the Lord must have provided something greater for His people than this petty daily grind of labor. The threat of hell-fire was no longer enough to keep the people quiet. They wanted a message.

There were other stirrings, of which the boy Breasted was unaware, but which might have affected some of his teachers as he moved into college, seminary, and university. The industrial revolution had reached a point at which proletarians were challenging the vested interests. The theory of evolution was changing science and setting off a debate about religion. Herbert Spencer was adapting the ideas of evolution to social history, attempting to trace the growth of the social organism from simple homogeneity to great heterogeneity, with the ultimate goal of individual human happiness. As with Breasted, Spencer discarded conventional religion and put his faith in science and in individual man. Each of them understood evolution as being change for the better, seeing an inevitably upward line. Further, the years of Breasted's youth were trembling with the High Criticism of the Bible and the consequent weakening of divine authority as manifested in one book.

Within this setting a boy of ambition and ability was born to a limited horizon; given only the resources of his family he might have achieved little. The kindly aunt who financed his education unwittingly released a great humanist on the world, one who had to preach a mighty message. The message announced that man had achieved great things over thousands of years. One might start with the beginnings in ancient Egypt to see how man had raised himself by his bootstraps time and time again. Each new human conquest was the promise of another. The line was straight, simple, and clear; from Egypt through the classical world, through western Europe, and on to the United States—on to little cities in the Midwest—the line of human progress was the string of buoy lights which led on into the future, toward the ultimate perfectibility of man. Careful scholarship on the early stages of human history might provide a sermon more powerful than any preached from the pulpit of a church. Man's course is upward!

FOOTNOTES

1. Charles Breasted, *Pioneer to the Past. The Story of James Henry Breasted, Archaeologist* (1943).

2. James H. Breasted, *De Hymnis in solem sub rege Amenophide IV conceptis* (n.d.), p. 63.

3. The work of the two seasons was reported in *AJSL*, 23 (1906), pp. 1–64; 25 (1908), pp. 1–110.

4. Charles Breasted, *op. cit.*, pp. 238 ff., 385.

5. *AJSL*, 35 (1919), p. 202.

6. W. F. Albright, "James Henry Breasted, Humanist," *The American Scholar*, 5 (1936), pp. 287–99.

7. *A History of Egypt*, p. vii.

8. *The Dawn of Conscience*, p. 401.

9. A specific parallel would be Amen-hotep IV's hymn to the sun and the 104th Psalm (*ibid.*, p. 367). Since this pharaoh's religion became heresy in Egypt, the hymn could not have survived there, to fashion the Hebrew Psalm. It must have gone into Asia in his own time, been translated into some Semitic dialect, and, in modified form, appeared finally in Hebrew.

10. *A History of Egypt*, p. 392.

11. H. R. Hall, *The Ancient History of the Near East* (1913), p. 298.

12. *Dawn of Conscience*, p. 301.

13. Mention might be made of a social scientist's attempt to put Breasted in his place by attacking the concept of the hero in history: Leslie A. White, "Ikhnaton: the Great Man *vs.* the Culture Process," in *JAOS*, 68 (1948), pp. 91–114: with p. 113: "We can come to no other conclusion than that the *general trend* of events would have been the same had Ikhnaton been but a sack of sawdust." If Breasted's hero worship seems dated back to the nineteenth century, the absurd dogmatism of the opposite viewpoint throws Breasted's treatment of history into happy relief.

14. James H. Breasted, *The Oriental Institute* (*University of Chicago Survey*, 12 [1933], p. ix).

15. In 1916 Breasted invented the term "Fertile Crescent" for the curve of land between the Syrian Desert and the mountains of Anatolia and Persia—a crescent including Syria-Palestine, northern Mesopotamia, Assyria, and Babylonia (*Ancient Times*, pp. 100 ff.).

16. Charles Breasted, *Pioneer to the Past*, pp. 117 ff.

17. Presidential Address, "The Place of the Near Orient in the Career of Man and the Task of the American Orientalist," *JAOS*, 39 (1919), pp. 182 ff.

18. Another exception to this generalization was the series of lectures ultimately published as H. Frankfort *et al.*, *The Intellectual Adventure of Ancient Man* (1946). The collaborative analysis of ancient oriental psychology also owed much to the persuasive personality of Henri Frankfort.

19. Breasted, *The Oriental Institute*, p. 144.

THE PHENOMENON OF ISRAELI
ARCHAEOLOGY

W. F. Albright

ONE of the most remarkable phenomena in the history of archaeology
is the extraordinary flowering of Israeli interest in it since Independence,
over twenty years ago. Jewish scholars were slow to enter the field, largely
because Rabbinic studies had tended to absorb them until the age of
Haskala (the Ashkenazi enlightenment in the late eighteenth and the
nineteenth centuries). Jewish intellectuals whose interests were wider than
Rabbinic scholarship generally took up philosophy and the arts, especially
music and later representational art. For men who were trying to break
away from the burden of their past dedication to ancient and medieval
Jewish literature, archaeology probably seemed too remote from the interests of the day which they were so avidly pursuing.

Jewish participation in archaeological research developed along two lines:
field exploration, and study of Jewish art and institutions—especially the
former. Among the greatest archaeological explorers of the nineteenth
century were Joseph Halévy and Eduard Glaser, who successively opened
up the virtually unknown world of South Arabian inscriptions. The former
was a Sephardi Jew from Turkey who became a French citizen; the
latter was an Austrian. Being a Levantine, Halévy was able to speak
Arabic and travel as a Yemeni merchant. Glaser was an Austrian as-
tronomer and Orientalist whose diversified talents allowed him to map
much of the still unknown territory of southwestern Arabia. Both were
brilliant innovators and became centers of violent scholarly controversy.
Between them they created the new scientific field of ancient South Arabic
studies—though the script itself had been previously deciphered by Rödi-
ger and Gesenius.

In the following period Jewish archaeological specialists arose in various
countries, as was to be expected, though no Jewish archaeologist seems
to have worked in Palestine until after the First World War. Among the
best known of the generation of archaeologists which grew up toward the

end of the nineteenth century was Raymond Weil, French Egyptologist, (who also directed a French campaign of excavation in Jerusalem after the war) and especially the brilliant American classical archaeologist, Hetty Goldman (who was recently awarded the second gold medal of the Archaeological Institute of America for distinguished work in archaeology).

Palestine was opened up to archaeological research after the end of the First World War, and especially after July 1, 1920, when the British Mandate was inaugurated with Sir Herbert Samuel as High Commissioner. No time was lost in setting up a Department of Antiquities, with a distinguished non-Jewish archaeologist, John Garstang, as director, and with an international archaeological advisory board to assist him in planning. For many years Professor Joseph Klausner represented Jewish interests on this board. The writer had the honor of sitting beside him as his interpreter, since the meetings were conducted in English and French, neither of which Klausner could speak, though he was, of course, perfectly at home in German and Russian. In those days there was an enthusiastic little group of Jewish scholars in Jerusalem; all were essentially amateurs except for Dr. Klausner, who was already well-known as editor and author of scholarly works, both in Russia and Germany.

Eliezer Ben Yehuda was then at the top of his form, bursting with vitality and enthusiasm; since he lived across the Abyssinian street—really an alley—from the house then occupied by the American School of Oriental Research, I saw him almost daily. He had begun his career in Poland, which he left to study medicine in Paris. He then became interested in Zionism and abandoned medicine in order to move to Jerusalem, where he edited a Hebrew newspaper for many years, devoting himself to the task of modernizing Hebrew and adapting it to daily use. Both Klausner and Ben Yehuda were interested in archaeology, but neither knew much about the field as such. As men of culture and broad interests they did much to make the pursuit of archaeology respectable.

The first Jewish excavation in Palestine was actually carried out at a ruined synagogue south of Tiberias by Nahum Slousch, who had become known as a historian of modern Jewish literature; he was known in France as a Semitic epigrapher who in collaboration with Philippe Berger published Punic inscriptions in the *Corpus Inscriptionum Semiticarum*. Unfortunately he had not received any real training in either epigraphy or archaeology, and his part was important chiefly because of his flair for publicity and his success in interesting the public in the Jewish archaeology of Palestine.

Among the group of intellectuals in Jerusalem was one who became greatly interested in archaeology, for which he showed natural talent—Eliezer Lipa Sukenik. Born in Bialystok (Byelorussia), he went from Russia to the University of Berlin to study botany, but he left abruptly for Palestine two years before the outbreak of the First World War. Here was a young scholar of broad intellectual interests who understood the scientific approach. He and I became fast friends in 1920 and were inseparable companions before long.

In 1922/23 he received a small grant enabling him to spend some time studying classical archaeology at the University of Berlin, having already gained some experience in excavating Jewish tombs in Jerusalem. In 1923/24 he attended courses at the American School of Oriental Research and took part in several archaeological undertakings. I then got into touch with Cyrus Adler, who invited him to come to Dropsie College (Philadelphia), where he received his doctorate in 1926.

In those years Sukenik had to struggle against the general prejudice of older scholars because he lacked the stereotyped classical education, without which he was not considered worthy of a university professorship. But in the end he fought his way through to complete success, becoming lecturer at the Hebrew University in 1935, professor at the Museum of Antiquities in 1938 and finally head of the department of Jewish Archaeology at the university in 1943. By then he was the foremost world authority on synagogues and Jewish archaeology in general. His great triumph came in 1947 when he recognized the Dead Sea Scrolls as genuine, and he acquired half of them for the university by a series of courageous moves at a very difficult time. Not having a good eye for form, he never succeeded in becoming a first-class epigrapher; this part of his career was continued brilliantly by his long-time assistant, who took the name of Nahman Avigad and became one of the foremost leaders in the field. Sukenik hesitated for months before fixing the date of the new finds. Over the years I had urged him to work out and publish the chronology of Hebrew and Aramaic inscriptions of the last few centuries BCE and the first centuries CE. At the time, I did not realize why he kept deferring execution of the plan and why he declined to take a stand on my dating of the Nash Papyrus and the ossuary inscriptions in 1937. For the same reason he delayed public announcement of the fabulous discovery until the American School had, quite innocently, reported its independent study of the complementary group of manuscripts (April 1948). There can be no doubt, however, that Sukenik's greatest achievement was to interest his son Yigael in his own field.

A still younger man who was to make an indelible imprint on Palestinian archaeology was Benjamin Mazar, who settled in Palestine after receiving his doctorate in 1928 from the University of Giessen, where he studied under Julius Lewy. After a dissertation on the history of Syria and Palestine in the second millennium BCE (published in 1930) he became interested at once in archaeology; after spending some time at Tell Beit Mirsim he decided that archaeology was to be his chosen career, if possible. It did become possible, and he has not only carried out many important excavations himself but has created a new school of ancient Near Eastern and biblical history. The enthusiasm with which he fills his students has been so widely diffused that he must be counted among the chief founders of Israeli archaeology.

With Independence in 1948 came a new Department of Antiquities headed by Shemuel Yeivin. Since the Palestine Archaeological Museum, founded by John D. Rockefeller, Jr., was in East Jerusalem, it became inaccessible to citizens of Israel and had to be replaced by a new one in West Jerusalem. The new Department of Antiquities was headed by Yeivin until his retirement, when his place was taken by Avram Biran (formerly Abram Bergman, who received his doctorate with me at Johns Hopkins University in 1935). Yeivin was not only an archaeologist of long experience but also a formidable administrator. He was a very good director of the Department, since he had tenacity and determination enough to override all kinds of administrative obstacles and property-owners' resistance. In the early enforcement of Israel's new law of antiquities, superseding the earlier Antiquities Ordinance of the British Mandate, firmness and stubborn determination were essential. Again and again he saved promising archaeological sites from being built over or otherwise exploited before archaeologists had a chance to excavate or at least make soundings. A weaker or more acquiescent director might have permitted all sorts of violations of the law, thus establishing a practice of accepting such situations as *faits accomplis*.

A. Biran, his successor, is ideally suited for the second phase of guiding the Department of Antiquities. As both a natural and a professional diplomat he gets things done without stirring up too much opposition; from long experience he knows how best to get along with the Arabs; he is very successful in interesting both Israelis and non-Israelis in the recovery and care of Palestinian antiquities.

Independence rapidly produced a new attitude toward archaeology among citizens of the new state. For the first time the ordinary Israeli felt a personal stake in the antiquities of his land. Archaeology had to do with the Bible. Israeli archaeologists speak and write the language of the Bible as well as that of the new nation. Archaeologists come from all ranks and groups of the mixed population; there are Ashkenazis and Sephardis, as well as Arabic-speaking Jews from such exotic countries as India and China. Besides, any schoolboy interested in collecting things can in Israel collect potsherds and beads as well as the usual shells and butterflies, and they also take less space. Coin collecting has become a hobby considerably more attractive than philately since a sharp-eyed boy can easily pick up ancient coins and start his own collection. Older people may purchase antiquities, or with enough money and influence may even subsidize digs in their own names. Archaeological meetings flourish and the Israel Archaeological Society is one of the groups most widely attended by amateurs.

Among literate Israelis in general, the influence of archaeology has not been restricted to collecting and sponsoring. Through archaeology one sees most vividly how cultures followed one another from the Middle Stone Age down to the present. Though archaeological remains may still not be as extensive or as impressive as in richer countries, their diversity is just as great as in any long-settled region of the Old World. What is true of chance finds and random distribution of sites is also true of major excavations. The late Clarence Stanley Fisher used to say that he found digging in Palestine more interesting than excavating in Egypt and Babylonia because the finds were much more diversified. The uniformity of cultural remains from the rich ancient centers of the Nile and Euphrates Valley often produces, in a given stratum, a rather dull repetition in types of objects found. In Palestine one is seldom bored by cultural homogeneity.

Above all, archaeology helps to produce, among Israelis, a sense of belonging. Objects from the last two millennia BCE illustrate the life of the People of the Book so perfectly that they tend to appear more and more as part of the continuing history of Israel. From Abraham to modern times there was no period in which the ancestors of modern Israel were not living in the land and living in the kinds of houses and using the kinds of artifacts found by excavators—whether or not the houses and artifacts in question were actually used by Hebrews, Israelites or Jews, or whether they were used by the neighbors living in a kind of symbiosis with them.

The modern Israeli is also increasingly struck by the fact that his ancestors were not true nomads in any known period. The great explorer of archaeological sites, Nelson Glueck, though not an Israeli, is one of the few men qualified to understand the relation between population and

settlement in antiquity. It is no accident that he was the first to identify
correctly the Age of Abraham with the Middle Bronze I period (also
known as Late Intermediate Bronze). Even then, as well as in all
subsequent periods, the Hebrews and their Israelite successors were
essentially sedentary, although they might occasionally have lived under
semi-nomadic conditions.

The two most important archaeological undertakings yet organized in
Israel have both been directed by Yigael Yadin (son of E. L. Sukenik):
the four seasons of work at Hazor and the two at Masada. Yadin, who
specialized in ancient weapons and warfare during his student days, and
has since published the best manual on the subject which we possess,
became an officer in the Hagganah, and at the end of the War of Independence was Chief-of-Staff of the Israeli Army. He is a natural organ-
izer, so it is scarcely surprising that these two digs were exceedingly well
planned and directed. He is also a master of detail with an ingenious
mind, as well as one of the most able lecturers in the entire archaeological
world. In addition, he possesses trained diplomatic skill—certainly un-
diminished by his experience at the negotiating table over twenty years
ago. Fortunately, he has no trace of his father's occasional *Stachelkleid,*
which sometimes handicapped his archaeological team-work and in his
younger years seriously hindered his advancement.

These two magnificently organized expeditions have shed more light
on ancient Palestine than almost any comparable excavations in the history
of Palestinian archaeology. The finds at Hazor were extremely well dated
by the skill of such experts in pottery chronology as Ruth Amiran and
Trude Dothan. The expedition architect, I. Dunayevsky, added greatly
to its success. Work at Hazor has clarified the history of Israel as well
as the history of Bronze Age Palestine, removing previous uncertainties
and increasing our understanding of the Israelite conquest of Canaan in
the thirteenth century BCE.

The excavation of Masada could be carried out almost completely
in two seasons because the surface of the site had been denuded to bedrock almost everywhere. On the steep slopes between vertical escarpments
there may still be caves or pockets of interesting debris to be cleared at
some future time. The excavators were helped enormously by a host of
selected volunteers from all over the world, thus introducing a new and
increasingly popular dimension into field archaeology. At Masada we
have before our very eyes, vividly pictured by the finds of buildings and
objects, the tragic end of the Jewish resistance in 73 CE, when the last
survivors killed their families and themselves in order to escape falling

into the hands of the Roman soldiers. Masada has driven the fundamental significance of archaeology home to the Israeli to an extent never approached by any past excavation anywhere in the world. The historian may think it more important to find fragments, large and small, of ancient Hebrew manuscripts. Masada has yielded such finds, giving the coup-de-grâce to both too early and too late dating of the Qumran Scrolls, since the latest script at Qumran is substantially the same, and in no case later, than the latest written remains of Masada. But from the standpoint of the impact of archaeology on national life Masada has no historical parallel; it remains unique.

ON RIGHT AND WRONG USES
OF ARCHAEOLOGY

Roland de Vaux, O.P.

ARCHAEOLOGICAL research in the Near East during the past one hundred years has completely reshaped our understanding of those countries mentioned in the Bible with which the ancient Israelites had contact. These "biblical countries," which are not limited to Palestine alone, run from Asia Minor to southern Egypt and from Iran to Crete. The pace of discoveries has been accelerating in the past forty years, and no slackening is anticipated. We now have knowledge of the peoples who inhabited these lands, of their writings and languages, their literature and art, their institutions, history, and religion; and this knowledge will increase. We know the cities they built, their houses and workshops, their furniture and tools. In short, we are now able to reconstruct— though not without many remaining lacunae—the human milieu, both intellectual and spiritual, in which the Bible was composed and was first heard and read. This flow of new information has produced a revolution which affects every branch of biblical studies: textual criticism and exegesis must take into account those languages which were not known or which were not understood a century ago, and those manuscripts which have been discovered in recent years in the region of the Dead Sea; literary criticism must compare the genres of the Bible with those of the literatures once believed lost; historical criticism must confront the biblical data with the texts and monuments which the excavations have uncovered.

The area of our investigation here, however, is less broad. Etymologically archaeology is the "science of antiquity," and it is in this sense that the word is used, for the first time, by Plato: "They are very fond of hearing about the genealogies of heroes and men, Socrates, and the foundations of cities in ancient times and, in short, about archaeology in general" (Hippias maj. 285d).* Archaeology, therefore, is synonymous with ancient history: the prologue to the history of Greece by Thucydides, dealing with origins, was called "The Archaeology"; the title of the history of Rome written in Greek by Denis of Halicarnassus is "Roman Archaeology"; the title of the history of the Jews by Josephus is "Jewish Archaeology." Understood in this sense archaeology should link together the study of texts with that of monuments; but the word did not pass into Latin, and it disappeared from post-classical Greek.

Scholars of the seventeenth century recreated the word, giving it a meaning it did not have in ancient Greece. In modern usage, despite occasional confusion, the word properly designates the study of the material remains of an ancient civilization as opposed to written sources, even if the latter have been provided by "archaeological" excavations. Such written sources are studied by the independent sciences of epigraphy, papyrology, palaeography, and philology. Archaeology, therefore, is limited to the *realia,* but it studies all the *realia,* from the great classical monuments to the locations of prehistoric fire-places, from art works to small everyday utensils, to the most primitive remains of any industry whatsoever; in short, everything which exhibits a trace of the presence or activity of man. Archaeology seeks, describes, and classifies these materials. But it does not stop there: it attempts to explain them; it compares them with each other and with the remains of neighboring civilizations; it arranges them in chronological order; and it places them in relation to texts and to history. Its final purpose is to reconstruct the conditions of life in antiquity, to trace the development and the circumstances of an extinct civilization. With reference to periods or peoples who have not known writing, archaeology takes the place of deficient history; where history based on written documents exists, archaeology verifies and completes the documents and puts them back into their living context. It is in this specific sense that the word is used here.

Archaeology is an auxiliary science of history in general, and archaeology of the ancient Near East has become an auxiliary science indispensable for biblical studies. The man to whom this volume is presented is at the same time an archaeologist and a biblical scholar, a man who has explored the country of the Bible and excavated its soil, and a man for whom the Bible is not only a subject of study but an inspiration for life. In the following pages, dedicated to him, our intention is neither

* Translator's note: this English rendering of Hippias major is from H. N. Fowler, *Plato with an English Translation* (1926), VI, p. 353 except for the word "archaeology," which is the actual Greek word used by Plato.

to present a summary of archaeology's contribution to a better understanding of the Bible, nor to detail the new problems it sometimes poses for the exegete and the historian. Because it is possible to make both good and bad uses of archaeology, we will propose only some methodological reflections. Archaeology can be used for other ends than those which are proper to it. One can ask of it more than it is able to give, and what it gives can be wrongly interpreted.

Let me quickly review some obvious abuses. In the nineteenth century certain excavations in Mesopotamia, in Persia and in Egypt were no more than plunder operations for the profit of European museums or private collections; the best of these systematically cleared large architectural structures, collected or copied inscriptions and preserved art objects, but even they neglected the stratigraphic observations which would have made dating the monuments or objects possible and made them useful for the historian. It has happened—and still happens in the midst of the twentieth century—that archaeology has served to conceal the activities of the intelligence services of certain major powers, or has provided the occasion to assemble information having nothing to do, or very little to do, with science. Between the two world wars archaeological research in mandate territories was generously subsidized and effectively supported by the mandatory powers for motives in which political prestige was not absent. Today in all the countries of the Near East, in those which have maintained their independence as well as in those which have recently acquired or recovered it, in the most ancient states as in the youngest, archaeology serves nationalism everywhere. It is used to establish links, real or contrived, with the past and to legitimize, through alleged ancient rights, the possession or acquisition of certain territories.

Fortunately, these intentions which are alien to science or contrary to it have not entirely deprived this archaeological research of any positive result. This is, in the first place, because excavations carried on without a proper scientific method have nevertheless brought to light a great deal of material which has thus been made accessible to study and has been preserved from possible destruction. Furthermore, many archaeologists working in these conditions have safeguarded their integrity as scholars. It must be stated, however, that the purpose of archaeology is neither to supply the galleries of museums nor to serve political interests.

I turn now to another abuse which is more difficult to detect and evaluate. It is evident that the extraordinary development in archaeological research in Palestine during the past one hundred years has not been motivated, as in other areas of the Near East, by the desire to resurrect some great civilization, nor by the hope of discovering many written documents or objects of notable artistic value. From this standpoint excavations in Palestine have always been very unproductive compared to those in Egypt, Mesopotamia, and, more recently, Syria and Asia Minor. Palestine has been explored and excavated because it is the "Land of the Bible."

A little more than a century ago, in 1865, the *Palestine Exploration Fund* was established in London "for the purpose of investigating the Archaeology, Geography, Geology, and Natural History of Palestine," and its first president, who was the Archbishop of York, laid down as principles the following: "1. That whatever was undertaken should be carried out on scientific principles; 2. That the Society should, as a body, abstain from controversy; 3. That it should not be started, nor should it be conducted, as a religious society." Nevertheless, the *Prospectus* announcing this new foundation to the public began with these words: "No country should be of so much interest to us as that in which the documents of our Faith were written, and the momentous events they describe enacted,"[1] and on the cover of the *Quarterly Statement* which the *Fund* began to publish in 1869 it was stated: "A Society for the accurate and systematic investigation of the archaeology, topography, geology and physical geography, natural history, manners and customs of the Holy Land, for biblical illustration."

With the English society as model, the *Palestine Exploration Society* was founded in New York in 1870, and its program added the "defense" of the Bible to its "illustration." The appeal to the public said: "The work proposed by the *Palestine Exploration Society* appeals to the religious sentiment alike of the Christian and the Jew . . . Its supreme importance is for the illustration and defense of the Bible. Modern skepticism assails the Bible at the point of reality, the question of fact. Hence whatever goes to verify the Bible history as real, in time, place and circumstances, is a refutation of unbelief . . . The Committee feels that they have in trust a sacred service for science and for religion."[2] The same year 1870 saw the birth in London of a new association, the *Society of Biblical Archaeology*, "to investigate and systematize the antiquities of the ancient and mighty empires and primeval peoples whose records are centered around the venerable pages of the Bible"; it set as its purpose "the investigation of the Archaeology, Chronology, and History, of Ancient and Modern Assyria, Arabia, Egypt, Palestine, and other

Biblical Lands"; its first president, Samuel Birch, declared: "Its scope is Archaeology, not Theology; but to Theology it will prove an important aid."[3] The American society was short-lived (see above, p. 10). The *Society of Biblical Archaeology* did not survive the first world war. The *Palestine Exploration Fund,* however, is very much alive; it has remained faithful to its principle of scientific objectivity, though its new organ, the *Palestine Exploration Quarterly,* still bears the words, "for biblical illustration," as the definition of its activities. Its undertakings, with those of younger institutions, have effectively contributed much "to illustrate" the Bible.

However, the biblical interest which has elicited and which continues to sustain explorations and excavations in Palestine may easily lead to an apologetic use of archaeology to "prove" the Bible. We have seen this intention expressed in the founding of the short-lived *Palestine Exploration Society.* More recently, this tendency has inspired expeditions to Mount Ararat to recover the remains of Noah's Ark, the interpretation of certain barren strata in Mesopotamian excavations as providing evidence of the Flood, an underwater exploration of the Dead Sea in search of Sodom and Gomorrah, and excavations in the neighborhood of Mount Nebo to locate the tomb of Moses. This apologetic preoccupation manifests itself in such books written for the wider public as Charles Marston's *The Bible Is True: The Lessons of the 1925–1934 Excavations in Bible Lands Summarized and Explained,* in 1934, and the "best seller" of W. Keller, *The Bible as History: Archaeology Confirms the Book of Books,* in 1956.[4] Such abuses are easy to recognize and denounce. But some scholars of great competence and complete integrity, although condemning such excesses, look to archaeology to "confirm" the Bible.

It must be understood that archaeology cannot "prove" the Bible.[5] The truth of the Bible is of a religious order; it speaks of God and man and their mutual relations. This spiritual truth can neither be proven nor contradicted, nor can it be confirmed or invalidated by the material discoveries of archaeology. However, the Bible is written in large part as history: those elements which deal directly with the history of the people of Israel from their origin (the Pentateuch and the historical books), or which have close links with history (the prophetic books), account for four-fifths of the Bible. It is concerning this "historical" truth of the Bible that one asks confirmation from archaeology. This matter is important for the Bible's "religious" truth. The faith of Israel in its God was founded on the interventions of this God in its history: it was faith in

Yahweh "who led Israel out of the land of Egypt" and who directs events toward the realization of his promises, executes his judgments, and fulfills his mercies. What the Bible recounts is a "sacred history"; it provices a religious interpretation of history, one that, again, archaeology can neither confirm nor invalidate. Archaeology can assist us only in establishing the facts that have been so interpreted.

But the manner in which they are reported and the amount of interpretation varies greatly. The exodus from Egypt and the return from exile are two salvific acts of God which have been construed as parallels, with the liberation from Babylonian captivity considered a new exodus; yet there is no comparison between the narrative of *Exodus* and that of *Ezra*. The conquest of Jericho and that of Ai are episodes of a holy war in which Yahweh delivers to Israel its Canaanite enemies; the destruction of Jerusalem is also a holy war in which Nebuchadnezzar is Yahweh's executor of judgment against his rebellious people, but one cannot treat in the same manner the narratives of *Joshua* and those of *Kings* and *Jeremiah*. These examples are extreme, but between them one is able to place many others. It is an illusion to attempt to force all these cases into the same "historical" category. The first duty of the historian is to undertake a critique of these narratives and to determine, as far as possible, the amount of reality and the amount of interpretation which each contains. Whatever the result, he is obliged to acknowledge that it is only his interpretation of a reality which he is not able to recover.

It would be naive to think that, because archaeology occupies itself with *realia,* it is more objective and hence nearer to historical reality. Actually, its results cannot be appropriated by the historian until they first are interpreted. If one takes archaeology in its specific sense, as we do here, it provides the historian only with mute documents. These documents have the advantage, over texts, of being contemporary with the events to which they witness and of having escaped the accidents of oral or written transmission and the changes introduced by successive interpreters. But they have the greater disadvantage of being mute, and thus they require interpretation. If they concern periods prior to writing they will never permit us to reach more than a sketchy and anonymous approximation of history. If they date from periods with written documents or with traditions which were later written down, it is the texts, whether historical works or short inscriptions, which explain the monuments, from palaces and temples down to the smallest objects. On the other hand, because of the advantages referred to, and also, paradoxically, because they are mute, the monuments of archaeology serve to illuminate, complement and control the written documents.

Texts and monuments are the two means of recovering historical actuality. They must be conjoined, but they must not be confused. The study of each is a distinct discipline which follows different methods that must be applied with equal rigor in both cases. There should be no conflict between a well established archaeological fact and a critically examined text. One and the same archaeological fact or one and the same text may allow a choice among several historical interpretations: the proper interpretation is then the one in which both ancient witnesses are in accord. But the judgment of the historian may be influenced, and warped, by the preference which he gives either to archaeology or to texts. The temptation may be to minimize the witness of archaeology which conflicts with his criticism of the texts, or to neglect the witness of the texts which do not occur with his archaeological conclusions. He may also be tempted to produce an artificial harmony between them by giving to the archaeological facts or to the texts a meaning which they do not have, and even to do violence simultaneously both to archaeology and to the texts. Finally, one must remember that the witness which archaeology and the texts afford is and always will remain incomplete. The earth's crust has preserved only a small portion of the monuments and objects of antiquity, and archaeology has recovered only a small proportion of these; also, those texts which we have represent only a very small part of that which was written, and even so would not represent everything necessary for the work of the historian. Thus archaeology can mitigate the silence of ancient texts to a certain degree, but one must also admit that lack of archaeological evidence would not be sufficient in itself to cast doubt on the affirmations of the written witnesses.

These methodological principles are applicable in scholarship generally, and the debate over the use of archaeology in the historical study of the Bible may be illumined by a comparison with analogous disputes in other areas of ancient history. Let us consider two examples.

The first is that of Phoenician expansion in the Mediterranean area.[6] The ancient authors have ascribed to this event very early dates: according to Strabo, the Phoenicians crossed the Columns of Hercules shortly after the Trojan War; according to Velleius Paterculus, they then founded Gades (Cadiz), and next, soon after, Utica. The founding of Utica is dated in 1101 BC according to the concurrent testimony of Pseudo-Aristotle and of Pliny. Once again, according to Pliny, Lixus, on the Atlantic coast of Morocco, would be older than Gades. All these settlements, therefore, would be considerably more ancient than Carthage, which traditionally is considered to have been founded in 814 BC. According to Diodorus, the Phoenicians were the first to exploit the silver mines of Spain; enriched by this commerce, they seemingly founded numerous colonies in Sicily and neighboring islands, as well as in Lybia, Africa, and Spain. According to Thucydides, the Phoenicians preceded the Greeks in Sicily and on the small coastal islands. Herodotus has the Phoenicians coming at an early date to Cythera, Thasos, and Thera. According to the Bible, Hiram, king of Tyre, a contemporary of Solomon, had a fleet equipped for the high seas; and according to Menander, as cited by Josephus, this same Hiram conducted a punitive expedition against a rebel colony (Utica?) which had refused to pay tribute.

These literary data, the accuracy of which was already doubted by J. Beloch, seemed contradicted as well by archaeology. In 1958 R. Carpenter summarized the results as follows: "We shall have to assert that Utica and Carthage were not settled before the latter part of the eighth century before Christ, and that the commercial expansion from Carthage as a base led thereafter to the settlement of Western Sicily early in the seventh century, of Sardinia late in the seventh or early in the sixth century, of Ibiza in the Balearic Islands and the southern coast of Spain still later in the sixth century, to be closely followed by the occupation of Gades outside the Straits and, at a considerable interval, the settlement of Morocco." Consequently, scholars have been willing to move the founding of Carthage down one century and have rejected the witness of the ancient authors. D. Van Berchem writes concerning this matter: "The Phoenician problem could serve as an example for a good discussion of method. It would be in order to ask, in particular, to what extent archaeological results authorize a correction of the statements of ancient authors. If it is evident that the results of excavations permit us to establish facts up to now unsuspected, it is much more doubtful that the absence of findings can, in itself, suffice to invalidate the witness of the literary sources."

This is in harmony with the considerations which I have proposed. In fact, during the past ten years a very definite about-face has occurred, required by the new interpretation of former discoveries and by the results of more recent excavations. A Phoenician inscription of Nora in Sardinia and an inscription of Cyprus are now dated in the ninth century BC (W. F. Albright); and the Phoenician ivories of Carmona in Spain have been attributed to the tenth or ninth century (W. F. Albright).

The excavations at Nora and at Sulcis in Sardinia have brought to light objects of the eighth century. In Sicily (Motya) and in Malta the Phoenician settlements go back as far as the eighth century. The tombs of Almuñecar in Spain, the Sexi of antiquity, contain Phoenician pottery of the eighth century and alabaster vases bearing the cartouches of the Pharaohs of the ninth century. The excavations at Mogador and at Lixus indicate that the Phoenicians had trading posts in Morocco during the seventh century.[7] The general claim of the ancient authors therefore regains its credence: the Phoenician colonization preceded the arrival of the Greeks. W. F. Albright now places the expansion of the Phoenicians in the tenth century. G. Garbini and S. Moscati are even disposed to accept a date closer to the one traditionally given for the foundation of Gades and Utica. I am not taking a position in this controversy; I want only to point out that it is unwise to dismiss texts for lack of archaeological support because new studies or new discoveries may provide that support.

My second example, that of the Trojan War, is even more relevant to our purposes.[8] Here is an event at the end of the thirteenth century BC, the historic memory of which was transmitted by oral tradition through the "Dark Age," taken on by epic singers as their theme, and received its final expression in the two cycles of the *Iliad* and the *Odyssey*, probably around the eighth century BC. The two poems were then written down and received their official, definitive form under Pisistratus in the sixth century. The presumed site of Troy, Hissarlik, has been excavated many times with the avowed intention of recovering the city of Homer. The earliest excavator, Schliemann, had first identified it with the most ancient of the nine cities superimposed upon Hissarlik, Troy I, then with Troy II. His successor, Dörpfeld, preferred Troy VI, where Mycenean pottery is abundant, and his opinion is still defended by some. But Troy VI was destroyed by an earthquake, not by an armed attack, and the Mycenean pottery is still extant in Troy VIIa. It is this level which the last excavator, Blegen, identifies with the city of Homer, and his conclusion has been accepted almost unanimously. Blegen thinks that "the tradition of the expedition against Troy must have a basis of historical fact" and this historical fact appears to him to have been proved by archaeology. "It can no longer be doubted . . . that there really was an actual historical Trojan War in which a coalition of Achaeans, or Mycenaeans, under a king whose overlordship was recognised, fought against the people of Troy and their allies."

This has prompted M. I. Finley to remark, "Blegen and his colleagues may have settled, insofar as such matters can ever be determined with finality by archaeology, that Troy VIIa was destroyed by human violence. However, they have found nothing, not a scrap, which points to an Achaean coalition or to a 'king whose overlordship was recognised' or to Trojan allies; nothing which hints at *who* destroyed Troy." He constructs the hypothesis that Troy VIIa was destroyed by, or in connection with, the invasions of marauders from the North called the "Sea Peoples" and he concludes: "New Hittite or North Syrian texts may yet produce direct evidence. Until then, I believe the narrative we have of the Trojan War had best be removed *in toto* from the realm of history and returned to the realm of myth and poetry." In response to this, J. L. Caskey recognizes: "Material evidence from the site of Troy has indeed not proven that the place was captured by Mycenaean Greeks . . . We are left without a compelling reason even to go on calling it Troy . . . The archaeological evidence, like the literary and historical, is incomplete and inconclusive."

This does not, however, justify a rejection of tradition. For his part G. S. Kirk concedes "that epic tradition can distort historical events." But to what extent? The Homeric tradition "is not just a vague legendary one; it preserves a great deal of accurate information, not only about Bronze Age social institutions but also about Bronze Age armour, buildings, and people." In its transmission it has assumed almost as many traits associated with the beginning of the Iron Age, it is true, "but can we believe that the interruption of the tradition, whether poetical or non-poetical, caused by the upheavals at the end of the Bronze Age, can have been so severe as to destroy not merely the details but the very outlines and whole substance of events belonging to the last heroic period of the Achaean civilisation? The *magnification* of a heroic past is common enough; how common is the virtual *creation* of a great heroic enterprise?" D. L. Page admits that "the evidence of Homer, that Greeks from the mainland sacked Troy (this I call the 'basic narrative'), cannot be proved to the exclusion of other possibilities," but he accepts the fact as historical because it accords with the results of archaeology and with the evidences of the Hittite texts. "The Homeric account has been confirmed since 1870 to an extent unimaginable before that time. It is very likely the true account; at least it is the only one which can claim the support of various and abundant evidence in both literary and archaeological records."

I have quoted at length because biblical scholars find here their own problems dealt with by means of the same arguments and resolved with the same diverse responses, from the total negation of Finley to the confident affirmation of Page. Even if one is disposed to follow the latter, he must recognize the limits of this "confirmation" that archaeology brings to the text.

A. Archaeology does not prove that the ruins of Hissarlik are those of Troy, but it shows that Hissarlik is the most important strategic site of the region which will later be called the Troad, and that this site was occupied in the epoch presumed to have been that of the Trojan War. The inscriptions found in the Hellenistic and Roman strata permit us to give to the site, at a later time, the name of Ilium or Ilias. It is Strabo who says that the inhabitants of Ilias believed their city to be the successor of Troy, and his testimony is confirmed by the coinage of Ilias bearing the figures of the heroes of the *Iliad*. Finally, it was Homer himself who employed the two names of Ilias and Troy to designate the city of Priam.[9] This line of argument may to some seem sufficient in itself, but it nonetheless rests on written documents later than Homer and these would not be different if Troy itself were but an invention of Homer's.

B. The *Iliad* depicts Troy as a large and rich city, heavily populated, protected by massive ramparts, reinforced with towers and gates and adorned with a number of palaces and temples. The city of Troy VIIa does not resemble this description at all: it is a poor settlement, built on the ruins of Troy VI after the destruction of the latter by an earthquake. D. L. Page describes it as follows: "An abject uncomfortable Troy, degraded and altogether pitiable. A network of unworthy lodgings spread to right and left . . . gloomy little bungalows, thin-walled, partly-walled, one-roomed, barely furnished . . . an offense to the eye, and an injury to pride."[10] Is it in this manner that Homer is "confirmed" by archaeology?

C. The ruins of Troy VIIa are difficult to date. Blegen, after holding various positions, fixed the date "by 1250 B.C., if not a decade or two earlier," and Finley prefers a date closer to 1190—to mention only two of the authors to whom I have already referred. The date depends upon which of the final phases of the Mycenaean Age Troy VIIa can be attributed to. Are we dealing here with Myc. IIIB still under the influence of Myc. IIIA, or of Myc. IIIB, or of Myc. IIIB already with some elements of Myc. IIIC? If one accepts the more common opinion that Troy VIIa has been destroyed at the end of Myc. IIIB, the problem is not solved; for the passage from Myc. IIIB to Myc. IIIC is dated in the neighborhood of 1240 by some, and of 1180 by others. One must harmonize this date with those of the ruins of Pylos, Mycenae or Tyrins,

which are not certain. If Troy VIIa was destroyed after the great Mycenaean centers of the continent, it is evident that the historicity of the
Trojan War, i.e., Page's "basic narrative," cannot be maintained.

D. Archaeology does not prove that Troy VIIa was destroyed by the
Achaeans. Our knowledge of the history of occidental Asia Minor in the
thirteenth century is very limited, but we do know that it was an epoch
of great troubles, the forerunner of the fall of the Hittite empire. Troy
could have fallen under the assaults of the Hittites, or of other local
enemies, or of invaders who crossed the Hellespont.

E. As for the relation of the Achaeans with the Mycenaeans and the
presence of Mycenaeans in Asia Minor, archaeology reduces these to a
minimum. In a recent publication, J. Mellaart pointed out that Mycenaean
influence in Anatolia was "ineffectual, peripheral, and exotic" and he
concludes his study thus: "I need hardly to point out that I find the
traditional account of the Trojan War archaeologically and historically
inacceptable."[11]

It is not my intention to take a position for or against the historicity
of the Trojan War. It has been my desire only to show how the same
problems have presented themselves in areas other than ours. If I have
seemed to dwell upon this second example, it is because it furnishes a
good parallel to a biblical question which, more than any other, puts
archaeology in conflict with the texts: it is the question of the "conquest"
of Canaan. The stages which separate these events of the thirteenth century from the final composition of the book of Joshua are similar to those
which separate the Trojan War from the "canonical" recension of the
Homeric poems of the sixth century BC. The principal cities mentioned
in the narratives of the conquest, Jericho, Ai, Bethel, Gibeon, Hazor,
Lachish, are identified in the field with at least as much certainty as
that of Troy at Hissarlik. These sites have been excavated. Archaeology
permits us to date the end of the Late Bronze Age and the beginning of
the Iron Age in Palestine in a manner considerably more precise than the
last phases of the Mycenean Age in Greece and the Aegean. The history
of Palestine in that epoch is better known to us than that of the Troad.
These advantages should permit a firmer judgment and an easier accord
concerning the "confirmation" which archaeology brings to the narratives
of the conquest. But, on the contrary, the same kinds of problems present
themselves, and the same kinds of arguments are exchanged between opposing camps.[12]

Most serious is the refusal to accept the historicity of the narratives, often expressed by the archaeologists themselves who have excavated the sites. In regard to Jericho the most recent judgment expressed by Miss K. Kenyon is: "It is impossible to associate the destruction of Jericho with such a date (the Exodus in the thirteenth century BC). The town may have been destroyed by one of the other Hebrew groups, the history of whose infiltrations is, as generally recognized, complex. Alternatively, the placing at Jericho of a dramatic siege and capture may be an aetiological explanation of a ruined city. Archaeology cannot provide the answer."[13] Concerning Ai, Judith Marquet-Krause concluded: "Chapters seven and eight of Joshua, which could be considered historical, are part of a legend."[14] The most recent excavator of Ai, J. Callaway, thinks that the long biblical narrative is based only on the capture by the Israelites of a small village established by other immigrants on the ruins of the city of the Ancient Bronze Age.[15] This leads to his more general conclusion that "we can no longer take for granted that the conquest of Canaan by invading Israelites accounts for the Late Bronze destructions of Bethel, Lachish, Tell Beit Mirsim, or Hazor."[16] In so far as Gibeon is concerned, J. B. Pritchard declares, "There can be no doubt, on the basis of the best evidence available, that there was no city of any importance at the time of Joshua." He continues, "The apparent anomalies found in the archaeological results from three sites which figure prominently in the narratives in the first part of Joshua (Jericho, Ai, Gibeon) suggest that we have reached an impasse on the question of supporting the traditional view of the conquest with archaeological undergirding."[17]

The situation at Hazor looks more favorable to the director of the excavation, Y. Yadin: "The excavations have shown in a decisive manner that the great Canaanite city was destroyed by fire, and was rebuilt, in the second part of the thirteenth century B.C. . . . This destruction must be attributed to the one described so minutely in the book of Joshua."[18] However, his assistant in the excavation, Y. Aharoni, discovered a number of settlements of the beginning of the Iron Age in Galilee and concludes: "This picture does not fit in with the theory that the Israelites penetrated Galilee in one big military campaign in which they defeated the Canaanites led by the king of Hazor. On the contrary, it fits with the views of those scholars who think that in Galilee, too, the penetration into unsettled regions preceded the decisive military encounter."[19]

I know, of course, that in each of these cases one could propose a solution which would put archaeology in accord with the biblical narratives: the remains of the Jericho captured by the Israelites may have been obliterated by erosion; tradition may have transferred to the neighboring site of Ai the historic memory of the capture of Bethel; several tombs and some sherds indicate that there was occupation of Gibeon during the Late Bronze Age which the too limited excavations did not bring to light; and the Israelite settlements of Galilee came after the fall of Hazor. My intention is not to discuss the validity of these explanations, but only to point out the single fact that when one is obliged to resort to them it clearly indicates that the "confirmation" brought by archaeology to the biblical narrative is rarely without ambiguity.

In certain cases the value of the archaeological evidence and the significance of the text which it is supposed to clarify have both been exaggerated. Bethel was destroyed in the course of the thirteenth century, but this does not authorize J. L. Kelso to write, "The last Bronze Age city was destroyed by Joshua's troops;"[20] because *a*) the date of the destruction has not been securely fixed; *b*) the capture of Bethel is not mentioned in the book of *Joshua;* c) its conquest by the house of Joseph was, according to the book of *Judges,* the result of treason and not of military attack; nor does the text say that the city was then destroyed. Lachish was destroyed at the end of the Late Bronze Age, but archaeology cannot be used to confirm either the date or the fact of an Israelite conquest. An hieratic inscription on a bowl dates from the fourth year of a Pharaoh; while it is possible that the Pharaoh was Merneptah this date provides only a *terminus post quem,* and one must also take into account the scarab of Ramses III found in the stratum of the destruction. Miss O. Tufnell, who participated in the excavation and published its results, accepts a later date, "some time during the first decades of the twelfth century B.C."[21] If other authors prefer a date somewhere around 1220 BC, it is because it is in accordance with a certain chronology of the Israelite conquest. But the book of *Joshua* contains no account of the capture of Lachish; the city is mentioned only in the summaries of the Conquest which are secondary literary compositions. The agents of the destruction of Lachish may have been the Israelites, or the Egyptians, or the Sea Peoples, or other Canaanites.

Similar choices are possible for other sites. This period is one of great turmoil in all the Near East: the collapse of the Hittite empire, the end of Egyptian domination in Asia, invasions from the north; the settlement of the Israelites is only one element in this whole movement. All the cities of the Late Bronze Age were destroyed, some several times, during this period; the phenomenon extends well beyond the limits of Palestine, and the Israelites are not the only ones responsible for it. In Palestine itself, the Bible prevents our attributing to the Israelites the destruction of the coastal cities or of cities such as Beth-Shan, Megiddo, Taanach and others, because it explicitly states that they were not conquered by Joshua.

The much poorer settlements which replace them at the beginning of the Iron Age provide no better evidence of the arrival of the Israelites, simply because archaeology is not able to establish the specifically Israelite character of any of the changes which then appear. One can only subscribe to the recent declaration of H. J. Franken: "Archaeologists would be totally unaware of any important ethnic change at the end of the Late Bronze Age were it not for the biblical tradition."[22]

But the biblical tradition exists. It may have overstressed the role of Joshua and the extent of the first conquests, but it cannot have completely invented the story that groups of Israelites entered into Palestine at that time and established themselves at least partly by violence. One will always have to reconstruct biblical history by starting with the texts, and the texts must be interpreted by the methods of literary criticism, tradition criticism and historical criticism. Archaeology does not confirm the text, which is what it is, it can only confirm the interpretation which we give it. (Editor's note: see below, pp. 331–41, for the same view from another perspective.) If the results of archaeology seem to be opposed to the conclusions of text criticism, the reason may perhaps be that not enough archaeological facts are known or that they have not been firmly established; the reason also may be that the text has been wrongly interpreted. Accord must finally be achieved between these two means of knowing historical reality, but it can not and must not be attained by a tendentious use of archaeological facts. If biblical studies have suffered from an excess of textual criticism, the remarkable and beneficial growth and progress of archaeology must not be permitted to lead to an opposite excess.

FOOTNOTES

1. The quotations are from C. M. Watson, *Palestine Exploration Fund. Fifty Years' Work in the Holy Land* (1915), pp. 17, 18, 22.

2. *Palestine Exploration Society, First Statement* (1871), pp. 34–35.

3. *Transactions of the Society of Biblical Archaeology*, 1 (1872), pp. i–ii and 12.

4. The title of the original German edition of 1955 was: *Und die Bibel hat doch Recht*, the subtitle of which was: "Forscher beweisen die historische Wahrheit."

5. Nelson Glueck himself has completely rejected "proving" the Bible: *Rivers in the Desert* (1959, 2d ed. 1968), pp. 30–31; "The Bible and Archaeology," *Five Essays on the Bible* (*Papers Read at the 1960 Annual Meeting of the American Council of Learned Societies* [1960]), pp. 60–80; the paragraph concerning "Archaeology and the Bible" in the new edition of *The River Jordan* (1968), pp. 3–9.

6. I refer here to W. F. Albright, "New Light on the Early Phoenician Colonization," *BASOR*, No. 83 (1941), pp. 14–22; R. Carpenter, "Phoenicians in the West," *AJA*, 62 (1958), pp. 35–53; W. Culican, "Aspects of Phoenician Settlement in the West Mediterranean," *Abr-Nahrain*, 1 (1959–60), pp. 36–55; W. F. Albright, "The Role of the Canaanites in the History of Civilization," *BANE* (1961), pp. 343–49, (1965), pp. 451–67; G. Garbini, "L'espansione fenicia nel Mediterraneo," *Cultura e Scuola*, 7 (1963), pp. 92–97; "I Fenici in Occidente," *Studi Etruschi*, 34 (1966), pp. 111–47; W. F. Albright, "Syria, The Philistines, and Phoenicia," CAH², ii, fasc. 51 (1966), pp. 33–43; S. Moscati, *Il Mondo dei Fenici* (1966), pp. 123–32, 241–301; D. Van Berchem, "Sanctuaires d'Hercule-Melquart. Contribution à l'étude de l'expansion phénicienne en Méditerranée," *Syr*, 44 (1967), pp. 73–109, 307–38. A large Phoenician temple built c. 800 BC has recently been excavated at Kition in Cyprus, V. Karageorghis, *CRAI* (1969), pp. 6–13.

7. A. Jodin, *Mogador, Comptoir phénicien du Maroc Atlantique* (1966).

8. I refer only generally to H. L. Lorimer, *Homer and the Monuments* (1950); D. L. Page, *History and the Homeric Iliad* (1959); C. W. Blegen, *Troy and the Trojans* (1963); C. Nylander, "The Fall of Troy," *Ant*, 37 (1963), pp. 6–11; G. S. Kirk, "The Homeric Poems as History," CAH², ii, fasc. 22 (1964); the discussion on "The Trojan War" between M. I. Finley, J. C. Caskey, G. S. Kirk and D. L. Page in *JHS*, 84 (1964), pp. 1–20.

9. This would be a paradigmatic exercise for biblical critics: Ilios 106 times in the Iliad and 19 in the Odyssey; Troy 50 times in the Iliad and 24 times in the Odyssey. Eleven different epithets are attributed to Ilios, 10 to Troy. Only one of these is common to both: Ilios (4 times) and Troy (2 times) is the city "with the beautiful ramparts." Literary critics might perhaps conclude that there are two sources or two traditions . . . and two cities. As a matter of fact, a Hittite geographical list mentions one after the other the two cities of Wilusiya and Tarusia, which *may* represent Ilios and Troy.

10. "The Historical Sack of Troy," *Ant*, 33 (1959), p. 27.

11. "Anatolian Trade with Europe and Anatolian Geography and Culture Provinces in the Late Bronze Age," *AnSt*, 18 (1968), pp. 189, 200.

12. I mention only the main contenders. On one side: A. Alt, *Die Landnahme der Israeliten in Palästina* (1925)=*Kleine Schriften* i (1953), pp. 89–125; "Joshua,"

Werden und Wesen des Alten Testaments (BZAW, 66, 1936), pp. 13–29=*Kleine Schriften,* I, pp. 176–92; "Erwägungen über die Landnahme der Israeliten in Palästina," *PJB,* 35 (1939), pp. 8–63=*Kleine Schriften,* I, pp. 126–75; M. Noth, *Das Buch Josua (Handbuch zum Alten Testament)* (1938, 2d ed., 1953); "Grundsätzliches zur geschichtlichen Deutung archäologischer Befunde auf dem Boden Palästinas," *PJB,* 34 (1938), pp. 7–22; "Hat die Bibel doch Recht?" *Festschrift G. Dehn* (1957), pp. 8–22; "Der Beitrag der Archäologie zur Geschichte Israels," *VT* Supplement 7 (1960), pp. 262–82; *The History of Israel*[2] (1960), pp. 68–80.

On the other side: W. F. Albright, "The Israelite Conquest of Canaan in the Light of Archaeology," *BASOR,* No. 74 (1938), pp. 11–23; *The Biblical Period from Abraham to Ezra* (1963), pp. 24–34; J. Bright, *Early Israel in Recent History Writing* (1956); *A History of Israel* (1959), pp. 117–20; G. E. Wright, *The Westminster Atlas of the Bible*[2] (1956), pp. 39–40; *Biblical Archaeology*[2] (1962), pp. 69–84; "Archaeology, History, and Theology," *HDB,* 28 (1964), pp. 85–96; P. Lapp, "The Conquest of Palestine in the Light of Archaeology," *CTM,* 38 (1967), pp. 283–300. The two theses are exposed and discussed by M. Weippert, *Die Landnahme der israelitischen Stämme in der neueren wissenschaftlichen Diskussion* (1967), in which he subscribes to the point of view of Alt and Noth.

    13. In *AOTS,* (1967), p. 273.
    14. *Les Fouilles de 'Ai (Et-Tell)* (1949), p. 24.
    15. "New Evidence on the Conquest of 'Ai," *JBL,* 87 (1968), pp. 312–20.
    16. *Loc. cit.*
    17. In *The Bible in Modern Scholarship,* ed. by J. P. Hyatt (1965), p. 319.
    18. In *AOTS,* p. 258.
    19. "Problems of the Israelite Conquest in the Light of Archaeological Discoveries," *Antiquity and Survival,* 2 (1957), pp. 131–50; *cf.* p. 149.
    20. *BA,* 19 (1956), p. 39.
    21. In *AOTS,* p. 302.
    22. "Palestine in the Time of the Nineteenth Dynasty. (a) Archaeological Evidence," *CAH*[2], II, fasc. 67 (1968), p. 9.

II
The Bronze Age

THE BEGINNINGS OF URBANIZATION
IN CANAAN

Ruth Amiran

Introduction

THE focal point of much of the following discussion is the Early Bronze I and II city of Arad.[1] The discovery of an EB large settlement, or city[2] in the semi-arid[3] Negev of Arad reveals two major points of great interest that bear directly upon the question dealt with here. (1). It seems to me that the only possible meaning of a large settlement emerging and existing in that marginal environment is that the areas with better climate, soil and rain—to the north of Arad (i.e., the whole of Canaan)—were already densely settled. We may deduce from the phenomenon of Arad some sort of "population explosion" in the country, resulting from a "prosperity" during the period in which this settlement was growing into a city. The logical question of why they settled in that area can hardly be answered otherwise. A further logical inference would be that the city of Arad, situated in a marginal area of settlement, should be placed *not* at the beginning of the process of urbanization, but well into its advanced phases. (2). The second major point is the city itself and the factual data it provides. These reveal aspects of the physical structure of a large settlement (=city) and should serve as the basis for sociological and non-physical inferences.

At the outset of the discussion it should be clearly stated that, to my mind, urbanism in Canaan seems *not* to have developed out of *purely and exclusively* local conditions.[4] An impetus from outside was necessary in the process. We have to connect this Canaanite phenomenon with the more general Near Eastern one, namely the dependence of Egypt's Dynastic beginnings (which were literate and urban[5]) upon Jemdet Nasr Sumerian stimulation,[6] a theory by now generally accepted. Thus, within the framework of what has been written[7] on urbanization in the ancient Near East in general, we shall try to focus on such phenomena as are mirrored in our area during the periods EB I[8] and EB II. In doing so there are four tasks: a) To examine the data of the EB I period with respect to the character of the settlements. b) To deal with those features in the material culture of EB I Canaan which are evidence of Mesopotamian influence upon the peoples of the land-route[9] (Canaan). c) To try to show with the aid of a map that Canaan was indeed densely settled in the EB I–II period as we surmise on the basis of the Arad settlement, which shows population expansion beyond its natural boundaries. It is superfluous to point out that thick population is synonymous with large settlements. d) To analyze and describe the physical elements of the phenomenon of a city, as exemplified by Arad, the evidence of urban planning as well as its non-physical implications.

A. Character of EB I settlements

Every scholar laments the fragmentary, scanty character of information on remains of the EB I period (which results from the fact that not enough digging has been done into these early remains that lie beneath thick accumulations of subsequent deposits). However, some conclusions of a provisional nature may be drawn from data available from various sites. Below we shall describe the main characteristics of the settlements on these sites: *Megiddo Stratum XIX*[10] (+Stages VII–IV) seems to be an unwalled settlement whose size is unclear. It contains Temple 4050 (or Temples 4050 and 4047) of the broad-room architectural style. The pottery includes, among other items, specimens of the Red-burnished and Gray-burnished wares. *Beth-Shan Strata XVII–XVI,*[11] whose size is also unknown, was probably unwalled. Its pottery context is characterized by Gray- and also Red-burnished wares. (Its architectural remains are as yet unpublished.) *Beth Yerah Strata I and II*[12] seem also to be an unwalled settlement, with pottery context of great similarity to that of Beth-Shan XVII–XVI. To the same general milieu (and in the same geographical area) is to be assigned *Tell Shuneh Stratum II* (and perhaps *III*),[13] constituting an interesting addition to the above information on Beth-Shan and Beth Yerah. The pottery context contains both Red- and Gray-burnished wares. *Tell Farah(N)*, which much clarified our knowledge of this period (as mentioned above in n. 8), presents a rich picture, but with some problems that must await more digging. From the point of view of the pottery context, the Strata *Chalcolithique Supérieur et Ancien Bronze Périodes 1 et 2* all apparently belong to EB I.[14] The size of the settlement in these periods is as yet unknown. Père R. de Vaux assigns the earliest phase of the city wall, with its gateway, to Période 1. *Ai, with* its rich harvest of excavations in the 1930s, is now being re-excavated and re-evaluated. The pottery from the EB I cemetery testifies to Red-burnished and Painted wares.[15] During the period of the cemetery Ai seems to have been an unwalled settlement, though Callaway is inclined to assign the first phase of the city wall to "Kenyon's EB I."[16] The context of pottery contemporary with this early phase of the city wall, when published, will be of utmost interest. *Jericho Strata VII–VI,* representing the earliest EB strata there, contain Shrine 420,[17] similar in its architectural style to the temple of Megiddo XIX. Possibly Kenyon's city wall and semi-circular tower would belong to these (Garstang's) strata.[18] *Tell Areni* (erroneously known as Gath) *Stratum V* seems to have been a very large (about fifty acres) walled city, dating to the time of Narmer[19] (judging by the sherd which carries an incision with the Serekh of Narmer). *Arad Stratum IV* is an unwalled settlement, the size of which is unknown as yet. Its pottery context is of the Painted Ware milieu of EB I, and judging by the fact that the Egyptian imported pottery found in it is from the very beginning of the First Dynasty (time of Narmer-Hor-Aha),[20] it should be placed at the end of EB I.

Though we have not surveyed all the EB excavations, some general conclusions may be drawn from the data so far observed. (1). Some of the settlements seem to have been walled cities as early as the latter phase of EB I. (2). A common feature of all these sites is considerable evidence of continuity between the stratum of the "unwalled village" and the following stratum of the "large and walled city." In each case (except at Shuneh, where only a brief sounding was made), continuity is confirmed by the architectural items themselves, for example, the continuity of building style and method between Farah(N) periods 1 and 2 and the following group of periods, 3, 4 and 5. (3). In each of these cases one may infer population continuity based on architectural and pottery styles, as well as on chronological considerations as in the case of Arad IV in relation to Arad III. We conclude there was an unbroken development from village-community to urban-society. If corroborated by further digging and thinking, this view will advance our understanding of the EB I period, especially its formative nature: new forms are shown in the making, forms that eventually became the fully developed EB II urban forms.

B. Evidence for Mesopotamian influence and Sumero-Egyptian contacts during EB I

It is of great interest to try to isolate those elements in the material culture of that village-society which, though assimilated and well-absorbed in it, are nonetheless recognizable as foreign and brought in by migratory-infiltrating movements[21] from Sumerian higher urban society. Helen J. Kantor has shown the EB I Spouted Vessel to be of Mesopotamian descent.[22] This type is known in Mesopotamia from Uruk in the south to

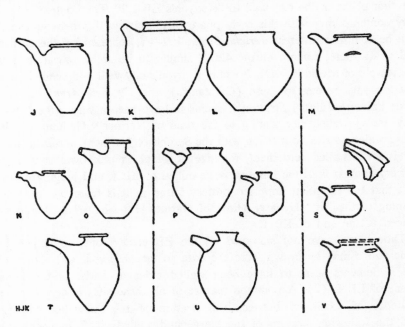

Figure 1. (Reproduced by permission of Helene J. Kantor, *COWA*,[2] fig. 4)

J – Diospolis, Petrie, *Corpus of Prehistoric Pottery* (1921), Pl.18:Fancy 58k

K – Khafaje, Delougaz, *Pottery from the Diyala Region* (1952), Pl.182:C 535.242

L – Khafaje, *Id.*, Pl.182:C 334.222

M – Ras el-'Ain, Iliffe, *QDAP*, 5 (1936), p. 121:No.63.

N – Badari, Brunton, and Caton-Thompson, *The Badarian Civilization* (1928), Pl.38:Fancy 581

O – Naqada, Petrie, *Corpus of Prehistoric Pottery* (1921), Fancy 59B

P – Warke VI, Noeldeke, "Vierter . . . Bericht . . . Ueber die Uruk Ausgrabungen (1931–32)," *Abhandlungen d. Preus. Akad. d. Wiss., Phil-Hist.* Kl.No.6 (1932), Pl.19:B z

Q – Warke VI, *Id., ibid.*, Pl.19:B w

R – Amuq, Braidwood, *Excavations in the Plain of Antioch*, I (1960), p. 272, Fig. 213:18

S – Farah(N), De Vaux, *RB* (1951), p. 584, fig. 12:2

T – Naqada, Petrie, *Corpus of Prehistoric Pottery*, Pl.18:Fancy 58a

U – Warka V, Noeldeke, *ibid.*, Pl.19:D c

V – Farah(N), De Vaux, *RB* (1951), p. 584, fig. 12:4

Nineveh in the north, during the Uruk and Jemdet Nasr periods. It seems to have taken root in the pottery complex of Canaan, developing into a series of variations with much local flair. This complicated problem is illustrated in figures 1–4 and Plates 1–4: fig. 1 is a reproduction of

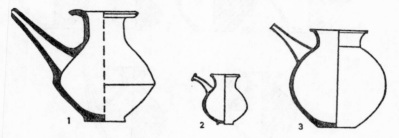

Figure 2. 1 – Warka VII, Noeldeke, *ibid.*, Pl.18:D g
2 – Nineveh, Ninevite 4, Mallowan, *AAA*, 20, Pl.LI:7
3 – Nineveh, Ninevite 4, Mallowan, *AAA*, 20, Pl.LII:12

Kantor's fig. 4. Fig. 2 shows three additional specimens in the Mesopotamian series, one from Uruk VII and two from Ninevite 4. Fig. 3 shows additional Canaanite specimens,[23] which manifest the variety of modes of assimilation. Fig. 4 shows Egyptian specimens. The Spouted Vessel reached Egypt in the same fashion, and is seen there in various manifestations. One (and perhaps more) of them had a complicated history: it follows, or rather imitates, a Canaanized version, elaborated and transformed on Canaanite soil. Plates 1–4, which contain three Canaanite[24] Spouted Vessels and one Egyptian,[25] clearly demonstrate the dependence of the Egyptian form upon the Canaanite.[26] Alongside the Spouted Vessel, many purely Canaanite vessels of various shapes and traits, went down to Egypt. We mention only a few, as all these features have been dealt with in detail by Kantor: the ledge-handled jars (W-Class of Petrie), the bowls with conoid projections, and Painted-ware vessels. There are other pottery items and traits of Mesopotamian descent as well as other kinds of objects which might be adduced to illustrate the tripartite contacts (Sumero-Egypto-Canaanite) on Canaanite soil. There, diversified ideas, styles, usages and customs intermingled, producing objects of a clearly hybrid character. The seal, both the cylinder-seal and the stamp-seal (and of course impressions of such), is definitely one of the foremost expressions of these complicated contacts or interrelationships. The story[27] of the cylinder-seal on Canaanite soil is an eloquent illustration of these tripartite contacts. Two cylinder-seals found in Palestine may serve as

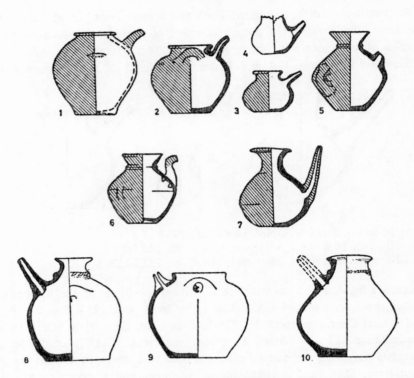

Figure 3. (Reproduced from Amiran-Beck-Zevulun, Pls. 9 and 12)
1 – Ras el-'Ain, Iliffe, *QDAP*, V, 1936, p. 121:63. (=fig. 1a:M)
2 – Farah(N), de Vaux, *RB* (1951), p. 584, fig. 12:1
3 – Farah(N), *ibid*, Fig. 12:2 (=fig. 1a:S)
4 – Farah(N), *ibid.*, (1952), p. 579, fig. 11:11 (=Pl.Ic)
5 – Farah(N), *ibid.*, (1949), p. 135, fig. 13:8
6 – Asawir, Israel Dept. of Antiquities, No. 53–537
7 – Beth Shan, *PMB*, 3, Pl.1:13 (new drawing)
8 – Jericho, Kenyon, *Jericho*, I, fig. 14:14
9 – Jericho, *ibid.*, fig. 18:17
10 – Jericho, *ibid.*, fig. 14:15

illustration. One, Pl. 5, was allegedly found in the Plain of Sharon, and is now in the Clarke Collection of the YMCA, Jerusalem (No. 524).[28] The other, Pl. 6, was excavated at Arad, Stratum II. The Sharon seal has the squat Jemdet Nasr form, and a design composed exclusively and purely of Egyptian signs, read by Petrie and Rowe as a name, Tekhi. It dates beyond any doubt to the First Dynasty. The Arad seal has the same squat form, is made of local (Arad) chalk, in crude workmanship, the design

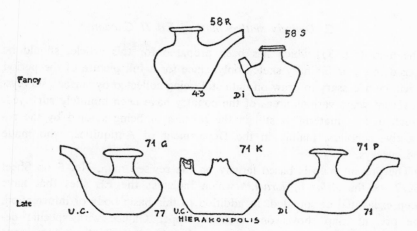

Figure 4. (Reproduced from: Petrie, *Corpus of Prehistoric Pottery*, Pl.XVIII: Fancy and Pl.LI:Late)

being of a general debased Jemdet Nasr flair.[29] These two seals, as explained, are not of pure Mesopotamian character; and though they clearly belong to EB II contexts (especially so in the Arad case), they imply that the cylinder-seal must have made its appearance in Canaan quite some time *before* the appearance of these hybrid creations, in order to allow some period of "incubation" for the intermingling elements. Thus, the first appearance of this cultural phenomenon together with the other Mesopotamian and Egyptian phenomena mentioned above is to be assigned to EB I. Quite a number of objects which came as pure traded imports from Egypt to Canaan may be enumerated, like the bull's amulet (Pl. 7) found in the Tomb of Assawir,[30] and the disc-like macehead from Stratum XIX at Megiddo[31] (Pl. 8). In a different area of material remains relating to higher cultural necessities, it should be pointed out that the imperative location of the temple in a well-defined area at the center of the community may also be considered evidence of Sumerian influence.[32] Though fragmentarily excavated, Megiddo XIX and Jericho VII, both EB I, and Arad III–II (as we shall presently see) and Ai,[33] both of EB II, reflect this conception of the location of the temple.

These features, taken as a whole, reflect a vital cultural and material intercourse that encouraged population growth and culminated in the emergence and progressive definition of cities and urban life.

C. *Densely settled map of EB II Canaan*

The map (fig. 5), which has been prepared for this article, should be considered a preliminary sketch only, since for a full picture of the period it will be necessary to draw on data still being collected by surface surveys. In recent years various areas of the country have been minutely surveyed. Much of that material is still in the process of being studied by the respective scholars, mainly in the Department of Antiquities, who made the surveys.

The present map is based largely on the revised map, No. 5 on Sheet IX/2, of the *Atlas of Israel*,[34] which indicates the EB sites that have been excavated or sounded. In addition to this basic body of information, the present map shows one area in Upper Galilee with specific details.[35] Practically every small plateau of arable land in the mountainous country of Upper Galilee was the *raison d'être* of a large-size settlement in this period. The map may serve as a hint of the possibilities and directions of investigations in other parts of the country. M. Prausnitz has in recent years collected data concerning the density of EB I–II large sites in the coastal plain, some of which appear on our map.[36] The central part of the hill-country (the Samaria of a much later time) has benefited from some information offered by R. Gofna,[37] which has been included in the map. In summing up the present state of our knowledge concerning the map of the country in the periods of EB I and EB II, we should stress two points: (1). Present information is insufficient for final conclusions, mainly because information gleaned from surface surveys must be very carefully analyzed. (2). On the other hand, present information is sufficient to point to growing populations and increasing usage of arable land on a scale that bespeaks large settlements.

D. *Structure of a city and pre-planning*

The physical structure of Arad, in all its aspects, raises the question to what extent we can read into it principles of town planning. Though not enough has as yet been excavated at Arad, and much more is required to validate our preliminary conceptions, there is already an appreciable volume of information that affords general hints about the "principles" followed by the builders of "cities" in the EB II period.

While analyzing and describing the factual data discovered at Arad we shall try to deduce the "principles" that apparently underlay them:

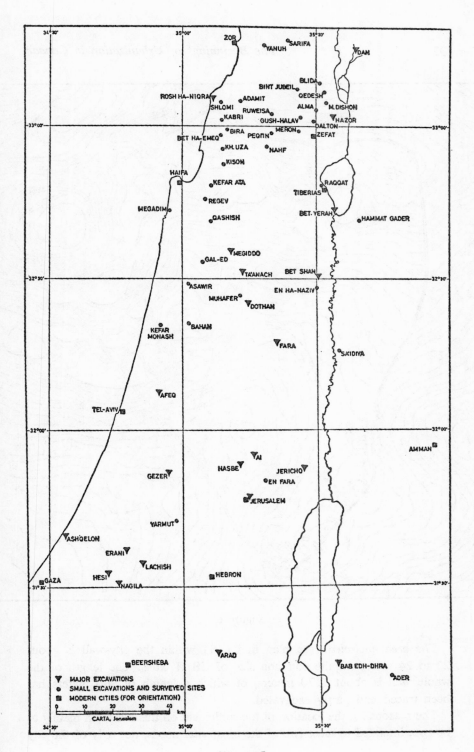

Figure 5

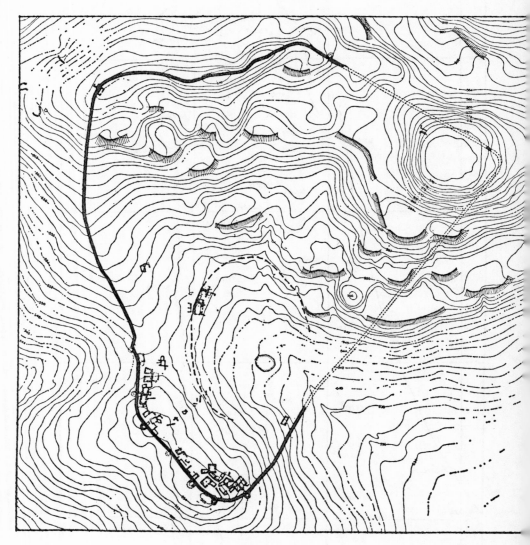

Figure 6

The area encircled (see plan in fig. 6) within the city-wall is about 23 to 24 acres, a quite common size of EB II cities. The length of the whole wall is about 1170 meters, of which a length of 900 meters has been traced and partly excavated.

The reasons for the location of the settlement on this hill seem mainly to be two, intended to meet two of the most vital needs, not only of the city of the EB II, but also of the village-settlement of the EB I (which constitutes the beginning of the city): water supply and building material. The solution to these needs evident at Arad betrays great ingenuity and planning capacities, of an extent unknown to date. The hill of Arad is one of a small group of Eocene chalk hills, situated in the northeastern part of the Beersheba-Arad basin, which has a deep fill of loess (yellow-gray loam). The round hill of Arad has the configuration of a horseshoe-shaped bowl, with slopes descending gently into the slight off-center bottom. This configuration was ingeniously chosen and exploited to collect the maximum possible amount of rain water that ran off into an artificially made central reservoir. Rain water, as we have seen, is scant and springs do not exist in this geological area. The chalk of the hill serves two purposes, easy quarrying of building material (cheaper in that area than brick-making, which requires much water), and preventing percolation losses of the reservoir, since the chalk is impervious.[38]

The city-wall, congruent with the bowl-like configuration, runs along the crest-line of the roundish hill and traverses the shallow saddles, gaining from this topography the best possible line of defense. At the same time the wall encloses the entire catchment area for the run-off water within the city.

The city-wall itself (fig. 6 and Plates 9–10) indicates a fully developed knowledge of city planning on a large scale, as well as its efficient execution. It has a readily identifiable style of military architecture seen also in other EB cities. A stretch of about 190 meters of the wall has been excavated, with the following results. The wall is 2.00–2.50 meters broad, made apparently all of stone, to judge by the well-preserved southwestern corner that rises to a height of 1.60 meters. Another proof of careful planning may perhaps be deduced from the fact that in a few places a straight and empty "channel" across the existing top of the wall was detected; this might perhaps be the impression left by wooden-beams put across the wall for reinforcement. Judging by the fact that in the stretch of about 190 meters seven towers were found, the wall was apparently appointed all along with semi-circular towers at intervals of 20–25 meters. The inner diameter, or width of the towers is 2.50–3.50 meters. Each is connected with the inside of the city by a passage of about 0.70 meter broad through the wall. One such tower was discovered in the walls of Ai, similar in dimensions, though its wall is much thicker, which belonged to the EB II defenses of Ai. At Jericho, as mentioned, one tower of this type similar in dimensions was found. The famous representation of a Canaanite city under Egyptian siege which decorates

one of the walls of the Tomb of Anta at Deshashe,[39] and dates to the
end of the Fifth or the beginning of the Sixth Dynasty, shows semi-circular
towers all along the city-wall.

The functional division of the city area was pre-planned, as is evident
from various features that have come to light in the excavations so far.
The areas dug adjacent to the city-wall seem to show that regular living
quarters (see below) covered the slopes of the hill. The center, or rather
the lower part of the slopes at the bottom of the horseshoe-shaped feature, seems to have been allotted to public buildings. Of this "center" we
have to date dug three buildings adjoining each other side-to-side. The
most interesting feature about them is a common back-wall, thicker than
usual, which encloses and at the same time separates them from the
living-quarter zone on the slopes. A street runs along this back-wall on
the other side of which an area of regular dwellings begins. All three
buildings face the center, toward the water-reservoir which, however, is
not very near. More public institutions may yet be discovered in this area.
It is not impossible, furthermore, that in this centrally situated area where
public functions took place an open space or piazza will be uncovered,
similar to the many piazzas that have already come to light in the living-
quarters (as we shall see). And one may be justified perhaps in identifying such a projected central piazza, due to its location, as a "public
market," or "bazaar"—an item of sociological connotation much discussed
by Kramer and Adams.[40]

The living-quarters, of which quite an area has been dug, show definite
evidence of city planning: streets and open spaces seem to have been laid
out according to guiding principles (cf. Pl. 10); an open space is left
along the city-wall with streets sometimes broadened into a sort of piazza.
Near one of the entrances into a tower is a large courtyard serving both
a house and the passageway into the tower. We have mentioned the
street along the dividing wall between the zone of dwellings and the
public-buildings center. The streets themselves follow the contours of the
hill parallel to the city-wall. The insulae of houses are between the streets,
with only one opening onto the street for every insula or block.

The architectural style of the public buildings, as well as those in
the living zone, is the most conspicuous feature of the phenomenon of
Arad. It is also the most intriguing feature in terms of its origins and the
reasons for its stereotypical appearance. Like other features we have mentioned, it appears fully developed, thus testifying to a long tradition. This
style of house (Pls. 10–12) is typical to all three strata of the history of
the walled city Arad. It is the broad-room style, with the entrance in the

PLATE 1. Spouted vessel from Beth Shan

PLATE 2. Spouted vessel from Nahal Tavor

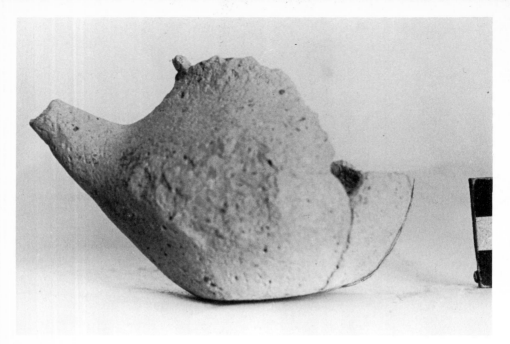

PLATE 3. Spouted vessel from Farah (N)

PLATE 4. Spouted vessel from Hu (Diospolis Parva)

PLATE 5. Cylinder seal allegedly found in the Plain of Sharon

PLATE 6. Cylinder seal from Arad, Stratum II

PLATE 7. Bull's amulet found in the Tomb
of Assawir

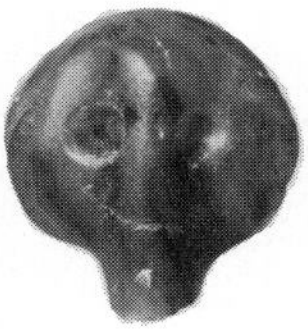

PLATE 8. Mace head from Stratum XIX
at Megiddo

PLATE 9. Arad, fragment of the wall with one tower

PLATE 10. Arad, a model of a section of the excavations showing the city-wall, three towers, streets and squares, various houses

PLATE 11. Arad, House 1234 with subsidiary room 1235

PLATE 12. Arad, House 1076 with kitchen 1502. Cooking place in the corner

PLATE 13. Jebel Qa'aqir. Tomb B54, chamber B, as seen with blocking-stone removed. Note disarticulated bones of three individuals and a sheep
(or goat). Seven of the eight vessels appear, three at center rear of
chamber; below the large storejar at left was found a copper pin.

long wall, a door-socket to the left of the entrance just inside the room, benches extending part way or all along the walls, and stone bases for wooden posts that support the flat roof. Having exactly the same features, but in larger dimensions, are the public buildings, two of which we have identified as temples because of their similarity to those of Megiddo XIX. The architectural composition of a typical house is also quite uniform. The smallest unit is one room of the type described with one subsidiary room which sometimes contained a cooking-place and sometimes served storage or other purposes. The two rooms never have a direct connection, but are perpendicular to each other, both opening on the courtyard. Larger units may also have a common courtyard. Still larger and more embellished units are enclosed by a wall or a fence; these have one large room of the above type, two subsidiary ones and one stone platform (the function of which still escapes us), all opening onto the central courtyard.

All these features are characteristic enough to constitute an architectural style decisive enough to point up a tradition of town planning and to define the settlement as a city. There is hardly a doubt that all this planning implies some degree of organization of public authority. The non-physical implications of such a structure—sociological and economic—are beyond the scope of this article.

Conclusions

The transformation from village-settlement to city should be considered a gradual process of local development, adapting outside stimulation and influences especially from the Sumerian sphere of higher civilization. That it was a slow, local process I would surmise from the fact that the city-strata sprang directly from the village-strata, whatever was the ceramic culture of the village: in the north of the country Red- and Gray-burnished wares were characteristic of the culture of these villages, while in the south Painted-ware culture predominated.

This bespeaks continuity of population, at least to a great extent, allowing for normal infiltration and migrations that were absorbed by the local stock.

As for chronological problems, Arad Stratum IV, an unwalled village of the Painted-ware milieu, dating to the very beginning of the First Dynasty (Narmer-Hor-Aha), demands the equation: latter part of the EB I overlaps the beginning of the First Dynasty. The excavations in progress at Ai, directed by Callaway, are bound to bring considerable clarification to problems of the Early Bronze Age in general, and in particular to the question of the beginnings of the city in regions of better climate, soil and rain, than the Arad region. In other words, it should be valuable to compare the pottery of the stratum of the earliest city-wall at Ai assigned by Callaway to "Kenyon's EB I" with the pottery of Arad Stratum IV, to learn whether these two different phenomena (walled-city and unwalled-village) are contemporary or consecutive.

It is surely not superfluous to conclude that the present state of knowledge of EB I requires much more digging and much more information as to the character of its settlements—their size, style of living, and regional differences—in order to be able to form a more reliable conception of the period and the milieu, which inherently formed every finished product encountered in the EB II period, as in the phenomenon of Arad.

We may quite safely assume, I think, that the information we have gleaned from Arad about city structure should be considered not as isolated data, but as characteristic of cities in EB II all over Canaan. We are far from being able to construct a reliable model of the general political organization of the country in EB II. However, the city-state option seems more logical and natural than any other model of the structure of the state.

FOOTNOTES

1. The final report on the excavations conducted at EB Arad from 1962 to 1966 was prepared by the members of the expedition, headed by the present writer, and will be published shortly in the series "Judaean Desert Studies," as *Ancient Arad, The Chalcolithic Settlement and the Early Bronze City*, by Ruth Amiran, Uzzi Paran, Yigal Shiloh, Raphael Brown, Yoram Zafrir and Amnon Ben-Tor; with contributions by Pirhiya Beck, Yehoshua Fuks, Yonathan Glas, George Haas, Nicu Haas, Maria Hopf, Naphtali Rosenan and Tama Schick.

2. I shall refrain from dealing with the widely discussed subject of the definition of a "city." For the purpose of this article I assume that a working definition is conditioned mainly by two physical factors: size and wall. All other factors, physical as well as human (organizational), I consider interrelated with and dependent on these two. (Editor's note: see Lapp's view below, pp. 101 ff.)

3. Average annual rainfall in the region of Arad is approximately 150 millimeters. The assumption that the climate of Arad has not changed in the last five thousand years is based on the following note by N. Rosenan (Deputy Director, Israel Meteorological Service): "We are not in the possession of any evidence which would prove that the climate (temperature and precipitation) was significantly different during the period around 3000 B.C. from that of today in the northern Negev. This statement is in line with evidence from various places in Israel, Egypt, Iraq and Iran, showing that no major change in climate of longer duration occurred during the last five thousand years. A significant proof is given by W. van Zeist and H. E. Wright, Jr., for western Iran. The constancy of climate which these scientists have found for Iran from pollen profile at Lake Zeribar may also be inferred for the area of Israel." Cf. *Science*, 140, No. 3562 (1963), pp. 65–67.

4. To quote R. M. Adams in *The Evolution of Urban Society: Early Mesopotamia and Prehistoric Mexico* (1966), as also quoted by S. N. Kramer in his review of Adams' book in *JNES*, 27 (1968), p. 326.

5. J. Wilson makes an interesting distinction between Mesopotamian city-states and the Egyptian nation-state in *City Invincible*, pp. 125 f. Cf. below, n. 7.

6. For a summary of this much-discussed problem cf. Helene J. Kantor in *COWA*[2], where her own work and that of other scholars is clearly presented.

7. A comprehensive book is: *City Invincible, A Symposium on Urbanization and Cultural Development in the Near East, Held at the Oriental Institute of the University of Chicago, December 4–7 1958*, ed. by C. H. Kraeling and R. M. Adams (1960).

8. I prefer to adhere to the old designation "EB I," which goes back to the work of Albright and Wright in the 1930s. Much material has been accumulating since then, adding new facets to this period's problems. The most important addition, pertaining to the *contents* of the period, not merely to its *terminology*, was the publication of the first annual reports of the excavations of Père de Vaux at Tell Farah(N) (excavated in the years 1946–60 and published yearly in *RB*, 54–69 [1947–62]). These excavations recovered and demonstrated the contemporaneity of two elements that had hitherto been considered successive: the Gray-burnished

and the Painted Wares. Subsequent discoveries tend to corroborate this conclusion (e.g., tombs at Assawir and Nahal Tavor, cf. below, n. 24; stratified deposits at Shuneh; etc.). The period here designated "EB I" the writer understands to comprise all three main and characteristic wares: Gray-burnished, Red-burnished and Painted Wares. The chronological sequence and regional interrelationships of these three wares are the basic problems of this period, and constitute the ground for the different systems suggested by scholars. Kenyon's system as expressed in her *Archaeology in the Holy Land* (1960) and in other works is: Proto Urban A—Red-burnished; PU B—Painted Ware; PU C—Gray-burnished ware, with not much chronological differentiation between them. Wright (in *Eretz Israel*, 5 [1958] and in the Albright *Festschrift*) prefers, or rather adheres to EB Ia, EB Ib and EB Ic. De Vaux, accepting to a certain measure Kenyon's conception, retains the old nomenclature with inner division into Ia and Ib. Besides changing the nomenclature of "EB I" into "Proto-Urban" Kenyon retains the designation "EB I" for a phase the contents of which I find as yet difficult to understand. A paradigm for the pottery of this newly created phase Dr. Kenyon sees in Jericho Tomb A 108 (*Archaeology in the Holy Land*, p. 124, fig. 17). Accepting or refuting the idea of this phase must await the material from the strata at Jericho in the final report of the excavations. J. B. Hennessy in *The Foreign Relations of Palestine during the Early Bronze* (1967) gives a brief sketch of the stratigraphy of this period at Jericho, but it is not enough quantitatively to judge the validity of this new idea. (See Lapp's correlations below, pp. 117–24—Ed.)

9. There is growing evidence that different routes should be assigned to that influence, both the sea route around the Arabian peninsula to Wadi Hammamat and the land route through Canaan and northern Sinai to the Delta. Sites in the eastern Delta where archaic material has recently been found are listed by H. G. Fischer (*Artibus Asiae*, 21 [1958], pp. 86–88, and *JARCE*, II [1963], p. 44, n. 2). According to Fischer they are "along the route from Lower Egypt to Palestine."

10. A stratigraphical-architectural reappraisal of the Holy Area at Megiddo, Section B-B was undertaken by the late I. Dunayevsky with A. Kempinsky; it covers all strata from XIX to VII, but is as yet only partially published (*Ḥadashot Archaeologiot*, 17 [1966], in Hebrew, and *IEJ*, 16 [1966], p. 142).

11. G. M. Fitzgerald, "Beth Shan: Earliest Pottery," *The Museum Journal*, 24 (1935), pp. 5 ff.

12. B. Maisler (Mazar), M. Stekelis and M. Avi-Yonah, "The Excavations at Beth Yerah (Khirbet Kerak) 1944–1946," *IEJ*, 2 (1952), pp. 165 ff. and 218 ff. More material has since been excavated by P. Bar-Adon in the 1950s and by P. Delougaz and H. J. Kantor in the 1960s—as yet unpublished.

13. H. de Contenson, "Three Soundings in the Jordan Valley," *ADAJ* IV–V (1960), pp. 12 ff., figs. 9–13.

14. Evidence for this is to be found in various figures in the reports, as e.g., in *RB*, 62 (1955), pp. 567–68, figs. 13–14.

15. Judith Marquet-Krause, *Les fouilles de 'Ay (Et-Tell), 1933–1935*, Paris, (1949).

16. *BASOR*, No. 178 (1965), p. 40.

17. J. Garstang, "Jericho, City and Necropolis, Report for the Sixth and Concluding Season," *AAA*, 23 (1936) pp. 73–74. We have to await the final publication of Dr. Kenyon's excavations to learn of the coordination between the strata of the two excavations.

18. Kathleen M. Kenyon, *Archaeology in the Holy Land* (1964), p. 107.

19. S. Yeivin, *First Preliminary Report on the Excavations at Tel "Gat"* (Hebrew, 1961); *idem*, "A New Chalcolithic Culture at Tel Erani and Its Implications for

Early Egypto-Canaanite Relations," *Fourth World Congress of Jewish Studies, Papers* (1967), pp. 45 ff.

20. Ruth Amiran, "A Preliminary Note on the Synchronisms Between the Early Bronze Strata of Arad and the First Dynasty," *BASOR*, No. 179 (1965), pp. 30 ff.; Ruth Amiran and Elise J. Baumgartel, *BASOR*, No. 195 (1969).

21. The exact nature of these contacts is yet to be understood.

22. *COWA²* (1965).

23. Reproduced from Ruth Amiran, Pirhiya Beck and Uzza Zevulun, *Ancient Pottery of Erez Israel*, Pl. 9.

24. Pl. 2 comes from a tomb in Nahal Tavor, dug by P. Delougaz, that contains vessels of all three wares. I am deeply indebted to Prof. Delougaz for his kindness in letting me publish this photograph.

25. The specimen Type Late 71 p (Pl. 4) is from *Diospolis Parva*, Pls. VI and XIX, in the collections of the Ashmolean Museum, Oxford. I am grateful to the director of the Museum for the photograph and permission to publish it.

26. This is not the place to go into detail to prove that a *vice versa* explanation is impossible. We shall mention only one point in that respect: the type of mushroom-like rim on this type is absolutely un-Egyptian.

27. This complicated "story" of the Palestinian cylinder seal has been uncovered by Dr. Pirhiya Beck in her as yet unpublished Ph.D. thesis.

28. According to Mrs. Helen Myer, in charge of the Clarke Collection in the Jerusalem YMCA, Clarke bought his objects in Palestine during the years before 1913. This seal was first published by W. M. Flinders Petrie (*Scarabs and Cylinders* [1917], Pl. IV, No. 87). Then A. Rowe republished it (*A Catalogue of Egyptian Scarabs, Scaraboids, Seals and Amulets in the Palestine Archaeological Museum* [1936], p. 30, Pl. XXVI, No. S 1). Since the provenances Clarke assigns to the objects he bought are to a great extent reliable, I am tempted to suggest a connection between this seal and the hoard of weapons and tools discovered in 1962 in the sands of Kefar Monash in the same Plain of Sharon (published by Ruth Hestrin and Miriam Tadmor, *IEJ*, 13 [1963], pp. 265 ff.).

29. Dr. Pirhiya Beck is preparing this seal and others for the final publication of Arad; cf. n. 1 above.

30. I am grateful to Dr. M. Dothan for permission to publish the photo here. Bull's amulets are dated to Pre-Dynastic times. Cf., e.g., Petrie, *Diospolis Parva, The Cemeteries of Abadiyeh and Hu, 1898–99* (1901), p. 26, dated to S.D. 46–67. Baumgartel thinks this amulet represents the fertility goddess (*The Cultures of Prehistoric Egypt*, II [1960], pp. 73 f., referring to Petrie, *Naqada and Ballas* [1896], Pl. LXI:4).

31. *Megiddo*, II, Pl. 270:2. This type of mace-head is dated by Petrie to: "S.D. 31–40, rarely found later, ending at 53" (*Diospolis Parva*, p. 24). It is known from many sites.

32. Temples I–V at Khafajah, dated by the excavators to Proto-Literate C–D (=Jemdet Nasr period; cf. P. Delougaz and S. Lloyd, *Pre-Sargonid Temples in the Diyala Region* [1942], Pls. 2–5) may be signaled here as specimens of Early Mesopotamian temples, which are all of the broad-room type, as specified by Delougaz, p. 12.

33. The large building on the acropolis has been variously interpreted as temple, citadel and palace. I am inclined to see it as a temple. Its original plan is of the EB II period.

34. *Atlas of Israel*, ed. by D. H. K. Amiran, J. Elster, M. Gilead, N. Rosenan (1969). Sheet IX/2 was compiled by M. Avi-Yonah and Y. Aharoni.

35. Compiled by the writer for a lecture read in a meeting of the Israel Ex-

ploration Society and published in Hebrew in *All the Land of Naphtali, The Twenty-fourth Archaeological Convention, October 1966* (1967), pp. 44 ff.

36. I am grateful to Dr. M. Prausnitz for this information.

37. I am grateful to Mr. R. Gofna for this information.

38. R. Gofna and J. Porath, in surveying the mountainous area of Samaria, came to the conclusion that Bronze Age settlements are situated in chalk areas (*Teva Wa'arez*, 10 [1968], pp. 295 ff.—Hebrew).

39. W. M. Flinders Petrie, *Deshashe* (1898), Pl. 4.

40. *JNES*, 27 (1968), p. 327. Cf. n. 4 above.

PALESTINE IN THE EARLY
BRONZE AGE

Paul W. Lapp

PRESTIGIOUS administrative responsibilities are a virtual death knell to academic pursuits in American higher education. Nelson Glueck provides a refreshing exception. His continuing dedication to the publication of his archaeological field work and to the elucidation of Palestinian history becomes increasingly admirable against the growing backdrop of poorer productions by colleagues with fewer responsibilities. A fact of life in Near Eastern archaeology is that most research is produced as an avocation, or at least is not the investigator's first responsibility. The result is that much archaeological material is never published; what is published often appears a decade or more after its excavation and is at least partly uninformed about a mass of comparative material yet to see the light of print. Some might be tempted to criticize the recent works of Nelson Glueck, and others, which have appeared under such circumstances. More appropriate is an appreciation of the perseverance which continues to produce under such trying circumstances and an effort to create academic structures leading to more efficient research production. If the physical sciences were confined to the research structures of Near Eastern archaeology, we would never have reached the moon!

The painfully slow progress in historical interpretation resulting from this research tradition is well illustrated in recent works on Early Bronze Palestine. J. B. Hennessy's admirable treatment of Early Bronze Palestine with a thorough and far-ranging examination of its cultural links and a preliminary presentation of stratified EB pottery from Jericho summarizes evidence published through about 1963.[1] This work did not appear in print until the very end of 1967, and is not referred to in the other recent literature cited immediately below.[2] Thus over a decade after the final campaign in 1958, even the preliminary publication of important stratified material from EB Jericho is only beginning to be utilized. It is especially unfortunate that the second edition of the Cambridge Ancient

History sections on EB Palestine[3] and Syria[4] were unable to make use of Hennessy's work, for they will be standard references for years. The same may be said of the magnificent treatment of "Préhistoire palestinienne" in *Supplément au Dictionnaire de la Bible*[5] and pertinent chapters of *Chronologies in Old World Archaeology.*[6]

Any agreement among these independent assessments is thus a good indication of areas where a professional consensus has been achieved. At a number of points the precision of this agreement is remarkable. A striking example is the close similarity of conclusions about EB Palestine's links with Egyptian history (apart from questions of absolute chronology).[7] The following is an attempt to summarize the areas of consensus, define major areas of disagreement, and indicate solutions preferred by the writer. The proposed solutions stem from the still largely unpublished evidence from the Early Bronze cemetery and town at Bâb edh-Dhrâ'.[8] No doubt the forthcoming final publications on Jericho and Arad will give evidence for conclusions described in preliminary reports. Therefore this seems a propitious time to attempt a perspective on Early Bronze Palestine.

The Cultures of Early Bronze Palestine

The Beginning of the Early Bronze Age. There is a sharp divergence between scholars who begin the Early Bronze Age immediately following Ghassulian and others who delay its inception until the beginning of the First Dynasty in Egypt. The disputed post-Ghassulian, pre-Dynastic period is called Early Bronze I (Wright, Amiran),[9] Proto-Urban (Kenyon, Hennessy),[10] and Late Chalcolithic (Albright, De Vaux).[11] The dispute is more than nominal. Wright began designating the disputed period Early Bronze I when pottery he classified as Upper (Late) Chalcolithic was found to be contemporary with a ceramic tradition he considered Early Bronze I.[12] De Vaux argues for the traditional Late Chalcolithic designation because "the culture of the red and gray burnished pottery in the north and centre of Palestine is very different from the Early Bronze Age culture and could not have been a preface to it" and opposes the newer classifications because "they divide two categories which represent the same stage of human development".[13] The ceramic typology displays a much sharper break at the beginning of the disputed period (see below) than at its end. The latest ceramic tradition to appear in the disputed period provides a "valid link"[14] and displays "marked continuity"[15] with the succeeding phase. Should the major division between the Chalcolithic and Bronze Ages be drawn at a point where there is substantial continuity in the ceramic tradition—the chief evidence for distinguishing cultures at this time? If we turn to architectural evidence, the traditional dividing line makes even less sense. At Gath an Egyptian jar bearing the name of Narmer, founder of the First Dynasty,[16] was discovered in Stratum V.[17] The major defenses of the site were first constructed in the previous Stratum VI, that is, before the beginning of the First Dynasty. Accordingly, the traditional Chalcolithic–Bronze division comes shortly after the innovation of heavily fortified towns—a development determining the character of Palestinian culture for centuries. Further, the traditional division linking the beginning of the Early Bronze Age with the beginning of the First Dynasty in Egypt could leave the misleading impression that the unification of Egypt under Narmer produced fundamental and immediately evident consequences in Palestine. The evidence just cited suggests that such was not the case; in fact, links with pre-Dynastic Egypt seem to have had more pervasive influence on EB Palestine than any contacts during the first six dynasties (see below).

The emergence of fortified towns at the end of the controversial period might seem to favor adoption of the "Proto-Urban" designation. "Proto-Urban" might imply that developments toward urban life could be traced through the period. The emphatic statement of De Vaux, quoted above, is indication enough that certain elements in this period cannot be regarded as steppingstones toward EB town culture. That postulating a unilineal evolution is an oversimplification is also suggested by evidence from Bâb edh-Dhrâ'.[18] This most intensively used cemetery in the Near East appears to have been utilized without a gap from the thirty-second century until near the end of the third millennium BC, that is, from well before the construction of the adjacent EB town until long after its end. There seem to be direct links between the pre- and post-town tombs in the dominant burial traditions of the town phase. These town phase traditions are best associated with the evidence of an extensive campsite occupation around the fortified town. These campers with their nonurban predecessors form a single population continuum paralleling the cemetery continuity. This evidence suggests that town life did not arise from but was imposed upon the nonurban folk of the disputed phase. If so "Proto-Urban" is a misnomer.

This same evidence favors Wright's classification, for in it the population continuum reflected at Bâb edh-Dhrâ' is coterminal with the EB Age. While Wright's typological basis for distinguishing three successive phases in EB I has been previously rejected, this framework may be profitably retained.[19] Accordingly, this paper includes treatment of the traditional Late Chalcolithic under the designation EB IA (=Proto-Urban A) and IB (=Proto-Urban B), and EB IC is to be identified with the EB I of the other classifications. In this way the three terminologies converge in their designations of Early Bronze II and III.[20]

The Transition from Ghassulian to Early Bronze IA. There are two phenomena to be noted when evidence for the transition from the Chalcolithic to the Bronze Age is observed. The first concerns the character of the links and relationships between the two cultures. The second focuses upon the extent of overlapping. Had the Chalcolithic culture reached extinction before the arrival of its successor, or was it pushed out by the newcomers, or was there a period when the two groups lived side by side, or did the transition involve more than one of these processes?

No scholar contends that the relationship between the Ghassulian culture (Ghassul–Beersheba–Tel Aviv–Neve Ur) and its successor is close. Some scholars emphasize a break between the cultures quite radically. De Vaux says that "the Ghassul-Beersheba culture, which made its appearance without any preliminaries, disappeared without any sequel".[21] Perrot concludes that Ghassulian culture disappeared abruptly "et ne semblent avoir joué aucun rôle dans la formation de la civilization cananéenne 3e millénaire."[22] Kenyon concludes that "their settlements seem simply to have died out. The recognisably Ghassulian forms of pottery and flint implements do not have their descendants in the forms of the Early Bronze Age."[23] Others describe the break in less radical terms. Hennessy lists a series of parallels between Early Bronze IB and Ghassul IV painted wares but concludes that "the parallels are close but not direct."[24] He does not consider the evidence sufficient to make the postulated connection certain. Albright considers the post-Ghassulian cultures "related, but definitely later."[25] Elsewhere he links a possible general devastation of Palestine with the final abandonment of Ghassul, and postulates a gap before "men began to settle down again."[26]

The evidence on which these general conclusions are based may be summarized as follows. Limited cranial material suggests a rather radical change in population type. The Ghassulians were Armenoid brachycephalics while their successors were predominantly dolichocephalic, and no Armenoids have been found in EB I contexts.[27] This observation by De Vaux has been strikingly confirmed by evidence from the Bâb edh-Dhrâ' cemetery, where hundreds of exclusively dolichocephalic skulls have been recovered from Early Bronze IA–C contexts.[28] The two cultures shared the practice of burying decarnated bones, but the distinctive ossuary containers of Chalcolithic burials (most often in the form of ceramic houses) are completely absent from EB I cemeteries.

Allusion has already been made to the indirect ceramic parallels between the two cultures cited by Hennessy. If the interpretation favored in the next section is accepted, the indirect character of the link between the painted traditions is emphasized by the fact that a period without a tradition of painted decoration intervened between them. There are similarities in the simple bowl forms of the two cultures, but the distinctive features of the two ceramic traditions are mutually exclusive. Chalcolithic painted decoration gives way to a tradition of red and dark[29] burnishing. The Chalcolithic churns and cornets are replaced by handled cups and small two-handled jars as characteristic forms.[30] The highly developed tradition represented in Chalcolithic stone vessels persists into the Bronze Age, but in a degenerate state, which produces no new forms.[31] The sophisticated metal artifacts, the remarkable artistic tradition revealed in the Ghassul frescoes, and even the rather poor architectural tradition of the Ghassulians were not reproduced by their immediate successors.[32]

Taken together this evidence suggests that the break between the Chalcolithic and Bronze Ages is one of the most thoroughgoing in the history of Palestine. The decarnated burial tradition might suggest at least a distant extra-Palestinian relation, and the persistence of the stone tradition indicates that there were minimal contacts in Palestine.

Given scholarly consensus on the radical differences between the Chalcolithic and EB I cultures, the basic disagreement on the character of the transition comes as something of a surprise. It is paradoxical that scholars who emphasize the discontinuities in the strongest terms are also those who lay most stress upon the temporal overlapping of the two cultures in Palestine,[33] while Albright, who recognizes some relationship, emphasizes their sequential character.[34] The extent of the disagreement is strikingly illustrated in the charts of De Contenson and Wright.[35] De Contenson has his latest Chalcolithic (Ghazzeh) material appearing alongside Megiddo XVIII. Wright draws a line at the end of Ghassul-related material about 3300 BC and has Megiddo XVIII emerging in the twenty-ninth century BC. What this means for the interpretation of archaeological evidence can be illustrated at Arad. Here Ruth Amiran has unearthed remains of a Late Chalcolithic settlement "somewhat nearer the Ghassulian than the Beersheba branch."[36] The next evidence of occupation comes at the end of EB I, but Amiran concludes that further excavation and more study are required before it can be decided whether there is a gap between the two occupations (see above, pp. 83 ff.—Ed.). The stratigraphic evidence from Arad by itself forces a reduction in the length of overlap postulated by De Contenson. Still, an overlap interpretation would make it possible to consider the Chalcolithic occupation as the immediate predecessor of the late EB I occupation, whereas with Wright's sequential interpretation there would be a gap of some four centuries between the occupations.

Stratigraphic evidence appears to support overlapping, and Carbon 14 dates fit this interpretation. The stratified evidence comes from Meṣer, where Ghassulian and late EB IA elements appear together in Strata II–I.[37] This evidence could be cited as one of the rare instances of contact between the separate contemporary cultures.[38] Contacts must have been few, if the two cultures preserved such radical distinctions after living side by side for centuries! Several C 14 dates suggest that the Chalcolithic culture disappeared during the thirty-second century BC, and the only C 14 date for EB IA, 3260±110 BC, comes from Jericho Tomb A 94.[39]

Albright has reacted strongly against the idea of a long overlap in a discussion emphasizing the improbability of interpretations based on regionalism and overlapping cultures in the small territory of Palestine.[40] He calls the Ghassulian–Early Bronze overlap an "impossible view." It is indeed highly improbable: there are no good examples of separate contemporary cultures of any duration in Palestine. The evidence from Meṣer needs to be considered alongside that from many sites where EB I groups are completely devoid of characteristic Ghassulian elements.[41] The preliminary reports, in which the Meṣer evidence is available,[42] do not provide conclusive evidence that the two cultures were in fact contemporary,[43] and more than a single C 14 dating is required in EB IA before its chronological limits can be suggested with any confidence.[44] Thus there is no convincing evidence to support the otherwise hardly credible postulation of substantial overlapping of the end of Chalcolithic and the beginning of the Early Bronze Age. The available evidence from C 14 datings suggests that Ghassulian disappeared in the thirty-second century BC. Any overlap with the Early Bronze culture should be limited to that century.[45]

The Cultural Elements of Early Bronze I. Until now there are only two sites which have produced a trustworthy stratigraphic sequence within Early Bronze I.[46] The evidence from the two sites, Jericho and Bâb edh-Dhrâ', is in complete agreement. Tombs K2 and A13 at Jericho have EB IB (Proto-Urban B) material superimposed on EB IA (Proto-

Urban A). This sequence is confirmed by stratified evidence on the mound.[47] In addition, tell stratigraphy confirms the assignment of Tomb A108 to EB IC (Kenyon–Hennessy EB I).[48] At Bâb edh-Dhrâ' there are three instances of Early Bronze IB tombs cut into those of EB IA, and there are tombs of EB IC situated in the stratigraphic sequence by their links with the mound sequence at Jericho.[49] A new element at Bâb edh-Dhrâ' is a group of shaft tombs predating the earliest EB IA tombs at Jericho.[50]

Most of the evidence for the EB I sequence is ceramic. Without examining typological details, the ceramic sequence may be sketched briefly from the Jericho and Bâb edh-Dhrâ' evidence.[51] At neither site is there a survival of distinctive Late Chalcolithic (Ghassulian) ceramic elements, and the earliest EB IA horizon at Bâb edh-Dhrâ' is typologically post-Ghassulian.[52] The pots are handmade, and the surface frequently finished with a highly burnished red to red-orange slip. There is absolutely no use of paint; common decorative elements are incised or stippled horizontal bands and sundry tiny handles, knobs, and raised dots. Late in EB IA there are typological developments accompanied by the emergence of a very poor tradition of painting occasional vessels with roughly spaced, reddish-brown lines. Along with the introduction of this painted tradition at Bâb edh-Dhrâ' is a new burial practice involving repeated use of a tomb for multiple articulated burial groups, in contrast to the earlier practice of chambers used once for a multiple disarticulated interment. The new practice persists as the most commonly found in the Early Bronze Age.

EB IB is marked by the appearance of a more developed and distinctive painted tradition alongside the repertory of EB IA. Characterized by clusters of parallel lines formed by what is called a multiple brush technique, the color of the paint tends to be darker, more of a dark plum red. The EB IB painted tradition introduced a few new forms (notably those with basket handle), but it is also used on EB IA forms. At Bâb edh-Dhrâ' the EB IB tombs attest both the articulated and disarticulated burial practices.

In EB IC a new kind of red-burnished ware appears especially on bowl and jug forms, which come to dominate the typology, though EB IB traditions persist. This burnishing is quite distinct from the EB IA technique in color (no orange hue) and texture (a more powdery surface), as well as by the new forms on which it occurs. The new EB IC tradition continues to predominate in EB II and III.

Esdraelon or Proto-Urban C ware is purported to represent the appearance of still another cultural group in Palestine in EB I.[53] This dark-burnished pottery is limited to a few cup and bowl forms which imitate basalt prototypes.[54] It is found in the later EB IA as well as in IB contexts, and a matte black finished imitation of a basalt cup at Bâb edh-Dhrâ' seems to be a precursor of this tradition.[55] It never occurs apart from the distinctive wares of EB IA and IB,[56] and is actually produced by a slight variation of the technique used to produce the red-burnished ware.[57] This evidence suggests that dark-burnished wares do not represent a separate population group, but the common (though not universal) employment of a variant technique by those who produced the characteristic wares of EB IA and IB.[58] Even a proponent of separate, contemporary population groups in EB I Palestine concludes that the Esdraelon pottery is more of "an additional ceramic type, in already well established cultures, than a hallmark of a large new group."[59]

If Esdraelon ware is dismissed, there are still four successive ceramic developments[60] to be interpreted in terms of population. Taken by itself the ceramic evidence is open to widely divergent interpretation. At one pole is the view that each development represents a population group of different origin; these entered Palestine successively but continued to dwell as separate groups, displaying some regional variance.[61] At the opposite pole would be the contention that the developments do not represent population movement at all, but merely the spread of techniques and skills.

Both extremes seem to be ruled out by other kinds of evidence from Palestine, as well as extra-Palestinian ceramic data.[62] Against the view of separate population groups is the cranial evidence from Bâb edh-Dhrâ'.[63] While it contains all four ceramic developments, this cemetery produced a single type of gracile Mediterranean skull throughout EB I. Further, the cemetery was in continuous use through EB I, and there are even instances in multi-chambered shaft tombs, and within individual chambers, of the mixture of two or more of the ceramic traditions. This agrees with evidence from the tomb groups and strata at Jericho with the persistence of the EB IA painted tradition into IB and of the IB painted tradition in IC.[64] This evidence points to the absorption of a population group or a tradition rather than the persistence of separate peoples. That we are dealing with more than a mere assimilation of new ceramic traditions is indicated by the association of a new ceramic horizon with innovation in burial practice at Bâb edh-Dhrâ'. This evidence points to a situation between the extremes: there is population movement, but the picture most compatible with the archaeological data is one of rapid absorption of successive and closely related population increments. If extra-Palestinian evidence were to suggest a similar origin for the ceramic innovations of EB I, as is suggested below, the correlation would produce a strongly buttressed hypothesis of successive population increments.

The Fortified Settlements and Towns of Early Bronze IC–III. Evidence bearing on the development of larger settlements and the introduction of fortifications in Early Bronze I is extremely difficult to interpret. With few exceptions, the excavated material is given scanty treatment in preliminary publications, and in even fewer instances are findings based on careful stratigraphic excavation. Our approach will be to examine the development of an architectural tradition and then attempt to relate this picture to the demographic situation proposed above.

From the earliest EB IA phase at Bâb edh-Dhrâ' campsite occupation has come to light in a very small sounding, and it is unclear if there was any kind of an architectural tradition in this phase. In later Early Bronze IA, massive buildings of stone and brick on heavy stone foundations attest a substantial architectural tradition at Jericho.[65] One is an apsidal structure, and the apsidal structures of Meṣer II may well belong to the same period.[66] Otherwise the architectural tradition of EB IA and IB is unimpressive. Subsequent strata in the area of the apsidal houses at Jericho reflect a decline in the architectural tradition, and Kenyon notes that only part of the mound was occupied in this period.[67] De Vaux catalogues evidence from a series of sites displaying evidence of occupation in this period but with few or no houses, and concludes that they "were conspicuous for their poverty and an almost complete lack of architecture."[68]

By a process nowhere as yet described, it seems that village houses multiplied rapidly about the beginning of EB IC and were soon surrounded by rapidly expanding defenses. This seems to be the conclusion to be drawn from Kenyon's observation that Jericho had a "fully developed occupation before the town was actually walled."[69] A similar situation occurs at Tell el-Far'ah.[70] Similar developments take place at many other sites, but in a number of instances it is clear that substantial occupation or defenses first occur in the EB II period.[71] Only for Tell Sheikh Aḥmed el-'Arênī is there the suggestion that the defenses might have been constructed before EB IC, but the pottery published from Stratum VI suggests that this is not the case.[72]

At several sites the earliest defenses were of mudbrick,[73] but these were soon strengthened with or superseded by defense lines of stone.

These stone defenses reach rather staggering proportions,[74] and frequently display numerous repairs, rebuildings, realignments, and additions. The stones used are comparatively small and undressed. The walls are composed of abutting, faced sections containing a stone screen. The only plan of a gateway belongs to the mudbrick defenses of Tell el-Far'ah. It is flanked by nearly square projecting towers.[75] Square, rectangular, and semi-circular projecting towers, frequently set at rather regular intervals, are characteristic of Early Bronze defense lines.[76] The fortifications were further consolidated and protected by sloping embankments or glacis in a number of instances.[77]

The impression of homogeneity produced by an examination of EB defensive masonry is underlined by an examination of the buildings inside the defenses and the associated pottery. Before EB IC, apsidal houses seem to have lost out entirely to rectangular units.[78] In fact, the rectangle seems to be the basic unit throughout EB IC–III for virtually all planned buildings—houses, palaces, temples, and even funerary buildings.[79] These units had a single entrance from one of the broad sides, commonly with a few downsteps to the level of the floor, and there were often plastered low benches along one or more of the walls. The charnel houses of Bâb edh-Dhrâ' did not have benches, but many of them shared another feature not uncommon in these buildings, a second story. They also provided the first evidence that these units had flat roofs.[80] A walk through the Arad excavations provides a vivid illustration of the fundamental importance of the rectangular unit in its domestic, public, and cultic buildings.[81]

The beginning of EB IC is distinguished primarily by the appearance of a new tradition of red-polished and -burnished ware associated with new ceramic forms, primarily bowls and jugs.[82] The beginning of EB II is defined more by the disappearance of the EB IB tradition, which persists through EB IC, than by typological shifts within the new tradition.[83] Similarly, the chief clue to the onset of EB III is the presence of Khirbet Kerak ware.[84] While there are a very few typological distinctions offering, at best, broad chronological delimitation, such characteristic forms as the flat-based Abydos jug occur without distinction of form or surface treatment from EB IC through EB III.[85]

The homogeneity of the EB IC–III period, suggested by the defenses and the architectural and ceramic traditions, appears to be disturbed by a single substantial intrusion, Khirbet Kerak ware. Its distribution in Palestine is very uneven; it is found in quantity at sites near the Sea of Galilee, more (Affuleh) or less (Megiddo, Taanach) common in the Esdraelon valley, more or less (Jericho) rare in central and southern Palestine, where only small bowls of this ware occur.[86] It is emphasized that at no site is the appearance of Khirbet Kerak ware associated with any kind of disturbance of the homogeneous features of EB IC–III.[87] Occupation of several town sites seems to cease before the beginning of EB III, but there is no evidence for associating this with the producers of Khirbet Kerak ware.[88]

The distribution of EB fortified sites in Palestine deserves attention before we turn to demographic considerations. West of the Jordan such sites are more common in the north than in the south; and the southernmost is Arad, at the northern edge of the Negeb. De Vaux describes this pattern and notes its importance in considering the character and origin of EB townfolk.[89] He neglects to mention the results of Nelson Glueck's explorations east of the Jordan, which are perhaps even more enlightening. Glueck's survey suggests that there were more fortified towns on the east bank than on the west, and he emphasizes the importance of the string of EB sites down the Jordan Valley and the Wâdī 'Arabah to Feinan, from which point the EB sites of Sinai are to the west.[90] This observation makes the lack of EB sites in the Negeb intelligible.

Another facet of Glueck's discoveries of importance for demographic considerations is the location of numerous unwalled settlements of the EB IC–III period. This should be examined along with the evidence from Bâb edh-Dhrâ' that there was a vast area around the walled site densely occupied by hut and hovel dwellers. Bâb edh-Dhrâ', of course, provides an important link in the string of Great Rift sites. Another, recently excavated, is 'Arô'er on the northern rim of the Wâdī Môjib, biblical Aroer on the Arnon. In this writer's opinion, evidence from the second campaign established that the original small fort (50 meters square), reconstructed by the Moabites and Nabataeans was originally built in the Early Bronze Age.[91] The size of the site precludes the role of a fortified settlement. It was more likely a garrison post, protecting the hazardous path through the majestic *wadi*.

The association of the EB IC–III defenses, architecture, and ceramic with a distinct population group seems inescapable. There is also abundant evidence that their appearance was a matter of peaceful infiltration, not warlike conquest.[92] That they were quite distinct from their predecessors in Palestine is obvious from the striking novelty of their pottery and defenses, but elements suggesting kinship with their predecessors also deserve attention. The rectangular building unit was apparently a tradition they shared with their predecessors,[93] and the cranial evidence from Bâb edh-Dhrâ', alluded to above, indicates that the two groups were of the same skull type. They seem also to have shared or adopted the stone maceheads of their predecessors, as well as a very limited skill in creating metal implements and weapons. Bâb edh-Dhrâ' evidence also suggests that they shared the tradition of successive burial of articulated groups in the shaft tombs. These suggestions of kinship are underscored by the juxtaposition of the EB IB and IC traditions in EB IC, even if it is considered a relatively short period.[94]

Similar observations may be made to interpret the appearance of Khirbet Kerak ware. At sites within a short distance of the northern Jordan Valley the ware appears in enough quantity and variety to postulate the arrival of a new population element, its size difficult to estimate. Elsewhere in Palestine it seems that its wares were carried by trade or sporadic individual movement. This element, too, seems in other respects to have had much in common with its Palestinian forebears.

It seems possible that the EB IB element was finally absorbed by the newcomers when their characteristic pottery disappears at the beginning of EB II. That the EB IC ceramic tradition triumphed is not to be denied, but the unwalled villages and the huts around the fortress at Bâb edh-Dhrâ' suggest that Palestine in EB IC–III

> was not an age of gradual and homogeneous evolution. From beginning to end there was general progress in the building of cities, in the material culture, and in daily life. But this was the result of the mixture and superimposition of different cultural traits, behind which were the various waves of newcomers of diverse origin arriving in Palestine. Tribal life was still going on in most regions; and in the vicinity of the cities some people still lived in villages, hamlets, huts, and tents.[95]

If there is any quarrel with Anati's view, it would be in emphasizing also the kinship of the waves of newcomers and the very probable numerical predominance of the population living outside the towns.

It remains to characterize the town life of the Early Bronze Age. The period reflects the emergence of Palestine's first urban civilization and the beginning of its city-state system.[96] This traditional view sees Palestine divided into independent city-states, each with its surrounding dependencies and spheres of influence. This structure leads to constant intrigue and frequent fighting between individual states or their coalitions, after the manner reflected in the Amarna correspondence for a later age. This traditional view deserves careful scrutiny.

First, the almost undelimited designation of this age as "urban"[97] and its fortified sites as "cities" appears to be more than slightly misleading. To ancients inhabiting the larger "cities" of Egypt, Mesopotamia, and even Syria, the fortified sites of Palestine were hardly more than "towns." Moderns worried about the current urban crisis could also be expected to shy away from applying such terminology to EB Palestine. Even a very large fortified site like Arad covers an area of only about one-thirtieth of a square mile. If "urban" terminology is retained, it should be divested of much of its modern meaning and connotation. The same applies to "town," but in a somewhat less radical manner. (Editor's note: compare Mrs. Amiran's view, above, pp. 83 ff.)

In the second place, the traditional view has failed to emphasize what appear to be two important phases in the development of the fortified sites. It was noted above that the earliest defenses were in certain instances built around already existing settlements. In the heading of this section these are called "fortified settlements." After fortification, such sites as Tell el-Farʿah display intensifying occupation, but only after a major destruction is something like town planning attested. EB III Megiddo provides striking evidence of such planning,[98] and the functional division of fortified Arad reflects rather well-organized town life.[99] To this writer it would be preferable to reserve the designation "fortified towns" for sites where the unplanned maze of village dwellings has been clearly superseded. Present evidence does not make it possible to decide whether the skills of town planning were imported or developed indigenously by the defense-builders. In any case the Neolithic fortification of Jericho is probably not unique, and cautions against calling the EB towns the earliest city-state system in Palestine.

The third problem with the traditional view concerns the purpose for which the defenses were originally built and subsequently strengthened. According to the traditional view it is possible to envision the gradual spread of city-states southward from Syria. The evidence from Gath, whatever its precise stratigraphy, shows that this southern site was among the earliest fortified. Accordingly, we must deal with the phenomenon of the fortification of a large number of towns throughout Palestine within a relatively short period. We are faced with a choice between seeing the newcomers as quickly taking hegemony, and just as rapidly dividing into warring factions building defenses against each other; or viewing the newcomers as a more unified and cooperating group, building defenses against a common threat whether indigenous or external. The homogeneity of the newcomers' culture, as emphasized above, favors the second alternative, and their peaceful coexistence with their predecessors in EB IC, when the first defenses were being built, points to an external foe. In fact, the only pertinent evidence available sustains this conclusion, for at Gath it is clear that the forces of Narmer overcame its earliest defenses.[99a] It will be proposed below that the fortified towns of EB Palestine might have been similar to the kingdom in Lower Egypt subjugated by Narmer.[100] The foreign foe gains further definition in Drower's interpretation of contemporary Egyptian records as referring to "royal raids into Palestine which had as their main object the capture of livestock both animal and human."[101]

A fourth consideration raising doubts about the traditional view is the relation between the newcomers and the indigenous population. It has been suggested above that the defense-builders did not entirely absorb the indigenous group, and that the latter represented the larger element of the population. Some undoubtedly became town-dwellers and a larger group became dependent upon town life, as the hovels outside the Bâb edh-Dhrâ' fortifications suggest, but the pre-EB IC pattern of village life persisted. The continuous tradition of shaft-tombs from EB IA to IV suggests that earlier practices persisted even among those who became town-oriented. The fact that this village culture persisted even after the destruction of the town system (see next section) underlines an element of separateness and independence maintained by the indigenous villagers throughout the period. This fits better a perspective of a unified ruling group over against the indigenous population than the polarization and the unification of populations within city-state territories.

The above arguments are intended to propose that, rather than suggesting an urban city-state pattern, the evidence suggests that Palestine became a fairly unified kingdom in the Early Bronze Age—no more enigmatic than other pre-literate kingdoms.

The Reversion to Village Life in Early Bronze IV. The designation "Early Bronze IV" requires explanation and defense, but this can be done more effectively after the sequence of events, reflected by archaeological evidence, has been described. Attention may be directed first to the destruction of the fortified towns. It is clear that their destruction is not the result of a decline and weakening of the town culture, for there is considerable evidence of robust life in the reconstructions and expansions of Early Bronze III towns.[102] With the possible exception of a few which may have been destroyed earlier,[103] all these flourishing towns appear to have been violently destroyed within a relatively short period of time.[104] This pattern of destruction provides another suggestion that the unity postulated for the town culture persisted to the end. The destruction of city-states of uneven strength and influence should have presented a more irregular pattern.

There are rather decisive archaeological clues to the identification of the people who destroyed town life. It clearly was not those who introduced Khirbet Kerak ware, for not a sherd of their ware has been found in the occupation layers or tombs of EB IV. At Bâb edh-Dhrâ', in the latest charnel houses of the town phase, there begin to appear a few new ceramic forms which become dominant during the course of EB IV. The charnel houses frequently contain several hundred pots, and the new ceramic is represented by less than half a dozen forms. It seems clear that these were the forerunners of the group that destroyed town life, and the new pottery suggests another wave of newcomers. Their extra-Palestinian identity is referred to below.

Evidence for the character of life in Palestine after the destruction of its fortified towns is not quite as meager as is usually thought.[105] The strongly built houses of EB IA–B became less sturdy during the period of fortified towns and thereafter deteriorated further or disappeared.[106] The earliest occupation at Tell Beit Mirsim (Stratum J) seems to have begun before the destruction of towns but flourished thereafter. It was more of a campsite, for there were no remains of masonry.[107] Evidence from Bethel suggests an identical sequence: slight occupation in EB III, somewhat more for EB IV, but no buildings.[108] The mounds of Lachish and Tell el-Ḥesi probably had similar histories, but the evidence is inconclusive.[109] Beth-shemesh[110] and Ader[111] are probable examples of sites at which camping occupation began after the towns had been destroyed. Ader is one of many sites in Transjordan at which Nelson Glueck discovered evidence of EB IV occupation.[112] Jericho provides an example of camping occupation immediately following the destruction of the EB town.[113] Excavation at Tell Ikhtenu, near Ghassul, has brought to light a village of this period with rather miserable walled mudbrick huts.[114] Here pottery of the newcomers was mixed with degenerate forms of the pottery of the town folk. A similar mixture occurs in two Bâb edh-Dhrâ' tombs, including a lamp, approaching the four-spouted type of the newcomers, red-burnished in the town tradition.[115]

This minimal and oversimplified sketch of EB IV evidence is necessary to understand the demographic developments of the period. It indicates, firstly, that the group responsible for the unified town culture was destroyed or left Palestine (see below). The defenses disappear and the architectural and ceramic traditions survive as a dim shadow. In the second place, even the minimal evidence just cited suggests a sizable post-town population. This population seems to have been concentrated in central and southern Palestine, especially in fringe areas. Third, the evidence points to two distinct elements in the post-town population. The ceramic repertory of the newcomers is distinctly limited and has as its basic unit a rounded-to-ovoid handmade body.[116] This repertory occurs in virtually pure form in cemeteries of the latter part of the period between EB and MB town life (traditional Middle Bronze I=my Intermediate Bronze II).[117] In EB IV this new pottery is found mixed with an indigenous ceramic horizon representing a degeneration of EB III. This is reflected especially in poor red burnishing, which subsequently disappears.[118] The mixture of the two ceramic traditions at the sites mentioned above suggests, as a fourth observation, that the two population elements mingled freely.

These observations make possible some speculative postulations concerning relations between the two groups. In the first place, it is likely that the indigenous group did not join the town folk in their struggle with the newcomers. In fact, the rash of major building operations in EB III towns might be associated with increased oppression in the form of corvée labor. As a result, the indigenous folk might have joined in the overthrow of the towns. Secondly, the mixture of the groups could hardly have occurred if they did not share a very similar way of life. Closer kinship than a common way of life is suggested by their joint use of the Bâb edh-Dhrâ' cemetery, where successive burials of articulated groups in shaft-tombs as well as single articulated cairn burials are both attributable to EB IV. Both, incidentally, have the same cranial types. This kinship appears to have been similar to that of the successive population increments throughout the Early Bronze Age, for the pattern of typological development is basically the same. The ceramic tradition of EB IA persists through EB IB; that of EB IB through EB IC; that of EB III through EB IV.

This kinship has a bearing on the Amorite problem. While a treatment of that problem would go beyond the boundaries of this chapter, a few remarks are required background for the discussion of terminology which follows. The close kinship between the newcomers of EB IV and those of traditional MB I is not in dispute. The kinship between these groups and the population increments going back to EB IA has been a dominant theme in this discussion. How can this kinship be related to Egyptian records which do not record Amorite names before the twentieth century BC (the latter part of traditional MB I)?[119] Dever's confidence in the traditional association of the Amorite Patriarchs with MB I appears to conflict with his perceptive emphasis on the complete ceramic break between MB I and MB II and his notation that Shechem, a site closely associated with Abraham, had no MB I remains on the mound and was only founded as a town in MB IIA (*circa* 1900 BC).[120] (Editor's note: for Dever's current analysis and view, see pp. 132 ff.).

To summarize, there are links between EB III and IV. There is a close link between EB IV and traditional MB I, but the break between MB I and MB IIA is at least as radical as that between Late Chalcolithic and EB IA. From EB IA through traditional MB I, Palestine received a series of related population increments, a pattern only partly obscured by that group which introduced town life. The terminology best reflecting this situation would include all the increments within Early Bronze. This would suggest that the post-town period should be called EB IVA and traditional MB I, Early Bronze IVB.[121] The problem with such a proposal is that it adds confusion to traditional terminology. Wright has correctly opposed arbitrary introduction of new terminology,[122] and yet in the same article he proposes that his earlier EB IV be changed to EB IIIB and prefers to reuse EB IV to designate something else—while sharply criticizing Kenyon for introducing new and confusing terminology.[123] My proposal to call EB IV Intermediate Bronze I and MB I Intermediate Bronze II[124] fails to reflect the link between EB III and IV and results with the beginning of the Middle Bronze Age in MB II. Dever proposes to call the non-town phase EB IV/MB I divided into two phases.[125] None of the recent proposals overcome the disadvantages of the traditional terminology without substituting new ones. Accordingly, I have designated the period just discussed EB IV and the succeeding period MB I, frequently with the determinative "traditional" to distinguish it from Kenyon's MB I (=traditional MB IIA). MB I represents the last in a series of distinct, but clearly related, groups which began arriving in Palestine in EB IA.

Early Bronze Palestine in Its Near Eastern Setting

The structure of this presentation has precluded marshaling in one place all evidence bearing on specific problems. It is hoped that the preceding review has contributed to a fair presentation of the evidence from Palestine rather than an arbitrary treatment based on broad preconceptions. There is no new evidence set forth in what follows, merely a brief summary of the material from the recent works cited in the introduction, especially Hennessy's. The world around Palestine in the third millennium BC is rapidly emerging from obscurity, but our knowledge of eastern Syria and parts of Anatolia is still extremely limited. Accordingly, some of the conclusions reached here will probably require revision and certainly be refined in the near future.

Relations with Syria and the North. It is worth noting that Mesopotamia is purposely excluded from this heading. There is no evidence of direct contact between Mesopotamians and Palestinians in the Early Bronze Age.[126] Artifacts in Palestine suggesting Mesopotamian connection can be explained as entering both Palestine and Mesopotamia from a common source or by mediation through the inhabitants of Syria. If Syria and Palestine were "the cultural intermediaries through which Mesopotamian influences streamed into Egypt in the period just before the First Dynasty,"[127] there is an amazing dearth of evidence for such Mesopotamian features in Palestine.[128]

In contrast with Mesopotamia, Anatolia appears to have been the source of most, if not all, the new groups reaching Palestine during the Early Bronze Age. These groups reached Palestine through Syria but their impact upon Syria varied considerably. There is very little evidence of newcomers arriving by sea, and none of immigrants from Egypt. A brief review of evidence concerning the origins of the new groups reaching Palestine in the Early Bronze Age follows.

If our analysis of the cultural sequence is correct, Hennessy's treatment of external parallels for EB IA materials needs reorganization. The Mesopotamian links for Canaanean flints and the metal industry are impressive, but these traditions originate in the Chalcolithic period. His separate treatment of black- and red-burnished traditions reaches somewhat different conclusions, but the parallels he cites retain their value and point to unmistakable conclusions. The loop handle was a common feature in the earliest EB IA tombs of Bâb edh-Dhrâ'; Hennessy cites parallels widely scattered in Turkey and concludes that it reached Palestine "from the north by way of Cilicia."[129] The common and characteristic large bowls of this phase seem to have their best parallels in South Russia,[130] suggesting an origin for the earliest EB group in northeastern Anatolia or even farther northeast. The distribution of dark-burnished (Esdraelon) wares has been conveniently plotted by Hennessy.[131] They have been found in north-central and eastern Anatolia, near the Cilician coast, and at Tabara el-Akrad in the Plain of Antioch, but evidence from Syria is scanty and limited.[132] For the red-burnished ware Hennessy cites parallels from the Syrian coast, the 'Amûq, and Tarsus, plus a number in ceramic features which have parallels northward.[133] Orthmann emphasizes the juxtaposition of red- and dark-burnished wares in inner Anatolia at this time,[134] but detailed parallels have not been collected. It would seem that evidence on the dark-burnished wares assures an Anatolian origin, but a more precise determination awaits a detailed typological comparison of the red-burnished wares. The scarcity of good parallels to both wares in Syria suggests that few of this group stopped in Syria on their path toward *Lebensraum* in Palestine.

Hennessy and others postulate a local origin for the multi-brush painted tradition of EB IB.[135] Elsewhere I have pointed to the closely-related Çıradere tradition and suggested that it is contemporary with EB IB on the basis of stratigraphy at Alishar Hüyük.[136] Certainly its relation to Sha'ar Hagolan's painted tradition is as remote as it is removed in time. While detailed parallels need to be compiled, it seems clear that this wave of newcomers also came from Anatolia. Syria seems to have had even less attractiveness for them than for their predecessors.

In the following EB IC–III period the situation in Syria is radically different, for, considering normal local differences, Syria-Palestine forms a single cultural area.[137] Hennessy proposes an origin for its ceramics in the 'Amûq spreading northeast to Tarsus and south along the coast into Palestine.[138] This point of origin could be stated with more conviction if a large area from northwest to northeast of the 'Amûq were not such an archaeological *terra incognita;* nor can a Phoenician origin be excluded. While postulating an 'Amûq origin for the pottery, Hennessy inconsistently favors the development of fortified towns as a natural development within Palestine.[139] That the uniform and dominant EB IC–III ceramic tradition was introduced by "a secondary infiltration" seems an awkward end to the preconceived evolutionary scheme inherent in "Proto-Urban." It seems clear that the close-bound unit of defenses–architecture–pottery reached Palestine from Syria in EB IC and was closely linked to Syria through EB III.

The northern origin of Khirbet Kerak ware has been accepted for some time. The literature is summarized by Hennessy, who provides a sketch map of proveniences attested so far.[140] There appears to be no argument with the proposed origin of this ware in northeastern Anatolia, and it is conveniently attested in a number of areas along the route to Palestine.

It seems likely that its bearers came through central Syria to the Jordan Valley, for Khirbet Kerak ware is common at Hama but rare on Syrian and Palestinian coastal sites. Khirbet Kerak ware provides clear evidence of the migration in EB III of still another Anatolian group to Palestine.

The EB IV invaders and their closely related MB I successors also came from the north. Elsewhere I have cited material from Soviet Central Asia which appears too similar to Palestinian material to be fortuitous.[141] Subsequently, the relation of this observation to M. Gimbutas' Kurgan invader hypothesis has been noted.[142] More evidence is needed to support postulations in this direction, but the evidence published and forthcoming appears sufficient to the writer to consider a northern origin the best hypothesis. My earlier treatment suffered from an overemphasis on a sea route by which this group reached Palestine.[143] In emphasizing the contrast between town life in Syria and its absence in Palestine at this time, I neglected to take account of the obvious and substantial elements of the pottery of the EB IV newcomers in Syria,[144] alongside the wares associated in Palestine with the townsfolk.[145] Many of the newcomers settled in Syria, though here the towns were apparently able to absorb them and avoid destruction. Many others reached Palestine by the Syrian land routes, though the evidence that some reached Palestine by sea should not be dismissed.

The trend of this evidence suggests that the successive population increments reaching Palestine during the Early Bronze Age originated in Anatolia or even farther north and east and arrived via Syria. Only the EB IC group seems more likely to have had north Syrian origins, a difference related to its unique associations with town life during the period. While there are considerable gaps of evidence along the routes by which these groups reached Palestine, especially in south-central Anatolia, there is ample evidence for postulating a series of related migrant groups from north of Syria reaching Palestine during the Early Bronze Age. This fits well the pattern of population increments required by the evidence from Palestine.

Relations with Egypt. Fundamental to understanding Palestine's relations with Egypt in EB IA is the perception that the southward migration spilled over into Egypt. The Palestinian ceramic elements of this period discovered in Egypt are usually attributed to trade.[146] Trade implies two-way movement, but there is no evidence of northward movement of expatriate goods or people during the entire Early Bronze Age in Syria-Palestine except from Dynastic Egypt. The best evidence of contact is found in large ledge-handled jars, which inspired "an entire class of Gerzean pottery."[147] This inspiration would seem better attributed to EB IA–B migrants, gradually absorbed in Egypt, than to mere trade. The thought that these large jars were transported regularly along the difficult route down the 'Arabah, across Sinai, and into Egypt is not attractive. Parallels to these jars from Early Chalcolithic contexts at Jericho and Beth-shan are cited in favor of a Palestinian origin,[148] but more contemporary counterparts can be noted.[149] Kantor's division of Gerzean into early and later phases (=earlier and later Naqada II) and her correlation of Gerzean and EB I in Palestine are largely confirmed by Bâb edh-Dhrâ' evidence. The types of ledge handles, knobbed bowls in plain ware, loop-handled jars, and twin cups imported into Egypt are all represented by good parallel material from the earliest EB IA tombs at Bâb edh-Dhrâ'.[150] These suggest a correlation between Early Gerzean and EB IA, though, for example, the knobbed bowl is assigned to Late Gerzean.[151]

Only three small vessels of the EB IB painted tradition have been found in Egypt, and one or more of these could be assigned to the end of EB IA.[152] Few, if any, migrants seem to have reached Egypt from Palestine in EB IB.

Relations with Egypt in the EB IC–III period are reflected in archaeological evidence from Palestine and Egypt as well as by Egyptian records. Except for two important groups, extremely few Egyptian imports have been found in EB Palestine.[153] The earlier group comes from Gath V, and is dated, by an inscription bearing this name, to the time of Narmer.[154] The choice between considering the Egyptian intrusion at Gath a raid or a conquest appears to be settled in favor of conquest by the evidence of Egyptian occupation of the site during Stratum V. Since there is no similar evidence elsewhere in Palestine, a third alternative cannot be excluded: it may have served as a protected base from which Egypt exploited its economic interests. Palestinian pottery in tombs of the First Dynasty could readily be connected with such activity (see below). The other group of Egyptian artifacts comes from an Ai sanctuary, dated by its Palestinian contents within EB III and by its Egyptian imports to the Second to Fifth Dynasties.[155] Outside the sanctuary there is nothing to suggest Egyptian occupation or control of Ai, any more than at other sites of EB Palestine except Gath V.[156]

In the period between Gath V and the Ai sanctuary, there are rather frequent references to the walled towns of Palestine, all of them hostile. There is no hint of any positive relation with rulers of certain "city-states." From the Narmer palette (attractively interpreted by Yadin as signaling

subjugation of Palestine and Transjordan[157]), to Djer's "Smiting of Asia,"
to the bound Asiatic in the tomb of Qaa, to Peribsen's epithet "He who
carries off Asia," to the Asiatic prisoners in the mortuary temple of
Sahure, to the sieges of Palestinian towns depicted in the tombs of Inti
and Kaiemhesit, to the five campaigns by land and one by sea of Uni
against Palestine in the reign of Phiops I—there is universal hostility
toward Palestine.[158] There are no hints that the pharaohs sought trade
or a safe trade route through amicable relations. Except for Narmer's
assault on Gath and perhaps Uni's campaigns, Drower's view of the action
more as raids than full-scale campaigns agrees with the fact that Egypt
had no standing army in Old Kingdom times.[159] This implacable foe
could well have given impetus to the defenses around Palestinian towns
and united the towns against their common threat.

It is in this light that I should prefer to view the Palestinian artifacts
found in Egypt during this period.[160] As in the Gerzean period, the
Palestinian pots found in the tombs of kings and nobles[161] are often
cited as evidence of trade.[162] De Vaux's suggestion of tribute would appear closer to the truth.[163] Perhaps even more to the point would be
the suggestion that the Palestinian imports were found in the tombs of
those who led or sent off raiding parties into Palestine. The more sporadic
occurrence of such imports after the Early Dynastic period might suggest
that there were less frequent or smaller scale raids into Palestine during
the Third and Fourth Dynasties. Perhaps the prosperity of EB III towns
attracted the stepped-up efforts of the Egyptians of the Fifth and Sixth
Dynasties that seem to be reflected in the records. Perhaps these in turn
were responsible for the several major phases of defense improvements
in EB III as reflected at sites like Taanach.[164]

If the evidence in general seems to fit our interpretation, there remains
a more exacting question for which precise evidence is lacking. This
concerns the relation between the EB IC pottery found in Egypt and the
rise of the First Dynasty which occurred during that period. The acuteness
of the problem may be illustrated at Ma'adeh, where Kantor assigns all
the pottery to the Gerzean period while for Baumgartel it is entirely
Dynastic.[165] As a matter of fact, both could be right, for such forms as
the first two in Kantor's Ma'adeh group[166] belong to EB IC, but it is impossible to distinguish early or late in this period. Ma'adeh is on the edge
of the Delta, which is a blank as far as our period is concerned. Hennessy
suggests that there may have been fortified towns like those of EB
Palestine in the Delta in the Late Pre-Dynastic period.[167] If there were,
and if they were somehow linked to those of Syria-Palestine, Narmer's

campaign at Gath may have been aimed at a direct threat to his newly unified kingdom of Upper and Lower Egypt, whose northern border was in the vicinity of Cairo. It is not impossible that this threatening enemy was an organized kingdom similar to that of Lower Egypt. This conclusion at least fits well with conclusions reached from Palestinian evidence.

A final problem is the most inscrutable of all. It concerns the situation in Egypt during the First Intermediate period and its relation to EB IV Palestine. De Vaux makes the perceptive suggestion that Uni's campaigns in Palestine are directed more against the force threatening Palestinian town life at the end of EB III than against Palestine itself.[168] It would also be congenial to the interpretations suggested here to speculate that Egypt retained its implacable hatred against Palestine and saw in the threat from the north an opportunity to join in dealing a death blow to Palestine. This would at least point a way out to the quite conflicting evidence in the Egyptian records that Asiatics poured into the Delta in the First Intermediate[169] and the archaeological evidence that there were "no unmistakably foreign types of objects . . . from the graves of the First Intermediate."[170] Perhaps tombs of those who destroyed EB town life in Palestine will some day be discovered in the Delta. Perhaps there was an accommodation between the newcomers and the Egyptians. In that case, perhaps the Asiatics entering Egypt were Amorites, an ephemeral group because it had no burial tradition.[171]

Egyptian Relations and Absolute Chronology. Whatever the circumstances by which Palestinian imports reached Dynastic tombs in Egypt, they have proved invaluable in establishing bonds with Egyptian evidence, and it is only through Egyptian evidence that any precision can be reached in the chronology of the ancient Near East.

Pre-Dynastic dates can only be broadly suggested from the results of C 14 tests. The datings for the latter part of Chalcolithic and the single date for an EB IA tomb suggest that the beginning of EB IA should be assigned to the thirty-second century BC.[172] We have noted just above that the beginning of the First Dynasty occurs during EB IC. There is only minor disagreement between Albright, who begins EB II with the third king of the First Dynasty (Djer),[173] and Hennessy, who makes the break with Djer's second successor (Den).[174] There is also general agreement that EB III comprises the Third to Fifth Egyptian Dynasties. Unfortunately, as a result of the weakness of records in the Early Dynastic and First Intermediate periods, these correlations can be assigned high, medium, or low absolute dates. These are conveniently summarized by Hennessy.[175] Following the moderately low chronology of Albright,[176] the following correlation may be suggested:

Early Bronze IA	3150–3050	Early Gerzean
Early Bronze IB	3050–2950	Late Gerzean
Early Bronze IC	2950–2850	Late Gerzean thru Djet
Early Bronze II	2850–2550	Den thru Second Dynasty
Early Bronze III	2550–2275	Third thru Fifth Dynasties
Early Bronze IV	2275–2050	Sixth Dynasty thru First Intermediate
Middle Bronze I	2050–1900	Ninth Dynasty thru Ammenemes II

Eight years have passed since the last *Festschrift* article with a somewhat more limited survey of the Early Bronze Age.[177] A quick perusal of that treatment will indicate what a vast wealth of new and exciting material has been excavated in the short space of eight years. There has been commensurate development, hopefully progress, in the interpretation of the material. Even in the face of such rapid development, the results of Nelson Glueck's topographical work continue to add an important dimension to our perspective on Palestine in the Early Bronze Age.

FOOTNOTES

(Editor's note: Professor Lapp refers to a number of key works more than once and to simplify his notations has developed his own set of sigla for this article. In each case he has given the necessary bibliographic information in the first reference, as follows: Hennessy in note 1; Lapp 1 and Lapp 2 in note 2; Lapp 3 in note 71; Lapp 4 in note 116; de Vaux 1 and de Vaux 2 in note 3; Drower and Bottéro in note 4; Wright 1 in note 9; Kenyon 1 in note 10; Glueck 1 in note 86; and Anati in note 95. In the cases of Wright, Kenyon and Glueck, Lapp refers to more than one of their works but cites only one of each more than once.)

1. J. B. Hennessy, *The Foreign Relations of Palestine during the Early Bronze Age* (1967).

2. Exceptions are Paul W. Lapp, "Bâb edh-Dhrâ' Tomb A 76 and Early Bronze I in Palestine," *BASOR*, No. 189 (1968), pp. 12–41 (Lapp 1); "Bâb edh-Dhrâ', Perizzites and Emim," in *Jerusalem through the Ages* (1968), pp. 1–25 (Lapp 2).

3. R. de Vaux, "Palestine During the Neolithic and Chalcolithic Periods," CAH^2 I, fasc. 47 (1966), pp. 35–43, and "Palestine in the Early Bronze Age," CAH^2 I, fasc. 46 (1966). Henceforth de Vaux 1 and 2 respectively.

4. M. S. Drower and J. Bottéro, "Syria before 2000," CAH^2 I, fasc. 55 (1968). Henceforth Drower and Bottéro.

5. J. Perrot, "Préhistoire palestinienne," in *SDB* (1968), esp. cols. 439–46.

6. Esp. Chaps. I–III in $COWA^2$.

7. Hennessy, pp. 85–90. De Vaux 2, pp. 25–26. Albright, $COWA^2$, pp. 49–50. Ruth Amiran, "A Preliminary Note on the Synchronisms between the Early Bronze Strata of Arad and the First Dynasty," *BASOR*, No. 179 (1965), pp. 30–33; "A Second Note on the Synchronism between Early Bronze Arad and the First Dynasty," *BASOR*, No. 195 (1969), pp. 50–53. The last reference appeared too late for comment in the text.

8. Lapp 1 and 2. Previous bibliography is cited in Lapp 1, note 1.

9. G. E. Wright, "The Archaeology of Palestine," in *BANE* (1961), pp. 81–83 (Wright 1). Ruth Amiran, *The Ancient Pottery of Eretz Yisrael* (1963), pp. 5, 61–79 (in Hebrew). (Editor's note: for Amiran's current view, see above, pp. 83 ff.).

10. K. M. Kenyon, *Archaeology in the Holy Land* (1965), pp. 84–100 (Kenyon 1); *Jericho*, II (1965), pp. 3–32. Cf. Hennessy, pp. 15–18, 26–47, and note Chart I, p. 21.

11. Albright, $COWA^2$, p. 51. De Vaux 1, pp. 35–43.

12. G. E. Wright, "The Problem of the Transition between the Chalcolithic and Bronze Ages," *Eretz Israel*, 5 (1958), p. 43. Cf. Lapp 1, pp. 31–32.

13. De Vaux 1, pp. 40–41. Cf. Albright, $COWA^2$, p. 51.

14. De Vaux 1, p. 41.

15. Hennessy, p. 18.

16. I. E. S. Edwards, "The Early Dynastic Period in Egypt," CAH^2 I, fasc. 25 (1964), pp. 5–10.

17. S. Yeivin, "Early Contacts between Canaan and Egypt, *IEJ*, 10 (1960), pp.

198–200; cf. Further Evidence of Narmer at 'Gat,'" *OrAnt*, 2 (1963), pp. 205–13. See also Albright, *COWA²*, pp. 49–50.

18. Lapp 1, pp. 26–31.

19. Lapp 1, pp. 31–36. Cf. below.

20. See Hennessy, Chart I, p. 21, for a tabular summary.

21. De Vaux 1, p. 35.

22. Perrot, col. 439.

23. Kenyon 1, p. 82.

24. Hennessy, p. 18.

25. W. F. Albright, *From the Stone Age to Christianity* (1957), p. 144.

26. W. F. Albright, *The Archaeology of Palestine* (1960), pp. 69–70. The insertion of a reference to the Beersheba culture continuing the Ghassulian tradition in the current edition of this work would appear to call for some revision also in postulating the general destruction.

27. De Vaux 1, p. 38; cf. p. 34.

28. Lapp 1, p. 13, n. 2; p. 20.

29. "Dark" is used instead of the usual "black" designation because the color varies from gray to black and has occasional cream-colored patches, depending upon the oven conditions that produced the dark color. Dark burnishing is limited to a very few forms, and these seem to be imitations of stone vessels. Cf. Lapp 1, pp. 33–35; and below.

30. On the stratigraphic juxtaposition of Chalcolithic and EB I forms see below.

31. Cf. Lapp 1, pp. 25–26, 34–35. Evidence on the relation between the respective flint traditions is inconclusive. Cf. Hennessy, p. 18.

32. No metal objects have been found in the EB IA tombs of Bâb edh-Dhrâ'. Cf. the virtual lack of metal in the later EB IA and IB tombs at Jericho.

33. De Vaux 1, pp. 41–42. Perrot, cols. 439–40. Kenyon 1, p. 96. Cf. Hennessy, p. 18.

34. Cf. n. 25. Albright, *COWA²*, pp. 48–49.

35. H. de Contenson, "Remarques sur le Chalcolithique Récent de Tell esh Shuna," *RB*, 68 (1961), Pl. 30, opp. p. 552. G. E. Wright, "The Archaeology of Palestine," in *BANE* (1961), Charts 1 (p. 80), 2 (p. 83), and 3 (p. 85).

36. R. Amiran and Y. Aharoni, *Ancient Arad* (1967), p. 6.

37. Cf. Lapp 1, p. 37 with refs. cited.

38. Perrot alludes to similar evidence from Gat-Govrin: *RB*, 69 (1962), p. 388.

39. The discussion below suggests that this tomb belongs to the end of EB IA. On the C 14 dates with pertinent references cf. Lapp 1, pp. 37–38.

40. Albright, *COWA²*, pp. 47–49. Cf. Lapp 1, pp. 32–33.

41. Note especially the copious material from tombs at Jericho and Bâb edh-Dhrâ', which is exclusively EB I.

42. M. Dothan, "Excavations at Meṣer, 1956," *IEJ*, 7 (1957), pp. 217–28; "Excavations at Meṣer, 1957," *IEJ*, 9 (1959), pp. 13–29.

43. Cf. Lapp 1, p. 37. In addition to observations suggesting the lack of empirical stratigraphic excavation (note especially the observation [*IEJ*, 9, p. 21] that only in the second campaign was it possible to differentiate the finds of Strata III and II–I), it should be observed that it is not sufficient to find the two pottery horizons in the same stratum or layer. Many layers consist of mixed fills or wash, and the Meṣer layers were complicated by numerous pits and intrusions. To be convincing, the pottery of the two cultures must be found in an undisturbed occupation or destruction layer.

44. Cf. Lapp 1, p. 38.

45. This dating has the result of reducing the overlap from 3300–29th century

to 32nd–29th centuries BC according to Wright's chronology, but the overlap is still much too long to be credible. The beginning of EB I in the thirty-second century fits well with chronological considerations discussed below.

46. On the unreliability of "stratified" material from other sites, cf. the remarks of Albright, *COWA*[2], p. 51, and de Vaux 1, pp. 38–39. On the rejection of Wright's use of the earlier "stratified" material and his related postulation of typological development for Esdraelon ware, cf. Hennessy, p. 16, and Lapp 1, pp. 31–37.

47. Hennessy, pp. 7–9.

48. Hennessy, pp. 11–12.

49. The Bâb edh-Dhrâ' evidence is unpublished; cf. Lapp 1, p. 36.

50. One of these is published in Lapp 1; cf. esp. p. 39.

51. For typological details and relations to material from earlier excavations see Hennessy, pp. 7–12.

52. Cf. Lapp 1, pp. 36–37.

53. Cf., e.g., de Vaux 1, p. 39; Kenyon 1, pp. 92–97.

54. For details cf. Lapp 1, pp. 34–35.

55. For its association with EB IA and IB and its distribution see Hennessy, Pl. 28. For the Bâb edh-Dhrâ' cup, cf. Lapp 1, pp. 25–26, and 30, fig. 13.

56. Hennessy's chart, Pl. 28, listing only Esdraelon ware from Kerak should not be construed as suggesting the absence of other ceramic groups. It merely reflects a passing reference to the presence of dark-burnished ware, Kenyon 1, p. 114. Cf. B. Maisler, *et al.*, "The Excavations at Beth Yerah (Khirbet el-Kerak) 1944–1946," *IEJ*, 2 (1952), p. 167.

57. Cf. Lapp 1, p. 34.

58. Cf. Lapp 1, pp. 33–35.

59. Hennessy, p. 46.

60. Two in EB IA, and those of IB and IC.

61. Cf. de Vaux 1, pp. 38–42; Kenyon 1, p. 97, and *Jericho* II, pp. 5–6; Hennessy, pp. 15–18.

62. Extra-Palestinian evidence is considered in the second major section below. Separating internal and external evidence is artificial, but it does point up the similarity of conclusions to be drawn from internal and external evidence considered independently.

63. Cf. above at n. 28.

64. Hennessy, pp. 17–19.

65. Hennessy, p. 6.

66. Cf. my proposal that Meṣer II–I consists of a mixture of Late Chalcolithic and late EB IA elements, in Lapp 1, p. 37. The apsidal houses are most naturally assigned that horizon in which such houses are clearly attested. Other apsidal structures of EB IA and IB are listed by de Vaux 1, p. 38, and Hennessy, pp. 44–45.

67. Kenyon 1, p. 98.

68. De Vaux 1, p. 38. Cf. Kenyon 1, p. 98.

69. Kenyon 1, p. 107.

70. Kenyon 1, pp. 109–10.

71. E.g., Lachish: Kenyon 1, p. 118; Taanach: Paul W. Lapp, "The 1966 Excavations at Tell Ta'annek," *BASOR*, No. 185 (1967), pp. 9–10 (Lapp 3).

72. S. Yeivin, *First Preliminary Report on the Excavations at Tel "Gat"* (1961), Pl. 7 (center). The large, deep bowl illustrated in the upper right does not occur at Bâb edh-Dhrâ' before EB IC. The spouted jar, upper center, makes its first appearance at Bâb edh-Dhrâ' in EB IB, but in a much more globular shape. The example illustrated here is typical of EB IC. Cf. Hennessy, p. 19, Type XV. He suggests that the form ("column handled jars") first appeared in EB IB, without

citing specific evidence. For his observations on the Gath fortifications, cf. Hennessy, pp. 61–62.

73. De Vaux 2, p. 9. Lapp, *RB*, 73 (1966), pp. 560–61.

74. The northern stone defense line at Tell el-Far'ah is 8.5 meters thick (de Vaux 2, p. 9), and a southern tower at Taanach measures 9.85 by 20.5 meters (P. W. Lapp, "The 1968 Excavations at Tell Ta'annek," *BASOR*, No. 195 [1969], p. 12).

75. R. de Vaux, "Les Fouilles de Tell-el-Far'ah," *RB*, 69 (1962), Pls. 19–21.

76. A most striking example is a 200-meter stretch of the EB defense line at Arad with seven semi-circular bastions spaced at 20–25 meter intervals: Amiran, *Ancient Arad*, p. 8.

77. P. Parr sees the glacis as a natural concomitant of the rising accumulation of mound debris and cites Taanach as an example: "The Origin of the Fortifications of Middle Bronze Age Palestine and Syria," *ZDPV*, 84 (1968), p. 42. The buttressing of the Taanach part way down the rocky slope tends to support this view for the EB glacis, but the complex MB glacis are built with a view to other considerations as well.

78. De Vaux (2, p. 14) suggests that apsidal houses belong to the beginning of the Early Bronze Age (our EB IC), but his earliest EB overlaps our EB IB. It seems clear that the apsidal houses in Megiddo Stage IV and the earliest level at Ai belong to a pre-EB IC horizon. Cf., e.g., Wright 1, p. 83, Chart 2.

79. De Vaux 2, pp. 14–15. Kenyon 1, p. 110. Lapp, *RB*, 73 (1966), pp. 556–57.

80. With de Vaux 3, p. 13, cf. Lapp, *RB*, 73, p. 556.

81. Until Ruth Amiran's forthcoming final publication appears, cf. her *Ancient Arad*, pp. 9–10.

82. Cf. p. 107 above. The designation "polished" is borrowed from Hennessy and used to designate a softer finishing technique without burnishing tools.

83. Cf. Hennessy, p. 20, who notes the introduction of broad platters as the only typological development isolated to distinguish the inception of EB II.

84. Cf. Hennessy, pp. 22–23, where, besides Khirbet Kerak ware, the typological developments distinguishing EB III are the introduction of a bowl type (hard to distinguish from EB II bowls), a typical painted decoration (rather ill-defined), and the elongation of stump bases (where only the occasional pronounced elongation is helpful).

85. Cf. Hennessy, pp. 20, 23. Similar evidence will be published from Bâb edh-Dhrâ'.

86. Cf. Hennessy, pp. 74–76; Ruth Amiran, "Khirbet Kerak Ware at Ai," *IEJ*, 17 (1967), pp. 185–86. Ai is an exception. Among sites to be added to Hennessy's distribution chart, Pl. 62, are el-Fakhât, Taanach, Bethel, and Bâb edh-Dhra'. N. Glueck, "Explorations in Eastern Palestine, IV," *AASOR*, 25–28 (1951), Pt. 1, pp. 142–43; Pt. 2, p. 426 (Glueck 1). Lapp 3, p. 2. J. L. Kelso, "The Excavation of Bethel (1934–1960)," *AASOR*, 39 (1968), p. 22. Lapp, *RB*, 73 (1966), p. 557.

87. Cf. Hennessy, p. 75, where pertinent literature is cited. (For Tell Taannek read Tell Ta'inat.)

88. Cf. de Vaux 2, p. 30; Wright 1, p. 86. The demise of towns before EB III is postulated primarily in light of Khirbet Kerak ware. The absence of the ware at a site in central Palestine like Tell el-Far'ah is not necessarily of chronological significance, and typology is not refined enough to exclude the persistence of occupation well into EB III. The small quantity of the ware at Megiddo is probably not correctly interpreted as indicating only a short persistence of occupation into EB III. Sherds of Khirbet Kerak ware are uncommon at neighboring Taanach (not more than thirty vessels represented), but here they are associated with the last two important phases of the defense system.

89. De Vaux 2, pp. 11–12.

90. N. Glueck, *The Other Side of the Jordan* (1940), pp. 68–69. Cf. details in his *AASOR* series "Explorations in Eastern Palestine" and his final conclusion, Glueck 1, p. 423.

91. E. Olávarri, "Sondages à 'Arô'er sur l'Arnon," *RB*, 72 (1965), pp. 77–94; "Fouilles à 'Arô'er sur l'Arnon. Les niveaux du Bronze Intermédiaire," *RB*, 76 (1969), pp. 230–59.

92. Cf. de Vaux 2, p. 27.

93. At Meşer the rectangular houses of Stratum I, which follow the apsidal structures of Stratum II, are clearly earlier than EB IC. Cf. Lapp 1, p. 37.

94. Hennessy, pp. 19, 49, 86.

95. E. Anati, *Palestine before the Hebrews* (1963), p. 325.

96. Kenyon 1, p. 103. De Vaux 2, p. 28. Wright 1, p. 81.

97. Anati, p. 318, wants to change the designation of the period from Early Bronze to Early Urban. Cf. Kenyon's Proto-Urban.

98. Cf. Kenyon 1, pp. 111–12.

99. Amiran, *Ancient Arad*, p. 8.

99a. Cf. n. 17 above.

100. Cf. n. 16 above and p. 122 below.

101. Drower and Bottéro, p. 42.

102. W. F. Albright, *Archaeology of Palestine*, p. 74. Kenyon 1, pp. 111–12. Anati, pp. 361–62.

103. Cf. n. 88. Note also that these sites suffered erosion for at least three or four centuries after their destruction at the end of EB III. Evidence for the latest town phase may have disappeared or been obscured.

104. Wright 1, p. 88. De Vaux 2, p. 30. Kenyon 1, p. 134.

105. E.g., W. Dever in this volume (below, pp. 136 ff.). I am indebted to Dever for an early copy of his manuscript and regret that mine was completed too late for his comment.

106. Kenyon 1, p. 108. It seems likely that the builders became attached or assimilated to the town builders and disappeared with them.

107. The description of Tell Beit Mirsim J provides a good illustration of what happens when secondary treatments do not stay close to their sources. Anati, p. 361, states that "at the lowest level of Tell Beit Mirsim, William F. Albright found that in the course of this period an open farming village evolved into a fortified town." Kenyon 1, p. 119, observes of the same stratum that "the architectural remains were fragmentary." In the final excavation report (*AASOR*, 17 [1938], p. 12) Albright summarizes that "no remains whatever of masonry have hitherto been found" in Stratum J.

108. The view of Albright that the Bethel material represented a later horizon than Tell Beit Mirsim J (*AASOR*, 17 [1938], p. 12) needs revision in light of Khirbet Kerak sherds reported in *AASOR*, 39 (1968), p. 22. Since Khirbet Kerak ware was also discovered at neighboring Ai, the suggestion that EB "Bethel then replaced Ai as the major city of that district" (*AASOR*, 39 [1968], p. 10) needs revision on more than one count.

109. Cf. Kenyon 1, pp. 118–19.

110. E. Grant and G. E. Wright, *Ain Shems Excavations (Palestine)*, Part V, Text (1939), p. 8. The pottery belongs to the EB IV horizon of the later sherds discovered at Bethel in 1934.

111. R. L. Cleveland, "The Excavation of the Conway High Place (Petra) and Soundings at Khirbet Ader," *AASOR*, 34–35, (1960), pp. 91, 93. The material from Ader C is scant but seems to belong to EB IV.

112. *AASOR*, 25–28 (1951), p. 423.

113. Kenyon 1, pp. 137, 153.

114. I am indebted to the excavator, Kay Wright, for showing me this material, which is as yet unpublished.

115. Tombs A 52 and 54, unpublished.

116. P. Lapp, *The Dhahr Mirzbaneh Tombs* (1966), pp. 63–64 (Lapp 4).

117. A convenient typology is provided by Kenyon in *Jericho* II (1965), pp. 38–47. Cf. Lapp 4, pp. 64–81 and the article by William Dever, below.

118. Dever (below, p. 145) recognizes this degenerate tradition but makes a somewhat different distinction.

119. Cf. Lapp 4, pp. 94–96, 114–15, and Lapp 1, pp. 26–31. Note also my postulation that a substantial part of Palestine's EB IV population entered Egypt in the First Intermediate, creating something of a void filled by MB I (Intermediate Bronze II) folk. Lapp 4, p. 100.

120. Dever (below, pp. 142–46). His description of the Amorite–Middle Bronze I relation (below, pp. 140–41) is similar to De Vaux's, to which I have reacted elsewhere: Lapp 4, pp. 92–96.

121. Cf. Lapp 1, p. 31, n. 24.

122. Wright 1, pp. 87–88.

123. Wright 1, pp. 86–88.

124. Lapp 4, pp. 115–16.

125. Dever, pp. 147–50.

126. De Vaux 2, pp. 23–26. Hennessy, pp. 85–90; cf. p. 66.

127. Albright, *Archaeology of Palestine*, pp. 71–72.

128. Cf. Kantor, *COWA²*, p. 13. De Vaux 2, p. 24.

129. Hennessy, p. 38.

130. Lapp 1, pp. 28–29, n. 19.

131. Hennessy, Pl. 30.

132. Hennessy, pp. 35–36.

133. Hennessy, pp. 36–40.

134. W. Orthmann, *Die Keramik der Frühen Bronzezeit aus Inneranatolien* (1963), pp. 66–68.

135. Hennessy, pp. 46–47. Cf. Perrot, col. 443.

136. Lapp 1, pp. 29–31, n. 22a.

137. Cf. de Vaux 2, p. 27.

138. Hennessy, Pl. 51, pp. 62–68.

139. Hennessy, pp. 67–68.

140. Hennessy, pp. 74–79, Pls. 62 and 74. Cf. Ruth Amiran, "Chronological Problems of the Early Bronze Age," *AJA*, 72 (1968), pp. 316–18.

141. Lapp 4, pp. 111–12.

142. Lapp 1, p. 29. For her most recent treatment see M. Gimbutas, "Die Indoeuropäer: Archäeologische Probleme," in *Die Urheimat der Indogermanen* (1968), pp. 548–61. In 1969 she raised her dates for the Kurgan movements (p. 556) to "second half of the fourth millennium" and 2400–2200 BC (personal communication).

143. Lapp 4, pp. 112–13. Cf. Dever, below, p. 141.

144. This is properly emphasized by Dever, below, p. 136.

145. The mixture of the degenerate ceramic tradition of the towns with that of the newcomers in Bâb edh-Dhrâ' Tombs A 52 and 54 is matched, for example, in Hama J8, which provides many good parallels. E. Furmann, *Hama II.1* (1958), p. 53, fig. 58: 4A859, 3H360, 3H491, 3H878, 3K211, 3H372, S No. bowls.

146. Hennessy, p. 47. Kantor, *COWA²*, p. 14.

147. Kantor, *COWA²*, p. 8.

148. Kantor, *COWA²*, pp. 7–8.

149. Hennessy, pp. 28–31.

150. Cf. Hennessy, pp. 28–31. The Bâb edh-Dhrâ' evidence is unpublished, except cf. Lapp 1.

151. Kantor, *COWA*², p. 27, fig. 3:43.

152. Hennessy, pp. 27–28, cites a good parallel to one of the three from EB IA Tomb A94, and all three belong to the same painted tradition.

153. Hennessy, pp. 60–61, 74. De Vaux 2, p. 25.

154. Cf. n. 17 above.

155. Hennessy, pp. 24–25, 69–71.

156. Even de Vaux's suggestion that the Egyptian gifts may have had the dual purpose of honoring a local deity and asserting power over local devotees of the cult does not contradict this assertion: de Vaux 2, p. 28.

157. Y. Yadin, "Egypt's Earliest Penetration into Asia," *IEJ*, 5 (1955), pp. 3–10.

158. Cf. Drower and Bottéro, pp. 41–47 and de Vaux 2, pp. 23–31.

159. Drower and Bottéro, p. 42. W. S. Smith, "The Old Kingdom in Egypt and the Beginning of the First Intermediate Period," *CAH*², I, fasc. 5 (1962).

160. Hennessy, pp. 49–60, 71–73, Pl. 46.

161. De Vaux 2, pp. 25–26.

162. Drower and Bottéro, pp. 41–42. Hennessy, pp. 60, 62.

163. De Vaux 2, p. 26.

164. Cf. n. 88 above.

165. Kantor, *COWA*², p. 27, fig. 3. E. Baumgartel, "Predynastic Egypt," *CAH*², I, fasc. 38 (1965), p. 23.

166. Kantor, *COWA*², p. 26, fig. 2.

167. Hennessy, p. 62.

168. De Vaux 2, p. 30.

169. Cf. Lapp 4, p. 100 and ref. cited.

170. Kantor, *COWA*², p. 19.

171. Lapp 4, pp. 94–100.

172. Cf. p. 106 and n. 39 above.

173. Albright, *COWA*², pp. 49–50.

174. Hennessy, pp. 49–52, 87, Chart 8.

175. Hennessy, p. 89, Chart 9.

176. *Archaeology of Palestine*, p. 71. It is worth noting that he has held this chronology with virtually no change for over twenty years.

177. Wright 1, pp. 81–88.

THE "MIDDLE BRONZE I" PERIOD
IN SYRIA AND PALESTINE

William G. Dever

THE "Middle Bronze I" period, *circa* 2150–1850 BC, is one of the most intriguing eras in the history of Syria/Palestine. It remained in many ways a "Dark Age" until a series of epoch-making excavations, beginning with W. F. Albright's work at Tell Beit Mirsim from 1926 to 1932, began to illumine it. The accumulation of material in the last thirty-five years has been so rapid and has reached such proportions that the time may be approaching when a synthesis is possible. The present article, however, can hope to do no more than summarize the main lines of research up to now, delineate the major problems now confronting the field, and after a resumé of some new and unpublished material, offer a suggested outline of the chronology, history and culture of the period.

I. In Retrospect: MB I Studies, circa 1930–60

The characteristic pottery of the period was first brought to light in Palestine (see fig. 1 for the following) by Watzinger in his excavations at Jericho from 1908–9, in levels which he termed *spätkanaanitisch*.[1] It was either neglected or misunderstood, however, until 1932, when W. F. Albright published the first volume of his excavations at Tell Beit Mirsim. Here on both stratigraphic and ceramic grounds he distinguished two phases, his strata H and I. He compared the pottery to the "caliciform" (Gk. *calyx,* "cup") of Syria just beginning to be known at that time, recognizing correctly that the wares were closely related and both should be dated *circa* 2100–1900 BC. He suggested that the period marked by these distinctive wares should be called "Middle Bronze I," in keeping with the chronological framework then being developed for Classical and Aegean archaeology.[2]

The same year as the appearance of *Tell Beit Mirsim* I, Nelson Glueck —who worked with Albright at Tell Beit Mirsim and succeeded him as

Figure 1. Map of major Middle Bronze I sites in Syria and Palestine. Dots represent sites discovered and explored by Nelson Glueck. (Diacritical marks eliminated on most place-names.)

Director of the American Schools of Oriental Research—began the extensive survey of Transjordan and the Jordan Valley which was to occupy him for the next fifteen years; as a partial result of this he eventually charted more than 100 hitherto unknown MB I sites in these areas, and later (1952 onwards) some seventy additional sites in the Negev (see fig. 1).[3] Already in the first volume of his *Explorations in Eastern Palestine* (1934), Glueck postulated widespread MB I occupation in these regions,[4] a phenomenon which he was later to demonstrate conclusively and which went far to corroborate Albright's thesis that the "caliciform" represented a culture common to Palestine as a whole in MB I. The latest studies[5] emphasize again the importance of Glueck's achievement for our understanding of this enigmatic period; Transjordan and the Negev now appear to be almost the only areas in Palestine where we can discern an actual pattern of settlement (but see below, section III), and for most of what we know of these areas we are indebted to Glueck's pioneer work beginning thirty-five years ago.[6]

In 1938, in the first comprehensive treatment of the period, G. Ernest Wright analyzed the materials of Albright and Glueck and properly classified previously unrecognized deposits at Beth-shan, Megiddo and Tell el-Harbaj in the Jezreel Valley, finally adducing parallels from the publications which had just appeared (1930–34) of Tell el-'Ajjûl, Bethel, Lachish and Megiddo.[7] Between roughly the time of this survey and the next treatment of similar comprehensiveness, that of Ruth Amiran in 1960 (see her article, above, pp. 83–96 as well as further discussion here), a flood of material appeared, of which we can only give the most cursory account here.

Major groups of MB I material from Palestine became available with the publications of Petrie's two "Copper Age" Cemeteries at Tell el-'Ajjûl, the tombs designated in the "100–200" and "1500" series (1931–32);[8] Fitzgerald and Rowe's publication of tombs from the "Northern Slope" and the "Great Northern Cemetery" and levels XII–XI at Beth-shan (1930–35);[9] the publication by Engberg, Guy and Loud of the multi-chambered shaft-tombs at Megiddo (1938) and the mixed deposits of Str. XV–XIIIB on the tell (1948);[10] Starkey and Tufnell's publication of 120 tombs in the "2000 Cemetery" and stratified *loci* in the "1500 Area" at Lachish (preliminary reports in 1934, final reports in 1958);[11] and Lankester Harding's publication of a large tomb group from el-Ḥuṣn, opposite Beth-shan across the Jordan Valley (1953).[12] We may also mention the publication of Albright's soundings of 1924 at Ader and Bâb edh-Dhrâ' (preliminary report, 1944, final report 1960)[13]; a tomb from

Yazûr (Azor) near Tel-Aviv (1944)[14]; and soundings by Peter Parr at Khirbet Iskander between Mâdeba and Dhibân (1960).[15]

The 1960s have seen a renaissance similar to that of the 1930s, much of the literature resulting from the renewed fieldwork of the post-war years. An important group of tombs from Ma'ayan Barukh, near the Lebanese border, with Syrian links, was published in 1961 by Ruth Amiran.[16] In 1962 there appeared a tomb group from Silwan,[17] on the outskirts of Jerusalem, as well as several tombs from Khirbet Kūfīn,[18] six miles north of Hebron in the southern Judean Hills. In 1963 James B. Pritchard published his excavation of fifty-five tombs in the cemetery at Gibeon (el-Jîb), northwest of Jerusalem, where most all of the tombs could be attributed originally to MB I.[19] The same year there appeared the first notice of what turned out to be a large MB I cemetery at Hazorea in the Jezreel Valley,[20] with exceedingly close parallels to the Megiddo shaft-tombs. With even closer correspondence to the imported Syrian wares of the Megiddo tombs, there also appeared that year the material of Str. XVIII at Hazor in Upper Galilee, excavated by Yigael Yadin and others.[21] A preliminary notice in 1963 of the excavations of M. Kochavi at Har Yeruḥam, eighteen miles south of Beersheba, gave indication of the first settlement of any size from the period yet discovered, with two clear phases of architecture, smelting and pottery kilns, cairn-burials, and other features.[22] Of special importance was the publication in 1960 and 1965 of Kathleen Kenyon's excavations from 1952–58 in the tombs of Jericho.[23] (Miss Kenyon's analysis of the 346 MB I tombs, with corresponding implications for the cultural phases of the period and its terminology, is so important that we shall return to it below.) In 1966 Paul Lapp's publication of a cemetery in the Dhahr Mirzbâneh, near 'Ain es-Sâmiyeh northeast of Jerusalem, offered carefully excavated evidence for the central hill country.[24] The latest publication (1968) gives another glimpse of the "Jezreel Family" in several tombs at Tiberias, on the Sea of Galilee.[25]

II. Major Problems of Current Research

With this brief account of the accumulation of material over the past several decades, let us turn to the problems this material presents and the theories advanced in treatments of the last ten years or so.

First, there are the related problems of chronology and terminology. Although Albright's initial dates of *circa* 2100–1900 BC appear in retrospect to have been remarkably accurate, somewhat greater precision may now be obtained. For the beginning of the period, the mass of recent data illustrating the end of the Early Bronze Age all across the Near East (and even into the Greek mainland), in most regions *circa* 2400–2300 BC at the latest, gives us for the MB I era a convenient *terminus post quem*.[26] In Mesopotamia, the interval following the First Dynasty of Akkad is marked by the Gutian invasions (*circa* 2180–2082 BC), the Ur III period (*circa* 2060–1950 BC), and then the Dynasties of Isin and Larsa (*circa* 1960 BC–), the latter called the "Second Intermediate Period."[27] In Egypt, the disruption results in the "First Intermediate Period" (Dynasties VII–X, *circa* 2175–2040 BC).[28] In Syria/Palestine, there is a long gap following the violent destruction of virtually every known site in EB II or III, and the archaeological record until very recently has been almost wholly silent for the post-destruction period except for a few scattered deposits—chiefly Tomb 351 at Jericho, Tell Beit Mirsim J, soundings at Ader and Bâb edh-Dhrâ', and surface material from the Jordan Valley, Transjordan, and the Negev—termed by Wright in his pioneer treatment in 1937 "EB IV" (*circa* 2300–2100 BC).[29]

Whether this material is significant enough to deserve the retention of "EB IV" as a separate phase will likely remain unclear until Paul Lapp's publication of the material from renewed excavations at one of the major sites, Bâb edh-Dhrâ' on the Lisan in Transjordan (see above, pp. 102 ff.—Ed.), where Albright first defined the phase from surface finds and brief soundings in 1924. Lapp's excavations in 1965 brought to light a fairly continuous series of tomb groups throughout EB and down to roughly the beginning of MB I. Of importance here is Lapp's contention in preliminary notices that the cairn-burials of "EB IV" should be taken together with the MB I shaft-tombs (only rarely found at Bâb edh-Dhrâ') to represent an "intermediate" period between EB III and MB II, the first phase of which he proposes to call "Intermediate Bronze I," and the second "Intermediate Bronze II," or "IB I" and "IB II."[30]

That the site of Bâb edh-Dhrâ' appears at present almost as the sole witness in Palestine to the twenty-third and twenty-second centuries BC should not mislead us. The uniqueness of Bâb edh-Dhrâ' may be due simply to the fact that it is precisely to Transjordan and the Negev—the fringe areas of the country—that one must turn to trace the vestiges of this elusive culture, and these areas are as yet barely known. It is significant that to the north, particularly along the bend of the Orontes in Syria, we have a growing body of material from the EB IV/MB I horizon. The striking thing is that the more of this material that comes to light the more it is clear that *proportionately* it represents a great bulk of what we know of Syria in the third and second millennia BC. Although we have only hints of it, the culture of this period in Syria was undoubtedly vigorous, fairly widespread, and largely urban in character in contrast to Palestine, where we have mostly tombs and some scattered surface material.

A provisional picture of this culture could already have been drawn from the sites on the Orontes known as long ago as the 1930s, particularly if one had properly assessed the apparently chance finds by du Mesnil du Buisson of extensive MB I tomb groups everywhere he turned (particularly Tell 'As, Dnebi, Khan Sheikhoun and other sites),[31] not to mention the stratified remains at Kadesh, Qatna and elsewhere. Had the Danish excavations at Hama (1932–38) been published more promptly, we might have drawn the picture in considerable detail. At Hama Stratum J, with eight well-defined phases of MB I over a considerable exposure, revealed a well-laid-out town with fairly elaborate domestic installations and an impressive stone, bronze, and ceramic industry. What is more, Radio Carbon 14 determinations produced dates as follows: Level J6:2310±140 BC; Level J5:2230±130 BC; Level J5/4:2210±120 BC.[32] As the goblets and other "caliciform" vessels which are the hallmarks of Hama J are increasingly well known from other sites in Syria and can be shown to be identical to certain imported vessels in the multi-chambered shaft-tombs at Megiddo and in sherds from Hazor XVIII,[33] we have an indisputable link between central Syria and northern Palestine at the very beginning of our period. More important, we have a fairly well-fixed date from which we can work out the relative sequence of the deposits which follow in Palestine (see fig. 2 below). This synchronism has been alluded to by Albright and others, particularly Amiran, but has not been worked out in sufficient detail; and in so prestigious a publication as the revised *Cambridge Ancient History* (1965) both the Hama and the 'Amûq evidence have been ignored entirely by Kenyon.[34]

The picture from Hama is corroborated and filled out by the excavations of Paolo Matthiae and an Italian team since 1964 at Tell Mardikh, forty-five miles north of Hama.[35] The surface collections, even before the start of the excavations, revealed a high proportion of wares identical to those of Hama J—simple, reserved-slip and painted wares in goblets and other forms of the "caliciform" repertoire.[36] In 1965 the remains of an apparently well-fortified city were brought to light, with an impressive cultic installation, and the next season a three entryway gate of MB II type was cleared, all these structures being attributed by the excavators to MB I on the basis of comparisons with Hama J and other Syrian sites.[37] However, a close examination of the report suggests that these installations belong to a very late phase of the Hama J horizon. Although even a date within the twentieth century BC would still fall with Palestinian MB I, this comparison is misleading in terms of *cultural* phases, as MB IIA appears to be already well advanced in Syria by the mid if not the early twentieth century BC, under the very rapid influence of the renascent Egyptian XII Dynasty (*circa* 1991–1786 BC).[38]

Farther north, the material from the Oriental Institute's "Syrian-Hittite Expedition" in the 'Amûq (1932–38) has now been made available in Braidwood's *Excavations in the Plain of Antioch* (1960).[39] It must be pointed out that the pertinent material from Phase J comes almost wholly from soundings at one mound, Tell Ta'yinat, and the exposure was too small to have produced significant architecture. Nevertheless, the pottery and the objects, exhaustively analyzed, are of considerable importance. "Smeared-Wash" wares and both painted and unpainted "Simple" wares continue from Phase I. There is the innovation of designs incised through dark paint, and goblet forms become abundant. There is a sharp decline in the use of stone implements and a significant rise in the use of metal.[40] A network of relationships based on comparisons of the most typical artifacts links Phase J clearly with Hama J and the Orontes sites. Both these areas in turn are part of a great cultural complex stretching to the north and east across Syria into Mesopotamia. On the Upper Euphrates and the Balikh, there are the tombs at Carchemish and the vicinity (el-Hammam, Kara Hassan, Şerrîn, etc.), the great *hypogéum* tomb at Til-Barsip, and the Akkadian/Ur III levels at Tell Chuera. In the Ḥabur region, we have levels 3–2 at Chagar Bazar and the "Sargonid" levels and the "Naram-sin Palace" at Tell Brak. The Mesopotamian sites are naturally more peripheral (especially in ceramics) and some of the relevant levels are slightly earlier; nevertheless, one should note on the Upper Tigris the Akkadian levels at Tepe Gawra and levels F and G at Asshur, and on the Lower Tigris "Cemetery A" at Kish and the "Royal Cemetery" at Ur.[41]

At least as far northeast as the Ḥabur, it must be stressed that the cultural links do not consist simply of isolated traits, but rather form a cultural unity (though, of course, with many local variations). Not only are the goblets and truncated conical cups ubiquitous, but the inventory of metals is even more highly standardized: bronze (or copper) toggle-pins with club, mushroom or rolled heads; small awls and pins; flat adzes and chisels; poker-butted pikes and leaf-bladed javelins, usually with curled tangs; and varieties of daggers.[42] In addition to these obvious links, some long-since noted, one may point to the frequent occurrence at many sites of such distinctive items as "hawk-beaked" female figurines and clay "wagon wheels."[43]

While the cultural complex just sketched has been known for some time, its relevance for understanding MB I in Palestine was not worked out fully until an important article by Ruth Amiran in 1960, the first attempt at an overall survey since Wright's 1938 treatment.[44] Amiran dated the Palestinian ceramics *circa* 2250–1850 BC and analyzed them in terms of three "Families." Her "Family A," which she thought the earliest, consists largely of the simple wares and particularly the band-combed wares, with a *flourit* in the central and southern regions *circa* twenty-third to twenty-second centuries BC. "Family B," *circa* twenty-second to twenty-first centuries BC, is largely northern (Ma'ayan Barukh and el-Ḥuṣn), and its characteristic decoration consists of knobs and single-tooth incision. "Family C," confined to the painted and red-slipped wares best illustrated from the Megiddo multi-chambered shaft-tombs and a few other sites around the Jezreel Valley (el-Ḥuṣn, Beth-shan, Hazorea, etc.), falls approximately in the twenty-first to the twentieth centuries BC. Almost immediately Albright pointed out that "Family A" is not the earliest, but the latest, a revision which Amiran now accepts.[45] Closer analysis indicates that the order and arrangement is even more complex—something like C–EarlyA–B–Late A—but we cannot go into details here (see below, section III).[46]

Some of the crucial material bearing on Amiran's argument appeared in publication too late to be utilized. Kathleen Kenyon's excavation of 346 MB I shaft-tombs at Jericho from 1952–58 (published in 1960 and 1965) has provided us with possibly the most important single body of evidence, and Miss Kenyon herself has offered some provocative interpretations of this evidence.[47] Already in the first preliminary report (1955) she suggested an analysis of the tombs that was eventually to divide them into seven categories: "Dagger," "Pottery," "Square-shaft," "Bead," "Outsize," "Composite," and "Multiple."[48] To her these imply the existence of several groups which only gradually came into contact with one another and thereby underwent a process of assimilation. The striking absence of stratified remains representing anything like town life at Jericho, plus the equally striking practice of burying disarticulated and incomplete skeletons in the tombs, suggested to Miss Kenyon that these groups were semi-nomadic and simply returned periodically to the ancestral burying ground in the course of their annual seasonal circuit. As the culture so represented has in Miss Kenyon's view little to do with either what precedes it in the Early Bronze period or what follows it in the Middle Bronze period proper, she proposes to call the interval "Intermediate Early Bronze–Middle Bronze" or "EB–MB."[49]

Kenyon connects the appearance of these newcomers with the irruptions of West Semitic peoples known in the Akkadian texts in the last quarter of the third millennium BC as "Amorites" (*amurrū*) or "westerners." These people are usually characterized in the texts as nomads from the desert steppes in the region of the Jebel el-Bishrī in northeast Syria who infiltrated the settled areas of north Syria and north Mesopotamia in ever increasing numbers; by the time of the Mari Texts (eighteenth century BC) "Amorite" proper names seem to indicate that they had become an influential element of the population in many areas, if not actually a majority.[50] The "Amorite" expansion during the period in question has recently (1965) received very impressive documentation in the revised edition of the *Cambridge Ancient History* in the fascicle by G. Posener and J. Bottéro (with Kenyon treating the archaeological evidence).[51] Here a mass of literary and other evidence is assembled to show the disruption of urban life in Syria, Palestine, and even as far as Egypt, where Asiatics are attested in historical records of the "First Intermediate Period" and are pictured on several wall paintings, in some cases (Beni Hasan) bearing copper or bronze weapons like those well known from Byblos, Ugarit and other Syrian sites. The earliest of the well-known Execration Texts (*circa* 1925 BC) depict a West Semitic population in Syria/Palestine bearing "Amorite"-type names and loosely organized in tribal fashion.[52]

It is difficult to withstand this mounting tide of epigraphic and monumental evidence, and, indeed, few scholars any longer oppose the "Amorite"–MB I equation. A typical reconstruction (though vastly oversimplified here) would see the destruction of the urban centers in Palestine at the end of EB II–III as due to a first wave of "invaders." The elusive "EB IV" period immediately following represents a nomadic or semi-nomadic culture removed from the old urban centers, and MB I proper is then the period of the gradual sedentarization of subsequent generations of the newcomers. Finally, a reversion to town life is suddenly accelerated with the beginning of MB IIA (*circa* 1875–1850 BC), perhaps due to still later waves of "Amorites."[53]

One recent treatment deserves mention here for being almost the only one to disagree with this interpretation. In the publication in 1966 of some thirty-five MB I tombs dug near 'Ain es-Sâmiyeh, fifteen miles north by northeast of Jerusalem, Paul Lapp uses the occasion of publishing the pottery to survey the period as a whole.[54] He attempts to connect the newcomers in MB I (or "IB II" in his terminology) with Cyprus, Anatolia, Greece and the Aegean, Sicily and Sardinia, and, finally, Spain. After having somewhat hesitantly suggested links of the Palestinian "caliciform" phases with a cultural complex long known in the Western Mediterranean area as that of the "Beaker Folk," Lapp finds the evidence inconclusive.[55] He rejects the "Amorite" hypothesis, however, and turns instead to theories of non-Semitic invaders from beyond the Caucasus in Central Asia, who, he thinks, made their way to Palestine via sea rather than overland. This explains the more distinctive wares and weapons at coastal sites like Ugarit, Byblos and Tell el-'Ajjûl; the "local" character of material from the inland sites of Palestine and Syria is due to the influence of surviving EB traditions as the newcomers moved inland and were gradually assimilated.[56] (Editor's note: see Lapp's response above, pp. 120 ff.).

While we cannot present here our detailed reasons for rejecting the analysis upon which Lapp's theory rests, we think it unlikely that many scholars will accept his conclusions.[57] The writer was also intrigued at one time with similar views, tempting ever since Childe's *New Light on the Most Ancient East* (1934), which linked Europe with the Near East. However, several weeks of research in Eastern Europe in 1966 with major collections of the Beaker and other materials and discussions with some of the specialists in the area have completely persuaded him that the "Near Eastern influences" in Europe are both sporadic and minimal. The parallels cited from Europe often refer only to isolated elements of the material culture (particularly the "torques" and a few other atypical bronzes), and, in any case, the appearance of these elements in Europe must be dated centuries after their occurrence in the Near East. Thus, even if direct influence could be proved (and not simply trade relations), it would have to be from the Near East to Europe, and not *vice versa.*[58]

We have tried to ascertain who the MB I peoples were, whence and when they arrived in Palestine, and how they settled. It remains to ask how long they flourished and what happened to them eventually. In the last decade Albright has returned to the subject of MB I in a series of articles concerned particularly with chronology.[59] Understanding the MB I period partly from Glueck's demonstration of its spread in Transjordan and the Negev, and interpreting this as evidence of the activity of donkey caravaneers along the trade routes, Albright sees the best setting for this culture as reflected in the nineteenth-century Cappadocian Texts, the eighteenth-century Mari Letters, and the nineteenth-century Serābīt el-Khādem inscriptions and various pictorial representations in Egypt (Beni Hasan and others). He accepts the general "Amorite" influence but sees such a long lag in the extension of this influence into Egypt that it is coeval not with the "First Intermediate Period" and the XIIth Dynasty (*circa* 1991–1786 BC), but with the "Second Intermediate Period," where it is reflected in the ceramic. Final threads in the argument involve identifying some of the names of the rulers of "Royal Tombs" I–IV at Byblos, the contents of which have long been identified with Palestinian MB IIA, dating the tombs *circa* 1800–1720 BC, and on this basis lowering the dates for the beginning of MB IIA (and thus the end of MB I) from *circa* 1900 BC to *circa* 1800 BC. The presence of XIIth Dynasty Egyptian officials and direct Egyptian influence at Shechem and Megiddo *circa* 1875–1850 BC (see below) is then related not to the MB IIA but to the MB I occupation of these sites.

We would prefer to place the beginning of Palestinian MB I at about 2100 BC, though the period may well begin earlier in Syria. Note that imported wares in the shaft-tombs at Megiddo, particularly the goblets, which fall early in the local sequence (fig. 2), are best compared with goblets of Hama J2-5, dated *circa* 2150 BC at the earliest.[60] (The only Palestinian material which might be slightly earlier would be Tomb 1101B–02 Lower at Megiddo.) For the end of the period, two factors are to be considered.

(1) Contrary to Albright's argument (above), there is considerable evidence that MB IIA cannot begin later than *circa* 1875–1850 BC, which would give us a suitable *terminus ante quem* for the end of MB I. At Megiddo there was found a basalt statuette of Thut-hotpe, the "Nomarch of the Hare Nome" well-known from his tomb at el-Bersheh, who served under Sesostris III (*circa* 1878–1843 BC).[61] The presence of a high-ranking Egyptian official at Megiddo is unlikely during MB I, when the scattered and mixed deposits of Str. XV show that the place was little more than a campsite.[62] We can only relate his activities to the flourishing MB IIA City State of Str. XIV–XIII; and, since he can hardly have functioned *after circa* 1850 BC, that city must have been founded by then at latest, and preferably somewhat earlier. (2) Similarly, a stela of another official of Sesostris III, Khu-Sebek, found at Abydos, mentions the conquest of *škmm*, undoubtedly Shechem.[63] As this conquest cannot have been later than *circa* 1850 BC, it must have been a conquest of the extensive MB IIA city known from the recent excava-

PLATE 14. Jebel Qaʿaqir. Pottery kiln built on bedrock. Note firing-chamber in foreground, with terra-cotta sidewalls and flues leading into hollow walls of the kiln

PLATE 15. Jebel Qaʻaqir. Cairn No. 4 partially excavated, linked by serpentine wall to Cairn No. 3 beyond, and smaller Cairn No. 2 in distance. Note mouth of cave with "cupmarks" in foreground, and outer curb-wall and inner chamber wall of Cairn No. 4

PLATE 16. Jebel Qaʻaqir. Cave G26; note "cupmark," low stone wall and store-jar in floor near entrance. Two storage bins are off to the right. Entrance to sleeping and storage chambers is above ledge at rear of terrace

PLATE 17. The top part of Kilamu's orthostat

PLATE 18. Two aediculae from Lilybeum

PLATE 19. The top part of Bar-Rakkab's orthostat

PLATE 20. The broken orthostat of Bar-Rakkab

PLATE 21. The Ba'al Haran orthostat

PLATE 22. A Punic stele from Carthage

PLATE 23. A Punic stele from Carthage

PLATE 24. A cult standard from Hazor

PLATE 25. A cult mask from Hazor

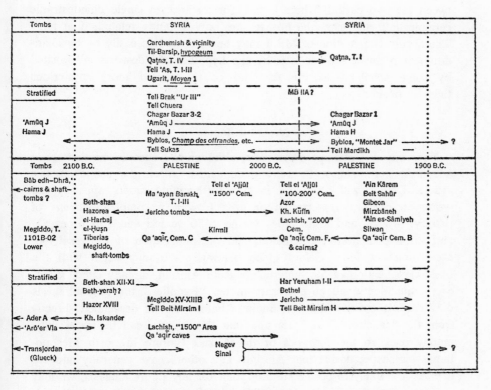

Figure 2. Relative sequence of MB I Groups in Syria/Palestine
circa 2150–1850 BC

tions of G. E. Wright and others. There were no MB I remains on the tell, and the city was founded only in MB IIA,[64] which in this case also must have been well underway by *circa* 1875–1850 BC.

Whether there is a gap preceding MB IIA, which would push the end of MB I even earlier, we cannot say in the absence of any well-stratified sequences. It is clear, however, that there is virtually no continuity between the two periods; there is not, for instance, a single demonstrable ceramic link, and even the bronzes are only distantly related, if at all.[65] The abrupt termination of MB I may be explained as easily by an abandonment of most sites as it is by the hypothetical "destruction" posited by some scholars—leaving the end of the period more mysterious than its beginning.

III. New Vistas

Now we must attempt a synthesis, although the conclusions tentatively advanced here cannot be fully documented within the scope of this article. Details will be found in two forthcoming monographs by the writer: a doctoral dissertation on MB I, with a complete *Corpus* of pottery, bronze, and tomb types (some 1450 vessels and 155 bronzes), and a full comparative discussion; and the publication of the results of excavations at Jebel Qaʿaqīr (see below).[66] We may begin with the basic classification of the material by Ruth Amiran, already cited. Whatever adjustments will be necessary in her "Families," the original thesis of Amiran's article—that the major "Family A" is descended directly from the "caliciform" of Syria and that this in turn can be traced ultimately back to the ceramics of the Akkad Empire in north Mesopotamia—is so persuasive that Albright and others have generally adopted it.[67] As it is likely to be the starting point for any future analysis, we may suggest certain revisions. (1) While the Syria-Palestinian link in this chain of evidence may now be regarded as conclusively proven, the linking in turn of the ceramics of central Syria with the Akkadian sites of Mesopotamia requires bridging a great gap. Granted the possibility of Akkadian influence on the ceramics of Syria, there remains the fact that the few sites we know in detail, for instance Hama, show very few *direct* connections. There are comparable individual features, such as incised decoration; but when the overall repertoire is studied in detail, the correspondences are not so impressive. Only in the bronzes, which have in any case an extraordinarily wide diffusion,[68] perhaps due to trade relations, are the comparisons really striking.

(2) If we are confined to Syria for our best overall comparisons, how do we understand the ceramic relationships? Albright has long insisted that "the incised ware of Palestine did not arise from the Syrian class until late in the history of the latter, after the combination of painting with incised ornament had yielded to a preference for incised decoration without painting."[69] This view seems generally accepted and would place all the incised and band-combed wares in Palestine at the end of the sequence. We propose rather that the use of incision or combing as a decorative motif *precedes* the incision through paint or "reserved-slip" technique,[70] and that it broke off comparatively early in Syria and enjoyed a separate and expanded course of development on its way to Palestine. (In Syria incision or combing never became dominant as it did finally in Palestine, paint remaining the preferred decoration.) Specifically, we must allow for the possibility that the "caliciform" of Palestine, while ultimately related to that of Syria and even of north Mesopotamia, underwent a period of "incubation" somewhere on the fringes of Syria/Palestine before it emerged in Palestine proper, probably via Transjordan and Jordan Valley sites such as Jericho.[71] (We may suppose that the "Amorites," who were semi-nomadic steppe-dwellers, deliberately avoided sustained contact with the great urban centers of Syria, which unlike those of Palestine were inhabited at the time; if the influence of the Syrian "caliciform" on them was only transitory, this would go far toward explaining the often-observed monotony and poverty of Palestinian MB I in contrast to that of Syria.) Somewhere in this vast, unknown area, the intrusive culture must have come in contact with the indigenous population of Palestine—perhaps the survivors of the destroyed Early Bronze sites in the heartland of the country—with its own ceramics clearly in decadent Early Bronze tradition, so that the end-product is obviously a hybrid. The basic MB I ceramic repertoire thus consists of Early Bronze Age survivals,[72] but with features which reflect the influence of Syria—albeit at one remove. From this we may conclude that the "caliciform" wares (Amiran's "A") must be subdivided, and that it is only the *early* group of true wheel-made ribbed wares[73] that is directly related to the Syrian "caliciform," whereas the later imitative technique of band-combing marks the indigenous and fully developed MB I wares of Palestine. Admittedly, this course of development is highly speculative, and until well-stratified sites in the vast lacunae of our map of MB I settlements are excavated, it must remain so.[74]

Much of what is suggested here concerning the character of the MB I period rests on unpublished material and is in part intuitive. The existence of large unpublished bodies of material is generally known, sometimes by hearsay—tombs from Rosh ha-Niqra', Ma'abaroth, Barqai, Azor, Hazorea, Beth-shan, the Wâdī Dâliyeh, and Tekoa. In addition, the writer has more than sixty pots and bronzes from tombs at 'Ain es-Sâmiyeh (which will greatly expand Lapp's *corpus* from nearby sites); an equal amount of material from the discovery of a partially-robbed ceme-tery of some two hundred eighty tombs at Khirbet el-Kirmil, four miles northeast of Samûa'; and information from the investigation of a robbed cemetery of nearly two hundred MB I tombs at Khirbet er-Râs, one mile west of 'Idhna. Still more important is the large necropolis and settlement on the Jebel Qa'aqīr, eight miles west of Hebron in the Judean Hills (see fig. 1; grid reference 145.7/103.4), discovered by the writer in 1967 and excavated for fourteen weeks in October–November of 1967 and August–November of 1968.[75] On the southern slopes below the ridge (near the Wadi Khâlit el-Fûl) were found four separate cemeteries and else-where several smaller groups of tombs. Of the one hundred fifty or so tombs noted, thirty-nine recently robbed tombs were cleared and planned and thirty-six undisturbed tombs were excavated. The collection from these tombs, including that acquired from the tomb-robbers, amounts to some two hundred fifty vessels and twenty-five bronzes. Burial customs were better attested and the skeletal evidence better preserved than at any other MB I site thus far (see Pl. 13).

It is the settlement on the ridge, stretching over a length of more than one thousand yards, that is our main interest here. Several sections of an enclosure wall which once may have circled the settlement were found, preserved as much as four courses high; on the western end of the ridge a secondary boundary wall enclosed a rocky plateau with several crude "standing stones." Just outside the wall at one point an almost perfectly preserved pottery kiln was excavated (see Pl. 14). Inside the enclosure wall, two of the numerous cairns were excavated, one of them (No. 4) about fifteen meters across (see Pl. 15). Of particular interest was a rectangular building immediately below the latter, probably a dwelling, with domestic installations and considerable pottery on the floor, from an earlier phase of MB I. Neither cairn produced any contents except for a few MB I objects and sherds, although the larger one had a rather elaborate inner structure, including a mysterious "tower."

Three of the several dozen caves on the ridge were cleared; from two of them, which appeared to have been used for storage or as pottery dumps, vast quantities of sherds were recovered. The third, Cave G 26, was clearly occupied; the terrace was surrounded by cupmarks, two stone bins were off to one side, a storejar was set into the earthen surface, and inside were two chambers for sleeping and storage (see Pl. 16). Two phases of both surfaces and walls could be discerned, although no chronological distinction could be observed in the pottery. (For pottery and objects, primarily from Cairn No. 4 and Cave G26, see figs. 3 and 4.)

Although this is probably no more than a hint of what is to be found in the settlement at Jebel Qa'aqīr, several points may be stressed. (1) We have here a sizable assemblage of domestic pottery and associated artifacts, to which only Jericho and Yeruham (also unpublished) appear to be comparable.[76] (2) The material is not only well-stratified, with two clearly discernible phases, but is from a one-period site where the attribution of a given item is never in doubt.[77] (3) Since the stratified material is extremely close to *Locus* 1529 and other *loci* in the caves of the "1500 Area" at Lachish (seven miles northwest)[78] and also to Str. I–H at Tell Beit Mirsim (five miles southwest), where most of the restorable pottery also came from caves,[79] we can now speak of at least a regional pattern of settlement by cave-dwellers in MB I. There are no springs within about two miles of the site, and that, plus an occupation exclusively in caves and open cave-terraces, points to no more than a seasonal settlement. The inhabitants were probably semi-nomads who ranged the northern Negev with their flocks in winter, coming north into the hills only when forced to in summer, just as the Bedouin of the Negev still do.[80] The pottery of the settlement appears to be slightly earlier than that of some shaft-tombs and is stratigraphically earlier than the cairn-burials,[81] which may suggest that the settlement was abandoned toward the end of the twenty-first century BC. Nevertheless, the exclusively disarticulated burials in the shaft-tombs, usually of two or more individuals interred simultaneously, suggests that for some time during the twentieth century BC either these or other semi-nomadic folk frequented the site to bury their dead.[82]

One of the results of the Jebel Qa'aqīr excavations is that the MB I ceramic and lithic industries, at least of domestic sites, are now seen to be in the EB tradition. "Canaanean" flint blades, the common "EB IV" inverted rilled-rim bowls, the exclusive use of "hole-mouth" cooking pots —all point to EB traditions (see figs. 3 and 4). It should be noted that this simply confirms the limited evidence from other settled sites recently investigated, such as Khirbet Iskander and Har Yeruham.[83] Perhaps, as Wright has suggested,[84] the period should be termed "EB IV." However,

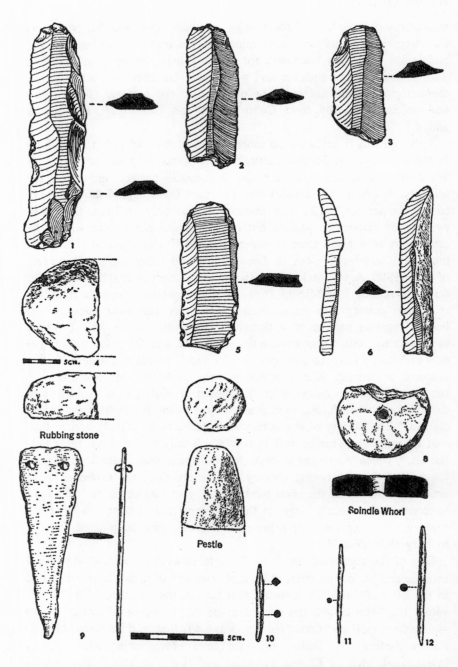

Figure 3. Jebel Qaʻaqīr: Copper and Stone Artifacts from *Cairn No. 4* (Nos. 3, 4, 6, 8, 10); *Cave G26* (1, 2, 5, 7); *Tomb B54 A* (9, 12) and *B* (11).

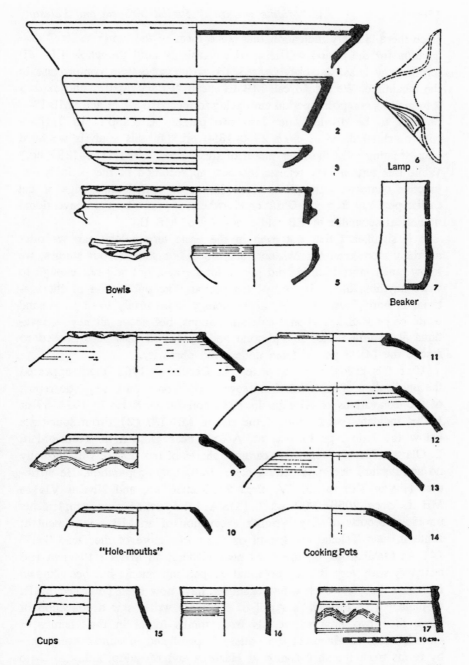

Bowls

Lamp 6

Beaker 7

"Hole-mouths"

Cooking Pots

Cups

10 cm.

Figure 4. Jebel Qa'aqīr: Sherds from *Cairn No. 4* (Nos. 1–3, 7–12, 14, 15);
Cave G26 (5, 6, 13); Probes in *Cemeteries B and F* (4, 16, 17).

since there is every indication that some form of the "intermediate" designation for the period will be used increasingly until the whole EB–MB terminology is satisfactorily revised, the writer suggests a compromise in the meantime. We should call MB I instead "EB IV/MB I" and expand it to make a composite period embracing former "EB IV"[85] and "MB I"— possibly to be divided later into two phases, as Lapp's "IB I–II"— with maximal dates of *circa* 2300–1850 BC. (In this analysis we have been treating only the later phase of this period, *circa* 2150–1850 BC.) While this terminology reflects the new appreciation of the period's disjunctive character and allows room for an expanded knowledge of the earlier phase at Bâb edh-Dhrâ' or elsewhere, it preserves the conventional numerical sequence of EB and especially of MB II.

It is significant that not even in the basic terminology can we offer anything more than a provisional scheme at this stage of our studies; we know much more than we did just a decade ago, but still not enough to write anything like a history of the period. The publication of the material in hand, new analyses, a chronology more firmly fixed by textual evidence or Radio Carbon 14 determinations, but above all new excavations at stratified sites in Palestine and Syria—all these are needed to rescue the MB I period from undeserved obscurity.

After this article was completed, in December 1968, there appeared the publication of materials from several additional sites. (1) The report of the excavations of Albright in 1934 and James Kelso in 1954–60 at Bethel indicates occupation of the site in MB I.[86] (2) From soundings below the Iron Age fortress at 'Arô'er, near Dhibân in Transjordan, E. Olávarri has recovered two ceramic phases of our period, with virtually no architecture but apparently a clear stratigraphic separation. He attributes Niveau VIb to EB IV, *circa* 2250–2050 BC, and Niveau VIa to MB I, *circa* 2050–1900 BC.[87] (3) A brief notice now supplements unofficial reports of Kay Wright's excavation of an MB I settlement at Ikhtenu, near Teleilat el-Ghassul on the north shore of the Dead Sea.[88] (4) At Ma'abaroth, on the coast near Hadera, an MB I settlement and cemetery with very striking pots and copper implements has been known for some time, of which a few examples have now been published by R. Gophna.[89] (5) Finally, in April of 1969 the writer saw a collection of more than two hundred vessels from tombs found in the vicinity of Gal'ed, south of Hazorea; the pottery is paralleled in almost every case by forms from the shaft-tombs at Hazorea and Megiddo, although there are a number of new ceramic forms, as well as a few copper pins of Syrian type.

FOOTNOTES

1. E. Sellin and C. Watzinger, *Jericho, die Ergebnisse der Ausgrabungen* (1913), pp. 14, 46–47, 108–12; for a horde of bronzes found in an amphoriskos, see pp. 116–20; for illustrations of pottery, see Pl. 22:1, 2a,b.

2. W. F. Albright, *The Excavation of Tell Beit Mirsim*, I: *The Pottery of the First Three Campaigns* (*AASOR*, 12 [1932]), pp. 8–14. See subsequently, IA: *The Bronze Age Pottery of the Fourth Campaign* (*AASOR*, 13 [1933]), pp. 62–67; II: *The Bronze Age* (*AASOR*, 17 [1938]), pp. 12–16.

3. The major results of the work in the Jordan Valley and in Transjordan were published in four Annuals of the American Schools of Oriental Research under the larger title of *Explorations in Eastern Palestine:* I (*AASOR*, 14 [1934]); II (*AASOR*, 15 [1935]); III (*AASOR*, 18–19 [1939]); IV (*AASOR*, 25–28 [1951]). Popular summaries are in *The Other Side of the Jordan* (1940; revised edition 1970) and *The River Jordan* (1946; revised edition 1968). For Glueck's work in the Negev from 1952 on, see preliminary reports in *BASOR*, No. 131 (1953), pp. 10–23; No. 137 (1955), pp. 10–22; No. 138 (1955), pp. 7–29; No. 142 (1956), pp. 10–21; No. 145 (1957), pp. 11–25; No. 149 (1958), pp. 8–17; No. 155 (1959), pp. 2–13; No. 159 (1960), pp. 3–14; No. 179 (1965), pp. 6–29. A semi-popular account will be found in *Rivers in the Desert: A History of the Negev* (1959); revised edition by W. W. Norton (1968); see also "The Age of Abraham in the Negev," *BA*, 18 (1955), pp. 2–9. The final publication is in process and will appear under the title *Explorations in Western Palestine*. This and the titles of the four volumes on Transjordan were deliberately chosen to complement the great *Survey of Eastern and Western Palestine* by Conder and Kitchener.

4. Glueck, *AASOR*, 14 (1934), pp. 81–82.

5. Note that Albright attributes his return to the detailed study of the period, with very provocative results (see below and n. 59), in part to renewed study of Glueck's collections in Cincinnati during a visit there in 1961. See also the study of M. Kochavi, *The Settlement of the Negev in the Middle Bronze (Canaanite) I Age* (unpublished doctoral dissertation, Hebrew University, 1967, a copy and permission to mention it kindly supplied by the author). While the latter treatment contains much that is new, chiefly from the writer's excavations at Har Yeruḥam (below), it assumes the basic work of Glueck. Incidentally, it was Glueck who first discovered Yeruḥam and identified it as an MB I site (Glueck's Site No. 361, "Bir Rekhmeh"); see *BASOR*, No. 149 (1958), p. 10; *BASOR*, No. 152 (1958), p. 22.

6. It will not be amiss, in a volume of essays in honor of Professor Glueck, to remind readers too young to know what Palestine was like in the 1930s that Glueck worked alone season after season in the most remote wilderness under extremely difficult conditions—coping with unstable political conditions, disorders accompanying the riots between Arabs and Jews, an almost complete lack of passable roads and communications, and frequent exposure to disease while living among the Bedouin. G. E. Wright has stated that "Glueck's work is to be rated as one of the two most important individual contributions to the field of Palestinian archaeology in our generation"; see "The Achievement of Nelson Glueck," *BA*, 22 (1959), p. 99. The greatest tribute to Glueck's pioneer work is that surprisingly little that is new can be

added to it, even after all these years. In Transjordan and the Jordan Valley, the only substantive work on our period is Peter Parr's sounding at Khirbet Iskander; the site was first discovered by Glueck, and the recent results of excavation confirm his views of its date. See Peter Parr, "Excavations at Khirbet Iskander," *ADAJ*, 4–5 (1960), pp. 128–33. Even in the Negev, where conditions since 1948 have favored very intensive research by the Israelis, relatively few MB I sites have been added to those charted by Glueck; see, principally, the surveys of Yohanan Aharoni (with E. Evanari, L. Shanan, and N. H. Tadmor) in the vicinity of Ramat Maṭred, just south of Avdat, "The Ancient Desert Agriculture of the Negev: Part V, An Israelite Agricultural Settlement at Ramat Maṭred," *IEJ*, 10 (1960), pp. 23–36, 97–111, and references there to earlier surveys in the Upper Niṣṣanah Valley. Aharoni's work with Benno Rothenberg and others in Sinai should also be mentioned, where several dozen MB I sites were found extending as far southwest as Serābīt el-Khādem; see Rothenberg, *God's Wilderness: Discoveries in Sinai* (1961), pp. 33–46, particularly the map on p. 34; and Aharoni, in the same volume, p. 182 and Pl. 89.

7. G. Ernest Wright, "The Chronology of Palestinian Pottery in Middle Bronze I," *BASOR*, No. 71 (1938), pp. 27–34.

8. W. M. F. Petrie, *Ancient Gaza*, I (1931), pp. 3, 9–12; for the pottery, see Forms 6R, 29, 30, and 33 (some) on Pls. XXXVII–XLIV and also the Register on Pl. LIX, all from the "100–200" Cemetery. *Ibid., Ancient Gaza*, II (1932), p. 2; for the daggers, see Pls. X–XIII; for the pottery, see Forms 30, 69 (some), Pls. XXIX, XXXV, and the group from T. 1573, Pl. XXXVI, bottom; for tomb plans, see Pl. LIII, and for the Register, Pl. LIX; all the above are from the "1500" Cemetery. See now the important re-publication of some of the 'Ajjûl material by Kenyon, "Tombs of the Intermediate Early Bronze–Middle Bronze Period at Tell 'Ajjûl," *ADAJ*, 3 (1956), pp. 41–55.

9. Alan Rowe, *The Topography and History of Beth-Shan* (1930), p. 2, Pl. XV:1, tomb group from the "Great Northern Cemetery." G. M. Fitzgerald, *Beth-Shan Excavations, 1921–23* (1931), p. 34, Pl. XXXV:1, 2, 4, 5, 10, 26, burial in "Trench on Northern Slope." *Ibid.*, "The Earliest Pottery of Beth-Shan," *Museum Journal*, 24 (1935), pp. 15–21, Pl. IX:13, 14; Pl. X:7, 9, 15, some from Str. XII–XI. While only the one shaft-tomb noted above (*Topography* . . .) has been published, recent reports indicate that the other tombs, several dozen in all, with very close parallels to the multi-chambered shaft-tombs at Megiddo, are finally being prepared for publication by an Israeli scholar, M. Oren.

10. For the tombs, see Robert Engberg and P. L. O. Guy, *Megiddo Tombs* (1938); references too numerous to indicate, but see pp. 135–37 for description of the multi-chambered shaft-tombs and for the pottery the following tombs: 16, 41, 58, 67, 217, 877, 878, 880, 884, 891, 911, 912, 922, 989, 1014, 1098, and 1120; Pls. 6, 7, 10–12, 15, 20–22, 31, and 33. Tomb 1101B–02 Lower is important but falls slightly earlier than the other tombs; see pp. 26–27 and Pls. 6–7. For the material from the mound, see Gordan Loud, *Megiddo II: Seasons of 1935–39* (1948): Str. XV, pp. 78–84, Pls. 8:2–4, 6, 7; 9:12, 13, 20; Str. XIV–XIII, pp. 84–87, Pls. 13:7, 12; 15:5, 6, 14, 16–18, 22: for the long-unrecognized MB I L. 4009, from Str. XIIIB, see Pl. 16:8, 16–18; finally, note miscellaneous sherds published only in photographs, including two large combed storejars with vestigial lug-handles, usually thought to be confined to the south; Pl. 109:2 (Str. XVI) and Pl. 115:7 (Str. XIV, apparently heretofore unnoticed).

11. John Starkey, "Excavations at Tell el-Duweir, 1933–1934," *PEQ*, 66 (1934), p. 165, Pl. III:a, 2. Olga Tufnell, *Lachish* IV: *The Bronze Age* (1958); for a description of "Cemetery 2000" and the Register, see pp. 275–79 and Pls. 88–89,

93; for the pottery, see pp. 171–75 and Pls. 20; 66:427–53; 67:454–98; for the bronzes, see pp. 74–76 and Pls. 21:6–10; 22:1–5. For a description of the "1500 Area," northwest of the mound, see pp. 253–75 and Pls. 88, 89, 94, 95; the MB I material comes from a number of EB caves subsequently occupied in MB I, esp. nos. 1510, 1512, 1513, 1518, 1527–29, 1536, 1541, 1551, and 1556. Only a selection of L. 1529 and two sherds from L. 1518 are published, out of what is described as "a great quantity"; see pp. 42, 171, 264, and Pls. 13:81–88 and 66:394–426; for daggers from L. 1513 and 1556, see Pls. 17:41; 22:6, 7; for degenerate flints of "Canaanean" type from L. 1556 (actually house of straggling walls), see Pl. 19:8–15; finally, see the crude copper ingots, surface finds in the "1500 Area," Pl. 21:11–15. The stratified material from the "1500 Area"—related to that from Megiddo XV–XIIIB (esp. L. 4009), Trench I at Jericho, Str. I–H at Tell Beit Mirsim, Khirbet Iskander, and Str. I–II at Har Yeruḥam—is now seen from the excavations at Jebel Qaʿaqīr and other unpublished material (see below and nn. 76–79) to be even more significant than first thought.

12. G. Lankester Harding and B. S. J. Isserlin, "An Early Bronze Age Cave at El Husn," *PEFA*, 6 (1953), pp. 1–13.

13. W. F. Albright, "Early Bronze Age Pottery from Bâb edh-Drâʿ," *BASOR*, No. 95 (1944), pp. 3–11; for later excavations, see below and n. 30. For the final publication of Ader alone, see Ray Cleveland, *The Excavation of the Conway High Place (Petra) and Soundings at Khirbet Ader (AASOR, 24–25 [1960]), Part II.* The Ader material is mostly "EB IV," despite Cleveland's attempt to assign Phases A and B to MB I (*op. cit.*, p. 88). Albright originally classed the material as MB I, but now (and apparently independent of the writer's views) prefers "EB IV"; see "Remarks on the Chronology of Early Bronze IV–Middle Bronze II A in Phoenicia and Syria-Palestine," *BASOR*, No. 184 (1966), p. 34, n. 34.

14. J. Ory, "A Bronze Age Tomb Near Yazûr," *QDAP*, 10 (1944), pp. 59–61. Recent excavations at Azor and at nearby Holon and Benayeh have brought to light numerous other MB I tombs, the unpublished material from which the writer has seen through the courtesy of Mr. Y. Shapira.

15. See n. 6.

16. Ruth Amiran, "Tombs of the Middle Bronze I Age at Maʿayan Barukh," *ʿAtiqot*, 3 (1961), pp. 84–92.

17. Y. Saʿad, "A Bronze Age Tomb Group from Hablet elʿAmud, Silwan Village Lands," *ADAJ*, 8–9 (1962), pp. 77–80.

18. Robert H. Smith, *Excavations in the Cemetery at Khirbet Kūfīn, Palestine* (1962); see T. 2, 3, Lower, pp. 8–16, Pls. X–XII.

19. James B. Pritchard, *The Bronze Age Cemetery at Gibeon* (1963); see discussion and tabulation, pp. 66–71; and T. 12–14, 22, 30–33, 37, 39, 42, 43, 46, 47, 52, 54, 56–59 and 62 (several tombs re-used in MB II–LB).

20. See E. Anati, *Palestine Before the Hebrews: A History From the Earliest Arrival of Man to the Conquest of Canaan* (1963), pp. 368–70. The excavations of Anati (carried out in 1956) have been supplemented by continued finds during construction work at Hazorea; the Curator of the local museum, Mr. E. Meyerhof, who is entrusted with the publication, has been kind enough to go over this large and exceedingly important collection with the writer and has given permission to mention it.

21. See Yigael Yadin, *et al.*, *Hazor III–IV: The Third and Fourth Seasons, 1957–1958* (1961), Plates only; the text volume has not yet appeared, but see, provisionally, sherds from Str. XVIII of Area A, Pl. CLVI:1–17. For the gap in "EB IV" and a brief sketch of the thin MB I occupation, see Yadin, "The Fourth Season of Excavation at Hazor," *BA*, 22 (1959), p. 18. The sherds of *Hazor*

III–IV, Pl. CLVI:1–7, are obviously of imported Syrian teapots identical to those of the Megiddo shaft-tombs. The only other site known thus far where similar imported teapots occur is Tell Bîr el-Gharbî, on the border of the Plain of Acco; see the brief notice of M. Prausnitz, *IEJ*, 12 (1962), p. 143.

22. See the brief notice by M. Kochavi in *IEJ*, 13 (1963), pp. 141–42; and also "The Excavations at Har Yeruḥam," *Yediot*, 27 (1963), pp. 284–92 (Hebrew). The Yeruḥam material is presented in full as part of the unpublished dissertation mentioned in n. 5 above.

23. Kathleen Kenyon, et al., *Excavations at Jericho*, I: *The Tombs Excavated in 1952–54* (1960); II: *The Tombs Excavated in 1955–58* (1965), pp. 33–166. The nearly four hundred vessels and more than forty bronzes from these tombs, plus other artifacts, constitute our largest collection from tombs of the period; although one may differ with the analysis and interpretation, it must be acknowledged that the material is published promptly and in exemplary fashion. The stratified evidence from the mound has not yet appeared, but see, provisionally, Kenyon, "Excavations at Jericho, 1952," *PEQ*, 85 (1952), p. 70 and fig. 6:36–45; *ibid.*, *Digging Up Jericho* (1957), pp. 189–94; *ibid.*, in G. Posener, J. Bottéro, and K. Kenyon, "Syria and Palestine, c. 2160–1780 BC," *CAH²*, I, fasc. 29 (1965), pp. 40–41.

24. Paul W. Lapp, *The Dhahr Mirzbâneh Tombs; Three Intermediate Bronze Cemeteries in Jordan* (1966). The material from the thirty-six round-shaft tombs consists largely of small jars with ledge-handles, amphoriskoi, four-spouted lamps, and small "bottles," the latter already familiar from el-Jîb, sites around Jerusalem, and particularly the "Pottery" tombs at Jericho. However, the excavation and publication are meticulously done, with particular attention to the often-neglected skeletal material. The comparative discussion is much fuller than the material actually warrants but is nevertheless welcome. For the author's controversial interpretations of the origin of the material, see below and nn. 57, 58.

25. V. Tzaferis, "A Middle Bronze Age I Cemetery in Tiberias," *IEJ*, 18 (1968), pp. 15–19. Not only is the painted pottery nearly identical to that of el-Ḥuṣn and Megiddo, but the plan of T. 1 (fig. 4, p. 17), with a stepped shaft, central chamber set off with stone walls, and four or five lateral chambers, is *strikingly* like that of T. 1120 at Megiddo (see *Megiddo Tombs*, fig. 48). The arrowhead and the three daggers with curled tang (Pl. 1:A) are unique thus far, but the curled tang is typical of pikes and javelins of the period.

26. For Palestine, see G. E. Wright, "The Archaeology of Palestine" in *BANE* (1961), p. 86. For Anatolia, see J. Mellaart, "Anatolia Before c. 4000 B.C. and c. 2300–1750 B.C.," *CAH²*, II, fasc. 20 (1964), pp. 28–50 and refs. there. For Greece and the Aegean, see J. L. Caskey, "Greece, Crete and the Aegean Islands in the Early Bronze Age," *CAH²*, I, fasc. 24 (1964), pp. 3–38 and refs. there.

27. On the Gutians, see C. J. Gadd, "The Dynasty of Agade and the Gutian Invasion," *CAH²*, I, fasc. 17 (1963), pp. 40–49. On the Ur III period, see *ibid.*, "Babylonia c. 2120–1800 BC," *CAH²*, I, fasc. 28 (1965), pp. 3–24. As background for the period, see especially D. O. Edzard, *Die zweite "Zwischenzeit" Babyloniens* (1957).

28. See Posener, Bottéro and Kenyon, *op. cit.*, pp. 3–8 and references there.

29. G. E. Wright, *The Pottery of Palestine from the Earliest Times to the End of the Early Bronze Age* (1937), pp. 78–81. Most of the additional material added to this phase after 1937 came from the explorations of Glueck (for references, see n. 3), who adopted the "EB IV" terminology, sometimes dividing it into "EB IVA" and "B." Wright now suggests that we speak instead of "EB IIIB," leaving "EB IV" perhaps to be used as an alternate term for MB I; see *BANE*, pp. 86, 88. De Vaux still

retains Wright's original terminology; see "Palestine in the Early Bronze Age," *CAH*², ɪ, fasc. 46 (1966), p. 8. Also see section III and n. 85.

30. For preliminary reports, see Paul W. Lapp, "The Cemetery at Bâb edh-Dhrâ', Jordan," *Arch*, 19 (1966), pp. 104–111; "Bâb edh-Dhrâ', Perizzites and Emim" in *Jerusalem Through the Ages*, ed. by J. Aviram (1968), pp. 1–25. The fullest defense of the new terminology is in the course of the publication of the Dhahr Mirzbâneh tombs, *op. cit.*, Preface, pp. 94–97, 115, 116. For our preference, see below, section III and n. 85.

31. See M. Pezard, *Qadesh: mission archéologique à Tell Nebi Mend* (1931); Le Comte du Mesnil du Buisson, "Compte Rendu de la Quatrième Campagne de Fouilles à Mishrifé-Qaṭna," *Syr*, 11 (1930), pp. 146–53; *ibid.*, "Une Campagne de Fouilles à Khan Sheikhoun," *Syr*, 13 (1932), pp. 171–78; *ibid.*, "Sourān et Tell Maṣin," *Berytus*, 2 (1935), pp. 121–32; *ibid.*, *Le Site archéologique de Mishrifé-Qaṭna* (1935).

32. E. Fugmann, *Hama. Fouilles et Recherches 1931–1938. L'Architecture des périods pré-Hellénistiques* (1958), pp. 281–82; for Str. Jl–8, see pp. 48–85.

33. For the imported pottery at Megiddo, see the teapots, *Megiddo Tombs*, Pls. 11:28–35; 12:1, 7, 12, 13; 15:1, 2, 6–9; 20:13; 22:3–5; 33:10; and for the goblets, see Pl. 11:26, 27; 22:19. For Hazor, and also Bîr el-Gharbî, see n. 21. For Hama, see n. 32.

34. For Albright and Amiran, see below, p. 139, and nn. 44, 67, 69. The publications of Hama and the 'Amûq are not alluded to in the text nor are they mentioned in the bibliography of Kenyon's treatment in the "Cambridge Ancient History" (cited in n. 23); the omission of the only stratified material we have for Syria in this period, whether by intention or oversight, is inexplicable in a publication that purports to be the authoritative treatment. The by-passing of this evidence is all the more surprising, since Kenyon *does* offer the most thorough discussion to date of such poorly excavated material as that of Byblos; see, *op. cit.*, pp. 54–58. For similar treatments of du Mesnil du Buisson's sites around Qaṭna (cited in n. 31), see p. 53 and her popular work *Amorites and Canaanites* (1966), pp. 44, 45.

35. Paolo Matthiae, *et al.*, *Missione Archaeologica Italiana in Siria; Rapporto Preliminare della Campagna 1964* (1965); *ibid.*, *Rapporto Preliminare della Campagna 1965* (1966); *ibid.*, *Rapporto Preliminare della Campagna 1966* (1967).

36. See *Rapporto . . . 1964*, pp. 23–33, Pls. XXXIV–XXXVII; XL; XLIV; XLVI; XLVIII; LIV; LV (fully half of all the surface finds illustrated).

37. *Rapporto . . . 1966;* for the three entryway city gate in Area A, see pp. 21–30 and fig. 1; for a large building in Area B, see pp. 31–61; for the temple in Area D, see pp. 63–75 and fig. 6. All these structures are dated to MB I or *circa* 2000 BC on the basis of parallels to Hama J and 'Amûq I–J; see esp. pp. 30, 45, 46, 59, 72. However, a careful study of the pottery and other objects will show that the material belongs to a very *late* phase of the 'Amûq/Hama J horizon, exceedingly close to phase H, i.e., twentieth century BC and MB IIA. Note that Albright also dates these levels to the twentieth to nineteenth centuries BC (see *BASOR*, No. 184 [1966], p. 31); however, since he has lowered his date for the end of MB I to *circa* 1800 BC (below and n. 59), he compares the Mardikh material with MB I in Palestine. We are strongly of the opinion that too few scholars have analyzed the mixture of materials of the 'Amûq/Hama J horizons; numerous pot-forms (esp. the painted forerunners of the Ḫabur Ware), the figurines, the bronzes—all point directly to the full-blown MB IIA culture of the 'Amûq/Hama K horizon which, since J must end circa 2000 BC, is probably fully developed shortly thereafter, or by the mid-twentieth century BC at latest. Nothing but confusion can result from

comparing Syrian material from the twentieth century BC—which is already MB IIA
—with Palestinian material from the same date, since the latter is still in MB I in
terms of *cultural* phases. It must be borne in mind that there is a lag of half a century
or so before XIIth Dynasty influence, and with it renewed urbanization, reaches
Palestine, which would place the MB I/IIA transition there *circa* 1900 BC or slightly
later; see below and nn. 61–64. Ward has shown that the scarabs of Sesostris I
(*circa* 1971–1928 BC) found in Palestine and cited by Schaeffer and others are all
from uncertain archaeological context, and in any case these scarabs were manufactured under later pharaohs. The earliest artifactual evidence of XIIth Dynasty influence in Palestine is from the time of Sesostris II (*circa* 1897–1879 BC); see W. A.
Ward, "Egypt and the Eastern Mediterranean in the Early Second Millennium BC,"
Or, 30 (1961), pp. 37–39.

38. Note that Braidwood puts the end of 'Amûq J no later than *circa* 2000 BC;
see Robert J. and Linda S. Braidwood, *Excavations in the Plain of Antioch,
I: The Earlier Assemblages, Phases A–J* (1960), pp. 522–23. See also now John
Van Seters, *The Hyksos: A New Investigation* (1966), pp. 14–20, esp. p. 18, where
a date of *circa* 1950 BC is advanced for the MB I/IIA transition (although the
author's utilization of the strictly archaeological evidence is sometimes open to
question). The new study of Tufnell, Ward and Porada of the contents of the
"Montet Jar" from Byblos raises the date to *circa* the twenty-first century BC, with
some of the cylinder-seals possibly falling as late as the twentieth century BC;
see Olga Tufnell and W. A. Ward, "Relations Between Byblos, Egypt, and Mesopotamia at the End of the Third Millennium B.C.: A Study of the Montet Jar,"
Syr, 43 (1966), pp. 165–241; and E. Porada, "Les Cylindres de la Jarre Montet,"
idem, pp. 243–58. Albright and others have long recognized that the horde
of bronzes and other artifacts, particularly the toggle-pins, is typical of MB IIA;
see *BASOR*, No. 184, p. 27, n. 3 and references there (though note that Albright
still holds to an absolute date in the early eighteenth century BC). Finally, note
that B. Mazar now adopts a "high chronology" for MB I in both Syria and Palestine,
circa 2200–2000 BC; see the valuable summary, "The Middle Bronze Age in Palestine," *IEJ*, 18 (1968), pp. 65–97, esp. pp. 67–72 and p. 97.

39. Cited in n. 38; for Phase J, see pp. 429–57. We consider Phase I, although
it is obviously related, as falling a bit early for close comparisons; note that it is
marked still by Khirbet Kerak wares, *op. cit.*, pp. 398–403 and figs. 304–6. See the
review-article by Miriam Tadmor, "Contacts Between the 'Amûq and Syria-Palestine," *IEJ*, 14 (1964), pp. 253–69.

40. For summary, see Braidwood, *op. cit.*, pp. 431, 453–56.

41. Space prohibits giving a full bibliography here; for references, see Braidwood,
op. cit., pp. 521–23; and Patty Jo Watson, in Robert W. Ehrich, ed., *Chronologies
in Old World Archaeology* (1965), pp. 79–81 and references there. We may add the
later reports from Tell Chuera: A. Moortgat, *Tell Chuera in Nordöst-Syrien;
Vorläufiger Bericht über die Dritte Grabungskampagne* (1962); *ibid., Bericht über
die Vierte Grabungskampagne 1963* (1964); *ibid., Vorläufiger Bericht über die fünfte
Grabungskampagne 1964* (1967). For Asshur, note the *Erdgräber*, shaft-tombs with
single burials rich in copper artifacts, dated to the Akkadian and Ur III period by
cylinder-seals in Graves 2 and 4; see W. Andrae, *Die Archäischen Ischtar-Tempel
in Asshur* (1922), pp. 5–10, Pls. 1, 7–9. For Kish, the "A" Cemetery is relevant;
see E. Mackay, *Report on the Excavations of the "A" Cemetery at Kish, Mesopotamia,
Pt. I* (1925), pp. 6 ff.

42. For a convenient summary and references, see Watson in Ehrich, *op. cit.*,
p. 81.

43. The "wagon wheels" from North Syria and Mesopotamia have not received

the attention they deserve. For examples from Hama J, see Fugmann, *op. cit.*, fig. 64: 3D492, 3H817, 3C608 (cart-body); fig. 85: 3C602; fig. 93: 3A339, 3A343 (body); fig. 98: 3B756, 3C368; fig. 103: 3A37. For similar examples, see A. Moortgat, *Tell Chuera in Nordöst-Syrien; Vorläufiger Bericht über die Grabung 1958* (1959), Abb. 44, p. 43; *ibid., Tell Chuera . . . 1962* (n. 41), Abb. 8, p. 13 (cart, wheels, and two draft animals). Striking parallels to these terra cotta carts can be assembled from Eastern Europe from the same period, identical to the Hama examples even in the decoration and representation of the spokes; see the valuable assembly of the material from fifty-two sites in I. Bóna, "Clay Models of Bronze Age Wagons and Wheels in the Middle Danube Basin," *Acta Archaeologica Academiae Scientiarum Hungaricae*, 12 (1960), pp. 83–111. M. Gimbutas dates these to the "Kurgan" expansion of the last quarter of the third millennium BC (below, n. 56); see *Bronze Age Cultures in Central and Eastern Europe* (1965), pp. 204–7.

44. Ruth Amiran, "The Pottery of the Middle Bronze Age I in Palestine," *IEJ*, 10 (1960), pp. 204–25.

45. W. F. Albright, "The Chronology of Middle Bronze I (Early Bronze–Middle Bronze)," *BASOR*, No. 168 (1962), pp. 37–41. The information that Amiran accepts this revision is a personal communication.

46. See the first of the two forthcoming works cited in n. 66, where an extensive analysis will be offered.

47. See the works cited in n. 23.

48. Kenyon, "Excavations at Jericho, 1955," *PEQ*, 87 (1955), p. 117; *ibid., PEQ*, 88 (1956), p. 78; and subsequent preliminary reports; the complete classification will be found in *Jericho* I–II, with the presentation of the full evidence. For a convenient summary, see Posener, Bottéro and Kenyon, *op. cit.*, pp. 41–43 and references there to earlier treatments.

49. The term seems first to have been used by J. H. Iliffe in his arrangement of the exhibits in the Palestine Archaeological Museum; however, it was first popularized —one might say, introduced unilaterally into the literature—by Kenyon, basing herself on the evidence of the Jericho tombs. With her adoption of it now in *CAH*[2] (*op. cit.*, pp. 38 ff.), it has been granted almost canonical status, although a full critical discussion has not yet appeared in the literature and the matter is far from settled. A variation, "Intermediate Bronze Age," is used by Smith and Lapp in the works cited in nn. 18 and 24. For other views, including the writer's, see below and nn. 84–86.

50. See, for instance, Jean Kupper, *Les Nomades en Mésopotamie au temps des rois de Mari* (1957), pp. 260–63; and also the more recent works cited in n. 51 below.

51. Cited in n. 23 above. We may add now: G. Buccellati, *The Amorites of the Ur III Period* (1966); esp. pp. 235–362; and H. Huffman, *Amorite Personal Names in the Mari Texts* (1965). For the new Execration Texts from Mirgissa, approximately contemporary with the Berlin Texts of Sethe, see G. Posener, "Les Textes d'envoutement de Mirgissa," *Syr*, 43 (1966), pp. 279–87.

52. *CAH*[2], pp. 26–29 and references there. The lowering of the date of the Berlin Texts by fifty to seventy-five years, with some scholars, would still not decrease their importance.

53. The particular statement here is the writer's, but the general "Amorite hypothesis" is adapted with variations by Albright, for instance; see summary and references to earlier work in "Abram the Hebrew: A new Archaeological Interpretation," *BASOR*, No. 163 (1961), pp. 36–54; *ibid., BASOR*, No. 184 (cited in n. 13), esp. pp. 34–35. See also De Vaux, "Les Patriarches hébreux et l'histoire,"

RB, 72 (1965), pp. 5–28. For similar views of Kenyon, see Posener, Bottéro and Kenyon, *op. cit.*, pp. 60–61; also *Digging up Jericho*, Chapter 8, "Nomadic Invaders." For Wright's views, see *BANE*, pp. 86–88.

54. See n. 24 and assessment there.

55. *Ibid.*, pp. 101–11.

56. *Ibid.*, pp. 111–13. The only other scholar to forward the view that the MB I people of Palestine are non-Semitic is Marija Gimbutas, the eminent specialist in East European archaeology; see *The Prehistory of Eastern Europe, Part I: Mesolithic, Neolithic and Copper Age Cultures in Russia and the Baltic Area* (1956), where she summarizes the evidence for a series of invasions of Eastern Europe in the last quarter of the third millennium BC by Proto Indo-Europeans who she believes came from beyond the Caucasus. Concerning the date and character of these "Kurgan" invaders (from the Russian *Kurgan*, "barrow," after their custom of burying in barrows), she concluded (*op. cit.*, p. 65) that "the correspondence between certain types of artifacts shows the persistent orientation of the northern Caucasus culture to the Near Eastern and Aegean civilizations and points to a date close to 2000 B.C." See also her more recent treatment in *Bronze Age Cultures* (n. 43). After visiting Israel in 1965 and becoming acquainted with the "Amorite" expansion and the MB I materials of Syria/Palestine, Gimbutas was inclined to dismiss the "Amorites" and see in the newcomers of MB I her "Kurgan" invaders (personal communication to both the writer and Lapp). Lapp did not originally take Gimbutas' views into consideration but now considers that she supports his position; see "Bâb edh-Dhrâ' Tomb 76 and Early Bronze I in Palestine," *BASOR*, No. 189 (1968), p. 29, n. 22.

57. The writer hopes to publish a review article of Lapp's *Mirzbâneh Tombs* in the near future. Meanwhile, it may be noted that no reviewer has been persuaded by Lapp's conclusions regarding ethnic movements, unless possibly Tufnell, who had independently suggested similar ideas.

58. For a brief report of the writer's research, sponsored by a grant from the American Philosophical Society in the summer and fall of 1966, see William G. Dever, "Ethnic Movements in East Central Europe and the Near East, ca. 2300–1800 B.C." in *Yearbook of the American Philosophical Society for 1967* (1968), pp. 500–3.

59. See works cited in nn. 13, 45 and 53, to which add now: Albright, "The Eighteenth-Century Princes of Byblos and the Chronology of Middle Bronze," *BASOR*, No. 176 (1964), pp. 38–46; *ibid.*, "Further Light on the History of Middle-Bronze Byblos," *BASOR*, No. 179 (1965), pp. 38–43.

60. See n. 33 for references.

61. For references see W. A. Ward, *Or*, 30, pp. 39–41. Although Ward minimizes the significance of XIIth Dynasty contacts with Palestine and thinks Thut-hotpe may have been simply an exile at Megiddo, he does not deny that he lived there for some time, so our argument is not affected.

62. This involves the rejection of Albright's use of this evidence (*BASOR*, No. 168, p. 39) and also the rejection of Kenyon's attempt to redate the monumental architecture of Str. XV, particularly the three *megaron* temples, to MB I; see Kenyon, "Some Notes on the Early and Middle Bronze Age Strata at Megiddo," *Eretz Israel*, 5 (1958), pp. 51–60, esp. pp. 55–59. The pottery of Str. XV is too badly mixed to date the stratum; most is MB IIA and a check of the find-spots will show that all but three of these vessels are from tombs, undoubtedly *dug down into* Str. XV, so that they must be eliminated. The balance of the pottery of Str. XV is MB I, but with earlier mixtures. Unfortunately, none of the pottery can

be definitely associated with the three temples. A detailed analysis of all the pertinent *loci* shows an EB III–MB IIA range. Wright thinks that the temples are MB IIA and the excavators simply dug the foundation down into MB I and earlier deposits; see *BANE*, p. 108, n. 71. The other alternative, a date in EB III, was proposed by the late Immanuel Dunayevsky on the basis of brief soundings done in 1965; see the notice in *IEJ*, 16 (1966), p. 142. On *a priori* grounds, it would be difficult to assign such monumental architecture to MB I, when elsewhere, as even Miss Kenyon admits, there is virtually no architecture of any kind for the period.

63. For full bibliography, see Posener, in Posener, Bottéro, and Kenyon, *op. cit.*, p. 9 and n. 2.

64. The insistence of Albright that "Shechem was inhabited in both MB I and MB IIA" (*BASOR*, No. 163, p. 47), repeated in his latest treatments (see *BASOR*, No. 184, n. 33), was apparently based originally on the very general preliminary report of the early campaigns of the Drew-McCormick excavations of G. E. Wright and others; see Wright, "The Second Campaign at Tell Balâṭah (Shechem)," *BASOR*, No. 148 (1957), p. 12. Albright's view was secondarily buttressed by casual statements of Lapp (*Mirzbâneh Tombs*, pp. 72, 83), which he quotes, mentioning MB I material at Shechem. What Lapp was referring to was the clearance in 1964 of a very few shaft-tombs disturbed by the bulldozer while cutting a road several hundred yards from the tell (see *BASOR*, No. 180, [1965], p. 33), which R. J. Bull in reporting took to imply a settlement, although he noted that no evidence for it was found on the mound. This is cited to put to rest the idea that there is an MB I "occupation" known from the tell at Shechem. The writer is responsible for the publication of the MB IIA and any MB I material in the final series and has all the material at his disposal; he can testify that there is no more than a handful of indeterminate "MB I" sherds from the tell and a very few pieces, including one teapot, from the tombs mentioned above. Note that in Field IX, the large quantities of MB IIA pottery directly overlay Late Chalcolithic on bedrock; elsewhere, MB IIA is basal and represents the first urban installation.

65. Wright and Kenyon have expressed this view independently; see Wright, in *BANE*, p. 88; Kenyon, *Digging Up Jericho*, pp. 187, 210, and Posener, Bottéro, and Kenyon, *op. cit.*, p. 39. Amiran has attempted to show continuity between MB I and IIA and on that ground to retain the traditional terminolgy (see *IEJ*, 10, p. 205, and fig. 1), but her ceramic arguments definitely do not carry conviction. It is true that the few red-slipped wares of Amiran's "Family C" have sometimes been seen as the forerunners of the red slip and burnish of MB IIA, but these wares are now proven to be the earliest in the MB I sequence and simply survivals in the EB tradition. Only the typical early MB II flat-bottomed cooking pots with completely pierced holes below the rim can be adduced; and the latest evidence indicates that most have probably been misattributed to MB I. Numerous examples were found in MB IIA fills in the 1967–68 seasons at Gezer, where there are no MB I levels. This leads us to suspect that most of the published examples have been misattributed, as for instance at Lachish and particularly at Tell Beit Mirsim, where MB I/IIA mixtures can be demonstrated in the case of other forms. Note that in the unpublished material from the stratified sites of Wâdī Dâliyeh, Khirbet Iskander, Har Yeruḥam, and Jebel Qa'aqīr—one-period sites—the exclusive cooking pots are hole-mouths in the EB tradition. As for the bronzes, the few types that do continue into MB II (toggle-pins and daggers) are much more highly developed and made of true bronze, while the most typical MB I bronzes (curled-tang javelins and pikes) do not seem to occur later, at least in Palestine.

66. The writer is indebted to Prof. Nelson Glueck for the opportunity to pursue

the research for the dissertation, under the direction of G. Ernest Wright, during 1964–65 as a Fellow of the Hebrew Union College Biblical and Archaeological School in Jerusalem, and for the school's sponsoring the Jebel Qa'aqīr excavations directed by the writer in 1967–68 while Resident Director. The two volumes will appear as numbers II and III of the new Annual series of the Jerusalem school.

67. See Albright, *BASOR*, No. 168, pp. 37–38; actually Albright himself as long ago as 1933 had proposed the extension to the territory of the Akkad Empire (*Tell Beit Mirsim* IA, p. 67), but had not traced the relationships in detail as more recent material accumulated.

68. For references, see Watson, in Ehrich, *op. cit.*, 79–81; to which should be added D. B. Stronach, "The Development and Diffusion of Metal Types in Early Bronze Age Anatolia," *AnSt*, 7 (1957), pp. 89–125.

69. Albright, *Tell Beit Mirsim*, II, pp. 15–16.

70. Note that the sites where we have any stratigraphic sequence—Hama, the 'Amūq, Tell Sukas—confirm this. See Fugmann, *op. cit.*, pp. 82–83; Braidwood, *op. cit.*, pp. 419, 431; for Tell Sukas, twenty miles south of Ras Shamra on the coast, see Ann M. Ehrich, *Early Pottery of the Jebeleh Region* (1938), p. 87.

71. While we cannot present the detailed evidence here, a network of ceramic relationships links Jericho with central hill-sites like Mirzbâneh and el-Jîb, with most southern sites such as Lachish and Tell Beit Mirsim, and even with the coastal site of Tell el-'Ajjûl. As the ceramic prototypes are at home in central Syria, and the intermediate links that we know are primarily in Transjordan and the Jordan Valley, the great oasis of Jericho—for millennia previously the natural gateway into Palestine—would most likely have been the *point d'appui*. This underlines again the importance of the several groups that Kenyon has recognized in her tombs at Jericho.

72. This phenomenon has been recognized, of course, but in our opinion most scholars underestimate the continuity. Thus Amiran says that "the break with the preceding period was indeed a sharp one and allowed only few left-overs of previous traditions to persist"; see *IEJ*, 10, p. 205. Kenyon speaks only of "some broad similarity" and "a remote common ancestry"; see *Archaeology in the Holy Land* (1960), p. 136. Much more preferable is Wright's view (*BANE*, pp. 87–88) that the newcomers "imported items from the 'caliciform' culture of Syria, but their most common pottery forms are survivals from, and adaptions of, Early Bronze forms, though made in a new way." See also below and n. 83.

73. We include in the early wheel-ribbed wares particularly the lug-handled carinated cups and some of the similar bowls from Megiddo, L. 4009; Tell Beit Mirsim, Str. I–H; and Lachish, L. 1529 (the above cited in nn. 2, 10, 11); as well as the new material from Jebel Qa'aqīr discussed below. Not enough attention has been paid to the fact that the shoulder and frequently nearly the whole body of these vessels is delicately made on a *fast wheel* in contrast to the technique of crude wheel-finishing only at the neck elsewhere in this period. We believe that these few sophisticated wheel-made vessels are not late in the period and in anticipation of the MB IIA technique, but rather belong among the earliest wares and are *directly* related to the universally wheel-made "caliciform" wares of Syria.

74. This highlights the considerable importance of the site of Jebel Qa'aqīr, discussed below, where we have a true settlement with stratified material.

75. An account of the discovery of the site and the unusual circumstances of excavation appeared in a newsletter of the Hebrew Union College Biblical and Archaeological School in Jerusalem in the fall of 1967. Both seasons of excavation were sponsored by the Hebrew Union College and its Jerusalem school. The writer is indebted not only to Prof. Nelson Glueck (n. 66), but also to Dr. Avraham Biran,

Director of the Department of Antiquities; to Mr. Zev Yeivin, Archaeological Liaison Officer with the Military Governor of the West Bank, who facilitated the obtaining of the salvage permit in accordance with the Geneva Convention regulations covering occupied territories; and to the professional staff, Dr. John Landgraf, Mr. Dean Moe, Dr. Elmo Scoggin (field supervisors), and Mr. Theodore Rosen (photographer). In early news reports the site was called Kh. el-Fûl.

76. For preliminary reports of Jericho, see n. 23; and for Yeruḥam, see nn. 5 and 22. The Jericho material is reported to be sizable, but the material from Yeruḥam, which the writer has gone over with Kochavi, is very limited in extent.

77. Extensive excavation plus surface exploration have yielded only a handful of Late Chalcolithic sherds, no EB, no MB II or LB, a very few Iron II sherds, and a scattering of late Hellenistic, Roman, and Byzantine. There is thus no room for doubt in the excavated material, enabling us to utilize the *corpus* from this site to tighten up that of Lachish and Tell Beit Mirsim nearby, where some stratigraphic mixture with EB III–IV and MB II was inevitable.

78. See material cited in n. 11.

79. In general, see references in n. 2. For the fact that much of the well-stratified H pottery and nearly all that was restorable came from a cave in SE 13, see Albright, *Tell Beit Mirsim*, IA, pp. 62–63 and Pls. 2–3. This and another cave in SE 22/23 Albright regarded simply as storage caves, though he noted that all had "entrances lined with rude masonry"—exactly like the Qaʻaqîr caves; see *Tell Beit Mirsim*, II, p. 15, Pl. 49, and also *BASOR*, No. 184, n. 34. Despite the attribution of a few crude walls to Str. I–H, we suspect that most of the MB I occupation at Tell Beit Mirsim was in caves, as at Lachish and now Qaʻaqîr.

80. The writer has noticed this especially at Gezer, where Bedouin from the northern Negev come in summer's drought because of the wells and springs near the *tell* and pasturage nearby. Some of them even live in the numerous large caves in the region, using others for storage and sheepfolds.

81. This sequence is apparently true also of Bâb edh-Dhrâʻ, where numerous cairns are reported. At Yeruḥam, the other well-known site with cairn-burials, some of the cairns overlay remains of the settlement of Str. 2 and belong probably with the latest settlement, Str. 1. In a personal communication Dr. G. E. Wright has called attention to the views of his student, Dr. Eric Meyers, in an unpublished dissertation, suggesting that the cairns may be the primary burial places. This would explain both the curious lack of bones in the cairns and the completely disarticulated bones of the shaft-tombs.

82. The whole question of a nomadic versus a sedentary society in MB I is still not resolved. Glueck has been of the opinion from the beginning that his EBIV/MBI sites in Transjordan represent "an advanced civilization" (*AASOR*, 15, p. 38). He considers that in the Negev a similar civilization flourished and that its people were probably agriculturalists as well as pastoralists (*Rivers in the Desert*, pp. 77–84). Kenyon thinks that these areas "were never occupied by a settled population and never could be" and that the culture represented is that of "nomadic pastoralists"; see Posener, Bottéro and Kenyon, *op. cit.*, p. 50. Albright stresses caravaning activity, but holds that the pattern of life of the traders in Palestine "shifted rapidly from prevailingly semi-nomadic to sedentary" (*BASOR*, No. 184, pp. 34–35), although elsewhere he regards these settlements as "purely seasonal" (*BASOR*, No. 163, p. 37). The settlement at Yeruḥam in the Negev effectively disposes of Kenyon's view; and new settlements farther up in the hills, like that at Qaʻaqîr, will undoubtedly show that settlements were far more widespread than formerly suspected and that their location and nature have simply made them largely inaccessible to archaeological investigation. We must stress that Kenyon's

insistence on a nomadic culture derives largely from the evidence of disarticulated burials at Jericho; see, for instance, Posener, Bottéro and Kenyon, *op. cit.*, pp. 43–44. This may indeed indicate nomadic—or, more likely, semi-nomadic—society during part of the period, but must not be taken, because of the lack of stratified sites, to characterize the period as a whole.

83. See references in nn. 5, 15, 22.

84. Wright opposes any change of terminology at present, but would prefer "EB IV," since this "is a new pottery, but it is the dying gasp of the last remnant of Early Bronze traditions"; see *BANE*, pp. 87–88. Of course, "EB IV" would not then refer to the same deposits that it did in Wright's 1937 treatment, since these are increasingly termed "EB IIIB" by Wright and others.

85. Former "EB IV" having come to be designated "EB IIIB" for the most part, there is considerable support for applying "EB IV" to our period, either in part or in its entirety. We have noted Wright's preference. Note also that Albright has recently proposed that we should use "EB IV" for Amiran's Families "B" and "C" (the forepart of the period) and "MB I" for her Family "A" (the main part of the period); see "Some Remarks on the Archaeological Chronology of Palestine Before About 1500 B.C.," in Ehrich, *op. cit.*, p. 54. Lapp, who earlier advocated "Intermediate Bronze I and II" for the period, has most recently suggested that if "Kurgan" invaders are involved, as Gimbutas (and apparently now Lapp) thinks, "EB IV A–B" might be preferable; see *BASOR*, No. 189, p. 31, n. 24. The one thing clear in the otherwise muddled picture is that our period in terms of *cultural* horizons belongs with Early Bronze rather than with Middle Bronze II, as it has substantial continuity with the former, virtually none with the latter. The only reason, in fact, for retaining "MB I" as part of our composite term is to salvage the traditional terminology of the Middle Bronze age. Otherwise, we should either have to drop "MB I" altogether, which would be awkward; or we should have to follow Kenyon's confusing usage of applying "MB I" to what everyone else calls "MB IIA." The problems of cultural and chronological relationships in this period are much like those of the Late Chalcolithic/EB IA period a thousand years earlier, where the traditional framework has likewise broken down. In both cases, the present scheme resulted from an archaeological congress in the 1920s, and it is clear that a similar congress is needed again to clarify these matters.

86. See Albright and Kelso, *The Excavation of Bethel (1934–1960)*, *AASOR*, 39 (1968). For the pottery (already known from a preliminary report in *BASOR*, 164 [1961], see Pl. 31, 48, 113; it is virtually identical to Tell Beit Mirsim I–H. Of the settlement reported, nothing can be affirmed except that the domestic occupation must have been thin and short-lived and that the town was probably unwalled. A "temple" attributed to MB I is too poorly published to analyze in any detail (pp. 22, 23; Pl. 105C, 106, 108), but it would appear to be nothing more than the substructure of an MB II complex, perhaps part of the northwest Gate.

87. See E. Olávarri, "Fouilles à 'Arô'er sur l'Arnon," *RB*, 76 (1969), pp. 230–59. Our impression is that the pottery of Niveau VIb and VIa shows too much similarity and continuity to represent more than two very close phases; since it is comparable to Ader C–A (as Olávarri correctly points out), we are inclined to date both to the very end of EB IV—not denying, of course, the possibility of an extension into the beginning of MB I (see our discussion of Ader, n. 13, and fig. 2). The striking thing is the *mixture* in Niveau VIa of clear EB IV forms with elements of classic MB I, including "caliciform" and band-combed wares—a picture identical to that at Kh. Iskander and (if the scanty evidence allowed a better view of it) at Ader B–A. I suspect that we are dealing with a cultural continuum from "EB IV" down through "MB I," the earlier phases of which flourished only in Transjordan. The fully de-

veloped "MB I" of Palestine proper derived from and naturally overlapped with these early phases. Since our terminology and chronology have developed largely from the later phases of this culture—which until recently have been the better known of the two—the categories are not wholly applicable to the Transjordanian material. A complete stratigraphic sequence from a single site would be desirable. But eventually typological developments within certain ceramic forms common to both banks of the Jordan may yield the best clues to the "EB IV"/"MB I" transition: the four-spouted lamps, the "hole-mouth" and flat-bottomed cooking pots, the grooved-rim teapots, and the inverted rilled-rim bowls. The disappearance of red slip and burnish may also become a major criterion. Older generalizations about the disappearance of ledge-handles and the "Canaanean" flint blades within the period will have to be re-examined. Note that flat-bottomed cooking pots are said to be typical at 'Arô'er (cf. fig. 5:12), in which case they would be the earliest well-stratified examples and would modify somewhat our conclusions in n. 65.

88. See Paul Lapp, *Biblical Archaeology and History* (1969), p. 73, Pl. 13. The MB I occupation at this site was first noted, incidentally, by Glueck; see *AASOR*, 25–28 (1951), pp. 394–98.

89. See Gophna, "A Middle Bronze Age I Cemetery at Ma'abarot," *Qadmoniot*, II (1969), pp. 50–51 (in Hebrew). Note also in the same issue the valuable survey of MB I pottery by Ruth Amiran (pp. 45–49); and Moshe Kochavi's résumé with further details on the settlement at Har Yeruḥam (pp. 38–44). The latter adds several new sites in Israel discovered by chance finds to his map of the period—among them: Qadesh, Meiron, Kh. Khalil, Chorazin, and Nazareth (all in Galilee); and Tell Regev (in the Valley of Jezreel, east of Haifa). Note that on this map Jebel Qa'aqīr is still referred to as "el-Fûl" (cf. n. 75 above). (Professor Dever notes that he made additions to his article in February 1970.—Ed.)

NORTHERN CANAAN AND THE
MARI TEXTS

Abraham Malamat

I

WHEREAS the royal archives at Mari fairly well document the broad ties with northern and central Syria, which have received considerable attention in recent studies,[1] the area farther to the southwest is only sparingly mentioned. The localities named in southern Syria and northern Canaan are the "land of Amurru," the "land of Āpum" (the Damascus region), Byblos on the Phoenician coast[2] and, within Palestine, Hazor and (as shall be seen below) Laish.

In our previous treatment on the kingdom of Hazor in the second millennium BC,[3] we dealt with the relevant epigraphic material which was known a decade ago, especially that from Mari: two letters and an economic text, as well as several still unpublished documents. In the two letters, Baḥdilim, prefect of the palace at Mari, reports to Zimrilim, the last ruler of the kingdom, of groups of messengers arriving at Mari from different directions. In one of the letters (*ARM* VI, 78)[4] missions from Mari and Babylon have arrived back from Hazor and Qatna (el-Mishrife, 18 km. north of Homs). Each mission was accompanied by a native escort (*ālik idi*) from Hazor or Qatna, following current diplomatic procedure.[5] In the second letter (*ARM* VI, 23), missions from six Mesopotamian cities have arrived at Mari on their way west to Yamḥad (capital: Aleppo), Qatna, Hazor and a fourth place, the name of which is illegible. The following damaged lines deal with the impending arrival of messengers from Yamḥad, a place whose name is broken here, and Carchemish, bound for various destinations south and east of Mari.[6]

In the economic tablet, Hazor is mentioned alongside Yamḥad as the destination of shipments of tin (*ARM* VII, 236). This metal, essential for the manufacture of bronze, was one of the major goods marketed in the west by Mari, which in turn imported it apparently from the mountainous region in northwestern Iran (and not Elam), by way of such places as Shemshāra (ancient Shusharrā) and Tell al-Rimah.[7] This accords with the archaeological evidence in Syria and Palestine, where there was a considerable production of bronze utensils in the Middle Bronze IIB Age—the earlier part of which corresponds with the Mari period (see below). In the above document, over ten minas (i.e. about five kilograms) of tin are sent to Hazor. As the ratio of copper to tin in the bronze alloy of this general period ranged between 6:1 and 9:1,[8] this tin shipment was sufficient for some thirty to forty-five kilograms of bronze utensils.

We also have an additional document from an administrative archive of the palace at Mari (*ARM* XII, 747) which mentions Hazor.[9] It contains a list of eighteen persons, messengers from various localities, artisans, singers and even a priest, who were supplied with cuts of mutton during their stay at the palace of Zimrilim. The list includes messengers who came from the southeast of Mari (Babylon and Esh-nunna), the Upper Euphrates (Carchemish and Emar on the Great Bend of the Euphrates) and from the west—two from Yamḫad and one from Hazor (*Ḫa-ṣú-ra-yu*^{*ki*}; line 3). Whether these persons were in transit or otherwise,[10] this is a clear record of the accommodation Mari afforded to messengers from places even as far away as Hazor.

Further, a letter sent by Shamshi-Adad, king of Assyria, to his son Yasmaḫ-Adad, viceroy at Mari, bears witness to the stay of messengers from Qatna, Hazor and the land of Amurru at Mari and refers to their subsequent return home. Shamshi-Adad instructs his son that the messenger of Ishḫi-Adad, king of Qatna, is to be entrusted with the care of messengers from Hazor and from four kings of Amurru for the leg of their journey homeward up to Qatna. It is unfortunate that this letter, of extraordinary historical importance, has not yet been published in full.[11] It contains the earliest reference to Hazor and, thus far, is the only one from the period of the Assyrian interregnum at Mari, prior to the restoration of Zimrilim to the throne of the local dynasty. It is witness also to the important status of Qatna at this time, the king of that city being a loyal ally of Shamshi-Adad and the father-in-law of Yasmaḫ-Adad (cf. *ARM* I, 77). (Rather noteworthy is a receipt of provisions [*ARM* XII, 10]—one of the few such records extant from the Assyrian interregnum—which deals solely with food supplied to a messenger from Qatna during his stay at the Mari palace.)

The center of interest in this letter, however, is its mention of "the messengers of four kings of Amurru" (*4 šarrāni* ^{*meš*} *A-[mu]-ur-ri-i*).

This most likely does not refer to "Amorite" kings in an ethnic sense, but rather to the rulers of four political units apparently spreading around petty urban centers in the country of "Amurru." Amurru as a definite geographical and political entity at that time is attested to in another Mari document which specifically mentions the "land of Amurru" (*ma-at A-[m]u-ri-im^{ki}*) alongside the "land of Yamḥad" and the "land of Qatna." The land of Amurru is again attested in several slightly later tablets from Alalaḫ as being the place of origin of horses and grooms, merchants and other persons.[12]

In the Mari period, Amurru was not headed by a single ruler, but rather comprised several independent districts—in contrast to the likewise extensive north Syrian "land of Yamḥad." It does resemble the "land of Āpum" to the east, where a northern and a southern district were each headed by a separate ruler, as evidenced in the later group of Egyptian Execration Texts. The generally contemporary Mari texts may also indirectly infer two kings in *māt Āpim^{ki}*.[13] The location of Amurru—to the south of Qatna but not so far as to include the kingdom of Hazor—may be deduced from two previously mentioned Mari documents. One gives the apparent geographical sequence Yamḥad–Qatna–Amurru in a sort of itinerary; the other mentions messengers from Amurru alongside and distinct from those from Qatna and Hazor.[14]

II

The Mari documents record established diplomatic ties between Mari and Hazor, two centers some seven hundred kilometers apart by the direct route from Terqa across the desert and through Qatna, or about nine hundred kilometers via the roundabout Emar–Aleppo route.[15] The flourishing political and commercial activity undoubtedly brought in its wake the penetration of Mesopotamian cultural influences into Hazor. Indeed, such are indicated by several epigraphic finds—in cuneiform script—from Hazor proper and quite unique for Palestine:

a) Several inscribed liver models used in haruspicy. Though these are later than the Mari period, dated by the editors to the end of the Old Babylonian period (i.e. the end of the seventeenth or mid-sixteenth century BC, according to the "middle" and "low" chronologies, respectively), they do, however, indicate an enduring literary and religious tradition at Hazor, apparently stemming from the Mari period.[16]

b) A fragmentary lexical tablet of the series ḪAR-*ra=ḫubullu,* a chance find in an excavational dump from MB II–LB I strata. Pending publica-

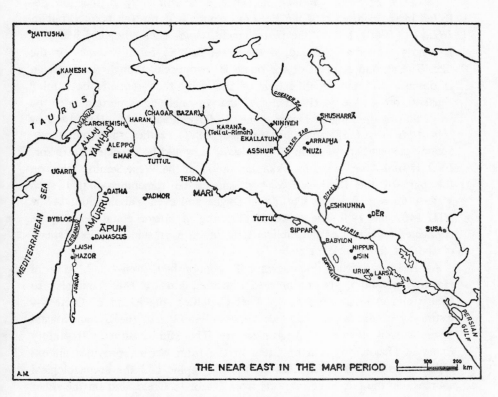

Figure 1. The Near East in the Mari Period.

tion, this seems to date generally to the Mari period.[17]

c) A personal name incised on a pottery jar (see below) found in the lower city of Hazor, in a context apparently from the MB IIB.[18] This inscription and the lexical tablet above are the earliest instances of cuneiform script yet found in Palestine.[19] Knowledge of this script reached Hazor probably in the Mari period, possibly from Mari itself.

Evidence of Mesopotamian influence at Hazor may further be detected in the character of the personal name, (c), for (as pointed out in *JBL*, 79 [1960], p. 18) the first element, *išme-* (i.e. "[he] has heard"), is clearly Akkadian, instead of the West Semitic form *yasmaḫ-* or the like. The second element of the name is theophoric, though the last sign is obscure and the identification of the deity thus remains doubtful.[20] Furthermore, in the Mari texts, of all the personal names pertaining to the west, that of the king of Hazor alone is of Akkadian form: *Ibni-Adad* or *Ibni-Addu* ("Adad/Hadad has created/built"), rather than the corresponding West Semitic form *Yabni-Addu,* as would be expected at Hazor. Even if Ibni-Adad were an Akkadianization of the West Semitic form on the part of the Mari scribes,[21] it should be remembered that such scribes did record names like Yabni-Dagan and even Yabni-Addu (*ARM* VII, 140, line 14). The name of this king of Hazor could possibly be connected with that of the biblical king Jabin, a presumed hypocoristicon of the full theophoric name.[22]

As is known from documents still unpublished, Ibni-Adad, king of Hazor, sent shipments not only to Zimrilim, king of Mari, but also to Ugarit and even to Kaptara (biblical Caphtor), the island of Crete[23]— testimony of the widespread ties between Hazor and the Syrian coastal towns as well as with the Aegean sphere. The Middle Minoan II pottery found at Hazor,[24] typical of Crete in the Mari period, provides an excellent case of correlation between the epigraphic and the archaeological sources: on the one hand, exports from Hazor to Crete, and on the other hand, imports in the opposite direction.

An important unedited text from the Mari administrative archives contains a long list of persons from various localities, amongst whom is Ibni-Adad, king of Hazor. In this same list appears the city-name Laish (*La-yi-iš*).[25] This city, later known as Dan, lies some thirty kilometers north of Hazor and is thus now the second site within Palestine proper to be mentioned in the Mari documents. Though a full evaluation can come only after actual publication of the text in question, the mere mention of this town is indicative of its status in this period.

Moreover, Laish and Hazor are the only sites in northern Palestine which have been excavated systematically in recent years—though on different scales—yielding important remains from the Middle Bronze II period. Thus, despite the relative wealth of archaeological and epigraphical data on Hazor as against that on Laish, the two together are most significant for comparative historical-archaeological research, and can serve as similar test cases in the confrontation of the various epigraphical sources with the archaeological evidence. Indeed, Hazor and Laish are mentioned also in the later group of Execration Texts from Egypt and, in spite of the great difference in size of the two sites, the excavations have revealed similar archaeological results concerning the Middle Bronze II strata. The hitch, however, is that since the absolute chronology of each of the factors is still under dispute there are several possibilities for a chronological correlation between the epigraphic sources themselves and between them and the archaeological evidence.

A. Mari and the later Execration Texts

All the references to Hazor (except one, as seen above), Laish, Āpum and Byblos in the Mari archives are, evidently, from the time of Zimrilim. These same four places also appear in the later group of Egyptian Execration Texts (but note here the "tribe" of Byblos, rather than "ruler" as with the other places). According to the "low" Babylonian chronology, Zimrilim reigned in 1720–1700 BC, whereas the "middle" Babylonian chronology, followed today especially by students of Mesopotamia, would put his rule in the years 1780–1760 BC—both in round figures.[26] If the "low" reckoning is followed, there is little relevancy to the various datings of the later Execration Texts since, in any case, they would antedate the period of Zimrilim. Following the "middle" chronology, however, their precise dating becomes crucial, for they are generally placed anywhere in the period from the third quarter of the nineteenth century BC down to a century later.[27] In other words, this very dating is the key factor in the proper correlation of the later Execration Texts and the Mari documents and thus also in the ensuing historical picture.

A case in point is whether the rulers of Hazor, Laish and Āpum mentioned in the Egyptian texts are earlier or later than those alluded to in the Mari archives—a matter which cannot as yet be settled.[28] In any event, there is a definite onomastic correspondence between the distinctly West Semitic name of the ruler of Laish in the Execration Texts and that of a private person at Mari: Ḥ(?)w3n'b[.] and *Ḥawrānabi*,[29] respectively.

B. Mari and the archaeological evidence at Hazor and Laish

The images of Hazor and Laish in the Mari documents, as a prime political center and a city worthy of commercial attention, should coincide with the well-fortified, flourishing settlements which rose on these sites early in the Middle Bronze IIB period. The absence of remains indicative of a true city in the MB IIA period at either site indeed furthers this assumption. In the upper city of Hazor, whereas the ceramic finds of the MB IIA period are quite meager and no contemporary fortifications or structures were found, the MB IIB period is represented by a wealth of small finds and the remains of a palace or fortress, a temple (found in the 1968 season) and a massive wall protecting the acropolis (stratum XVII). At the beginning of the MB IIB, an immense lower city—a rectangle of some seven hundred by one thousand meters was founded on the north of the tell, fortified with mighty ramparts and uniquely large gates (stratum 4 in the lower city).[30] It was this newly established, bustling lower city which must have attracted Mari and the other Mesopotamian kingdoms to the Hazor of Ibni-Adad.

The situation at Laish was the same in essence. The excavations carried out in 1966–69 at Tel Dan (Tell el-Qādi), one of the largest mounds in Palestine, have revealed an extensive and flourishing MB IIB settlement.[31] Terre pisée ramparts, outstanding in plan and execution, enclose an area of some two hundred dunams. The inner slopes of these defenses were settled already at an early stage, and the pottery found there notably includes wares of North Syrian (e.g., Tell Atchana) type.

The synchronization between the Mari texts and the archaeological evidence from Hazor and Laish articulates the matter of absolute chronology relating to both the archaeological and the historical data. For if the start of the MB IIB period is fixed in the mid-eighteenth century BC (e.g., Yadin, at Hazor) or, all the more, at the end of that century (e.g., Albright in his latest publications), the "low" chronology must be applied to the Mari period.[32] But adopting the "middle" Babylonian chronology, this archaeological period must be dated earlier, as recently suggested by K. Kenyon and B. Mazar who put the transition between MB IIA and MB IIB (MB I and MB II, in Kenyon's terminology) around 1800 BC, or thereabouts.[33] Even if the "low" Babylonian chronology is accepted, it would seem (especially in the light of the case of Hazor) that the start of MB IIB could not possibly fall as late as the end of the eighteenth century BC. A dating such as the latter would necessitate the doubtful conclusion that the contacts between Hazor and Mari in the days of Shamshi-Adad be related to the meager, open settlement on this site in the MB IIA period. For Shamshi-Adad ruled over Mari until *circa* 1720 BC, at latest, even according to adherants of the "low" chronology (and according to Albright to only 1728 BC, or somewhat earlier; see above, n. 26).

III

A further facet of the Mari texts touching upon northern Canaan can serve to elucidate certain biblical traditions[34] on pre-Israelite Palestine, in particular on Hazor and Laish. We have already assumed that the parenthetic remark in Josh. 11:10—"for Hazor *beforetime* was the head of all those kingdoms"—may refer to the city's traditional pre-eminence starting back in the Middle Bronze Age.[35] Indeed, the very wording calls to mind the central kingdoms of the Mari period—besides Mari itself, Babylon, Larsa and Eshnunna in southern Mesopotamia, and Qatna and Yamḥad in the west—each of which held sway over ten to twenty vassal kings.[36]

Another Canaanite city, Hebron, is definitely the subject of a biblical tradition harking back to the MB II period: "Now Hebron was built seven years before Zoan in Egypt" (Num. 13:22). As Tanis (Zoan) is known to have been established as the Hyksos capital around 1720 BC, the "founding" of Hebron must have occurred in approximately the same distant period—and possibly in similar historical circumstances—as that of the expanded Hazor of MB IIB.[37] And, indeed, archaeological soundings in 1964–66 carried out at Jebel er-Rumeideh, one of the sites of ancient Hebron, revealed several occupational phases and remains of a massive rampart from the MB IIB.[38]

As for Laish, this erstwhile name in the biblical tradition 'And they called the name of the city Dan, after the name of Dan their father. . . . howbeit, the name of the city was Laish at the first' (Jud. 18:29) is now confirmed in the Mari texts as well as in the later Execration Texts (E 59) and the topographical list of Thutmes III (No. 31). But whereas the Egyptian sources give the name in the untidy forms *3wsy* and *r/lws,* the Akkadian transcription at Mari exactly renders the Hebrew form (but compare also the form Leshem, possibly corrupt, in Josh. 19:47). Several additional examples of change of early Canaanite place-names are preserved in the Bible, the closest typologically to the Laish/Dan case being those of Bashan/Havvoth-jair and Kenath/Nobah, made to conform with the names of the tribal groups who had conquered and occupied these sites (Num. 32:41 f.; Deut. 3:14). Lacking relevant external sources from the second millennium BC, however, the other biblical changes of place-names are deprived of the substance present in the renaming of Laish/Dan.[39]

The occurrence of the name Dan in the Patriarchal narratives (Gen. 14:14) is a clear anachronism. Dan may originally have been paired here with Laish (or Leshem), like the several other paired toponyms in the unique source comprising Gen. 14 (cf. vv. 2–3, 7, 17), but in this case the archaic element has fallen by some editorial wayside. Despite the late form of the chapter as it stands, it obviously incorporates an early tradition on the campaign of Chedorlaomer and his allies to Transjordan and the Negev, which in turn preserved certain archaic historical features.[40] One such feature seems to be the phenomenon of four kings of the east (as well as the nature of their names) rallying in a joint military venture. This is actually a faithful reflection of the political circumstances typical of Mesopotamia and Syria in the Old Babylonian period, when the area was divided among several central powers, which would enter from time to time into military alliances.

Mutual ventures to the west on the part of Mesopotamian rulers—though of a quite different character from the episode in Gen. 14—are evidenced in one of the Mari letters mentioning Hazor (*ARM* VI, 23). As seen above (pp. 164–65) Syria-Palestine was the destination of missions making rendezvous at Mari from six widely separated kingdoms: Babylon on the Lower Euphrates; Ekallātum on the Tigris north of the city of Asshur; Eshnunna, Qabrā and Arrapḫa, all three beyond the Tigris; and Karanā, recently identified with Tell al-Rimah between the Tigris and the Upper Habur (see map, p. 167).[41] In sum, we have in this letter an informative picture of the historical reality which may have served as the setting for epic or pseudo-historical compositions such as the biblical account of the four eastern kings joining in a campaign to the far west.

FOOTNOTES

1. Cf. F. M. Tocci, *La Siria nell'età di Mari* (*Studi Semitici*, 3 [1960]); J. R. Kupper, "North Meospotamia and Syria," *CAH²*, II, fasc. 14 (1963); H. Klengel: *Geschichte Syriens im 2. Jahrtausend v.u. Z. I—Nordsyrien* (1965) (and bibliographical references in all these); cf. also A. Malamat, *Eretz-Israel*, 5 (1958), pp. 67–73 (Hebrew) on the ties between the local dynasty of Mari and the Aleppo region.

2. The documents on Byblos and Āpum have not yet been published; for G. Dossin's preliminary remarks, cf. *Syr*, 20 (1939), pp. 109 ff. Byblos in this context will be treated on another occasion; the land of Āpum mentioned here must be differentiated from another country of the same name occurring in the Mari and Cappadocian texts, located in the Habur region (cf. M. Falkner in *AfO*, 18 [1957], p. 2)—a fact recently re-emphasized by W. F. Albright, *YGC* (1968), p. 58, n. 30, and cf. his earlier "The Land of Damascus between 1850 and 1750 B.C.," *BASOR*, No. 83 (1941), pp. 30 ff.

3. A. Malamat, "Hazor 'The Head of All Those Kingdoms,'" *JBL*, 79 (1960), pp. 12–19.

4. *ARM=Archives Royales de Mari*, ed. by A. Parrot & G. Dossin (1950–).

5. Cf. J. M. Munn-Rankin, "Diplomacy in Western Asia in the Early Second Millennium B.C.," *Iraq*, 18 (1965), pp. 106 ff., where, in addition, failure to supply such escorts is shown to have been contrary to usual diplomatic practice. For *ālik idi*, cf. also *CAD* A/1, p. 343.

6. This is the probable restoration of lines 28–30, parallel to the construction of the previous paragraph (lines 19–24). The last destination in line 29 should be restored [*Ar-ra-*]*ap*(!)-*ḫi-im*—Arrapḫa across the Tigris—parallel to the last city in the first list of messengers who arrived at Mari (line 22).

7. For the geographical source of tin in the Mari period, see now W. F. Leemans in *JESHO*, 9 (1968), pp. 201 ff. For Tell al-Rimah as a tin emporium, see now D. Oates in *Iraq*, 30 (1968), pp. 137 f.; and cf. H. W. F. Saggs, *ibid.*, p. 154 as well as D. J. Wiseman, *ibid.*, pp. 175 ff. For tin trade at Shemshāra, see J. Laessøe, *Acta Orientalia*, 24 (1959), pp. 83 ff.

8. Cf. H. Limet, *Le travail du métal au pays de Sumer* (1960), pp. 67 ff.; B. Landsberger, *JNES*, 24 (1965), p. 292.

9. See M. Birot: *Textes administratifs de la salle 5 du Palais*, *ARM* XII (1964), pp. 4 f., 238 f.

10. J. M. Sasson, *BASOR*, No. 190 (1968), p. 53, interprets the *entire* group as artisans working at Mari, which is stretching the evidence.

11. See *Or*, 19 (1950), p. 509; J. R. Kupper, *Les nomades en Mésopotamie au temps des rois de Mari* (hereinafter Kupper, *Nomades*) (1957), p. 179, n. 1, for a first report of this document (No. A. 2760). Additional details of its contents have subsequently been published; cf. G. Dossin, "Kengen, pays de Canaan," *RSO*, 32 (1957), pp. 37 f. Another form of contact with the far west is found in Shamshi-Adad's campaign to the Lebanon and Phoenician coast; cf. A. Malamat in *Studies in Honor of B. Landsberger*, *Assyriological Studies*, 16 (1965), pp. 370 ff.

12. For the second document from Mari, see Dossin's article (above, n. 11), as

well as A. Parrot, *RHPR*, 30 (1950), p. 7. For Amurru here and in the Alalaḫ texts, see *JBL*, 79 (1960), p. 16; Kupper, *Nomades*, pp. 179 ff., and now also *CAD* A/2, p. 94a.

13. For Āpum in the Mari documents, see above, n. 2. Since the texts are as yet unpublished, it is not clear whether the two kings—Zuzu and Ḫayabum—were contemporaries ruling over neighboring districts or successive rulers over one realm. The name Ḫayabum was recently discussed by E. Lipinsky in *Syr*, 44 (1967), pp. 260 f. For Āpum in the Execration Texts, see G. Posener, *Princes et pays d'Asie et de Nubie* (1940): E 33 (name of ruler broken), E 34 (name of ruler either *'ḫwk3k3* or *'ḫwkbkb* [Albright]).

14. Cf. I. J. Gelb, *JCS*, 15 (1961), pp. 43 f. In this important study, Gelb further argues, on linguistic grounds, that Hazor and Amurru were two distinct areas, the former within the Canaanite sphere (with its *ā>ō* shift), and the latter within the "Amorite" sphere (with long *ā* preserved)—a geographical application that here, however, seems too rigid. Gelb regards the Akkadian transcription of *Ḥaṣūra* in the Mari texts as the oldest example of the *ā>ō* change, and thus the earliest evidence for the Canaanite language. No such shift, though, is necessitated if *Ḥaṣūr* is regarded as a *qatūl* formation, as would be the place-name *Naḫūr* (biblical Naḫōr) in Mari and other early cuneiform texts, a parallel form.

15. While the safer route through Aleppo was generally preferred, the desert route was used in the time of Shamshi-Adad, as he was on hostile terms with Yamḫad; see Kupper, *op. cit.* (above, n. 1), pp. 19 ff.

16. B. Landsberger and H. Tadmor, "Fragments of Clay Liver Models from Hazor," *IEJ*, 14 (1964), pp. 201 ff. The Hazor livers contain elements characteristic of the "archaic" type of liver models from Mari, the latter dating from the beginning of the second millennium BC. The editors of the Hazor livers note that scribal craft and extispicy may have spread to Hazor from Mari. For the various categories of liver models, see now also J. Nougayrol, *RA*, 62 (1968), pp. 31 ff. It is interesting to note that in *ARM* I, 66, lines 5–8, a liver model (*šērum*) is sent through Mari to Qatna by Shamshi-Adad; for UZU=*šērum* in this sense, rather than "oracle," cf. now *CAD* A/1. p. 346 (s.v. *aliktu*).

17. I thank Profs. Y. Yadin and H. Tadmor for these details and the permission to mention them here. The tablet is to be published by Professor Tadmor.

18. See Y. Yadin *et al.*, *Hazor*, II (1960), p. 115. This is a locally manufactured vessel found in a stratum 4 (the earliest occupational stratum in the lower city—MB IIB) or stratum 3 (MB IIC) context. The first possibility is preferred by the excavators.

19. From apparently the same general period is an arrowhead from Lebanon (now Musée de Beyrouth No. 2951), bearing two cuneiform signs, as shown by F. M. Cross in *Eretz-Israel*, 8 (1966), pp. 19*-20*. Still earlier (evidently Ur III period) are, from Byblos, a cuneiform syllabary, cf. W. F. Albright, *BASOR*, No. 163 (1961), p. 45 and n. 46 (dated there by W. W. Hallo); and a cylinder seal with cuneiform inscription, cf. M. Dunand, *Fouilles de Byblos*, I, Texte (1939), p. 313, No. 4183; *idem, Atlas* (1937), Pl. CXXV, now read by W. W. Hallo (in a private communication to the author, dated December 1968): Ušumgal/dumu *ir-ra-ba-ni*/ dam-gàr(a).

20. For this inscription see P. Artzi and A. Malamat, *apud* Y. Yadin *et al.*, *op. cit.* (above, n. 18), pp. 115 f.; Pls. CXII: 9; CLXXX; and the suggested readings by W. F. Albright and F. M. Th. de Liagre Böhl given there. The last sign, following Böhl, is closest to LAM, though it should not be taken as a phonetic complement of the preceding symbol, which would result in a form contrary to normal Akkadian syntax. In a letter dated April 1967, Böhl now proposes that **Lam* is a dialectic

variant of *Lim*, the West Semitic deity so prominent in the onomasticon of the Mari texts. The name would thus read *mIš-me-dLam* ("the god Lam has heard"). For other readings of the theophoric element, see R. Tournay, *RB*, 69 (1962), p. 475: *dLibittum* (=SIG₄); G. G. Cameron, *apud* H. B. Huffmon, *APN* (1965), p. 16: *dTišpak*. Albright has abandoned his former reading *mIš-me-dAdad* and now renders the name *mIš-me-ilum*, by entirely dismissing the last sign; see *BASOR*, No. 159 (1960), p. 38.

21. Kupper (*Nomades*, p. 237, n. 1) regards the name as truly Akkadian, while Gelb (*JCS*, 15, p. 39, n. 37) and M. Noth (*Die Ursprünge des alten Israel im Lichte neuer Quellen* [1961], pp. 23 f., n. 41) consider it only as an "Akkadianized" form of a West Semitic name. However, Noth's similar conclusion concerning the name of the Hazor jug is justly refuted by Huffmon, *APN*, pp. 16 f.

22. See W. F. Albright, *The Biblical Period from Abraham to Ezra* (1963), p. 102, n. 83. If so, the name Jabin, which appears in two different episodes in the Bible (i.e. in the stories of Joshua and Deborah) is based on an early onomastic archetype that may have been used at Hazor as a dynastic name, like Ben-Hadad in the later kingdom of Aram-Damascus.

23. Cf. G. Dossin, *Comptes rendus, Ire rencontre assyriologique internationale* (1951), p. 21; *Or*, 19 (1950), p. 509.

24. For the Aegean "Kamares" ware uncovered in the lower city of Hazor, see Yadin *et al.*, *op. cit.* (above, n. 18), p. 91; Pl. CXV: 12–13.

25. I am obliged to Prof. G. Dossin who kindly communicated to me details of this document, which he is about to publish. Cf. A. Parrot, *Enciclopedia de la Biblia*, IV (1964), col. 1308; and A. Malamat, *XVe rencontre assyriologique internationale (La Civilisation de Mari)*, ed. by J. R. Kupper (1967), p. 138 (postscript).

26. The several chronological systems have been appraised recently by, e.g., M. B. Rowton, "Chronology," *CAH²*, II, fasc. 4 (1962), pp. 23 ff. (and the bibliography there) and H. Tadmor, "The Chronology of the Ancient Near East in the Second Millennium B.C.," *The World History of the Jewish People*, II (ed. by B. Mazar, 1967), pp. 40 ff. (Hebrew). Both these tend to accept the "middle" chronology, as did, e.g., Mrs. H. Lewy in her specific study "The Chronology of the Mari Texts," *XVe rencontre assyriologique* (1967), pp. 13 ff. In contrast Albright, an adamant adherent of the "low" chronology, dates Zimrilim's reign to 1728–1697 BC, attributing to him thirty-two years on the basis of the known year formulae; see *YGC*, p. 232 (k). But for a shorter reign for Zimrilim, see now W. Röllig, *XVe rencontre assyriologique*, pp. 97 ff.

27. For the dating of the later Execration Texts, and their historical significance, see most recently Albright, *BASOR*, No. 184 (1966), p. 28 (later part of the XIIth Dynasty, 1850–1825 BC); W. Helck, *Die Beziehungen Ägyptens zu Vorderasien* . . . (1962), p. 53; J. van Seters, *The Hyksos: A New Investigation* (1966), pp. 78 ff. (start of the XIIIth Dynasty=the first half of the eighteenth century BC); and B. Mazar, *IEJ*, 18 (1968), pp. 75 (n. 23), 81 (reign of Neferhotep=third quarter of the eighteenth century BC).

28. For the Execration Texts, see G. Posener, *op. cit.* (above, n. 13): E 15—Hazor; E 33–34—Āpum; E 59—Laish. According to Mazar's scheme, the *Gt'* of these texts reigned at Hazor after Ibni-Adad, and was possibly the founder of a new dynasty there; see *IEJ*, 18 (1969), p. 83, n. 51.

29. The correct rendering of this name, *Ḥa-aw*(PI)-*ra-an-a-bi* instead of *Ḥa-wi-ra-an-a-bi*, is given by Huffmon, *APN*, p. 32 and n. 44. For the prominent Canaanite god Ḥoron appearing as the theophoric element in this name, see M. H. Pope and W. Röllig: *Wörterbuch der Mythologie*, I, ed. by E. W. Haussig (1965),

pp. 288 f.; R. Stadelmann, *Syrisch-palästinensische Gottheiten in Ägypten* (1967), pp. 76 ff.

30. For the most recent summaries of the Hazor excavation, see Y. Yadin, in *The Encyclopaedia of Archaeological Excavations in the Holy Land* (Sample Fascicle, 1964), pp. 8 ff.; *idem*, "Hazor," *AOTS* (1967), pp. 245 ff. For the 1968 season of excavations at Hazor, see *IEJ*, 19 (1969), pp. 1 ff.

To the huge lower cities at Hazor, Qatna and Carchemish (cf. Malamat, *JBL*, 79 [1960], p. 19; Mazar, *IEJ*, 18 [1968], p. 83), we may now add that at Tell Mardikh, some seventy kilometers south of Aleppo on the way to Qatna. The ramparts of the lower city surrounding Tell Mardikh enclose an area of seven hundred by nine hundred meters; see P. Matthiae *et al.*, *Missione archaeologica Italiana in Siria (Tel Mardikh), Campagna 1964* (1965); *Campagna 1965* (1966); *Campagna 1966* (1967). The excavators have ascribed the fortifications of the lower city to the MB I period (no later than 2000–1900 BC); P. Parr, *ZDPV*, 84 (1968), pp. 33 ff., has suggested a later date, analogous with the other lower cities mentioned above.

31. For preliminary details on the four seasons of excavations, directed by Dr. A. Biran on behalf of the Israel Department of Antiquities and Museums, see A. Biran in *All the Land of Naphtali* (1967), pp. 21 ff.; *Ḥadashot Arkheologiot*, 22–23 (1967), pp. 4 ff.; 25 (1968), pp. 1 ff.; 28–29 (1969), pp. 1 ff.; 31–32 (1969), pp. 1 ff. (Hebrew); and *IEJ*, 16 (1966), pp. 144 f.; 19 (1969), pp. 121 ff.

32. For Yadin's opinion, and the chronological considerations he raises concerning Hazor in the Execration Texts, see his contribution in *AOTS*, p. 258. For Albright's latest views, see *BASOR* No. 176 (1964), p. 44; No. 184 (1966), p. 27; and cf. G. E. Wright in *BANE* (1961), pp. 88 ff. (MB IIB±1750/1700–1650/1625 BC).

33. See Mazar's comprehensive study, "The Middle Bronze Age in Palestine," *IEJ*, 18 (1968), pp. 65–97, and the Chronological Chart on p. 97. Mazar relates the later Execration Texts with MB IIB, which would certainly fit the archaeological situation at Hazor and Laish. Miss Kenyon, though she, too, fixes the start of the MB IIB (her MB II) at the beginning of the eighteenth century BC, places the founding of the lower city at Hazor late in the same century. See K. Kenyon, "Palestine in the Middle Bronze Age," *CAH*[2], II, fasc. 48 (1966), pp. 13, 24 f. For a review of the various chronological systems proposed for the phases of the Middle Bronze Age, and their possible ethnic attributions, see now also C. H. J. de Geus. "De Amorieten in de Palestijnse archeologie: een recente theorie kritisch bezien," *NedTTs*, 23 (1968), pp. 1–24.

34. For the genealogy of Nahor (Gen. 22:20–24) in this light, see our remarks in *XVᵉ rencontre assyriologique* (above, n. 25), pp. 129 ff.; to this we may add that the territory represented by the four sons of Nahor's concubine corresponds roughly with that of the (four) kings of Amurru mentioned in one of the above Mari texts.

35. See *JBL*, 79 (1960), p. 19. In contrast, Yadin assumes that this passage relates to the period of the Israelite conquest "from the [biblical] narrator's point-of-view"; see *AOTS*, p. 261, n. 12.

36. This political situation is depicted in an illuminating report sent to Zimrilim by Itūr-Asdu, one of his agents; see G. Dossin, *Syr*, 19 (1938), p. 117.

37. The "former" name of Hebron—Kiriath-(ha)Arba, seemingly having the literal meaning "city of four (sides or quarters)"—may allude to a giant city resembling Hazor, for in the biblical tradition the name Arba is ascribed to "a great man among the Anakim (i.e. giants)" or "the father of Anak" (Josh 14:15; 15:13; cf. also 21:11). For the Hyksos foundation of Hebron, and the meaning

of "Kiriath-Arba" as a "Vierstadt," see S. Mowinckel, "Die Gründung von Hebron," *Donum Natalicium H.S. Nyberg Oblatum* (1955), pp. 185 ff. See also B. Maisler, "Hebron," *Dinaburg Jubilee Volume* (1947), pp. 310 ff. (Hebrew).

38. See P. C. Hammond, *RB*, 72 (1965), pp. 267 ff.; 73 (1966), pp. 566 ff.; 75 (1968), pp. 253 ff.

39. For this and the other topographical renamings in the Bible, see the author's paper "The Danite Migration and the Pan-Israelite Exodus-Conquest: A Biblical Narrative Pattern," *Biblica*, 51 (1970), pp. 1 ff. We have attempted to demonstrate there that the literary account of the land-hungry tribe of Dan, culminating in the conquest of Laish (Jud. 18), was a model in miniature of a biblical narrative pattern serving for campaigns of inheritance—which pattern was followed on a much larger, pan-tribal scale in the Exodus-Conquest cycle.

40. Thus, for instance, N. Glueck has repeatedly pointed out (e.g., *Rivers in the Desert* [1968], pp. 71 ff.) a link between the occupational suspension on the MB I sites in Transjordan and the Negev and the military campaign of the four eastern kings; the tradition in ch. 14 could thus go back to the beginning of the second millennium BC. Among recent advocates of the early date of Gen. 14 are E. A. Speiser, *Genesis* (1964), pp. 102 ff. (who even assumed an Akkadian origin for the chapter); Albright, *BASOR*, No. 163 (1961), pp. 49 ff.; *YGC*, pp. 60 f.; K. A. Kitchen, *Ancient Orient and Old Testament* (1966), pp. 43 ff.; and cf. N. M. Sarna, *Understanding Genesis* (1966), pp. 110 ff.

41. The site of Qabrā is somewhere to the north of the Lesser Zab. As for the location of Ekallātum, see now W. W. Hallo, "The Road to Emar," *JCS*, 18 (1964), p. 72. For Karanā as Tell al-Rimah, and the hundreds of tablets from the Old Babylonian period (including some sent by Zimrilim, i.e., from approximately the same time as our Mari letter) found there in 1967, see S. Page, *Iraq*, 30 (1968), pp. 87 ff.; and cf. D. Oates, *ibid.*, pp. 136 f.

THE SALTIER OF ATARGATIS RECONSIDERED

Marvin H. Pope

THIS paper attempts to shed light on an item of dress or decoration found on numerous representations of goddesses over a wide range of space and time, from the Levant to India, beginning in the third millennium BC— the saltier or chest bands in the form of the *crux decussata* or St. Andrew's Cross. This brief study is offered as a token of personal esteem and gratitude for the long and distinguished career of Nelson Glueck, whose lively archaeological interests extend beyond potsherds and walls to deities and dolphins, and include the trappings of Atargatis.

In 1947, M. le Comte du Mesnil du Buisson[1] devoted a study to this feature and demonstrated the extraordinary range, persistence and fixity of this *bijou divin,* as he termed it. The documentation of this feature could be extended considerably with additional specimens, published and unpublished (including an excellent example on a terra cotta figurine recently excavated at Gezer), but the present interest is to explain the motif rather than to augment the already ample documentation of it.

The explanation offered by du Buisson[2] was not wholly persuasive. He suggested that the ornament was perhaps inspired by the use of the cross as a symbol of the planet Venus which came to be regarded as an amulet or preservative against the evil eye, a symbol intended to arrest or neutralize every sort of charm inimical to fecundity and love, or other evil enterprise. He emphasized the potency of the cross as a magical symbol, noting that among certain peoples it was even considered dangerous to cross one's legs. The knot or protuberance, sometimes seen at the intersection of the crossbands between the breasts, according to du Buisson, served as a sure defense against sorcery. The knot of the saltier of Atargatis he related to the knot of Isis and to the magical knot of the *ankh* sign, the Egyptian symbol of life, which supposedly served as the model for amulets.

In 1960 a more detailed study of the cross chest bands was made by

Figure 1

Figure 2

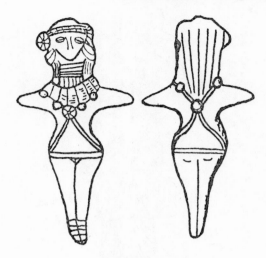

Figure 3

George F. Dales as part of a doctoral dissertation dealing with the elaborate necklaces, bands and belts which decorate Mesopotamian terra cotta female figurines.[3] The chest bands appear first on Mesopotamian figurines of the Obeid period but are found later in Anatolia, Syria-Palestine, and Iran. Farther west, they are seen on statues and paintings of the Roman (fig. 1)[4] period, while to the east they occur as an important item of Hindu iconography of the first century BC, in the so-called *channavīra* garment of the Yakshīs, or fertility goddesses (fig. 2).[5] The link between occurrences in Mesopotamia and in India, Dales suggested, may be provided partly by the clay figurines of uncertain date from northern West Pakistan (fig. 3)[6] and the exquisite blue schist figurine of the Scytho-Parthian period from Sirkap (Taxila) (fig. 4).[7] The probability that the chest bands spread from the West to South Asia is enhanced by the association of the bands with hip-belts and girdles on similar figurines from both Mesopotamia and India.[8]

Although Dales was unconvinced by du Buisson's explanation of the origin and function of the chest bands, he was unable to provide much additional clarification. Trying to ascertain the names of the various necklaces, bands, and belts, Dales did adduce some evidence tending to support du Buisson's suggestion of magical function, at least for the *dudditu*[9] pectoral pendant. The girdle or hip-belt in Indian art, called the *mekhala,* which appears often in connection with the *channavīra* (to which it is sometimes attached), is said in the Atharva-Veda to be a long-life

Figure 4

charm.[10] The chest bands, however, in spite of their ancient, persistent, and widespread importance, remained "incomprehensible" to Dales.[11]

The significance of the chest bands thus remained elusive despite the intensity of Dales' investigation, or rather, we think, because of its limitation to clay figurines and plaques. Had the research been extended to include glyptic and painting, as attempted here, some of the mystery might have been dispelled. The writer's attention was drawn to the problem of chest bands in the course of investigating certain parallels between the goddess Anat of the Western Semites and the Indian goddess Kali. The well-known mural of the palace at Mari supplied the clue to the explanation for the puzzling chest bands herewith proposed.

In the scene depicting the investiture of the king (presumably Zimri-Lim) on a wall of the palace at Mari, (fig. 5),[12] the goddess (generally assumed to be Ishtar, although she could as well be taken for Anat) stands with her right foot on her lion, a sickle sword in her left hand, and in her right hand the rod and ring, emblems of authority.[13] The goddess wears the cross bands with the lower ends of the bands at the front—extending to and presumably attached to a belt at her waist. We may reasonably suppose that the bands are similarly connected to the belt at the back. At her back, extended above each shoulder in line with the cross bands, are weapons that are presumably attached somehow to the cross bands across her back; they may be held in a receptacle at-

Figure 5

tached to the bands. The heads of the weapons above the left shoulder
are damaged in the painting, but those above the right shoulder appear
to be a mace between two sickle swords.

Also, from Mari, a representation on the seal of Mukannishum (fig. 6)[14]

Figure 6

depicts the goddess with cross chest bands, holding a sickle sword and
standing on corpses behind a male figure who also tramples on corpses
while dispatching another victim with his sickle sword. As in the "investiture" scene on the palace mural, a goddess looks on, her arms raised
in an attitude of intercession or benediction. The war goddess, instead of
having weapons protruding behind her shoulders, has outstretched wings.

This, according to P. Amiet,[15] is the first example to date of the Winged Victories.

There are a number of representations of the goddess with weapons showing at her back but with no indication as to how they are attached and with no sign of the chest bands.[16] It may be assumed, however, that the weapons were understood to be attached to some sort of harness or contained in some kind of receptacle which in turn must have been held to the body with cords, bands or straps. An Assyrian cylinder (fig. 7),[17]

Figure 7

shows the goddess standing on her lion with bow and arrows in her left hand, a peculiar weapon at her side, and two quivers on her back at the same angle as the weapons that rise above her shoulders in the Mari mural and on a number of seal-cylinders; but no harness for holding the implements is visible. Two quivers could be worn with the slings crossed at the chest, although the arrangement of the quivers on one's back might be cumbersome and awkward. On some seals the goddess's weapons appear behind one shoulder only, but always approximately at

Figure 8

Figure 9

the angle that would correspond to the slant of a diagonal chest band (fig. 8).[18]

The same sort of chest bands worn by the goddess appear also occasionally on gods; e.g., Seth (Baal) of the famous "Stela of the year 400" (fig. 9)[19] wears cross bands decorated with circlets. Resheph (fig. 10)[20] on a stela of the Oriental Institute of the University of Chicago

Figure 10

wears plain cross straps apparently attached to a belt at the waist.

The cross chest bands, moreover, were not restricted to deities; human warriors over a large area of the ancient Near East wore them. Representations of warriors and war scenes from Egypt and Mesopotamia af-

ford ample illustration. A Theban noble of the twenty-first century BC
is represented on his funerary stela armed with bow and arrow and wearing a saltier.[21] An archer on an Eleventh Dynasty painted relief from
Deir el Bahri (Collection of the Peabody Museum, Yale University) wears
white bands crossing high on the chest and running under the arms (fig.
11).[22] Archers depicted on the wall of the tomb of Khety at Beni Hasan

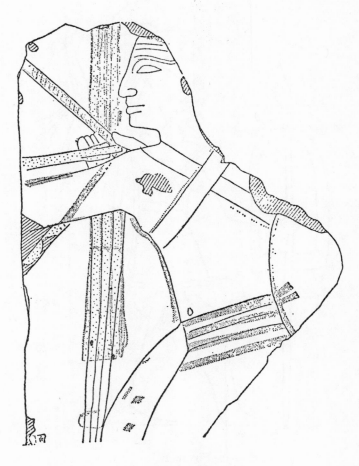

Figure 11

(*circa* 1900 BC) wear cross chest harnesses, as do the enemy in the
besieged tower. The belts with which the bands connect are not at the
waist but high on the chest, only a little below the armpits (fig. 12).[23]

Figure 12

Reliefs on the sides of the chariot of Thutmose IV show the Pharoah with wide crossed bands on his chest; some of the Syrian enemy also wear crossed bands, others a single diagonal band.[24] Ramses II is depicted in his chariot at Beit el-Wali in Nubia, bands crossing his chest and end-

Figure 13

ing in wings at the shoulders.[25] The same Pharoah, wearing the same sort of wing-tipped cross bands, is shown on foot in another Beit el-Weli painted relief, smiting a Libyan captive with the sickle sword. The hapless Libyan wears narrow cross bands of blue and a waist band of the same sort, tied at the side, but some distance below the lowest reach of the bands. Whether the waist band is entirely separate or connected with the cross bands at the back, cannot be seen.[26] Since both the royal executioner and his victim wear the cross bands, one may wonder about what their efficacy as an amulet was thought to be.

A cylinder-seal of Ramses II (fig. 13)[27] shows the king practicing archery, shooting at a copper target with a couple of apparently Asiatic prisoners bound beneath the target. The king wears chest bands similar to those representations mentioned above. The god Resheph, brandishing a sickle sword, stands facing away from the king. The god here does not have the chest bands he sometimes wears.

Turning to Mesopotamian martial scenes, we find cross bands having a circular medallion at the intersection worn by spearmen of several Assyrian kings (fig. 14).[28] A boundary stone (*kudurru*) from Babylon

Figure 14

depicts Marduknadin-akhe (*circa* 1100 BC) armed with bow and arrows and wearing narrow cross bands which appear to terminate at the base of a wide belt or waistband. There is no decoration at the intersection of the bands.[29] Similarly, Shamshi Adad V of Assyria (823–811 BC) is depicted wearing two shoulder straps that cross his chest diagonally. Suspended from his neck and reaching almost to the intersection of the crossed straps is a large medallion in the form of the "Greek" Cross. In his left hand he holds a mace.[30] Some of Sennacherib's archers at the siege of Lachish wear wide cross bands attached to a wide belt, without decoration at the intersection of the bands, while other warriors (both archers and slingers) have a single diagonal band over the right shoulder connecting on the left side with a belt to which are attached a scabbard and sword.[31]

The necklaces and girdles decorating the terra cotta figurines treated by Dales present no great problem in view of the universal feminine penchant for adornment. However, the chest harness on nude female figurines is indeed puzzling at first and, viewed in isolation, would remain incomprehensible. But, when the same sort of trappings are observed on representations of the war goddess Ishtar or Anat (the two names are later blended in Atargatis), and similar trappings are worn by human warriors, a purpose other than the magical or ornamental suggests itself.

It is admittedly difficult to tell from the graphic representations whether or how implements or receptacles for such were attached to the bands, or to belts with which the bands are sometimes connected. A strap running over the shoulder diagonally across the chest and attached to a belt makes an efficient harness for carrying arms and equipment while leaving one's hands free. The shoulder band helps to distribute the weight and relieves pressure on the waist and hips. The single bands were certainly used in this way, as is clear from the Mesopotamian war scenes. Two bands over the shoulder would be better, presumably, than a single band, especially if more than one weapon or weapon carrier had to be supported. The bands would not need to be crossed (there are, in fact, representations of uncrossed shoulder straps that extend to the belt in a V-shape) (fig. 15),[32] but the crossing tends to prevent slipping and reduces the need for additional bands to keep the harness snug. Since the single diagonal band was certainly used for supporting weapons, it seems likely that the double bands served the same purpose. When the bands appear to be attached to a waistband or belt, they might be supposed to serve as suspenders to support the skirt. But this could not be the case when the bands do not reach to the waist (figs. 6, 11, 12, 13). On some figurines and statues the bands extend below the waist, even to the hips or thighs, and there is little or no clothing to be supported (figs. 2, 3, 4).

Both the single and the double strap harness have served as basic ac-

Figure 15

coutrement of the field soldier for centuries; they continue in use to this day.[33] The single diagonal band and the double crossed bands, both functional and ornamental, continue as a common feature of military dress. It is, thus, quite possible that the harness may have become, at an early date a vestigial, non-functional item of martial dress, perhaps with magical or talismanic significance. The appearance of the cross bands, with circle or rosette at the intersection, or quivers (fig. 16)[34] suggests magical as well as ornamental purpose.

The cross bands under consideration and the similar cross on the

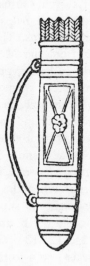

Figure 16

labarum, the war standard of the Emperor Constantine, may be related. This standard, comprising a monogram of the letters X (*chi*) and P (*rho*), was not originally a Christian symbol since it appears on pre-Christian coins.[35] The emperor regarded this emblem as the safeguard of the Empire itself and treated it with respect like that accorded the celebrated Palladium, the relic of the goddess Pallas Athena, which had formerly protected Troy but had been transferred to Rome and was tended by the Vestal Virgins. Constantine's pagan background may well have influenced his choice of the symbol and his attitude toward it.[36] A panegyric by Eumenius, delivered in 310 in the presence of Constantine, mentions the emperor's visit to the Apollo temple at Autun in anticipation of a renewed attack on the Franks. Apollo, according to the panegyrist, accompanied by Victory, appeared to the emperor and offered him the laurel crowns.[37] The timing of this apparition a few years before the vision in which the cross was revealed as a victory standard is provocative of speculation.

The winged goddess of Victory (fig. 17)[38] was the most highly

Figure 17

honored among deities of the Roman State, the symbol of Roman power. This goddess was the Roman equivalent and counterpart of the Greek Athena, Atargatis, Ishtar-Anat of the Semites, Inanna of the Sumerians —the warrior goddess who wore the cross chest bands. It seemed likely that Constantine's familiarity with the goddess, and presumably with her characteristic cross chest bands, would have influenced his choice of the same type of cross as his standard. It is striking that the Roman Victoria is often represented wearing the same sort of cross bands with circular medallion at the intersection as those worn by Mesopotamian warriors (fig. 18).[39] Eusebius was apparently aware that the emblem for Con-

Figure 18

stantine was a charm, or fetish and symbol of life and immortality, rather than a token of Christ's sacrifice and vicarious death.[40]

Cross marks in various forms have been used as sign and symbol in all times and places, but it is often very difficult to determine their specific significance as a symbol.[41] It has often been taken as a symbol of life. In Ezek. 9:4, e.g., the mark (*tāw*) (presumably in the primitive X form of the letter[42]) on the foreheads of the faithful was intended to save them from destruction.[43]

The X of Constantine's war standard was manifestly a symbol of victory and thus also of life. If the origin and meaning of its name were known, we would perhaps have a better understanding of the symbol's

significance. The word *labarum,* however, remains a mystery despite
the torture of many languages in vain efforts to extract an etymology.
Among far-fetched proposals, Akkadian *labāru,* suggested more than a
century ago, seems as good as any; the association with life follows from
the meaning "grow old," "endure." The noun *lubārum* in Akkadian
designates a garment, but it is not clear whether the term is general or
specific. My cuneiformist colleagues, W. W. Hallo and H. A. Hoffner, Jr.,
have called to my attention an unpublished lexical text in the Yale
Babylonian Collection (YBC 13524) which lists *lubārum* among terms
connected with bands and bandages. This may turn out to be an important
clue to the nature of the garment.

The connection of Anat and Athena with Life and Luck is abundantly
attested; it may suffice to cite a few examples. In the Ugaritic Tale of
Aqhat, the goddess Anat tries to get the marvelous composite bow from
the young hero by offering him immortality:

> Ask life, O hero Aqhat
> Ask life and I will give it (to) thee,
> Immortality and I will extend it (to) thee;
> I will make thee count years with Baal
> With El's sons thou wilt count months.[44]

A Greek and Phoenician bilingual inscription from Larnax Lapethos
dating to the end of the 4th century BC makes particularly explicit the
connection of the two goddesses with Life, Fortune, Victory and Salvation.
The Greek version is dedicated "to Athena, Saviour, Victory" and the
Semitic version "to Anat Strength of Life," while both versions end with
the words "to Good Luck."[45]

Victory is also associated with the Virgin Goddess in the Ugaritic Anat
text (col. II, 1. 27). The goddess slaughters mankind, wades hip-deep
in blood and gore, decking herself with severed heads and hands while
her inwards swell with glee, joy and victory (*tšyt*). The biblical uses of
the cognate of this latter term suggest the meaning "success" or "victory."[46]
The bloodthirsty Indian goddess Kali, who likewise wears a necklace of
heads and a girdle of hands, is also called the giver of victory and a
cry of her devotees is "Victory to Mother Kali."[47]

The association of the saltier with goddesses of war and love, victory
and life, is also amply documented. It thus appears that du Buisson's
surmise that the saltier of Atargatis was a symbol of Life is in the main
correct. The same sort of saltier worn by the goddess we have seen on
representations of other warriors both divine and human. We have sug-

gested an originally practical function as well as ornamental and symbolic development. The saltier on the nude fertility figurines naturally suggests a different aspect of life and luck from that worn by the armed goddess, but both types represent different aspects of the same goddess of love and war; even in her most benign apparition as patroness of fecundity and sexual pleasure she retains martial trappings, the harness for carrying her weapons, reflecting the inseparable and irrepressible violence of her ambivalent character. She is the terrible queen who loves the clash of battle, who stirs up fury, leads the armies and never retreats; at the same time she is the goddess of the even more powerful passion of love which produces and provides the continuation of life itself.

Originally simply a harness for supporting weapons, the saltier became an attribute of the great goddess of war and love and thus a symbol of life, luck and victory. Its persistence as a feature of military dress and an emblem of war standards and national flags suggests a tradition of at least four thousand years.

Christians dismayed by the use of the cross as a war standard since the days of Constantine[48] may take only scant comfort in the long-known fact that its origin and meaning is wholly pagan, a *crux diaboli*,[49] diametrically opposed to the cross of Christ, of whatever form, which symbolizes self-sacrificing love.

FOOTNOTES

1. *Le sautoir d'Atargatis et la chaine d'amulettes* (1947).
2. *Op. cit.*, pp. 11, 22–24. E. Goodenough, *Jewish Symbols in the Greco-Roman Period*, v, p. 73, asserts that the Egyptian *ankh* symbol became the Christian cross.
3. *Mesopotamian and Related Female Figurines: Their Chronology, Diffusion, and Cultural Functions* (1960). The most common iconographic details seen on the figurines are necklaces, chest bands, and hip belts or girdles; these features Dr. Dales treated in an article based on his dissertation "Necklaces, Bands and Belts on Mesopotamian Figurines," *RA*, 57 (1963), 21–40.
4. Bronze statuette of goddess with saltier, Roman period, after du Buisson, *op. cit.*, p. 22, n. 74, p. 23 (fig. 9).
5. Yakshi with *channavīra* garment, after du Buisson, *op. cit.*, p. 22, n. 73, p. 23 (fig. 11).
6. Figurine reportedly from the vicinity of Peshawar, after Dales, *op. cit.*, p. 28 (fig. 16).
7. Cf. Dales, *op. cit.*, p. 37 (fig. 31), n. 3.
8. *Ibid.*
9. *Ibid.*, pp. 31–33.
10. *Ibid.*, p. 40, n. 4.
11. *Op. cit.*, p. 36.
12. Marie-Thérèse Barrelet, "Une peinture de la cour 106 du Palais de Mari," *Studia Mariana*, ed. by A. Parrot (1950), Pl. 1, pp. 9–35. A. Parrot, *Mission archéologique de Mari*, II, 2: *Le Palais, Peintures murales* (1958), pp. 53–56, Pl. XI. *ANEP* 610, *AWBL*, p. 173.
13. E. Douglas Van Buren, "The Rod and Ring," *Archiv Orientální*, 17 (1949), pp. 434–50.
14. P. Amiet, "Notes sur le répertoire iconographique de Mari à l'époque du palais," *Syr*, 37 (1960), p. 230 (fig. 12).
15. *Ibid.*
16. Cf. Marie-Thérèse Barrelet, "Les déesses armées et ailées," *Syr*, 32 (1955), p. 227 (fig. 2); p. 231 (fig. 7a).
17. M. T. Barrelet, *op. cit.*, p. 258 (fig. 23).
18. After M. T. Barrelet, *op. cit.*, p. 227 (fig. 2, a, b, c, d).
19. *ANEP*, 555.
20. *ANEP*, 476.
21. *AWBL*, p. 163.
22. H. G. Fischer, "Eleventh Dynasty Relief Fragments from Deir el Bahri," *Yale University Art Gallery Bulletin*, 24 (No. 2, Oct. 1958), p. 32, fig. 4; "The Nubian Mercenaries of Gebelein," *Kush*, 9 (1961), p. 70, fig. 9.
23. *AWBL*, p. 159.
24. *AWBL*, pp. 192–93.
25. *AWBL*, pp. 234–35.
26. *AWBL*, p. 232.
27. *AWBL*, p. 201.
28. *AWBL*, p. 294.
29. *AWBL*, p. 358.
30. *ANEP*, p. 442.

31. *AWBL*, pp. 430–31.

32. *AWBL*, p. 72.

33. Cf. F. G. Blakeslee, *Army Uniforms of the World* (1919), p. 39. The white cross belts on the uniform of the Connecticut Governor's Foot Guard, founded 1771, support the cartridge box and bayonet scabbard. The Scots in the Middle Ages favored the blue tunic decorated with the Cross of St. Andrew, p. 79. Major R. Money Barnes', *Military Uniforms of Britain and the Empire 1742 to the Present Time* (1960), in nearly every figure and plate shows chest bands either single or double crossed, either ornamental or functional, or both. In Paul Martin and Hans-Joachim Ullrich, *Military Costume: A Short History* (1963), *passim*, note the St. Andrew Crosses on the chest and shoulders of a coat of arms of Burgundy, p. 23. The bandolier, either single or double, slung over the shoulder and across the chest, unconnected to a belt, is still a convenient means of carrying ammunition for firearms. The uniform of the cadet of the U. S. Military Academy at West Point has wide white cross bands with a clip at the intersection; cf. *Military Uniforms in Color*, written and illustrated by Preben Kannik, English ed. by William Y. Cowan (1965), fig. 510.

34. *AWBL*, p. 296.

35. Cf. E. Rapp, "Das Labarum und der Sonnencultus," *Jahrbücher des Vereins von Alterthumsfreunden im Rheinlande* (1866), pp. 116–45. C. B. Coleman, *Constantine the Great and Christianity*, Columbia University Studies in History, Economics and Public Law No. 146, 60 (1914), pp. 79–81.

36. Cf. M. A. Huttmann, *The Establishment of Christianity and the Proscription of Paganism*, Columbia University Studies in History, Economics and Public Law No. 147, 60 (1914), "Constantine's Personal Religion," pp. 13–30.

37. C. B. Coleman, *op. cit.*, pp. 75–76.

38. After S. Reinach, *Répertoire de la statuaire grecque et romaine*, II, p. 388, No. 9.

39. After S. Reinach, *op. cit.*, II, p. 319, Nos. 5 and 8.

40. Eusebius, *Life of Constantine*, i., 32; cf. C. B. Coleman, *op. cit.*, p. 80.

41. Cf. B. Goff, *Symbols of Prehistoric Mesopotamia*, p. 49. "A cross when used as a symbol has no single explanation."

42. Cf. W. W. Hallo, *JBL*, 77 (1958), p. 337.

43. Cf. E. Dinkler "Zur Geschichte des Kreuzsymbols," *ZTK*, 48 (1951), pp. 148–72, especially Part IV, "Die Interpretation des jüdischen Kreuzzeichen," pp. 162–69.

The haggadic interpretation of Ezek. 9:4 in Talmud Babli Shabbath 55a makes no distinction between *tāw* as protective or life symbol and the opposite, since the *tāw* in ink on the forehead of the righteous meant *tiḥyeh*, "thou shalt live," while the same sign in blood meant *tāmût*, "thou shalt die."

44. For the Ugaritic text cf. A. Herdner, *Corpus des tablettes en cunéiformes alphabétiques*, text 17, VI 26–29. On the term for immortality (*blmt*), lit. "non-death," cf. M. Dahood, *Ugaritic-Hebrew Philology*, BibOrPont, 17 (1965), p. 74; and M. Pope, *JBL*, 75 (1966), pp. 462 f.

45. *CIS* 195. G. A. Cooke, *A Text-Book of North-Semitic Inscriptions*, No. 28. H. Donner and W. Röllig, *Kanaanäische und Aramäische Inschriften*, No. 24.

46. Cf. M. H. Pope, *Job* (Anchor Bible, xv) on Job 5:12b, 11:6b, 12:16a, and 30:22b.

47. Cf. J. Campbell Oman, *The Brahmans, Theists and Muslims of India* (1907), pp. 10 and 16.

48. Cf. James J. Macintyre, *The Cross and Crescent as Standards in War* (1854).

49. Cf. J. Freccero, "The Sign of Satan," *Modern Language Notes*, 80 (1955), p. 21, on the *crux diaboli*.

III
The Iron Age

SYMBOLS OF DEITIES AT ZINJIRLI, CARTHAGE AND HAZOR*

Yigael Yadin

WE SHALL deal first with several monuments from Zinjirli, set up by the kings of Samal and bearing inscriptions in Phoenician and Aramaic; above the writing appear several symbols of gods mentioned in the inscriptions proper. The monuments have been well known since their discovery during the excavations carried out on the site from 1888 on.[1] Several detailed studies have been devoted to the connection between the divine symbols and the names of the gods mentioned in the inscriptions, attempting to identify the symbols and to reveal the nature of these gods on the basis of their attributes.[2]

In spite of the many efforts, these studies seem to me to have missed their mark and failed to provide a satisfactory solution to the problem. It appears to me that this was caused by several scholars having sought a solution mainly on the basis of the gods' *names*, while largely ignoring the importance of the symbols themselves;[3] in other cases, scholars devoted too much importance to the symbols and were misled in their understanding of the names.[4] Moreover, because of a lack of conformity between the number of symbols on the monuments and the number of divine names mentioned in the inscriptions, some of these scholars simply reached an impasse.[5]

In the study below, we shall first attempt to re-examine the epigraphic and iconographic material and then to prove that the reason for the numerical discrepancy is rooted in the fact that several symbols may be attributes of a single god. We shall also attempt to use comparative material from other sites, where such symbols, or parts of them, are accompanied by inscriptions specifically mentioning divine names. This clarification will lead us, for reasons to be explained below, to an assess-

* Published in Hebrew in *Yediot*, 31 (1967), pp. 29–63.

ment of the Punic stelae from Carthage and its general region, as well
as of the divine symbols in the "stelae temple" at Hazor.

ZINJIRLI–SAMAL
KILAMU ORTHOSTAT⁶

We start with this monument not only because it is the earliest (second
half of the ninth century BC) of the Zinjirli monuments bearing both
names and symbols of gods, but principally because it is the only one
which specifies exactly the names of the deities of the royal dynasty at
Samal, no mention being made of the names of the gods included in the
usual pantheon of the peoples surrounding this locality. The most important part of the Phoenician inscription, for our purposes, is at the
end:

15. ומי. ישחת. הספר ז. ישחת. ראש. בעל. צמד. אש. לגבר.

16. וישחת. ראש. בעל חמן. אש. לבמה. ורכבאל. בעל בת.

The three gods mentioned here, none of whom appear in contemporary
inscriptions from neighboring lands, are mentioned chronologically according to the reigns of the kings of Samal:

  Ba'al-Ṣemed=of Gabbar

  Ba'al-Ḥamman=of BMH

  Rakkab-El=of the House, i.e., Kilamu's dynasty.

  This chronological order of the kings of Samal is mentioned at the start
of the inscriptions

מלך גבר על יאדי ובל פ[על] כן במה ובל פעל.

This fact should be remembered from the outset, for it leads to the
conclusion that the mention of the gods at the end of the inscription is
not in the order of their importance but rather according to the reigns
of the kings of Samal—each king with his peculiar god. Of course, this
order is not necessarily identical with the order of the divine symbols
at the head of the orthostat. Even so, we may assume that the king,
in setting up this monument allotted the principal position to the symbols
of "his" god.

  There are four symbols carved at the head of the orthostat (see fig. 1;
Pl. 17). Their order is from left to right even though the inscription is
written from right to left. This is evident not only from the fact that the
first symbol also faces in this direction.

  First symbol: Peaked cap with pair of horns.

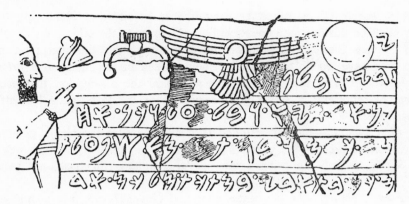

Figure 1. The top of Kilamu's orthostat.

Second symbol: Bow-shaped object, the extremities pointing downward, each terminating in a knob. At the center is a third knob and above is a sort of grooved or roped bar.
Third symbol: Winged sun-disc.
Fourth symbol: Crescent with full-moon disc.

Before analyzing the meaning of these symbols and their connection with the divine names mentioned in the inscription, the second symbol must be discussed, for it is the only one of which the iconographic meaning is not self-evident.

Landsberger[7] suggested that this is the symbol of the Hittite-Luwian moon-god (i.e., that it is a sort of crescent pointing downward), though he did not ignore the difficulty caused by the clear fact that a moon appears as the fourth symbol.

I believe it was Eduard Meyer,[8] however, who first correctly perceived its meaning: a chariot yoke. This interpretation was accepted by Donner,[9] who further demonstrated that this symbol has in fact no practical resemblance to the Hittite-Luwian one, in which the points of the crescent although pointing downward are not rounded as in the Zinjirli symbol but are rather pointed. Meyer's interpretation was also accepted by Galling.[10] However, credit must be given to Barnett not only for accepting this meaning but also for providing proof for it on the basis of many parallels.[11]

With at least the outward meaning of the symbols clarified, it is possible to proceed to identify them with the gods mentioned in the inscription. At this stage we shall be as inductive as possible, drawing upon the meaning of the divine names only when absolutely necessary. Moreover, we shall limit ourselves, as much as possible, to identifying the symbols on this one monument, with no reference to the others. We should first review Barnett's suggestions[12] to demonstrate that the interpretations to date have led up a blind alley, being based in the main on *a priori* interpretations of the nature of the gods and the assumption that each symbol represents a single god mentioned in the text. Thus Barnett's hypothesis:

First symbol:—the cap=*Hadad* (not mentioned in the text).

Second symbol:—the yoke=*Baʻal-Ṣemed*

Third symbol—the winged disc=*Baʻal-Ḥamman* (Shamash, not mentioned)

Fourth symbol—the crescent=moon-god (*Baʻal-Ḥarran,* not mentioned in text)

Thus, it is evident that Barnett identified several symbols with gods who are not mentioned within the text. Moreover, according to this method *Rakkab-El* (the dynastic god) has no symbol whatever! There is an additional, external difficulty pointed out by Barnett himself: "(there are) only three names—Baʻal-Ṣemed, Baʻal-Ḥamman, Rakib-el—but there are *four* symbols" (his italics!).[13]

Let us now attempt to identify the symbols in a different manner, starting first of all with that of Rakkab-El. *Rakkab-El* was the god of Kilamu and its dynasty, and it can be assumed that his symbol would occupy an important position among the others. Moreover, *Rakkab-El* is the only god mentioned in each of the Zinjirli inscriptions and it is most likely that his symbol should appear on all the Zinjirli monuments. Finally, it should not be difficult to determine his nature on the basis of his name. Though scholars are at odds over the reading of the name—*Rakkab-El* or *Rakib-El,* etc.[14]—today it is generally agreed that the meaning of the name is the "Charioteer of El"[15] and not the "Chariot of El" or "That Which is Ridden by El," i.e., the animal bearing the god.[16]

From the above we readily arrive at the assumption that the symbol of Rakkab-El should be in the principal position among the symbols, and that there is thus little doubt that the yoke (the second symbol) belongs to this god; and this both because of the connection between the nature of the god and that of this symbol, and the prominent position the symbol holds.[17] However, we immediately recognize that the central symbol *next* to the yoke is the winged disc, identified by Barnett *with* *Baʻal-Ḥamman* (Shamash). But it is difficult to assume that *Baʻal-Ḥamman* should hold a central place here, and thus it would seem much more logical to ascribe the symbol to *El* himself. For not only does it always symbolize the supreme *El* in the Mesopotamian, Canaanite and Hittite pantheon,[18] but it also appears as the attribute of El on the famous stele from Ugarit.[19] Since the second element in the name *Rakkab-El* is *El* I suggest that the two symbols together be regarded as the symbol of *Rakkab-El: Rakkab*=the yoke+*El*=the winged disc.

This receives confirmation from another document from Zinjirli, the seal-impression of king Bar-Rakkab son of Panamu (fig. 2).[20] There is no

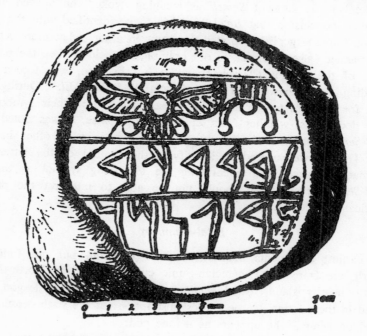

Figure 2. Seal-impression of king Bar-Rakkab

doubt that the principal god of Bar-Rakkab was *Rakkab-El*. This is evident not only from his name, Bar-Rakkab (-El), but also from his monument (the symbols of which will be dealt with below), on which he states: "My lord *Rakkab-El* and my lord Tiglath-Pileser enthroned me on the seat of my father." It is proper, therefore, that the symbols of *Rakkab-El* should appear on his seal; and, indeed, above the inscription "belonging to Bar-Rakkab son of Panamu" appear the two symbols, the winged disc and the yoke (see fig. 2). We shall deal later with the symbols of *Rakkab-El* in discussing the other monuments. Let us now return to Kilamu's orthostat in order to identify the other two symbols

(the first one on the left, the cap; and fourth one, on the right, the crescent) with the other two gods mentioned in the text, i.e., with *Ba'al-Ḥamman* and *Ba'al-Ṣemed*. Even before attempting to ascertain the nature of
these gods through the meaning of their names, we shall identify the symbols through comparative morphology. This should facilitate arriving at a
clear conclusion, without becoming entangled in the problems of the significance of the names.

As already pointed out, since Barnett interpreted (in our opinion
mistakenly) the element *Ṣemed* as meaning "yoke," he arrived at an
erroneous conclusion that *Ba'al-Ṣemed* is to be identified with the yoke
symbol. Landsberger[21] interpreted the name in a somewhat more reasonable manner (also incorrect, in our opinion; see below), i.e., the pair of
beasts of the chariot ("Zweigespann"); but he, too, was forced into
regarding *Ba'al-Ṣemed* as a sort of twin of *Rakkab-El*.[22] During our
quest for parallels to the names of these gods and to their symbols in
other documents, whether from Zinjirli or otherwise, it was noted that
Ba'al-Ṣemed, unlike *Ba'al-Ḥamman,* is mentioned in no other inscription. Thus if we succeed in identifying the symbol of the latter, we
automatically succeed in identifying the remaining symbol as that of
Ba'al-Ṣemed, even if we should not be able to interpret the precise
significance of the name.

Ba'al-Ḥamman

The earliest documents mentioning *Ba'al-Ḥamman,* but not found at
Zinjirli, are from the Phoenician-Punic cultural realm in North Africa
and the nearby islands. *Ba'al-Ḥamman* is almost the sole male god mentioned in these latter. In the earliest inscriptions of the sixth century BC,
found on Malta,[23] he appears as a lone god:

נדב מלכבעל אש שם נחם לבעלחמן אדן כי שמע קל דברי

Later, from the fifth century BC on, he is sometimes mentioned alone
לאדן לבעל־חמן and sometimes together with his companion תנת פנבעל
who is generally referred to in this period in that very manner.[24] Several
scholars[25] have indeed concluded that the origin of the Punic *Ba'al-
Ḥamman* is the *Ba'al-Ḥamman* mentioned on the Zinjirli stele, but,
surprisingly, no attempt was made to compare the symbol on the Punic
stelae with the series of symbols from Samal. One of the reasons for this
may be the fact that on the Punic stelae three symbols generally appear
(see fig. 3), and the scholars dealing with this material have not connected
any one of them with *Ba'al-Ḥamman* or *Tanit* (TNT) in particular.
However, there is little doubt (and we shall return to this matter below)

Figure 3. The three symbols of the deities in Punic monuments.

that the symbol of *Tanit* is that commonly called the "sign of *Tanit*," i.e., the figure with outstretched arms, and that she may also be represented by the "caduceus."

Thus, the third symbol, i.e., the crescent with disc, appearing generally at the top of the stele, should be that of *Ba'al-Ḥamman*. The extremities of the crescent mostly point downward, though this is not of cardinal importance, as indicated, e.g., by the two miniature funerary temples from Lilybeum:[26] on one the crescent points upward, but on the other it points downward (see Pl. 18).

From the above, we may assume that the fourth symbol on the Zinjirli stele, i.e., the crescent with disc, is the symbol of *Ba'al-Ḥamman*. It would be most coincidental if, in the two cases where *Ba'al-Ḥamman* is mentioned alongside a symbol, the crescent and disc should symbolize two different gods. Of course, this identification nullifies Barnett's suggestion (based on Ingholt's study) to interpret the name of *Ba'al-Ḥamman* as meaning "Lord of burning (altar)," and to identify him with the winged disc.[27]

If our suggestion is correct, the first symbol (the horned cap) must necessarily be identified with *Ba'al-Ṣemed*. Moreover, this serves to point out a further fact, one much more basic: the symbols on this stele are solely the divine attributes of the royal dynasties of Samal.

In the light of these conclusions, we shall now proceed to examine another stele from Zinjirli, bearing an Aramaic inscription of *Bar-Rakkab*.[28] Before describing the symbols at the top of the inscription and to the

Figure 4. The symbols of the deities on the Bar-Rakkab orthostat

right of the head of the king (see fig. 4 and Pl. 19), it should be remembered
that this inscription mentions only one god, i.e., *Rakkab-El:*

הושבני מראי רכבאל ומראי תגלתפליסר על כרסא אבי

The symbols and their order (from left to right) are identical with
those on the above mentioned orthostat of Kilamu: the cap, yoke, winged
disc and crescent with disc. The only difference is the addition of a
further symbol: a five-pointed star within a circle, placed between the
yoke and the winged disc.

In keeping with the accepted interpretation which regards these symbols,
as on the rest of the Zinjirli monuments, as attributes of gods of the
Canaanite pantheon, and not as symbols of gods especially peculiar to
the kings of Samal, there have been various attempts to identify the
symbols. Thus, for instance, Donner and Röllig suggested the following
identification (from left to right): *Hadad* (cap), *Rakkab-El* (yoke),
Reshef (star?), *Shamash* (winged disc) and Sin (=*Ba'al Ḥarran;* crescent with disc; and see below). This is based on the names of the gods
mentioned in the inscription of Panamu, engraved on a statue of Hadad
but without any divine symbols:[29] הדד. ואל. ורשף. ורכבאל. ושמש or
להדד. ולאל. ולרכבאל. ולשמש or הדד. ואל. ורכבאל. ושמש וארק רשף
The faults of this system are quite apparent, not only because of the
erroneous interpretation of the symbols (see above), but mainly because
the symbol of El, who is mentioned in the inscription, does not at all
occur; whereas *Sin* or *Ba'al-Ḥarran,* who is not even mentioned, has a
symbol (see below). Moreover, it is clear that all the gods mentioned
except *Rakkab-El,* who is the dynastic god, do not belong to the group
of gods peculiar to the kings of Yadi-Samal. This is most evident at the
end of another inscription (without symbols) of Bar-Rakkab,[30] dedicated to his father Panamu:

הדד. ואל. ורכבאל. בעל. בית. ושמש. וכל אלהי יאדי . . .

It is, thus, clear that except for *Rakkab-El* none of these gods could be
defined as gods of Yadi. They are most likely—together with *Rakkab-El*
—*Ba'al-Ṣemed* and *Ba'al-Ḥamman* (for *Ba'al-Ḥarran,* see below).

No less forced is Barnett's suggestion[31] identifying the symbols as follows: *Hadad* (cap), *Ba'al-Ṣemed/Reshef* (yoke), *Rakkab-El* (star), *Ba'al-Ḥamman/Shamash* (winged disc). According to this hypothesis, not only is there no identification of the crescent—here and on the other orthostats —with one of the gods mentioned in the inscriptions, but the star is to be identified with *Rakkab-El.* Of course, the star does not appear on any other document, and thus the very symbol of *Rakkab-El,* the dynastic god, appears only here!

Our supposition, in contrast, enables identification of all the symbols exactly by the same method used on the Kilamu orthostat (from left to right): *Ba'al-Ṣemed* (cap), *Rakkab-El, Ba'al-Ḥamman* (crescent with disc). The symbol of *Rakkab-El* is comprised of two parts, as stated above: the yoke and the winged disc. In this instance, and on the basis of our axiom that these symbols belong solely to the kings of Yadi-Samal, the star does not signify another god, but rather serves as a determinative signifying the divinity of the double symbol: yoke+winged disc.[32] Our hypothesis of dividing the symbols and identifying them is summarized as in fig. 8.

We must now examine a fragment of the most interesting orthostat yet found at Zinjirli, published recently by Donner[33] (see fig. 5; Pl. 20).

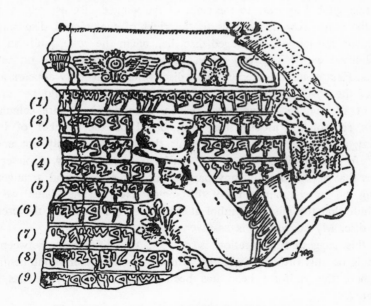

Figure 5. The broken orthostat of Bar-Rakkab

This stele, set up by Bar-Rakkab, was discovered broken (the lower and left hand parts are missing). However, at the right of the extant fragment we see the figure of Bar-Rakkab facing left (unlike the other monuments where the king of Samal is on the left side facing right). Above his head and above the inscription are the symbols of the gods from right to left, as indicated by the first one (the cap) which faces to the left. Unfortunately, the inscription is largely lost and one cannot be sure which gods were mentioned in it. In any event, it seems that no additional gods are specifically mentioned except *Rakkab-El*.[34]

The major importance of this inscription to the matter at hand is, of course, the row of symbols, which differ in several details from those on the other monuments. Briefly, they are, from right to left: horned cap, janiform with horned cap, yoke, winged disc, yoke (see below, fig. 6). The first question arising is, naturally, how to restore the missing part of the row of symbols to the left. Barnett, who evidently assumed that the symbol farthest to the left was the last one in the original row of symbols, identifies it in his comparative chart[35] with the crescent of the other monuments. This is difficult to accept, not only because the symbol is entirely different from the crescent symbol, but also because it is essentially identical with the yoke to the right.[36] Donner, on the other hand, in whose opinion the yoke is an independent symbol signifying *Rakkab-El,* sees in the fact that this symbol appears to the right of the winged disc as well, a proof that the entire row of symbols to the right of the winged disc was repeated on the left of the winged disc, i.e., again the yoke, janiform head and horned cap.[37] This suggestion, too, seems unreasonable on several counts. First of all, the crescent with disc, which constantly appears at the end of the row of symbols on the other monuments, would not appear here at all, and for no apparent reason. Secondly, a precise calculation of the size of the missing fragment, based on the number of letters missing at the end of line 2,[38] reveals that there is simply not enough room for an additional cap and janiform head. Finally, Donner too agrees that he did not find any parallel for this symmetrical arrangement among the many monuments of the ancient Near East.[39] Thus, we may conclude that the missing symbol at the left of the stele was the crescent with disc. My suggestion is as given in fig. 6.

If this suggested restoration is correct, the differences between the symbols on this orthostat and the symbols on the other monuments are that here the janiform head has been added and the yoke has been repeated.

For the identification of the symbols, here too Donner and Barnett

Figure 6. A suggested restoration of the symbols of the deities in the broken
orthostat of Bar-Rakkab

apply their methods (i.e., that each symbol signifies a single god and
that the symbols do not necessarily apply solely to the gods of Yadi-
Samal), but they differ in their interpretations. Donner identifies the
symbols as follows (from right to left): *Hadad* (cap), *El* (janiform
head), *Rakkab-El* (yoke), *Shamash* (winged disc), *Rakkab-El* (yoke),
etc. Even according to his method, the symbol of *Reshef* is missing here.
By contrast, Barnett identifies the symbols as follows (from right to
left): *Hadad* (cap), *El* (janiform head), *Ba'al-Ṣemed* (yoke with
knob), *Ba'al-Ḥamman* (winged disc), *Sin, Ba'al-Ḥarran* (yoke without
knob). This latter method, in my opinion, fails with all the faults of
Donner's method and with the addition of a few of its own, as we have
already observed. In the present instance additional problems arise: the
lack of a symbol for *Rakkab-El* (the principal god of Bar-Rakkab); the
identification of *Ba'al-Ṣemed* and *Reshef;* and the identification of the
yoke (without knob) with the crescent.

Let us now examine the row of symbols in the light of the conclusions
arrived at in our discussion of the other monuments, beginning with the
central group: we have concluded that the yoke and winged disc together
form the attribute of *Rakkab-El*. The orthostat before us not only serves
to strengthen this assumption, but only by this assumption can the group
of three symmetrically arranged symbols be explained, i.e., the yoke+
winged disc+yoke as a whole signifies *Rakkab-El*.[40] If we do not accept
this explanation, we are forced to assume that the entire series of symbols was repeated to the left, as in Donner's opinion (which we have
attempted to disprove on several counts), or that only the yoke—as a
military symbol—is repeated, a phenomenon which would be unique
and without a reasonable explanation.

Since in our opinion there was on the missing left side the crescent
symbol with disc, which we identified with *Ba'al-Ḥamman,* we have only
to identify the two symbols on the right, i.e., the horned cap and the
janiform head with horned cap. The cap, as stated above, signifies
Ba'al-Ṣemed. Who is indicated by the janiform head? Donner and Barnett
have identified it with *El*.[41] This is unacceptable, not only because only

on this monument would it signify *El* (and thence the symbol of this god would appear on no other stele), but also because of the axiom which we have tried to prove above, that the symbols appearing on these stelae are divine attributes peculiar to the god of Samal. Thus we arrive at the conclusion that the janiform head, too, signifies *Ba'al-Ṣemed*. In other words, the horned cap is the general symbol of the various "Ba'als,"[42] including *Ba'al-Ṣemed;* whereas, the janiform head with the horned cap is the symbol peculiar to *Ba'al-Ṣemed*.[43]

In closing this part of our discussion, before going on briefly to the matter of the meaning of the names of the gods, two additional monuments should be noted.

The first is a tomb-stele found at Ördek-burnu, some twelve kilometers south of Zinjirli.[44] On its lower part is a blurred inscription, above which appear two figures. Above one of the figures is a row of symbols, also somewhat blurred, though the yoke undoubtedly occurs in the center. Above the yoke there seem to be traces of an additional symbol, possibly the winged disc. To the right a vague symbol can be made out, possibly a horned cap; whereas, on the left there appears to be a crescent.[45]

In fig. 7 (based on a photograph), I have attempted to suggest the order

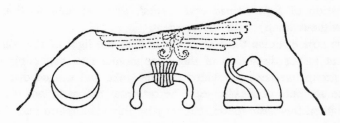

Figure 7. A schematic restoration of the symbols in the Ördek-burnu monument.

of the symbols in a strictly schematic manner.[46] Even though the reading of the inscription is most difficult, there is no doubt that in line 5 there is written לרכבאל אלה, and in line 7 there is possibly ברכבאל (!). This stele adds to our discussion the important fact that the yoke appears clearly at the center of a stele mentioning *Rakkab-El*.

The second, especially important to the matter at hand, is a stele of Bar-Rakkab, devoted to *Ba'al-Ḥarran* (see Pl. 21). In the relief appears Bar-Rakkab enthroned; above him is the inscription.אנה ברוכב בר פנמו In the center, atop a pole with a tassel hanging down on either side, is the crescent symbol with disc; above it to the right is the inscription

מראי בעל חרן. Here, at least, there is no doubt that this is the symbol of the well-known moon-god *Ba'al-Ḥarran*. It is also clear that in the days of Bar-Rakkab this god was introduced into the pantheon of Samal under Assyrian influence.[47] The symbol itself greatly resembles that of the crescent with disc which appears on the other Zinjirli monuments (and which we have identified with *Ba'al-Ḥamman*). The additional details (the pole with tassels) are truly the distinguishing features of *Ba'al-Ḥarran*. It is possibly because of this general similarity that Bar-Rakkab saw the need to deviate from the normal practice on the monuments and to write the name of the god next to the symbol. In any event, it would seem that *Ba'al-Ḥarran* is parallel to (or even replaces) *Ba'al-Ḥamman,* but not *Rakkab-El.*[48]

Our suggestions for the identification of the symbols on the Zinjirli monuments are summarized as in the table in fig. 8.[49]

So far we have seen that it is possible to identify the divine symbols with the gods of Samal mentioned in the Kilamu stele even without resorting to the meaning of the divine names. Now, however, after having arrived, as we believe, at their identifications, we should briefly examine the connection between these symbols and the nature of the gods with whom they are identified.

As for *Rakkab-El,* we have already slightly touched upon this as a point of departure for our discussion. It is evident that the people of Samal regarded this god as the charioteer of *El.* Thus, his symbol clearly expresses his capacity. Since this god is not mentioned in any other source, and since he is denoted as the dynastic god by the later kings of Samal, it might be concluded that this god was introduced by the kings of Samal. This could also explain the fact that the pair of symbols is not found on any monument outside Samal.

The problem of the literal meaning of the name *Ba'al-Ṣemed* is much more complex. Not only is there no other occurrence of the name in sources outside Samal; even on the Zinjirli monuments it occurs but once, as the god of Gabbar (on the Kilamu stele). On the face of it, it is possible to interpret the name as the *"Ba'al* (of) *Ṣemed,"* similar to the names of Baals in the Bible, e.g., *Ba'al-Haṣor, Ba'al-Ḥermon, Ba'al-Ma'on, Ba'al-Pe'or, Ba'al-Ṣafon* and *Ba'al-Tamar,* or the names of the Baals in extrabiblical sources, e.g., *Ba'al-Lebanon, Ba'al-Ṣidon, Ba'al-Ḥarran,* and *Ba'al-Ṣor.* Of course, there is a difficulty in giving this interpretation, for no mountain or city of this name (Ṣemed) is known. Though this interpretation cannot be entirely overlooked, it certainly does not free us from the necessity of looking into this second element more fully;

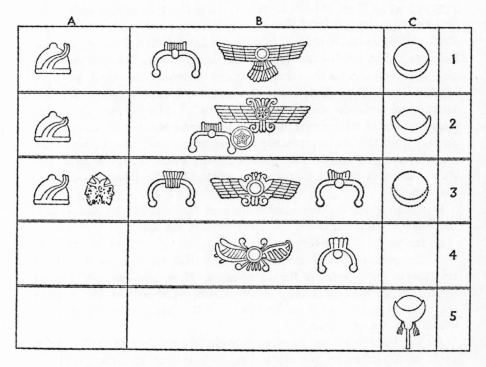

Figure 8. The symbols of the deities on the monuments of Zinjirli and their
possible identification:
col. a – Ba'al Ṣemed. col. b – Rakkab-El. col. c – Ba'al Ḥamman (no. 5 – Ba'al
Ḥarran). line 1 – Kilamu (cf. fig. 1). line 2 – Bar-Rakkab (cf. fig. 4). line 3 –
Bar-Rakkab (cf. figs. 5–6). line 4 – Seal impression of Bar-Rakkab (cf. fig. 2).
line 5 – Bar-Rakkab: the symbol of Ba'al Ḥarran (cf. Pl. 21)

for it seems indeed to reflect the character of this particular Baal. Actually,
this is the method used by most of the scholars who have approached
it. As stated, Barnett interprets *ṣemed* as meaning "yoke," but this word
does not denote the yoke proper but rather the team of beasts har-
nessed to the yoke. Thus, Landsberger interpreted the name "Herr der
Zweigespanns," i.e., *ba'al* of the team (of beasts) of the chariot.[50] This
is certainly possible, but it should be noted that in this case *Ba'al-Ṣemed*

would be of a character too close to that of *Rakkab-El,* a difficulty which Landsberger himself foresaw.[51]

Several scholars have proceeded in a different manner and have suggested interpreting the name as a weapon in the hands of the god; this suggestion is based on the fact that a weapon denoted *ṣemed* is mentioned in the Ugaritic texts in connection with *Ba'al* (see below). Thus, for instance, it has been suggested to translate the name as "Herr der Keule," i.e., Baal of the mace.[52] However, this meaning too is problematic, for it is not at all certain that the Ugaritic weapon *ṣemed* is indeed a mace. On the contrary! It seems that the semantic development of the word in the Semitic languages, including Ugaritic, would demand that it be a "tied" weapon,[53] double[54] or paired[55] in nature. Actually, even at Ugarit this term denotes, among other things, the chariot's pair of wheels.[56] In this light, we should re-examine the meaning of the weapon *ṣemed*. First of all, we may note that it appears only as a weapon of gods.[57] The most important passage for the understanding of this word is in the well-known text (III ABA=68) dealing with Baal's struggle with *Yamm* and with the peculiar weapon prepared for him by the craftsman-god *ktr w ḫss*. Herewith several lines from the relevant passage (the translation is taken for the most part from ANET, p. 131):

11. Kothar brings down two *ṣemed* and gives them names. Thou, thy name
12. is Yagrush ("chaser"). Yagrush, chase Yamm! Chase Yamm from the throne,
13. Nahar from his seat of dominion. Do thou swoop in the hand of Baal like an eagle
14. between his fingers; strike the back of Prince Yamm, between the arms
15. of Judge Nahar. The *Ṣemed* swoops in the hand of Baal like an eagle
16. between his fingers. It strikes the back of Prince Yamm, between the arms of the Judge
17. Nahar.[58]

Gray has already noted[59] that reference here is to a weapon of double nature, and thus he translated the term as "a double mace." We may ask, however, whether it truly refers to a mace. It is peculiar to the gods and swoops like an eagle. Moreover, Baal had two of them (*ṣmdm*). In this light, and taking into account the etymological-semantic meaning of the word (double and tied together) would

it not be possible to regard it as the weapon peculiar to several of
the storm-Baals, etc., symbolizing the double lightning tied at the middle? There are reliefs showing gods holding such double symbols, one
in each hand[60] (see fig. 9).

Figure 9. "Storm-god" from Arslan-Tash (cf. *ANEP* No. 501)

If we connect the Ugaritic word *ṣemed* with the meaning of the name
of *Ba'al-Ṣemed* of Samal, the god is not to be regarded as the *ba'al* of the
mace, but rather as the *ba'al* of the mythological weapon which is double
and which "swoops."

We must point out the interesting fact that on the Bar-Rakkab orthostat the symbol of *Ba'al-Ṣemed* is not solely the horned cap, held
in common by all the ba'als, but also the double janiform head! Could
this have some connection with the meaning of the god's name? The
janiform god has a long history indeed, and his various incarnations
have not yet been sufficiently studied.[61] In any event, it appears from
glyptic art that the janiform figure was the "vizier" of Ea, and in
this capacity appears on many Akkadian cylinder-seals.[62] His image
appears also on the Cappadocian seals.[63] What is important to us is
the fact that the janiform deity appears in Hittite seals as well[64] (see
fig. 10), in a form very similar to that of the Samal stele. No less

Figure 10. Janiform deity (enlarged) from an Anatolian cylinder-seal (cf. H. Frankfort, *Cylinder Seals* (1939), p. 123

interesting is the fact that this figure also appears in the art of Urartu in Anatolia, in a period quite close to that of Bar-Rakkab.[65]

In sum, unless *Ba'al-Ṣemed* is to be connected with a place-name, we may assume that his name reflects the double nature of his head or the peculiar nature of his characteristic weapon, or that these two features are, in themselves, connected. In any event, whether these possibilities are accepted or not, there is nothing in this to undermine the identification of the cap and the janiform head with this god, a conclusion arrived at by other means.

Earlier in this discussion I mentioned that we cannot ignore the fact that the symbol of *Ba'al-Ḥamman,* the crescent with disc (see also below), appears on the Phoenician-Punic stelae, and that this symbol at Samal is to be identified similarly. It follows that the suggestions to connect this name with the sun-god are unacceptable;[66] on the contrary, this symbol indicates that *Ba'al-Ḥamman* is primarily a moon-god. It appears that we should accept Halevy's suggestion—as have many scholars[67]—and interpret the name *Ba'al-Ḥamman* as referring to the *ba'al* of Mt. Amanus, a mountain undoubtedly of great importance in Samal and its surroundings. If this is the case, then the name *Ba'al-Ḥamman* can be included among the usual group of mountain-*ba'als* such as *Ba'al-Ḥermon, Ba'al-Lebanon*, the ba'al of Mt. Carmel and many others. In any event, since *Ba'al-Ḥamman* holds a most central position in the Phoenician-Punic pantheon and since the crescent with disc appears in the stelae temple at Hazor, we should now re-examine the Phoenician-Punic pantheon and its divine symbols and compare them with the evidence from Hazor.

CARTHAGE AND HAZOR

One of the most interesting discoveries at Hazor is, without doubt, the "stelae Temple" found in area C. This temple, in its two phases, is of the fourteenth to thirteenth centuries BC.[68] All the stelae are plain except the central one, which bears a relief with two motifs: a crescent with disc and two hands stretching upward (fig. 11).[69] In the excavations report I dwelt upon the similarity between the crescent with disc and the symbol on the Bar-Rakkab monument devoted to *Ba'al-Ḥarran*,[70] from which I concluded that the chief god at the Hazor temple was a moon-god. This was further strengthened by the fact that a crescent with its points facing downward[71] is depicted on the chest of a statue standing near the stele. I was unable at that time to find any parallel for the two hands, but I noted that two hands in a similar position appear on Punic stelae from North Africa, though of a much later period, and that they might possibly represent the continuation of a tradition which we cannot as yet trace in all its phases.[72] A more thorough search among the Punic material has revealed additional points of similarity. Clarification of this matter can lead not only to further light on the problem of Hazor and Carthage, but can also prove, if I am not mistaken, that several aspects of Canaanite worship found their continuation at least from the Late Bronze Age till the end of the Punic period. Thus we shall start our discussion with finds from Carthage and the Punic area in general.

Ba'al-Ḥamman and Tanit

In the earliest stelae from the Punic sphere, including those from Carthage, *Ba'al-Ḥamman* alone is mentioned.[73] From the fifth century BC

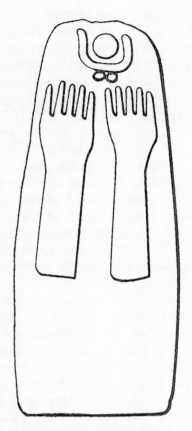

Figure 11. The central stele from Hazor

on, he is mentioned together with his consort Tanit (see below).[74] His title is האדן בעל חמן whereas Tanit is called רבת. There is no doubt that *Ba'al-Ḥammon* has his origins in the Phoenician mother-culture, in which he appears on the above mentioned Zinjirli monument, apparently in an inscription from the vicinity of the Lebanese border,[75] and in an inscription from Palmyra.[76]

Before treating the symbol of *Ba'al Ḥamman,* we should discuss the problem of his consort, *Tanit.* From the fifth century BC on, this goddess holds the prime position on thousands of stelae. She is mentioned mostly with the following formula: לרבת לתנת פנבעל ולאדן לבעל חמן.[77] *Ba'al Ḥamman* is occasionally mentioned by himself as well.[78]

Many studies have been devoted to *Tanit.* The common consensus holds that the name is Libyan.[79] In my opinion there is no doubt that *Tanit* was connected with moon worship, as may be learned from an inscription from 400 BC found at Athens[80] מצבת סכר בחים לעבדתנת בן עבדשמש הצדני. In the Greek translation, עבדתנת appears as 'Αρτεμιδώρος, and thus according to this inscription, *Tanit* was equated with *Artemis*, who was often identified with *Selene*, the Greek moon-goddess.[81]

In addition, there is no doubt that *Tanit* is very closely connected with *Ba'al Ḥamman*. Her title, the "Face of Baal," leaves little room for doubt in this matter, and indicates that her powers were derived from *Ba'al-Ḥamman*, even after worship had become centered around her, she being only his "face." But before going into the problem of her name and the cult objects connected with her worship, we should deal with her symbols and that of *Ba'al-Ḥamman*.

The series of symbols on the thousands of stelae from Carthage and its neighborhood comprises, in actuality, three symbols (see above, fig. 3): (a) the crescent with disc;[82] (b) the symbol generally called the "sign of *Tanit*" by scholars; and (c) the symbol generally identified with the caduceus.

There seems to be little doubt that the crescent is the symbol of *Ba'al Ḥamman*, for it appears not only at the head of most of the stelae on which he and *Tanit* are mentioned, but also at the head of most of the stelae on which he alone is mentioned (see below, fig. 15). Moreover, it does not appear at all on many of the stelae devoted to *Tanit* alone. This is further strengthened by the fact that the crescent is the only symbol mentioning *Ba'al-Ḥamman* appearing on both the Zinjirli monuments and the Punic stelae. This conclusion can be reached through elimination, as well: if it is proved that the "sign of *Tanit*" (fig. 12) truly belongs to *Tanit*, then the symbol of *Ba'al Ḥamman* would in any event be the crescent with disc. On some of the coins of Ashkelon, there appears the figure of a goddess accompanied by the inscription φανηβαλος and the symbol in question.[83] There is no doubt that "phanebalos" is to be identified with פנבעל, the title of *Tanit*,[84] thus further strengthening the identification of this symbol with *Tanit*.[85] Scholars are divided on the meaning of this symbol as well, but it would seem that it should be regarded as a figure with arms stretching upward.[86]

An interesting development took place in the symbols on the Punic stelae; in many stelae there appear two hands stretched upward alongside the symbol of Tanit, a motif mentioned at the start of this discussion. These hands seem to be connected with the worship of *Tanit*. Not only can they be regarded as representing the figure of *Tanit* herself,

Figure 12. The "Tanit Symbol"

pars pro toto, but in most of the stelae of this type there is no indication of a symbol representing *Ba'al-Ḥamman;* the symbol of *Tanit* appears at the head of the stele or between the two hands (see Pl. 22–23).[87] We shall return to this problem when discussing the symbols on the stele from Hazor.

The Caduceus Symbol. The third symbol, appearing on almost every Punic stele, is that called the caduceus. It is difficult to decide whether it symbolizes *Ba'al-Ḥamman, Tanit* or both of them together. Again, scholars are divided on the interpretation of the symbol proper. In spite of the great similarity between it and the caduceus of Hermes, i.e., the scepter terminating in snake-heads, there are scholars who consider it to consist of a disc surmounted by a crescent, atop a pole and tied to it by means of ribbons (see Pl. 22–23).[88] Even so, it should be noted that because of the clouded origin of the caduceus of Hermes, on the one hand, and the clear connection between the moon-god(dess) and snakes, on the other hand (see below), it might be possible to assume that this symbol has taken a little from both, i.e., that the symbol is basically connected with the crescent and disc motif atop a pole with ribbons (similar to the symbol on the Bar-Rakkab monument dedicated to *Ba'al-Ḥarran*), with an additional connotation having to do with snakes. In the light of the frequency of this symbol on the stelae dedicated to both *Tanit* and *Ba'al-Ḥamman,* it might be best to assume that it is connected with their common worship. A fuller exposition of this matter, interesting in itself, is beyond the purpose of the present paper.

Another interesting question is the meaning of the name *Tanit*. As already stated, scholars generally tend to ascribe it to some unknown Libyan source. It would seem, however, that a Semitic origin should be looked for. Thus, we should briefly review the material from the third sphere in which *Ba'al-Ḥamman* appears, i.e., at Palmyra. The worship of *Bel (Ba'al)-Ḥamman* at Palmyra has long been known through a number of inscriptions, among the earliest found on the site.[89] Additional important inscriptions were recently found in the temple of *Bel-Ḥammon* there.[90]

From previous inscriptions, but even more so from the latest, it appears that alongside the worship of *Bel-Ḥammon* there was another important cult, connected with his consort, *Manawat:* לבל חמון עבדו . . . היכלא דנה . . . וואף קרבו היכלא די מנות[91]. There is even evidence of a connection between the cult of *Manawat* and that of פנבעל.[92] Most interesting is the fact that this *Manawat* is also mentioned in Nabatean inscriptions,[93] and even in the Qur'an.[94] The meaning of the name of this goddess was connected already by Wellhausen[95] with "lot," "portion," "specific gift," similar to Tyche and גד. In this light, the question arises whether the name *Tanit* also was derived from such a root, signifying a specific lot, i.e., that she is a goddess of fate?[96] In any event, it should be noted that one of the attributes of the Palmyrian *Manawat* is the snake, as indicated by a figure appearing on a bulla from Palmyra (see fig. 13).[97]

Figure 13. MNWT from Palmyra (cf. n. 97)

In this connection, further interesting parallels are to be found in the cult of the "stelae temple" at Hazor, as we shall see below.

We shall now turn to another find which can serve to connect the Punic cult with that at Hazor, i.e., the many masks discovered at various sites.[98] These are generally considered to be female masks[99] used in apotropaeic capacities. However, a most important fact for our discussion should be noted here. Occasionally on the forehead of such masks there appears the crescent with disc (see fig. 14). It would seem

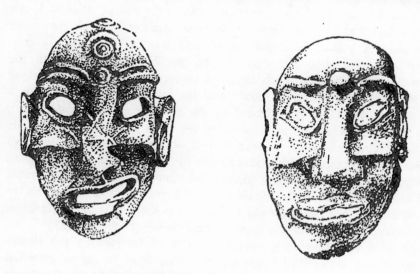

Figure 14. Two Punic masks (cf. n. 98)

that these masks are connected with the *Ba'al-Ḥamman* cult. But in the light of the fact that on the Punic stelae the standard title of *Tanit* is פנבעל, the "face of *Ba'al*," it may be asked whether these very masks were the "face of *Ba'al*" proper, i.e., the representation of *Tanit* in the form of פנבעל? If this assumption is correct, these objects are then connected with the cult of *Tanit*.[100] In summary, we can state that the Punic cult features the following points:

a) Worship connected with stelae.

b) The principal god is *Ba'al-Ḥamman* whose symbol is the crescent with disc.

c) His consort is *Tanit*, פנבעל, whose symbol is the figure with upraised hands, near which are (often) a separate pair of upraised hands.

d) This goddess is evidently connected with a snake cult.

e) Among the cult objects are masks possibly signifying *Tanit*/פנבעל.

As we have stated above, the point of departure for the second part of this study is the stele from Hazor with the two symbols: the crescent with disc and the two hands. Having reviewed the principal symbols of the Punic cult, along with its cult objects, we now proceed to the cult symbols and objects at the "stelae temple" of Hazor.

It appears immediately that there is an amazing similarity between Hazor and Carthage, and not only in the two-hands symbol. Iconographically, the most important feature among the row of stelae at Hazor is the fact that only the central stele bears symbols, whereas the others are plain. As stated, the Hazor symbol consists of two parts: a) the crescent with disc (and two small knobs, possibly volutes, beneath the crescent); and b) two hands stretched upward in an attitude of prayer (see fig. 11). There is no doubt that the temple is connected with a moon-god cult. This is evidenced by the above mentioned male statue, on whose chest a pendant appears in the form of a crescent with its points facing downward, a clear symbol of the moon-god.[101] We have seen that the crescent with disc is similar to the symbol of *Ba'al-Ḥamman* (according to our hypothesis) on the Zinjirli monuments and to the symbol of this same god on the Punic stelae. Of course, it is impossible to ascertain whether the moon-god at Hazor was specifically *Ba'al Ḥamman* or some other *ba'al*, of the type of *Ba'al-Ḥazor* (II Sam 13:23).

Another very interesting question is that of interpreting the significance of the two uplifted hands on the Hazor Stele. In the excavational report,[102] I noted the connection between this symbol and the Punic "hands," and assumed that the meaning behind the gesture of the hands was one of supplication before the divine symbol above them. However, it now seems that this symbol should be re-examined, comparing it with the parallel symbol on the Punic stelae on which the hands are given, *pars pro toto*, for the consort of *Ba'al-Ḥamman*. If this is the meaning of the hands at Hazor,[103] we must assume that the cult of this temple, too, was devoted to a god and his consort, whose iconographic expression is the raised hands.

This assumption might possibly explain another important object found near the "stelae temple." In locus 6211,[104] related to the temple complex, a cult "standard"[105] of silver-plated bronze was found within a unique jar. The lower part ends in a tang, probably meant for fastening it to a wooden pole (see Pl. 24). This standard is undoubtedly connected with the cult of the above temple, as witnessed by the crescent at its top. Further, there is no doubt that the standard was not dedicated to the moon-god, but rather to a goddess connected with his cult. This is indicated by the peculiar symbol of the goddess appearing within the crescent (a pattern curled at either end), a symbol appearing also on the lower part of the standard. This seems simply to be a stylized snake.[106] However, the most important feature of this standard is at its center, the face and part of the body flanked by a snake on either side. The present state of the silver plating makes it difficult to determine the connection between the figure and the snakes, though it is clear that the figure is holding them. Thus we have before us a parallel to the known goddess figure of the "Qadesh" type, holding snakes in her hands.[107]

In light of the above, it may be assumed that the standard is connected with the cult of the moon-god's consort, a goddess holding snakes in her upraised hands.[108]

Another cult object found within the temple area is also of considerable interest, a clay mask found in the court of a potter's workshop attached to the temple.[109] This mask (Pl. 25) was meant to be tied in one manner or another, as is indicated by the holes at its edges. It should be noted, however, that it is quite small (length twelve centimeters), and probably was not meant to be placed over a human face. Could it have been intended for placing over the face of a statue? The mask lacks a beard or moustache, but it is not clear whether a young male or a female is meant here. A similar mask was found in area D at Hazor as well,[110] but the latter is much cruder in execution.

These masks indicate another connection between Hazor and the Phoenician-Punic rite, in which similar masks are also found. We might assume that here, as well, the mask signifies the "Face of *Ba'al*" and is directly connected with the cult of the consort of this temple's *ba'al*.

Finally, we must not overlook the similarity between the character of the "stelae temple" itself and the Punic cult places. Both there and at Hazor the stelae were the principal cult equipment.[111] In this connection, we should note a famous Punic stele (see fig. 15) from Lilybeum in Sicily.[112] On this stele, which is dedicated to *Ba'al Ḥamman,* in addition to the usual symbols of Tanit and her cult objects, there also appears the form of the temple itself, a row of stelae resting upon a raised dais. Above this appear the symbols of *Ba'al Ḥamman,* the crescent with disc.

If we examine the stelae of the temple at Hazor as they were discovered, *in situ* (Pl. 26), we can observe the great similarity between them and the depiction on the Lilybeum stele, including the symbol at the top of the central stele in both cases.

The discussion of the symbols of the gods at Samal (Zinjirli), the point of departure for this general review, has brought us to the conclusion

Figure 15. A Stele dedicated to *Ba'al Ḥamman* from Lilybeum in Sicily
(cf. n. 112)

that there are certain connections between the names of the gods, their
symbols and their cult objects, as evidenced by the finds from Hazor,
Zinjirli and in the far West-Semitic sphere, i.e., the Punic world. This in
turn raises a most interesting question, the answer to which lies beyond
the scope of the present paper, that of the religious-cultural connection
between these cultural focal-points, as well as the missing links in our
knowledge of the development of the Canaanite culture from the second
millennium down to the end of the first millennium BC. Our discussion
may serve as the impetus for further clarification of the important problems initially raised by Albright in his basic study of the position of the
Canaanites within the history of civilization.[113]

FOOTNOTES

1. F. von Luschan *et al.*, "Ausgrabungen in Sendschirli," *Königliche Museen zu Berlin—Mitteilungen aus den orientalischen Sammlungen* (henceforth *Sendschirli*), I (1893); II (1898); III (1902); IV (1911); V (1913). Donner has recently published an additional orthostat: H. Donner, "Ein Orthostatenfragment des Königs Barrakab von Sam'al," *MiOr*, 3 (1955), pp. 73 ff. (henceforth *Donner*).

2. Full bibliography in this matter is found in H. Donner and W. Röllig: *Kanaanäische und aramäische Inschriften* (henceforth *Donner & Röllig*), I (1962); II–III (1964), Nos. 24–25, 214–21. The inscription numbers in the present article follow those given by the editors.

3. E.g., B. Landsberger, *Sam'al, Veröffentlichungen der türkischen historischen Gesellschaft*, 7 (1948), (henceforth *Landsberger*).

4. And see the basic study by R. D. Barnett, "The Gods of Zinjirli," *Compte rendu de l'onzième rencontre assyriologique internationale* (1964), pp. 59 ff. (henceforth *Barnett*).

5. See especially *Barnett*, p. 65.

6. See *Donner & Röllig*, no. 24.

7. *Landsberger*, p. 45.

8. E. Meyer, *Geschichte des Altertums*, II² (1931), pp. 428 ff.

9. *Donner*, p. 79.

10. K. Galling, "Erwägungen zum Stelenheiligtum von Hazor," *ZDPV*, 75 (1959), p. 6.

11. *Barnett*, pp. 69 ff.; figs. 5–7. Though he correctly identified the symbol, Barnett erred, in my opinion, in ascribing it to *Ba'al-Ṣemed*, interpreting *ṣmd* to mean "chariot yoke"; we shall return to this matter below.

12. At this point we give only Barnett's suggestions, for his study is the most recent on this subject and is far more detailed than any of the previous treatments. The opinions of Landsberger and Donner will be mentioned below in connection with the other monuments and the significance of the names of the gods.

13. *Barnett*, pp. 65–66.

14. For the basis of the reading *Rakkab-El*, see *Landsberger*, pp. 45 ff.; *Donner & Röllig*, notes to the inscription; see also *Barnett*, p. 65. These readings are based both on an Akk. inscription—[d]Bé-'-li-ra-kab'biᵃᵃ, and on a Hittite seal—Bar-r(a)-ki-ba(sa).

15. "Streitwagenfahrer des El" (Landsberger); "Charioteer" or "rider of El" (Barnett); etc.

16. This opinion was recently expressed by L. Y. Rahmani, "Two Syrian Seals," *IEJ*, 14 (1964), p. 183.

17. This has already been assumed by Landsberger (though he believed the symbol to be that of the moon-god, and that *Rakkab-El* was thus a moon-god), Donner and others.

18. On this symbol in general, see E. Douglas van Buren, "Symbols of the Gods," *AnOr*, 23 (1945), pp. 94 ff.

19. See *ANEP*, No. 493.

20. See *Sendschirli*, v, Pl. 38:6.

21. *Landsberger*, p. 46.

22. Dublette zum Be'li-rakkabi=Gott des Streitwagens=Rakkab-El), *ibid.*, n. 116.

23. *Donner & Rӧllig*, No. 61; for additional bibliography, see *ibid.*, II, p. 77.

24. For the problem of *Ba'al-Ḥamman* and *Tanit* and their series of symbols, see below.

25. See *Donner & Rӧllig, loc. cit.* (above, n. 23).

26. See, e.g., V. Tusa, "La Questione Fenicio-Punica in Sicilia," *Eretz-Israel* 8 (1967), pp. 50*-57* and Pl. XVII, 1-2; and see *ibid.*, p. 56*, n. 40, for additional references.

27. *Barnett*, pp. 62 ff. This explanation is unacceptable for other reasons as well; see below.

28. *Donner & Rӧllig*, No. 216; for further references see *ibid.*, II, p. 232.

29. *Donner & Rӧllig*, No. 214; see also below.

30. *Ibid.*, No. 215.

31. *Barnett*, p. 68, table.

32. For the star see Douglas van Buren, *op. cit.* (above, n. 18), p. 82.

33. See *Donner; Donner & Rӧllig*, No. 217; and *Barnett*, p. 64, fig. 3.

34. The beginning of the inscription, as restored by Donner, is as follows:

1. אנה. ברדכב.בר. פנמו. מלך. שמא[ל עבד תגלתם]
2. ליסר. מרא. רבעי. אר[קא עבד] 3. ואלהי. בית אבי]   [

Donner conjectures that at the end of line 2 there was possibly mention of the name of the gods of Asshur, while in his opinion the phrase ואלהי בית אבי refers to the entire pantheon of Samal: *Hadad, El, Rakkab-El, Shamash* and *Reshef*. However, this supposition seems unlikely for several reasons: In Bar-Rakkab's other inscription (see above), where he defines himself as the servant of Tiglath-Pileser, no mention is made of any Assyrian god. On the contrary! The text reads מראי רכבאל ומראי תגלתפילסר. It is difficult to suppose that after the name of Tiglath Pileser the name of *Rakkab-El* would be lacking, especially as *Rakkab-El* is mentioned at the end of the inscription: ר] (8) כבאל חני קד]מ . . . (7) Moreover, the phrase ואלהי בית אבי connotes a plurality of gods, but certainly this does not include *Haddad, El*, etc., for these, as we have already seen, though part of the Canaanite pantheon, were definitely not among the dynastic gods of Bar-Rakkab. Thus if we restore the end of line 2 as [. . . ועבד. מראי. רכבאל] the intent would be to *Ba'al-Ṣemed* and *Ba'al-Ḥamman*, the sole dynastic gods of Samal. Somewhat hesitatingly we could restore the first lines as follows: [אנה. ברדכב. בר. פנמו. מלך. שמא[ל עבד. תגלתם] .1 . . . ליסר. מרא. רבעי. אר[קא. ועבד. מראי. רכבאל] 3. ואלהי. בית. אבי . .2 The phrase רכבאל ואלהי בית אבי would then tally with that of the monument that Bar-Rakkab set up in memory of his father Panamu (*Donner & Rӧllig*, No. 215); . . . הדד ואל. ורכבאל. בעל. בית ושמש. וכל אלהי יאדי (and see above). Though my restored version may not be accepted word for word, it does fit the lacuna exactly. In any event, it is clear that no mention was made here of the names of the gods as in the longer version, which lists the entire Canaanite pantheon.

35. *Barnett*, p. 68.

36. This yoke differs from that to the right of the winged disc only in one detail: Instead of the knob at the center there is a series of lines, as if binding it. It is difficult to assume that this minor difference signifies another god. We can, therefore, agree with *Donner* that this symbol is intrinsically identical with that to the right of the winged disc.

37. *Donner*, p. 80, n. 30.

38. About nine letters and dividing points. *Donner* concurs (and see *Donner & Rӧllig*).

39. *Donner*, p. 80, n. 30.

40. This order conforms with the denoting of the chariot beasts if four are used; see the yoke in a relief of Sennacherib, *Barnett*, pp. 368, 373.

41. See especially *Donner*, p. 81.

42. See, e.g., the famous *Ba'al* stele from Ugarit, C. F.-A. Schaeffer, *Ugaritica*, II (1949), Pls. XXIII–XXIV.

43. This identification may also serve to explain the peculiar fact that the symbol under discussion is extremely rare (and see below) and that the name *Ba'al-Ṣemed* is unique.

44. See especially M. Lidzbarski, *Ephemeris*, III (1915), Pl. XIII, pp. 192 ff.

45. Lidzbarski (*ibid.*, p. 196) also identified the left-hand symbol with the crescent and disc, and considered the right-hand one to be the sun-disc. The latter is very vague, but on the basis of parallels on the other monuments and fragments, this is none other than the horned cap.

46. *Donner & Röllig*, No. 218; and the additional bibliography there. See also *ANEP*, No. 460.

47. *Landsberger* (p. 46, n. 114) has already touched upon this, but according to his interpretation it is a substitute of *Rakkab-El.*

48. Concurring with *Landsberger* (*ibid.*).

49. The symbols in col. 3 of fig. 8 are given from left to right, in conformity with the order on the other monuments.

50. *Landsberger*, p. 46, n. 116.

51. *Ibid.*

52. *Donner & Röllig*, II, p. 34.

53. Cf., e.g., חרב מצמדת על מתניו (II Sam 20:8); and thus in other Semitic languages.

54. Of course such phrases as צמד חמורים (Judg 19:10), צמד בקר (I Sam 11:7), צמד פרשים (Isa 21:7) and (II Kings 5:17) צמד פרדים. stem from the actual yoking of pairs of beasts; thus also in Akk., etc.

55. In this connection it should be noted that the biblical expression הנצמדים לבעל פעור (Num 25:5) and others similar to it refer to ritual coupling connected with *Ba'al*; Cf. Num 25:8.

56. See, e.g., Document No. 15.83 in the administrative texts from Ugarit, *Le Palais Royal d'Ugarit*, II (1957), p. 154:arb'-ṣmdm-apnt.

57. *Ṣemed-El*, similar to מרח אל etc. See Cyrus H. Gordon: *Ugaritic Textbook*, (*AnOr*, 38 [1965]), Glossary, s.v. Gordon, however, translates this as "a stick, war club;" and see below.

58. *Ibid.*, *Texts*, p. 180. See also the translation by H. A. Ginsberg: *ANET*, pp. 130–31.

59. J. Gray, *The Legacy of Canaan, VT*, Supplement 5 (1957) p. 24, n. 5.

60. F. Thureau-Dangin, *Arslan-Tash* (1931), Pl. 2; see also *ANEP*, No. 501; and cf. *ibid.*, No. 500 and especially No. 538. The "doubling" of the weapons is evident also in the weapons of the famous "Ba'al" from Ugarit (*ANEP*, no. 409), the one part of which is like a spear and the other like a thunder-bolt. For the possible connection between the *ṣemed* under discussion and the "thunder and lightning," see also P. D. Miller, Jr.: "Fire in the Mythology of Canaan and Israel," *CBQ*, 25 (1965), p. 257. Miller especially mentions Gaster's opinion (T. H. Gaster, *Thespis²* [1961], pp. 164 ff.) that the two maces are "symbolizations of thunder and lightning."

61. See Donner, p. 80, and the additional bibliography there.

62. See H. Frankfort, *Cylinder Seals* (1939), p. 123 and the additional bibliography there. It should be noted that the two-faced god is generally identified with the Sumerian Isimud. Could there be some connection between this name and *Ṣemed*?

Could the Sumerian here have borrowed the name of a Semitic god? Or is the Semitic name Ṣemed a sort of "translation" of the Sumerian word, following a folk-etymology? Because of considerable interest stirred by this name, I approached Professor N. Kramer (through Professor Edith Porada) for an explanation of the form of this name in the Sumerian documents and its connection with occurrences in the Akkadian. This is his answer (May 1965): "When it is the subject of a transitive verb and the root of the word must therefore be followed by the grammatical element -*e*, the sign used is d é, which means that the -*e* was combined with final consonant *d* of the root; hence the root must have ended in *d*. Since the vocabularies give i s i m u as the reading of the sign, we must assume that the root was actually i s i m u d, but the final *d* was dropped, unless followed by a grammatical element beginning with, or consisting of a vowel." For Professor Kramer's opinions on this matter, see *AASOR* Supplementary Studies, 1 (1945), p. 25, n. 50. I must thank my colleague H. Tadmor for his help in clarifying this matter and for the relevant bibliography dealing with the connection between Sumerian Isimud and the later Akkadian form Usmû or Usumû. And see G. Furlani, *AnOr*, 12 (1935), pp. 130–62; A. Ungnad, "Der Babylonische Janus," *AfO*, 5 (1928–29), p. 185; R. Franken, *Takultu—De Sacrale Maaltijd in het Assyrische ritueel* (1954), p. 118. The name and title—the Vizier of Ea—are already mentioned in an Akkadian inscription of the king of Malgium on the Tigris from the beginning of the second millennium BC; see T. Jacobsen, "The Inscription of Takal-ili-su of Malgium," *AfO*, 12 (1937–39), p. 365, l. 34.

63. Frankfort, *op. cit.* (above, n. 62), p. 254.

64. *Ibid.*, p. 285, fig. 92.

65. See E. Akurgal, *Die Kunst Anatoliens* (1961), p. 46, figs. 25–26.

66. See *Barnett*, p. 62, and the additional bibliography there.

67. See F. M. Abel, *Géographie de la Palestine*, ι (1933), p. 335.

68. See Y. Yadin *et al.*, *Hazor*, ι (1958), pp. 83 ff.

69. *Ibid.*, Pl. XXIX, 2.

70. *Ibid.*, p. 89.

71. *Ibid.*, p. 89; Pl. XXXI, 1.

72. *Ibid.*, p. 89; see also Galling, *op. cit.* (above, n. 10), p. 2.

73. See *Donner & Röllig*, No. 61; *CIS*, ι, No. 123.

74. For a thorough discussion of this subject, as well as further bibliography, see *Donner & Röllig*, ιι, p. 77.

75. Here mentioned under the name אלחמן; see *ibid.*, p. 26.

76. See further below.

77. E.g., *ibid.*, No. 79, etc.

78. See further below. For the convenience of the reader, I refer him to the index in *Donner & Röllig*. Below I shall give the sources only in special instances.

79. *Donner & Röllig*, ιι, p. 90 (No. 72); G. A. Cooke, *North-Semitic Inscriptions*, (1903), p. 132.

80. *CIS*, ι, No. 116; *Donner & Röllig*, No. 53.

81. See *The Oxford Classical Dictionary* (1949), s.v. Artemis, Selene. For the connection of *Tanit* with the queen of heaven, cf. also her Latin titles (*Donner & Röllig*, ιι, p. 90). For an additional connection between the cult of Artemis and that of *Tanit* (the masks), see below, n. 100.

82. Even though the extremities of the crescent are generally turned down, they occasionally appear facing upward; see Pl. 18.

83. G. F. Hill, *Greek Coins of Palestine* (1914), pp. lix ff., Pl. XIII, 18.

84. *Ibid.*

85. The cult of פנבעל in the Ashkelon region is also witnessed by a lead weight recently found south of Ashdod-Yam. On the one side, it clearly bears the "sign of *Tanit*." This weight is at present under the study of M. Dothan, whom I must thank for allowing me to examine a photograph of the object. See *Hadashot Arkheologiot*, 10 (1964), p. 18 (Hebrew).

86. G. Picard, *Le Monde de Carthage* (1956), p. 41; see also D. Harden, *The Phoenicians* (1962), p. 89. A similar phenomenon, as far as the iconographic development is concerned, is found in a much later period, among the Bogomils living in Bosnia in the Middle Ages. On their tombstones there are often figures with outspread arms, depicted in a realistic style. In several instances, however, the figures are quite schematic, recalling very much the "sign of *Tanit*." For these monuments and the problem in general, see O. Bihalji-Merin and A. Benac, *Bogomil Sculpture* (1962), especially Pl. 37. Other symbols appearing on these stones are also most interesting, e.g., the crescent, sun, etc.

87. See, e.g., *CIS* I, Nos. 585, 603, 647, 783 etc. See especially J. Euting, *Sammlung der Carthagischen Inschriften*, I (1883), Pl. 56:93, and *CIS*, I, Nos. 183, 199, 240. In these inscriptions one may observe many interesting variations: the hands-up top, the full symbols of *Tanit* below, etc. Of course, at the same time, the hands also signify the supplicant position also expressed in the "sign of *Tanit*" itself with its two arms stretched upward.

88. See, e.g., Harden, *op. cit.* (above, n. 86), p. 88.

89. For a full discussion of this problem, as well as for additional bibliography, see R. du Mesnil du Buisson, *Les Tessères et les monnaies de Palmyre* (1962), pp. 198 ff., *et passim* according to the subject. The author's interpretations of the symbols there (crescent with disc, etc.) hardly agree with mine.

90. *Idem*, "Première campagne de fouilles à Palmyre," *CRAI* (January–March 1966), pp. 158 ff.; and especially the chapter "Temples de Bel Hamman et de Manawat," pp. 165 ff.

91. *Ibid.*, p. 170.

92. See especially the Latin inscription from Dacia in which a person from Palmyra dedicates a temple to various of his native gods: "diis patris Malagbet et Bebellahamon et Benefal et Manawat." Starky (at Milik's suggestion) has already noted that we should read "Fenebel" (i.e. פנבעל) instead of "Benefal." For the problems of this inscription and the relevant bibliography, see du Mesnil du Buisson, *op. cit.* (above, n. 89).

93. See, e.g., Cooke, *op. cit.* (above, n. 79), Inscription No. 79 from El-Hejra (*CIS*, II, 197) of the ninth year of Aretas IV: ילענו דושרא ומנותו וקישה
94. The "star" sura 43:18–19.

95. See the full discussion in Cooke, *op. cit.* (above, n. 79), p. 219.

96. A similar form, with the meaning of a legal and defined portion, was recently found in the Nabatean documents from Naḥal Ḥever in the Judean Desert (not yet published), in which the legal rights of a landowner are defined as follows: מן צדק ... ותחום ... וחלק ותחף ותנת (Doc. No. 2 of the twenty-eighth year of Rabel II). At this point, we should mention the female sphinx bearing the inscription תנת among the proto-Sinaitic monuments from Serabit el-khadem, dedicated to *Ba'alat*, the consort of *Ba'al*. See most recently Albright's extensive study "The Proto-Sinaitic Inscriptions and their Decipherment," *HTS*, 22, (1966), fig. 6: 347, p. 17: *TNT* "gift"; p. 44; *tnt* . . . "offering." Could there be some connection between the Punic *TNT* and this word *tnt* in Sinai? [After writing the above, it happily came to my atention that Cross regards the Punic Tanit as stemming from a Semitic root; see Frank M. Cross, Jr., "The Origin and Early Evolution of the Alphabet," *Eretz-Israel*, 8 (1967), p. 12*, n. 27. Cross further compares it with *tnt* in the proto-

Sinaitic inscriptions. However, in the light of the above, it is understood that I do not tend to accept Cross's intriguing suggestion to interpret the name *TNT* as the feminine of תנן, with the meaning of "the one of the (sea) serpents" or "the Dragon Lady." Among the difficulties raised by this suggestion one should note, once again, the name *Manawat*, the consort of *Ba'al Ḥammon* of Palmyra, with its close relationship in meaning to the name *Tanit* and which undoubtedly has no connection with תנן, etc. The appearance of the word תנת in the Nabatean papyri (which of course have not been known to Cross), with the clear meaning of a defined and absolute gift-portion, negates his suggestion. However, it should be noted that both Cross and myself reached the conclusion, on differing and opposing grounds, that *Tanit* is a goddess connected with snakes (in his opinion תנן; in mine, actual snakes).

Thus there is no doubt that it is possible to interpret the titles *dt bṭn* etc. (in the meaning of "the Lady of Serpent") on the Serabit el-Khadem monuments (see Cross, *ibid.;* Albright, *op. cit.,* this note) as an indication, in my opinion, of the attribute of TNT, but not her actual name. For in the last instance the name of the goddess would undoubtedly stem from the word בתן bṭn etc., and not תנן. In any event, this matter, important in itself, does not interfere with our suggestion that *Tanit* is a goddess whose attribute is the snake (and see also below).

97. See du Mesnil du Buisson, *op. cit.* (above, n. 89), p. 169.

98. See especially P. Cintas, "Amulettes Puniques," *Publications de l'Institut des Hautes Etudes de Tunis,* I (1946), pp. 37 ff.; figs. 69–71, 74–77, 78–83. Most of the masks were found in tombs. However, it should be noted that two very small masks of ivory were also found in the temple of *Tanit* (*ibid.,* p. 49, fig. 73). See L. Poinssot and R. Lantier, "Un Sanctuaire de Tanit à Carthage," *RHR,* 87–88 (1923), p. 58. I must thank Prof. D. Harden for this reference.

99. E.g., Harden, *op. cit.* (above, n. 86), p. 199.

100. This can also support the assumption that a part of the masks are female, as is based on the fact that on some of them there are traces of ear-and nose-rings; see Harden, *ibid.* Actually, there is a sort of mixture of male and female in these, a feature noted in treatments of the cult of *Tanit;* see, e.g., Hill, *op. cit.* (above, n. 83), p. lx, on the figure of Fanebalos on the coins. See also G. A. Cooke, The *Religion of Ancient Palestine in the Light of Archaeology* (1930), pp. 178–79. We should also note here the male-female centaur figures (with arms upraised) in several of the statues in the Aya Irini temple in Cyprus. It is interesting that there, too, these figures are connected with snake-worship. I must thank Dr. V. Karagheorgius for calling my attention to this fact.

In this connection I should also mention that Barnett regards these masks (including those from Hazor and Carthage) as figures of the monster Hubaba mentioned in the famous Gilgamesh Epic; see R. D. Barnett, "Some Contacts between Greek and Oriental Religions," in *Eléments orientaux dans la religion grecque ancienne, Colloque de Strasbourg, 22–24 Mai 1958* (1960), pp. 143 ff. Though this suggestion is interesting, it is difficult to grasp the connection between Hubaba and the Canaanite-Phoenician masks. We should also note the interesting clay mask of the eleventh century BC discovered by Dr. V. Karagheorgius some time ago at Kition (I thank him for permission to mention this find). The mask was found in a structure (temple?) very close to a later temple dedicated to *Artemis.* In this connection mention should be made also of the famous masks found in the Artemis temple at Sparta; see Barnett, *ibid.* For the possible connection between the *Tanit* cult and that of *Artemis,* see above, n. 81.

101. Yadin *et al., op. cit.* (above, n. 68), p. 89.

102. *Ibid.*

103. Could there be a similar cultic significance to the ivory hand found in the temple at Lachish? See O. Tufnell *et al.*, *Lachish II: The Fosse Temple* (1940), Pl. XVI, 7; see also below.

104. Y. Yadin *et al.*, *Hazor*, II (1960), pp. 104 f., 117 ff.

105. *Ibid.*, Pl. CLXXXI.

106. For this symbol and its parallels, see *ibid.*, p. 118.

107. For this problem see *ibid.* See also *ANEP*, figs. 469–74. See also the figures of the gods from Ugarit, also lifting their arms, *ibid.*, figs. 464–65.

108. See our remarks on the snake as a symbol of *Manawat* at Palmyra, above, n. 96. We should possibly note here that in area C at Hazor, near the temple, we found a fragment of a Mycenean figurine depicting a woman with her hands uplifted (Yadin *et al.*, *op. cit.* [above, n. 104], Pl. CLXXIX, 7). In any event, it would seem that there is a connection between the type of goddess lifting her hands (*Tanit*) and the famous statues from Crete of the Late Minoan III age; see S. Marinatos, *Crete and Mycene* (1960), Pls. 128–31; and the additional bibliography there.

109. No. C 1136; see Yadin *et al.*, *op. cit.* (above, n. 104), p. 115, Pl. CLXXXIII.

110. Yadin *et al.*, *op. cit.* (above, n. 68), p. 138; Pl. CLXIII. Masks of this type were very rare in this period. In the final report of *Hazor*, I (*ibid.*) we noted a very similar parallel from Gezer (M. A. S. Macalister, *Gezer*, II [1912], p. 233; fig. 383). To this we should now add a stone mask with similar characteristics found a little while ago in the Hebron region (not in scientific excavations); see *Bible et Terre Sainte*, 49 (1962), p. 10; see also F. Winzinger, "Die Steinmaske aus dem Heiligen Land," *Pantheon*, 2 (1964), pp. 151 ff.; figs. 1–2.

111. See Harden, *op. cit.* (above, n. 86), pp. 94, 305. For the hypothesis that these stelae in the temple at Hazor are a בית במות, see especially W. F. Albright, "The High Place in Ancient Palestine," *VT*, Supplement 5 (1957), pp. 16 ff.

112. *CIS*, I, Pl. XXIX, No. 138. See also H. Gressman, *Altorientalische Texte und Bilder zum Alten Testament*, II (1909), 13, fig. 14; and V. Tusa, *op. cit.* (above, n. 26), Pl. 17, 3.

113. W. F. Albright, "The Role of the Canaanites in the History of Civilisation," in *BANE* (1961), pp. 328 ff. This article is a new, revised version of his original article.

ISRAELITE JERUSALEM

Kathleen M. Kenyon

JERUSALEM did not become Israelite until the time of David. At the stage of the entry into Palestine it is recorded as occupied by the Jebusites, a tribe otherwise unknown; apparently they belonged to the general group regarded by the Israelites as Amorites.[1] The comparatively late period at which the town succumbed to the spread of control by the infiltrating Israelite tribes is established by literary evidence, both by the record of its capture by David[2] and by the specific statement[3] that it was not captured in those phases of Israelite spread recorded in the Book of Joshua.

The history of Jerusalem is thus like that of Megiddo, Bethshan and Gezer, in that its absorption into Israel comes only at the time of the monarchy. Early Jerusalem, however, could not compare with these great towns of the Bronze Age, being only a fraction of their size and providing little evidence of rich and prolonged occupation. It had nevertheless a significance for Israelite development that the other sites lacked, for it lay in the center of the hill country in which was the early nucleus of the Israelite tribes, whereas the other sites lay on its fringes. In character it was probably little different from a number of other hill towns or villages, some of which certainly exceeded it in size. The very deep ravines that bordered it on two sides undoubtedly helped to give strength to its defenses, but other towns also had strong walls. Jerusalem's significance was geographical. The physical configuration of Palestine is such that from the central mountain backbone, at a height of 2700 feet near Jerusalem and at 3000 feet at Mount Ebal above Shechem, the terrain drops westward from Jerusalem to the coastal plain at near sea level in a distance of only twenty miles, while to the east the drop is even more rapid, to sea level in the upper Jordan Valley in a distance of ten miles, and then on to 1300 feet below sea level at the Dead Sea. As a result, the flanks of the mountain range are deeply cut by ravines and valleys, which make lateral communication along the flanks of the range almost impossible, or at best extremely laborious. Continuous north-south communication in the Jordan Valley is blocked by the Dead Sea, and the coastal plain was under the control of the Philistines. The only north-south route in the area occupied by the Israelite tribes was along the mountain crest. Jerusalem is situated just beside the crest at a point where this is very narrow, and at a point, moreover, where the important route from the Jordan Valley that starts near Jericho up the Wadi Qelt and the route from the west up the Wadi es-Sikke both reach the summit to form one of the few convenient east-west lines of communication.

The inhabitants of Jerusalem could, if they wished, control these routes, especially the north-south one. In effect, they lay between the southern and northern Israelite tribes. It is now usually accepted that the entry of the Israelites was a process of infiltration that created two main groups. The separate history of, and even antipathy between, the two groups is clear from the biblical record. David became king of the southern group and the northern group by two quite different contractual acts.[4] The existence of alien Jerusalem between the two groups must have contributed to the separation. It could also be that no particular effort was made to capture Jerusalem earlier because it was on the periphery of the area of either group. But for David, called to kingship by both groups, its capture was essential in order to clear his lines of communication. Its capture, moreover, gave him the site for a capital that was neither northern nor southern, and could be regarded as his own personal property.

The excavations of 1961 to 1967 have established with reasonable certainty the position of the earliest city and its wall. The Jerusalem of the Jebusites and David lay at the southern end of the eastern of the two ridges that run south from the present Old City of Jerusalem. The two ridges are bounded to the east and west by wadis that take their origin a few hundred yards away to the north as shallow depressions, and in those few hundred yards deepen into steep-sided ravines, good examples of the physical configuration referred to above. The eastern valley, the Kedron, is the main one. The western valley, the Wadi-er-Rebabeh (usually identified as the biblical Hinnom or Gehenna), curves round to meet the Kedron. Between the two is a central valley, known to Josephus as the Tyropoeon, originally almost equally deep and ravine-like, but now much silted up. The Tyropoeon enters the Kedron just north of the mouth of the Wadi Rebabeh, creating with the Kedron a narrow V-shaped ridge. On this ridge was situated the first Jerusalem.

Earlier excavations have traced walls running along the summit of the eastern ridge, and connecting with walls that also enclosed the western ridge. The ascription of these walls to the early periods of the Israelite monarchy was purely subjective, because the excavations did not have available the criteria of modern stratigraphical methods, nor modern knowledge of pottery. The accumulated evidence for the dating of pottery is of the greatest importance, but the crucial link is the establishment by modern, exact, stratigraphical methods of the relation of the occupation levels to the structures.

In the 1961–67 excavations, it was very early established that the walls on the crest of the eastern ridge could not possibly belong to the period of David and Solomon, ascribed to them in the 1923–25 excavations,[5] for they overlay houses occupied in the seventh century BC, and almost certainly destroyed by Nebuchadnezzar in 587 BC.[6] The excavations of 1961–67 did in fact face an initial improbability in dating the walls on the crest to the Jebusite-Davidic period. The sole advantage that the lower, narrower, eastern ridge has over the western ridge is that at its foot is the only permanent natural water supply within the area with natural defenses, the Spring Gihon, today known as the Virgin's Fountain or 'Ain Umm el-Daraj. The importance of this perennial spring in ancient times is shown by the number of ancient channels connected with it. The most famous is the Siloam Tunnel, dated with very great probability to the time of Hezekiah, *circa* 700 BC, to which reference will be made later. The archaeological evidence concerning the earlier channels is regrettably scanty; what there is depends on the observation of Père L. H. Vincent of the 1909–11 excavations;[7] there is good reason to suppose that Père Vincent's conclusions are convincing. These conclusions indicate that the original access to the spring from the summit of the ridge was by a combination of channels, shafts and passages (figs. 1, 2) that provided access to the water from high on the flanks of the ridge. The problem posed in 1961 was that the summit of this approach system must have come to the surface some twenty-seven meters outside the line of the walls hitherto ascribed to the Jebusite-Davidic period.

This conclusion was an improbable one, for an additional element of improbability was introduced if one accepted that the most likely interpretation of II Sam. 5:6–8 is that Joab climbed up the water channel and thus penetrated the city and took the defenders by surprise from the rear. This is a perfectly reasonable thesis, but makes no sense at all if the Jebusite system of access to the spring terminated outside the contemporary walls.

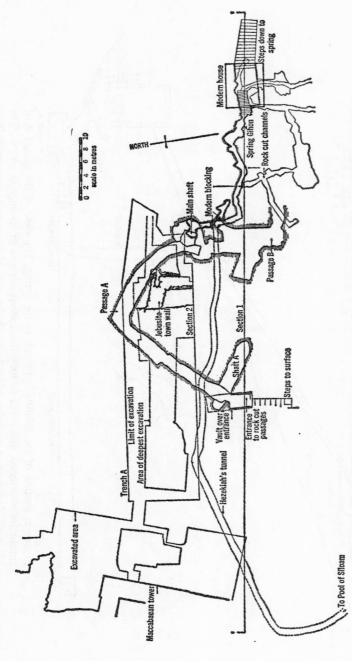

Figure 1. Plan of the Jebusite rock cut water channel, shaft and tunnel which provided access in wartime to the spring in the valley. The angular course of the tunnel was presumably to reduce the steepness of the route.

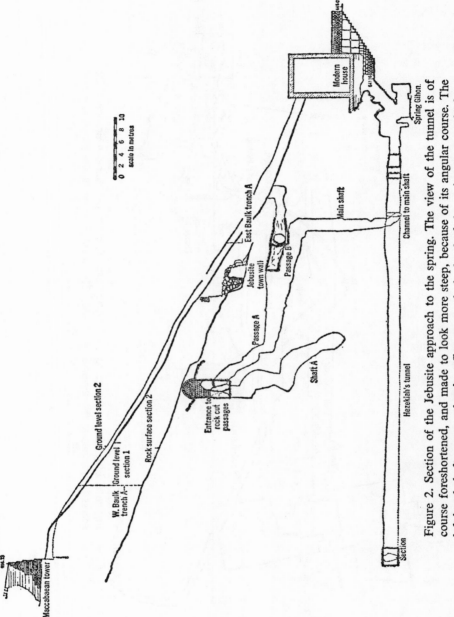

Figure 2. Section of the Jebusite approach to the spring. The view of the tunnel is of course foreshortened, and made to look more steep, because of its angular course. The left-hand shaft was an abortive effort to reach the level of the spring, apparently frustrated by difficult rock conditions.

As has already been said, the 1961–67 excavations early established the fact that the walls on the crest were, at earliest, Post-Exilic. From beneath them extended the seventh to sixth century BC houses which provided a basic certainty that the earlier limit of the town lay to the east, farther down the slope. This reasoning led to the excavation down the slope of a trench running east from the so-called Davidic tower. To reach intact structures involved working through layers of silt and tumbled stones to a great depth. The first intact structures reached were certainly late, in use until the seventh to sixth centuries BC, and though massive, they were clearly not defensive. It was only at a distance of forty-eight meters from the "Davidic" tower, and 27.25 meters lower, that what can be claimed as the ancient town wall was reached. The dating evidence from its foundation trench was clear, evidence confirmed by subsequent extension of the excavated area. It was built fairly early in the Middle Bronze Age, perhaps *circa* 1800 BC. It was the wall of Bronze Age Jerusalem. There are traces of occupation in the Early Bronze Age, but no town wall can be ascribed to that date. The traces of the contemporary Middle Bronze Age town are scanty, but they exist, though erosion has removed most of the evidence. The important point about the town wall is that, from its origin in the Middle Bronze Age, it existed until well into the Israelite period (Pl. 27). The excavation evidence shows that below it, to the east, the rock surface was kept clear until the seventh century BC. The wall found was massive, but it survived only as foundations. At least one rebuild on its top could be traced, but many more may have been necessary to maintain it in use until the building of its seventh century BC successor. David certainly repaired the walls after capturing the city.[8] Of his repairs there is no definite evidence, but it is certain that here was the line of the walls of the city of David.

The evidence just described for the boundaries of the city of David concern the eastern wall. To provide evidence for the northern limits of the city, it is necessary to refer to the structural characteristics of the preceding Jebusite town. The extension of the town walls far down the slope of the Kedron Valley was dictated by the necessity of controlling access to the Spring Gihon. The area on the steep slope that had thus to be enclosed was not inviting for any except the simplest type of structures. The Middle Bronze Age remains discovered were in fact of this character. In about the thirteenth century BC,[9] there was a major town-planning operation in Jebusite Jerusalem. The eastern slope was converted into a series of terraces with massive substructures[10] that provided a basis for relatively well laid-out houses. Of these houses nothing survives, for the terrace substructures were dependent on retaining walls; any destruction of these, by hostile attack or natural disaster such as earthquake or torrential rain, inevitably involved the collapse of the terrace and all it supported. The archaeological evidence is clear that the terrace structures were repaired on a number of occasions from early in the Israelite period, and that the only houses surviving on them belong to the seventh century BC. It is a reasonable suggestion that this is the *millo* or "filling" that David repaired,[11] as did a number of his successors; the claim of this interpretation is at least as convincing as the numerous other proposals put forward.

The reason why it is necessary to describe this element in the structures of Jebusite and Davidic Jerusalem at this point is that these terraces were found in the area immediately east of the so-called tower of David, east of the earlier excavations on the crest of the ridge and in Trench I of the 1961–67 excavations (fig. 3). In Square A XXIV, only ten meters to the north, there were no traces of them. Houses that date at the earliest to the eighth century BC[12] were based on bedrock. Between the two areas must have run the wall of the early town. Similar bracketing evidence is provided between Site P and Site H. In Site P, strata dating (on preliminary assessment) to the thirteenth century BC were found, though all later levels had been removed by earlier excavations. Site H lies immediately to the north, though its southern edge, forming the effective boundary with Site P, was a complicated succession of walls, so complicated and so massive that the area available for excavation did not provide clear stratigraphic evidence. The conclusive point is that in the northern half of Site H, north of this succession of massive walls, were deposits going down to bedrock that are at the earliest tenth to ninth century BC. Though exact dating must depend on further work on the finds, there is no doubt of the broad dating. The southern boundary of Site H divides the earliest town from its later development. It is on this basis that the line of the northern boundary of the Jebusite-Davidic town is drawn on fig. 3.

The southward extension of the eastern defenses from the east of Trench I is conjectured as following about the same contour, but no investigations have been carried out on the presumed line. The southern limit is given by the contours of the ridge, though the actual tip has been somewhat truncated. The line of the western defenses is based on negative evidence only. The excavations of Site K, in particular, and Site N showed that the Iron Age town did not extend onto the slopes of the ridge at these points. The eastern end of Site K touched the foot of the

PLATE 26. The steles' temple at Hazor

PLATE 27. Town Wall of Jebusite and Davidic Jerusalem

PLATE 28. Cave, mazzeboth and altar of the extramural cult center on the eastern slope

PLATE 29. Wall probably of the period of Nehemiah built on scarp at summit of eastern slope

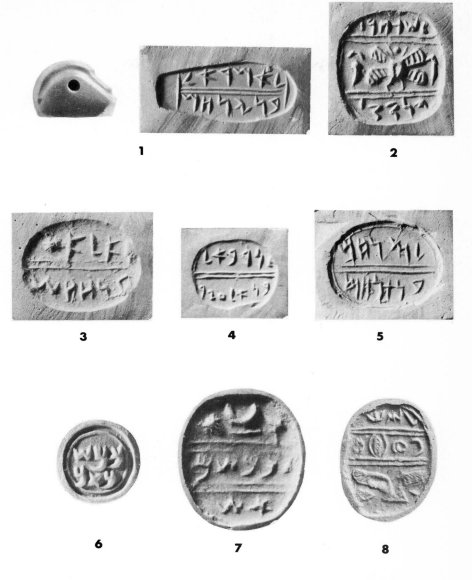

PLATE 30. Nos. 1–5 are Ammonite seals, Nos. 6–8 Moabite seals. The profile of the seal, No. 1a, is actual size while the impressions are all twice actual size

PLATE 31. Submycenean krater, P66.119. Sardis, House of Bronzes

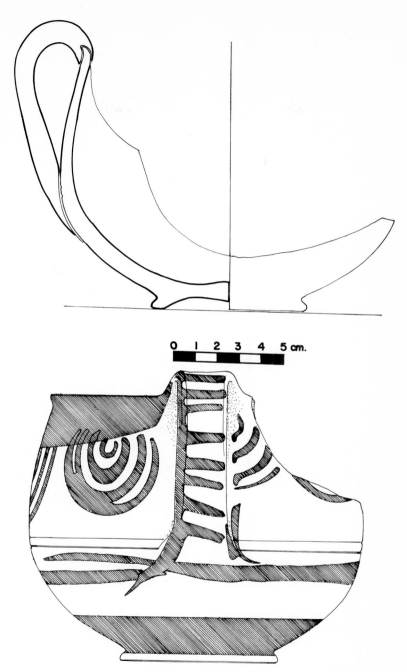

PLATE 32. Protogeometric cup, P66.107. Sardis, House of Bronzes

PLATE 33. Mycenean IIIA krater from Ephesus

PLATE 34. Cupels 5, 6, 7. Sardis, Pactolus North. Used for purifying gold of base metal impurities

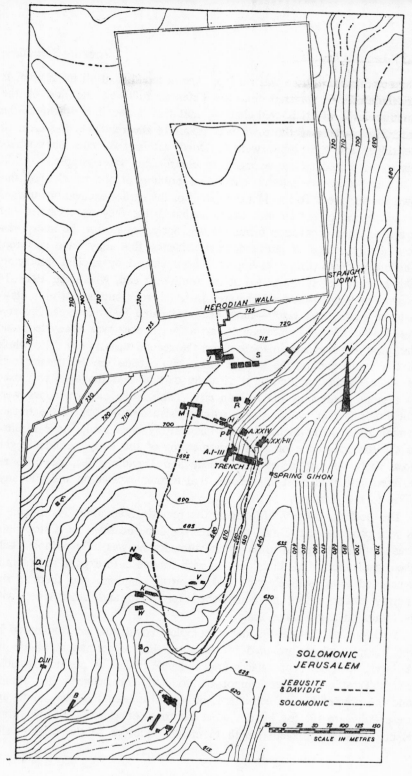

Figure 3. Solomonic Jerusalem.

summit scarp, and there was no Iron Age occupation at all in its area. It can therefore be inferred that the defenses followed the line of the summit scarp, which is well defined, and this is the line drawn in the plan. The nucleus of the town was therefore the relatively flat crest of the ridge, and the slopes were included within the walls only where this was required by the necessity to control the water supply.

It has become regrettably clear that nothing of the interior of this town has survived. To this fact the extent of the earlier excavations toward the north end of the summit has contributed, for they were carried out at a time when excavation technique was not adequate for the interpretation of any scraps of stratigraphical evidence that may have survived. The major destruction has, however, been caused by ancient quarrying. This is most clearly illustrated at the south-east end, where the 1913–14 excavations[13] uncovered a large area in which rock cuttings of all sorts— cisterns, baths, and vats[14]—have been truncated by widespread quarrying. In the 1961–67 excavations, an adjacent area was excavated, and the quarrying was shown to be from the second century AD. The whole of the south end of the eastern ridge lay outside the Hadrianic town of Aelia Capitolina, and it is virtually certain that the area was used as a stone quarry for the Roman city. Though the eastern slopes were not thus quarried, collapses due to successive destructions of the terrace retaining walls, to which reference has already been made, have resulted in the disappearance of all superstructures of the early periods in this area. Only the outline of the Jebusite and Davidic cities has been recovered, and it is most improbable that further excavation will add anything to the picture.

The position is very little better as regards Solomonic Jerusalem. It is very probable that David took over the Jebusite town as it stood and made little contribution to its architecture, for he was fully occupied with the organization of his kingdom and with conquests to expand it. Solomon succeeded to a relatively rich and powerful kingdom, and there is full literary evidence that he embellished Jerusalem and other cities with buildings on a grandiose scale.

To Jerusalem Solomon added a complete royal quarter, dominated by the Temple, which provided for the first time a permanent abode for Yahweh, with adjacent palaces and audience hall. The position of Solomon's Temple enclosure cannot be doubted, for between his Temple and the present Haram esh-Sherif, of which at least the east, south and west walls are formed by the great platform of Herod's Temple, there is no break of sufficient length to create doubt as to the original site.

As to where, however, the original Temple stood on the Solomonic platform, and as to its plan and that of the adjacent Palace building, there is no archaeological evidence; attempts to compensate for the lack of facts with theories and reconstructions are innumerable.

From the archaeological evidence for the limits of the original town, it must be accepted that Solomon's Temple lay to the north outside the walls of the Davidic city. It seems probable that the area between the Temple and the original north wall would have been enclosed within an extension of the town walls, though it has been suggested[15] that the Temple-Palace complex formed a separate acropolis area. An original theory[16] that this extension was made from the south-east corner of the original town proved to be wrong, for the excavation of Square A XXIV (fig. 3) showed that this area was outside the town at least until the eighth century BC.[17] The extension must have been confined to the summit ridge. Of this, some scanty evidence has been found. The existence in Site H, immediately north of the presumed line of the north wall, of deposits of the tenth to ninth century BC, has already been mentioned. Along the eastern crest of the summit ridge in Site H was found the almost destroyed remains of a casemate wall,[18] which could belong to Solomon's extension; this plan for a defensive wall would be entirely suitable for the period. A further hint came from the Trench SII farther north. The trench was against the inner side of the Byzantine wall exposed by the road cutting at this point. Beneath was an earlier wall, in use in the eighth century BC.[19] This earlier wall was built of re-used stones with margins and bosses reminiscent of the Phoenician-type masonry of the Omri-Ahab buildings at Samaria. They could well be derived from a Solomonic wall also built by Phoenician masons, and it would not be unreasonable to deduce that this Solomonic wall had been nearby.

The evidence therefore suggests that the Davidic town was joined to the Solomonic Temple by an extension along the summit of the ridge. Again, structures of any early occupation of this area have unfortunately not survived; again the reason is quarrying. In the trenches in the western part of Site S and in Site R, bedrock had been extensively quarried; the quarrying here, however, appears to have been Herodian.[20] Herod the Great must have destroyed the adjacent area of the original town to obtain the stone for his great rebuilding of the Temple and for all his other structures.

Solomon's Temple, like its successors, must have been supported by massive terrace walls to provide an adequate level space on the summit of the ridge. Much of Herod's platform wall still survives at the south end, at the south-east corner to a height of about 40 meters above bedrock. Recent clearance just north of this south-east angle has shown that at a distance of about 32 meters from the corner there is a straight joint between the typical Herodian masonry to the south and an older building stage to the north. The closest parallel to the older masonry is that of buildings of the Persian period in Lebanon. It would thus seem extremely probable that what one sees is the work of Zerubbabel, in his reconstruction of Solomon's Temple completed *circa* 516 BC, on the return of the exiles from Babylon in the reign of Cyrus the Great. Zerubbabel's Temple was a repair, to the best of the ability of the returned exiles, of Solomon's Temple, and it is to be expected that the enclosure walls would follow the lines of the ruined Solomonic walls; certainly they would not have extended the limits of the enclosure. It can thus be claimed with some assurance that the straight joint provides evidence of the position of the south-east corner of the platform of Solomon's Temple.

On the western side of the Haram platform there is no corresponding straight joint, and Herodian masonry is visible at the Wailing Wall and Wilson's Arch, at least 130 meters north of the south-west corner. It could be possible that the earlier wall here needed greater rebuilding at the time of Herod. It is more likely that the east-west width of the original platform was less, for Josephus states that Herod greatly increased the area of the Temple enclosure. Herod's platform extends on the west right across to the far side of the central valley,[21] and it is much more probable that Solomon's platform was confined to the eastern ridge. A rather tenuous possibility is that the wall of the salient running south from the Haram platform (now forming the east wall of the Old City and of its ancestor Aelia Capitolina) represents the line of the *west* wall of Jerusalem down to the time of Herod.[22] It is reasonable to suppose that just as the east wall of Solomon's extension seems to have run to the south-east corner of his Temple enclosure, so the west wall would have run to the south-west corner. A position for the south-west corner deduced as described from the line of the salient would balance the south-east corner quite nicely with reference to the crest of the ridge. It is on these grounds that the plan on fig. 3 has been drawn. The west wall is shown running from the point in Site M where there is some evidence for the position of a wall of the Solomonic period.[23]

Owing to the quarrying described above, archaeological evidence for most of the rest of Jerusalem's history in the period of the Monarchy is derived only from remains on the eastern slope. The Jebusite-

Davidic town wall continued in use to at least the eighth century BC, for clearance at the base of Trench I showed that the rock at its foot was kept clear until that period. The immediate successor to this wall has completely disappeared, and it can be inferred only from levels, including a cobbled street, that cross its top, which must have been retained by a wall farther to the east.[24] These levels were cut into by a later wall, an appreciable length of which has been uncovered, which in date cannot be earlier than the beginning of the seventh century BC, and which had several stages of repair.[25] A full analysis of the pottery evidence is required before one can say how closely it can be dated, and whether the first build can be early enough to belong to the time of Hezekiah. At least one stage of the defenses must certainly belong to Hezekiah, together with the cutting of the Siloam Tunnel, in face of the Assyrian threat of *circa* 700 BC.

The construction of the Siloam Tunnel, carrying the waters of the Spring Gihon from the Kedron Valley on the east through the eastern ridge to the western side of the city has long been associated with the biblical description of Hezekiah's measures to meet the Assyrian threat.[26] The tunnel today discharges water into the Pool of Siloam in the central valley. This fact caused no difficulty until the 1961–67 excavations showed that the adjacent southern end of the western ridge was certainly outside the town at this period.[27] A supply of water in an open pool here would have been very little safer than at the foot of the eastern slope. It is similarly inconceivable that the wall enclosing the eastern ridge should have been carried out into the central valley to enclose the Pool, for this would have brought it right under the threatening slope of the western ridge. The clue to the interpretation of this anomaly is provided by the channel that today carries the overflow from the Pool. Instead of running down the center of the valley, as might have been expected, overflow is carried round to run in a channel cut into the rock at the foot of the eastern ridge. This channel was clearly originally completely rock cut, and its outer side has been removed by subsequent quarrying. The original engineers would not have gone to the trouble of concealing the overflow in this way unless the water reservoir itself had been concealed, and had in fact been a great rock cut cistern. Access to this from within the walls by means of a shaft or stairs would have been perfectly simple and have been all that was required.

Remains of the eighth to seventh century BC even on the eastern slope have survived only scantily. Reference has already been made to

Square A XXIV. Here was found a substantial building founded on bedrock, and dating from the eighth to seventh century BC at the earliest, the exact dating again depending on the detailed analysis of the pottery. The existence of this building is evidence of the inclusion within the city of this date of the northern part of the eastern slope. It is probable that this was associated with one of the later walls already described, but this cannot be proved. The line shown on fig. 4 is made to climb the slope obliquely to the south-east corner of the Temple platform. It could be that in fact it continued north at a lower level, and just possibly might be represented by the wall found by Warren forty-six feet east of the Golden Gate in the Haram Wall;[28] Warren's tunnels, however, could not provide stratigraphic dating evidence.

The most interesting finds of this period made on the eastern slope were, however, extramural. Beneath the levels associated with the vanished wall that immediately succeeded the original wall, were found two caves in a rock scarp. Both served as a repository for a large number of pottery vessels and other objects. The one first found was unimpressive as a cave, but was associated with a complex of other structures (Pl. 28). The cave itself, little more than a shallow scoop in the rock, was surrounded on its outer side by substantial walls, and the aperture between the walls and the rock had been covered by mud-plaster. Adjoining the enclosure walls was a small room with two standing stones, almost certainly to be interpreted as *mazzeboth* (cultic pillars or monoliths), for the room was too small to require them as roof supports. The back wall of the room was separated from the rock scarp by a space only about thirty centimeters wide, yet a doorway, subsequently blocked, opened from the room into this slot-area. On the rock above the scarp was a small square structure, much too small to be a room. The probable explanation is that the square structure was an altar, and the doorway was to enable libations to be poured at its foot from the *mazzeboth* room. The only possible interpretation of the cave is that it served as a repository, a *favissa,* for vessels used for offering in this sanctuary complex, which could not thereafter be used for profane purposes.

The second cave, ten meters to the south, was a much more elaborate affair, impressively well cut.[29] It might originally have been a tomb, though there was no evidence of this. In it, in a veritable cascade down from the entrance, were well over a thousand objects, mainly pottery vessels, including a fine incense stand. There were also many figurines, a number of them pillar-type fertility figurines and horses with discs on their foreheads, perhaps to be associated with the "horses of the sun."[30]

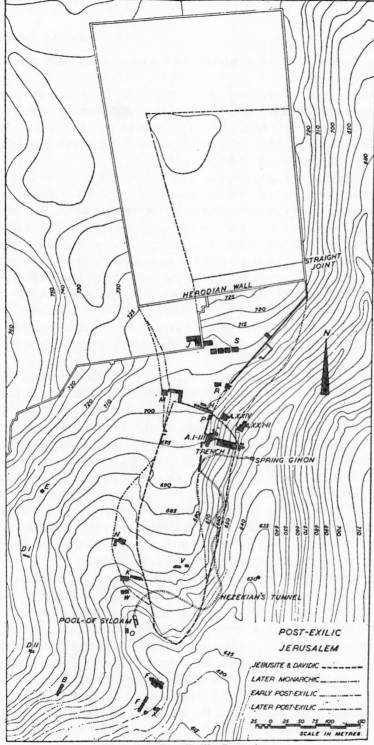

Figure 4. Post-Exilic Jerusalem.

Again, the cave is to be interpreted as a *favissa* of the same or another sanctuary.

Thus we have a sanctuary or sanctuaries of an unorthodox cult at Jerusalem itself, almost under the shadow of the Temple. It is a most vivid illustration of the heathen practices with which Josiah had to deal.[31] The *favissae* were in use for a period of which the central date, on the pottery evidence, cannot be far from 700 BC.

The expansion of Jerusalem on the eastern slopes has already been described. There is no evidence that the city of the period of the Monarchy ever extended onto the western ridge. Extensive excavations were carried out in the south-west corner of the Old City, within the Armenian Quarter, between 1962 and 1967. A considerable amount of Iron Age II pottery was found here, but on rock there was only evidence of extensive quarrying. This cannot be ascribed to the Herodian or Hadrianic periods, like the quarrying on the eastern ridge, and thus be claimed to have removed Iron Age structures, as there were intact Post-Exilic levels overlying it, also associated with quarrying.[32] All the evidence points to the inclusion of any part of the western ridge only in the Maccabaean period.

The only domestic architecture from the period of the Monarchy to survive belongs to the very end of the period and is situated at the upper western end of Trench I, on the crest of the ridge. The remains consisted of a number of rooms, mostly small, of the unimpressive rough stone masonry typical of Iron Age II. One room was larger, with the common tripartite plan divided by two rows of monoliths. Only one of these survived, the easternmost row having collapsed down the hill in the final destruction. The period of use of the rooms was the seventh century BC. The destruction of the rooms, which involved the collapse of the retaining walls of the terraces, Jebusite in origin, on which they were based, and covered the surviving floors with great mounds of stone, was certainly that of the Babylonian capture of Jerusalem in 586 BC.

The archaeological evidence was clear that this destruction terminated the occupation on the eastern slope. The excavation of Trench I showed that the latest buildings to survive were the substructures of terraces that in their last stages had supported the seventh-century buildings. Above them were only layers of tumble, stone layers interspersed with silt layers, derived in the first place from the seventh-century buildings and then from buildings on the summit of the ridge of the Post-Exilic, Maccabaean, and Herodian periods, down to the first century AD. The whole complex of buildings on the slope within the area of the original town had been too precariously dependent on the retaining walls of the terraces, with the town wall at the base as their ultimate support, to survive a major destruction such as that of the Babylonians, followed by virtual abandonment for sixty years. During this abandonment, the man-made breaches in the walls would have been enlarged by the torrential rains of most Jerusalem winters and gradually, or even very rapidly, all the houses would have collapsed in the cascade of stones revealed by the excavations.

The possibility of reconstructing the town walls did not arise until the time of Nehemiah, probably *circa* 440 BC. This cascade of stones was what Nehemiah found in his inspection of the site so graphically described in Nehemiah 2:12–16. Nehemiah's resources were inadequate to restore the elaborate terrace complex. The needs of the much reduced population did not require this additional area, and since the waters of the Spring Gihon were now conducted through the Siloam Tunnel to a reservoir in the central valley, it was no longer necessary to have walls sufficiently low on the slopes to protect the spring, the external access to which was no doubt at this time carefully blocked up.

Nehemiah's wall was therefore built on the eastern crest of the ridge and established the line of defenses now visible, which thereafter constituted the boundary of the city in this area. The biblical account is consonant with a wall on the eastern side which did not follow the earlier line.[33] Excavations in Square A XVIII, east of Site P on the plan, fig. 4, were against the portion of the wall on the crest which was clearly structurally the earliest (Pl. 29); against the foot of the scarp were midden deposits of the fifth to fourth century BC. This wall is with great probability to be recognized as the wall of Nehemiah. To it were added the other structures on the crest.

The most important of these structures so far uncovered is the tower ascribed to the time of David, with a repair in the time of Solomon, in the 1923–25 excavation.[34] It is shown as such to tourists today. Reference has already been made to the impossibility of this ascription since the tower overlies the ruins of the seventh century BC just described. Absolute stratigraphical proof for the dating of the tower has been destroyed by the trench of the 1923–25 excavations along its line, which cuts the junction of the strata with the structure. The surface belonging to the structure could, however, be inferred with great probability. The tower can be taken as a second century BC, Maccabaean, addition to the line of walls established by Nehemiah. The rather mysterious bulge to its north, built in a stepped form, given a too rigid aspect by the conservation measures of the Department of Antiquities of the Mandate, is visually quite certainly later than this second-century BC tower. The 1923–25 excavators quite rightly interpreted this structure as plugging a breach in the fortifications of the crest,[35] though their conclusions about the date were erroneous. The structure of the tower shows that it protruded from a steep slope. To its north a weakness in the support of structures above this slope developed; all the available evidence suggests that this could occur frequently in ancient Jerusalem. This so-called Jebusite bastion was purely subterranean, and belonged at earliest to the second century BC.

For the rest of the history of Israelite Jerusalem, evidence concerning the core of the city is lacking, for the same reasons as for that of Jerusalem in the period of the Monarchy—the whole site has been destroyed by quarrying. As is the case in the earlier periods, the only evidence comes from the flanks of the eastern ridge. Within the Hellenistic-Maccabaean period, there was certainly an expansion on the western side of the eastern ridge. The clearest evidence was provided by Site K of the 1961–67 excavations (fig. 5). The eastern limit of the site was against a high scarp which delimits the present summit area. It has already been inferred that the absence of any Iron Age II deposits below (west of) this scarp, means that the Israelite city was bounded by this scarp. The excavation of Site K showed that at a later period there was a considerable expansion in the area, involving an intrusion into the central valley. Little or nothing of any superstructures survived, but the massive foundation walls showed that there were buildings of some substance in the area in the second to first century BC. The western boundary of this intrusion into the central valley was barely touched in the excavations, but at the extreme western edge of the area a wall was touched which from its dimensions, a minimum width of 3.50 meters, could well have served the dual purpose of a defensive wall and a retaining wall for the terraces needed for this new quarter.[36] Further north, the 1927 excavations discovered a gateway certainly in use in the Maccabaean period.[37] The excavator's belief that this gateway dated back to the Bronze Age because of the crudeness of the masonry can be discounted, in the light of present knowledge of the architecture of Jerusalem. Just to the north again of the area investigated in the 1927 excavations, Site M (fig. 5) provided evidence of a succession of walls, presumed to be town walls, within the second to first centuries BC.[38]

The evidence is therefore clear that the southern part of the eastern ridge was still an entity, with its defensive walls to the east and to the

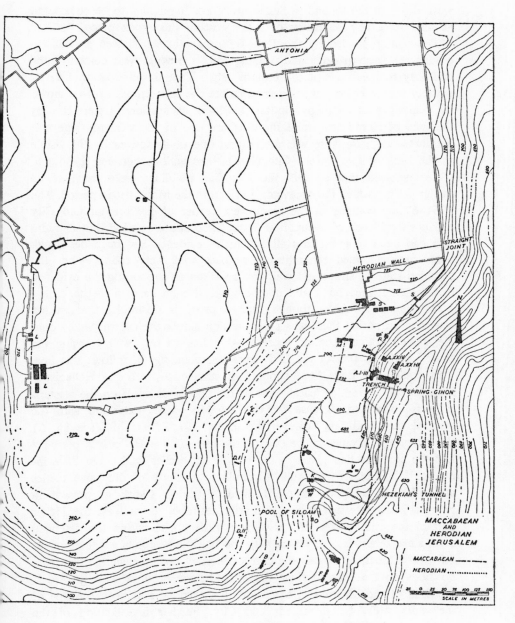

Figure 5. Maccabaean and Herodian Jerusalem

west, down to the second to first century BC. It remains to be considered at what stage any expansion onto the western ridge took place.

The plan produced by the 1894–97 excavations[39] showed a wall enclosing the western ridge and running from the south-west corner of the Old City to the point of the eastern ridge. That this line of wall in its entirety cannot belong to any period before the first century AD was shown by a number of soundings in the 1961–67 excavations.[40] Certainly by the time of Herod the Great the northern end of the western ridge was within the city, for here was his palace; one of its towers is still visible as the base of the present Citadel. The excavations between 1934 and 1948[41] showed that beneath the Herodian buildings were those of an earlier period, which the excavator ascribed to the Maccabaean period. The 1961–67 excavations in the south-west corner of the present Old City produced evidence of occupation in the Maccabaean period, but denudation had been so great that all conclusive evidence had been destroyed. Some very denuded remnants of a town wall were found,[42] but the denuded state of strata and wall can be taken as supporting the evidence in the citadel area but could not be conclusive on its own merits.

It remains probable, though further proof is desirable, that in the Maccabaean period there was an expansion across the central valley onto the western ridge. The only present-day line of city wall crossing the central valley is that of the Old City. The plan, fig. 5, follows this line. This could well have little support in connection with the Hellenistic-Maccabaean period, at least as far as the line of defenses on the western ridge is concerned. A case for the junction of the extension with the original west wall can, however, be made,[43] for in Site M, (see fig. 5) the valley area seemed to be outside the town in the Hellenistic period,[44] and the configuration given to the site by an earlier wall could have influenced the builders of Aelia Capitolina. A study of defensive tactics and offensive weapons in the Hellenistic period (work at present in progress) suggests that it was militarily desirable for at least the higher part of the middle area of the western ridge to be within the defended area, since otherwise, an attack with the ballistic weapons available could have been mounted against the core of the city on the eastern ridge from positions on the western ridge that would have been in dead ground if the limit of the Maccabean extension to that ridge had been the line of the south wall of the present Old City. Further investigation of the problem is planned in the area that was not available in the 1961–67 excavations, since it was part of the demilitarized zone.

My brief for the contribution to the present volume is Israelite

Jerusalem. I have taken this as continuing to the period of the Maccabees, but as excluding the Jerusalem of Herod the Great. Maccabaean Jerusalem represents, on present archaeological evidence, the most important expansion of Jerusalem after the period of Solomon. Herod the Great made Jerusalem more magnificent, but, on present evidence, he did not increase its area. The greatest territorial aggrandizement of the city came in the time of Herod Agrippa, and the life of the city of Herod Agrippa lasted a bare forty years before the city was obliterated by Titus.

FOOTNOTES

1. Kathleen M. Kenyon, *Amorites and Canaanites* (1966), p. 2.
2. II Sam. 5:6–8; I Chron. 11:4–7.
3. Josh. 15:63.
4. II Sam. 2:4; II Sam. 5:1–3. Cf. M. Noth, *The History of Israel* (1958), p. 187.
5. *PEFA*, 4 (1926).
6. *PEQ*, 93 (1961), pp. 76–81.
7. L. H. Vincent, *Jérusalem sous terre* (1911).
Editor's note: figures 1 and 2 are the same as figures 3 and 4 in Miss Kenyon's *Jerusalem* (1967) and used here by permission of the author.
8. I Chron. 11:8.
9. A precise dating must await the diagnosis of the 1961–67 pottery.
10. For details see *PEQ*, 95 (1963), pp. 12–13; *PEQ*, 97 (1965), pp. 4–6.
11. II Sam. 5:9; I Chron. 11:8.
12. The exact dating is dependent on the detailed analysis of the pottery.
13. R. Weill, *La Cité de David*, 2 vols. (1920 and 1947).
14. The excavator's interpretation of some of the cuttings as the Royal Tombs is improbable and unconvincing. My own view is that the cuttings were cisterns.
15. *Ant*, 42 (1968), p. 238.
16. *PEQ*, 98 (1966), fig. 2.
17. *PEQ*, 99 (1967), pp. 68–69.
18. *PEQ*, 95 (1963), p. 17.
19. *PEQ*, 100 (1968), p. 104.
20. *PEQ*, 100 (1968), pp. 98–101.
21. K. Kenyon, *Jerusalem* (1967), pp. 14–15, fig. 1.
22. *PEQ*, 95 (1963), pp. 102 and 105.
23. *PEQ*, 98 (1966), pp. 80–83.
24. *PEQ*, 98 (1966), pp. 80–81; Kenyon, *Jerusalem*, pp. 66–67.
25. *PEQ*, 98 (1966), p. 81.
26. II Chron. 32:4, 30.
27. *PEQ*, 94 (1962), pp. 84–86.
28. C. Warren, *Recovery of Jerusalem* (1871), pp. 156 ff.
29. *PEQ*, 100 (1968), Pls. XXXIII–XXXVI.
30. II Kings 23:11.
31. II Kings 23:1–14.
32. *PEQ*, 100 (1968), pp. 109–10.
33. *PEQ*, 95 (1963), p. 15.
34. *PEFA*, 4 (1926), pp. 56 ff.
35. *Ibid.*, pp. 51–52.
36. *PEQ*, 98 (1966), p. 84.
37. *PEFA*, 5 (1929), pp. 12–23.
38. *PEQ*, 98 (1966), pp. 33–34; *PEQ*, 99 (1967), p. 69.
39. F. J. Bliss and E. C. Dickie, *Excavations at Jerusalem 1894–1897* (1898).
40. *PEQ*, 94 (1962), pp. 84–86.

41. *QDAP*, 14 (1950).
42. *PEQ*, 100 (1968), pp. 110–11.
43. *PEQ*, 100 (1968), p. 102.
44. *PEQ*, 98 (1966), pp. 83–84; *PEQ*, 99 (1967), p. 69.

NEW ASPECTS OF THE ISRAELITE
OCCUPATION IN THE NORTH*

Yohanan Aharoni

AMONG those heroes who came to the aid of Israel during the period of the Judges a prominent place is reserved for "Jael, the wife of Heber, the Kenite, of tent dwelling women most blessed" (Judges 5:24). To all appearances her great renown stems from her slaying of Sisera, the commander of Jabin's army, but examination of the Song of Deborah would suggest that her principal work preceded that deed. In the song a particular era is designated by Jael's name: "In the days of Shamgar, son of Anath, in the days of Jael, caravans ceased and travellers kept to the byways, the peasantry ceased in Israel, they ceased . . ." (Judges 5:6).

An important detail about the figure of Jael became known to us from the excavations at Arad. Her clan, Heber, the Kenite, draws his importance from the ancient desert traditions through his relation to Hobab, the father-in-law of Moses. Similar traditions are also preserved in connection with Arad: ". . . and the descendants of (Hobab LXX), Moses' father-in-law, went up with the people of Judah from the City of Palms into the wilderness of Judah which lies in the Negeb of Arad; and they went and settled with the people" (Judges 1:16). This apocopated chronicle has received new illumination by the discovery of the Israelite temple at Arad.[1] It becomes likely that the two dwelling places chosen by the descendants of Hobab in the land were both cultic sites:[2] Arad, in the light of the discovery of the sacred cult center; and "the Oak in Zaanannim" (Judges 4:11), in keeping with the significance of the name as an example of similar places called after the sacred oak, e.g., אלון בכות, "Allon-bacuth" (Gen. 35:8), אלון מעוננים, "the Diviner's Oak", (Judges

*Part of this paper is based on a lecture delivered at the twenty-fourth convention of the Israel Exploration Society and published in Hebrew under the title "Jael the Wife of Heber the Kenite and Shamgar the Son of Anath" in *All the Land of Naphtali* (1967), pp. 55–61.

9:37), אלוני ממרא "the Oaks of Mamre" (Gen. 13:18), and אלון מורה, "the Oak of Moreh" (Gen. 12:6), where Abraham built an altar and witnessed a theophany (Gen. 12:7).

On the basis of this assumption we can understand the propriety of the biblical emphasis upon the descendants of Hobab, the father-in-law of Moses, as having settled precisely in these places since they were evidently serving in a sacerdotal capacity. The highest of all pedigrees for an ancient priesthood was a family connection with Moses, as exemplified most succinctly by Jonathan, son of Gershom, son of Moses, i.e., Moses' grandson, who founded the dynasty of priests at the cultic center of Dan. Micah said to the lad: "Stay with me, and be to me a father and a priest" (Judges 17:10). A similar understanding is required for the enigmatic reference to the Kenite settlement in the Negeb of Arad which I would complete as follows: ". . . and he went and settled with the people (and became their priest)" (Judges 1:16).

These considerations bring the figure of Jael even closer to that of Deborah. Jael was seated beneath a sacred tree, the oak in Zaanannim, and was related to a venerable priestly family. Thus her meeting with Sisera is more readily understood. Her family was respected by both Canaanites and Israelites, "for there was peace between Jabin, the king of Hazor, and the house of Heber, the Kenite" (Judges 4:17). Jael was a well known personality, and Sisera probably expected to obtain sanctuary for himself as was the custom in any sacred precinct. Jael's deed was in a sense a breach of trust, but justifiable, nevertheless, for a charismatic figure operating under divine inspiration.

Just as Deborah was linked with Barak, the son of Abinoam, so Jael was paired with Shamgar ben Anath, about whom it was recorded: "And he slew six hundred of the Philistines with an ox-goad" (Judges 3:31). It was apparently as a result of that heroic deed that communications became disrupted and the security of the northern settlements was threatened, as described in the Song of Deborah. What was the nature of the historical act alluded to in those laconic passages, and why were its results so important that the Song of Deborah should see them as a prelude to the great armed conflict that followed? And what was Shamgar's distinction that the period in question should be called "the days of Shamgar, son of Anath, . . . the days of Jael . . ." (Judges 5:6)?

The unusual name, Shamgar son of Anath, has helped not a little to weave the variegated web of legend around his person and his marvelous deeds. The first element, Shamgar, is non-Semitic, apparently Hurrian.[3] As is well known, one finds many bearers of Hurrian and Indo-Aryan personal names in the aristocracy of the el-Amarna Age; Shamgar was more than likely a descendant of that class. The second element is Semitic, and specifically Canaanite at that. Does this refer to a son of the famous Canaanite goddess Anath? Most recently it has been suggested that the phrase be taken as a title awarded to Shamgar after his victory over the Philistines.[4] Others have conjectured that this is perhaps a shortened form of the name בן בית ענת, "son of Beth-anath," and that his place of origin was the Canaanite city Beth-anath in the district of Naphtali.[5] In the meantime, however, the name Ben-anath has been found in various inscriptions including both Ugaritic and Egyptian texts.[6] It is worthwhile to recall at this point the inscription on an arrowhead from *circa* the eleventh century BC, discovered in the Lebanese Beqa' and published by Milik.[7] On both sides of the blade the following inscription was engraved: חץ זכרב/כן בנענ. Milik reads: "the arrow of Zakkur, son of Bin' ana," and assumes that the letter *beth* at the end of the first line should be disregarded as a doubling of the first letter in the second line. However, the photograph of this arrowhead reveals quite plainly that the front part is abraded and one or perhaps two letters are missing, evidently at the end of each line. Thus, the restoration suggested by Yeivin[8] seems more probable: חץ זכרב[על]/בן בנענ[ת], "the arrow of Zakir-Ba['al]/son of Ben-ana[th]."

From this evidence one may deduce that "the son of Anath" was an ordinary Canaanite name, and need not be taken to mean that Shamgar was either the son of the goddess or a resident of the town Beth-anath. The biblical formulation is apparently a shortening of "Shamgar (son of) Ben-anath." Milik also stressed that some of the men bearing the name Ben-anath were professional soldiers.

Therefore, it would seem that Shamgar Ben-anath was a military leader of Canaanite origin who was led to smite the Philistines by the inspiration of Jael, wife of Heber, the Kenite, who was from a sacerdotal family highly respected both by Canaanites and Israelites and dwelling in the vicinity of the Yavneel Valley on the border between Issachar and Naphtali.[9] According to the testimony of the ancient song, Shamgar's deed provided the background for the crisis which preceded the battle because, as a result of the temporary deliverance, security for the inhabitants in the northern zone was weakened. If it were within our means to determine the nature of Shamgar's mighty act, this might lead to a better understanding of the events preceding this greatest of the conflicts with the Canaanites in the north, and might perhaps reduce the outside possibilities of its much debated date, opinions still varying from the late thirteenth to the early eleventh centuries!

A commonly accepted view connects Shamgar's deed with the main penetration of the Philistines into Canaan during the first half of the twelth century BC. Subsequently they gained a foothold in the land and settled in the south. However, we know nothing about wars with the Philistines in the north of the country. There are some scholars who have gone so far as to conjecture that Sisera himself was a descendant of the Sea Peoples, who was trying to oppress the Israelite tribes.[10] Shamgar's deed is thus explained as an ephemeral event that took place at the beginning of this struggle.

But these theories have no foundation in the sources. The battle description of Ramses III states that he smote the Sea Peoples in northern Lebanon, viz. in Amurru, but the texts contain no allusion to their penetration into Galilee or the northern valleys. In the ancient Song of Deborah the enemies are the kings of Canaan, and not the Philistines or other peoples. The nine hundred chariots at their disposal represented the Canaanite city states in the fullness of their strength while they still dominated the northern valleys and the related trade routes; there is no hint of their having been weakened in strength as a result of the Sea Peoples' invasion.

Philistine pottery was found during the excavations at Megiddo and Beth-shan, but in such small quantities that one cannot accept it as evidence of Philistine occupation. The Canaanite population in these towns continued to maintain their existence, and even the Egyptian hegemony was carried down to the middle of the twelfth century. It seems methodologically wrong to deduce conclusions about the preceding period from the Philistine control of Beth-shan during the reign of Saul, more than a century later.

The only evidence of which I am aware pertaining to the presence of Sea People elements in the northern part of the country during an earlier period is that of the anthropoid coffins from Beth-shan. From the time when these coffins, designed to resemble human forms, were discovered, the idea was expressed that they had belonged to a group of the Sea Peoples and perhaps the Philistines in particular.[11] Similar burial practices have been found at several places in Palestine and Egypt.[12] Albright has pointed to the apparent influence of Egyptian burial practices as well as to their clear relationship with the Aegean region.[13] Thus it is accepted now by most scholars that these peculiar coffins belonged to mercenaries of the Sea Peoples who were serving in the Egyptian ranks. This assumption is quite likely with regard to Beth-shan in that period, since the latter was being used as an Egyptian base.

The pottery found in the burial places has yet to be published, so we do not have reliable data for establishing their date. The scholars who have examined this ceramic material have conjectured that it belongs to the period between the thirteenth and eleventh centuries.[14] Stirrup vases were present, but they seem to have been predominantly of local manufacture executed according to the Mycenean ceramic style.[15] Of much significance is the fact that in the Beth-shan burials none of the typical Philistine pottery, so much in evidence in the anthropoid burials at Tell el-Far'ah, was found.[16]

One should remember also that at Beth-shan two different types of anthropoid coffins were found. The first of these (fig. 1) is charac-

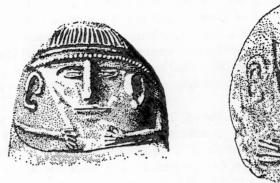

Figures 1 and 2. Anthropoid coffins from Beth-shan

terized by special ornamentation around the head, which, as Trude Dothan has pointed out, has great similarity to Philistine helmets on the reliefs of Ramses III.[17] This gives strong support to the assumption that they were related to the Philistines.[18] They must be associated with the earlier phase of the twelfth century at the latest, prior to the broad dissemination of Philistine pottery in their own areas of occupation. We may not rule out the possibility that Philistines, or members of some ethnic group closely related to them, served as mercenaries in the Egyptian army prior to the days of Ramses III, inasmuch as the presence of Aegean mercenaries in Egypt was a widespread phenomenon beginning with the El-Amarna Age.

The second type of anthropoid coffins is typified by a finer and more realistic execution (fig. 2) reminiscent of the coffins that were found in Egypt and the burials from Anibah in Nubia in particular.[19] It seems unlikely that two types so different from one another were contemporary,[20] and it is plausible that the second type (the Egyptian) is older.[21] It is, therefore, most probable that at least some of the anthropoid burials at Beth-shan belong to the days of the nineteenth dynasty, i.e., to Level VII of the excavations.

The Egyptian base at Beth-shan was destroyed towards the end of the thirteenth century and re-built during the reign of Ramses III. Aegean mercenaries served in the garrison there. Are these perhaps the Philistines who were smitten by Shamgar Ben-anath? Even if they were not true Philistines but some other segment of the Sea Peoples, it would not be surprising that they should be called Philistines since that became the standard biblical terminology for all the Aegean races that appeared in the land.

It seems that such an assumption fits best all the available evidence. After the decline of the nineteenth dynasty the Beth-shan garrison became isolated. The Egyptian hegemony imposed by force had undoubtedly been a thorn in the flesh for both Canaanites and Israelites, and its abolition would have been well received by all. The tribal territory of Issachar, on the northern boundary of which Jael dwelt, bordered on Beth-shan. One of the stelae from the reign of Seti I, discovered at Beth-shan, contains information about the suppression of semi-nomadic tribes in Mount Yarumtu=Yarmuth, the later city of Issachar, by an Egyptian army division.[22] One could hardly argue against this interpretation of Shamgar's deed, that the biblical reference would have taken on a local coloring devoid of any allusion to the Egyptian rule. It has been thus with all of the traditions from that period preserved in the Bible.

The liberating hero is portrayed as a deliverer, and his association with Jael, the Kenite, who belonged to the family of Moses, made him acceptable to the Israelite tribe in spite of his Canaanite origin. Furthermore, it is understandable why this deliverance served as a prelude to the great struggle between Canaan and Israel in the north. After the Egyptian hegemony was abolished and the two segments of the population were left without a ruling overlord, the struggle for dominance which broke out between them was inevitable. This is exactly what is stated: "In the days of Shamgar, son of Anath, in the days of Jael (after the Philistines had been smitten), caravans ceased and travelers kept to the byways; the peasantry ceased in Israel, they ceased . . ." (Judges 5:6–7).

From this we also obtain a chronological frame of reference for the series of battles that took place in the north. If we accept the conclusion that Shamgar Ben-anath destroyed Level VII of Beth-shan,[23] then his activity must have begun towards the end of the thirteenth century. The great decisive clashes in the north must have taken place soon afterwards, which permits a date that well suits the sudden decline and final destruction of Hazor in that period.

This conclusion conforms very nicely to a recent archaeological discovery: in the light of the new excavations being carried out by P. Lapp at Taanach, the excavator reports an occupational gap there between *circa* 1125 and 1000 BC.[24] That conclusion has far-reaching implications for the chronology of the conquest and the various stages of settlement in the north; and perhaps it would be advisable to await the full publication of the excavation. However, inasmuch as there is a definite revelance to our discussion, we have chosen to summarize in brief the implications of this new evidence and place it in its proper perspective.

Lapp has already noted[25] that this occupational gap contradicts Albright's interpretation of the well known passage in the Song of Deborah, "at Taanach by the waters of Megiddo" (Judges 5:19). Albright suggested that this alluded to a situation in which Megiddo was in ruins while Taanach enjoyed the position of prominence in the region.[26] If the destruction and abandonment of Taanach took place at about the same time as that in Megiddo, Stratum VII A, then there was obviously no such situation as Taanach being a strong city due to the decline of Megiddo. Thus for determining the chronology of Deborah's battle, the date of approximately 1125 is changed from a *terminus a quo* to a *terminus ad quem:* the event had to take place when both Taanach and Megiddo were still strong Canaanite cities in the region, and more precise geopolitical details cannot be extracted from the biblical account.

The Song of Deborah is not the only biblical source whose dating is affected by this new information. Taanach and Megiddo appear in Judges 1:27 among the un-conquered Canaanite cities; these towns were reckoned with the inheritance of Manasseh, although they had formerly been counted in the area of Issachar (Josh. 17:11). We also have a mutual concern between this text and that which describes the tribal boundaries in Josh. 15–19, as Alt has noted.[27] Both combine the actual tribal situation with the hypothetical assumption that the unconquered Canaanite cities belonged to the various tribal areas. Most remarkable is the absence of Issachar from both documents. The list of Canaanite cities in Judges 1 only touches on six tribes: Benjamin, Menasseh, Ephraim, Zebulon, Asher and Naphtali. Cities of the tribe of Dan that are added at the end of the list are reckoned to the house of Joseph. These are the tribes of Mt. Ephraim and Galilee, the northern tribes that comprised "Israel" in the limited sense common to documents from the period of the Judges and the Monarchy.

I have tried to show elsewhere that in reality the tribal boundary descriptions were concerned with the same six tribes.[28] Not only are Issachar and the Trans-jordan tribes missing from this document, as Alt had noticed, but the inclusion of the southern tribes, "Judah" as distinct from "Israel," is fictitious. In fact, only the northern border of Judah is given. Without going into the complex question of that segment's origin, it is obvious that Judah's northern boundary had to be the southern border of its neighbors to the north; and thus at least its eastern part reappears as the southern border of Benjamin. The remaining borders were taken from another source which fortunately has survived in the Bible, viz., the description of the boundaries of Canaan (Num. 34). The various scholars who have dealt with this problem have all given due emphasis to this resemblance, but without attempting to draw chronological conclusions, or else accepting the boundary description of Judah as the primary source.[29] It seems that no doubt can be cast on the antiquity and independence of Num. 34, or on its claim to be the source for the southern boundary of Judah (and not the opposite). The settlement of the southern tribes did not penetrate farther south than the general vicinity of Beersheba during the period of the Judges. On the other hand, the boundaries of Canaan correspond to the territory of the Egyptian province as crystalized during the fourteenth to thirteenth centuries BC; there is no later historical reality suitable to these borders which include Lebanon and Damascus and exclude Gilead.[30] The covenant community of the tribes of Israel viewed itself as the heir of the land of Canaan, which would explain its preservation of such an ancient document.

The tribal inheritances, even with the Canaanite enclaves, occupied only a portion of that territory. Thus the concept of "the land that remains" (Josh. 13:2–6; Judges 3:3) came into being as a definition of that same area from the "Land of Canaan" that was not taken in by the Israelite occupation. It included the Philistine territory to the south and the Canaanite territories to the north, assigned to the Sidonians=Phoenicians in the west and to the Hivites (Horites or Hittites with the LXX?) in the east.[31] The Canaanite enclaves listed in Judges 1 do not belong to "the land that remains," as is clearly seen from the boundary of Asher that reaches as far as Great Sidon (Josh. 19:28; cf. also Josh. 13:4, Judges 3:3 and especially Josh. 11:8).[32] In the south, the northern limit of the "land that remains" fits at least partly the *northern* border of Judah (Josh. 15:10 ff.)! The fictitious inclusion of Judah in the tribal boundary descriptions is achieved, therefore, by adopting the southern boundary of Canaan. This resolves the difficulty presented by a document purporting to unite the tribes on both the north and the south, even though there was no co-operation between them in any of the traditions from the period of the Judges. It follows that the basic document containing the boundary descriptions belonged originally to a league of northern tribes, "Israel," in the restricted sense of the term, which was made up of the same six tribes mentioned in Judges 1.

Even one who rejects the reciprocal relationship between the various ancient geopolitical sources must certainly admit that Judges 1 reflects a different reality from that depicted in the Song of Deborah. Menasseh has replaced Machir in the northern part of Mt. Ephraim, and the change in the Issachar region is particularly striking. That tribe, which attained its place in the eastern part of the valley by submission to the Canaanite cities in that region,[33] eventually lost its place in the tribal league as proven by its absence from Judges 1 and from the tribal boundary descriptions as alluded to in the blessing of Jacob (Gen. 49:14–15). Issachar is still listed among the tribes in the Song of Deborah (Judges 5:15), even though the biblical account stresses the role of Zebulun and Naphtali as the two Galilee tribes that took a leading part in the battle (Judges 4:10; 5:18). As a consequence of the conflict, Issachar certainly must have been relieved of the heavy yoke of his enslavement by the Canaanite cities, but it was his stronger neighbors and not he who gradually took over the Canaanite territories as expressed unmistakably in Josh. 17:11. This is the situation reflected in the story of Gideon: he calls for action from Menasseh, Asher, Zebulun and Naphtali (Judges 6:35) and sends messengers throughout Mt. Ephraim (7:24), i.e., his call is addressed to the tribes of Mt. Ephraim and Galilee. Gideon himself belonged to the families of Menasseh which had moved northward,[34] and Issachar, in whose territory the battle took place, is not mentioned at all. The period of Gideon, therefore, represents most closely the conditions reflected in Judges 1 (and in my opinion, the document containing the tribal boundary descriptions).

With the help of the new archaeological data, approximate dates for the various sources may be established. The alleged destruction of Tanaach, *circa* 1125 at the latest, provides a *terminus ad quem* for Judges 1. In other words, this literary source (and the other sources reflecting the same situation) cannot be later than *circa* the middle of the twelfth century. The battle of Deborah, which reflects a different, earlier situation, must be at least a generation older. These considerations also point, therefore, to the late thirteenth or early twelfth century as the probable date for the great battles in the north, a date that agrees well with the assumption that Shamgar Ben-anath destroyed Beth-shan VII and fits the destruction of Canaanite Hazor (Stratum XIII) at approximately the same time.

Finally, the question must be raised anew as to the nature of Megiddo VI. Between Strata VII A and VI B one finds one of the most complete cultural breaks noted anywhere in the history of that city. Stratum VI was a poor, unwalled settlement, and the great public structures that typified Megiddo for centuries—the city-wall, the palace near the gate, and the temple in the eastern quarter—are gone entirely. This last detail is of special importance. In the "sacred precinct," the tradition of the sanctuaries and their ritual was preserved from the beginning of the third millennium BC down to Stratum VII A in spite of all the vicissitudes of the city. From Stratum VI on, there is not the slightest hint of sacral buildings in the area, and afterwards it was covered by one of the stables. Is it possible that the same populace suddenly adopted such an attitude of indifference and disdain for that ancient tradition? Could we expect any more decisive proof that with the destruction of Stratum VII A the Canaanite city at Megiddo came to an end?

Such was the original assumption of several scholars, and Albright saw in Stratum VI the first Israelite settlement at Megiddo. He also pointed out that in Stratum VI there is an abundance of the collared-rim jars so typical of Israelite settlements in the hill country during the twelfth and the first half of the eleventh centuries BC.[35] Albright later retracted this view, as a consequence of Engberg's argument that much of the pottery of Stratum VI still represented the older ceramic tradition while level V is typified by a completely new style.[36]

Today, in the light of various later excavations and surveys, we know that the definition of the collared-rim jars as most typical of the Israelite settlement during the period of the settlement is surely justified. However, local variations appear in the ceramic traditions of the Israelite settlements because of the local influences to which they were subjected; note, e.g., the local early Iron Age pottery in Upper Galilee, which was influenced by the Canaanite culture in the north,[37] or that at Beth-shemesh, which was affected by its proximity to Philistia.[38] Thus it is not surprising to find local influence from the Canaanite culture of the Jezreel Valley in the Israelite settlement there. On the other hand, the sharp differences that typify the pottery of Stratum V indicate that there was an occupational gap which began after the complete and heavy destruction of Stratum VI A; that was what the excavators originally assumed.[39] Today we know very well that in the Israelite sphere of occupation there took place many decisive and rapid changes in the styles and methods of manufacture of ceramic vessels at the beginning of the monarchial period, just when there was no likelihood whatsoever of ethnic changes. One may also cite the special brick construction typical of Stratum VI, which testified to a different building tradition among the occupants.[40] On the other hand, the destruction or the occupational gap which separates Strata VI A from V B is no proof in itself of a change in the ethnic composition of the population. Circumstances likely to explain the destruction of settlements in the plain were certainly not lacking during the 11th century. A most illuminating parallel was found at Hazor. The last Canaanite city (Stratum XIII) was replaced by a poor, primitive settlement, and with its destruction, the site saw an occupational gap that continued until the founding of the Solomonic city.[41] Yet, notwithstanding the gap, there is no doubt that Hazor XII represents a first Israelite attempt to settle the site, both because of its simplicity in contrast to the sophisticated Canaanite urban center that preceded it and because of the similarity between the pottery found and that of the many newly founded sites in Upper Galilee.[42]

Alt was fully aware of the fundamental difference between Megiddo VII A and VI B. However, influenced by the arguments set forth by Engberg, he hesitantly considered VI to be a last remnant (letzter Ausläufer) of the Canaanite city.[43] In order to escape from this contradiction, he suggested that the rehabilitation of the fallen city was done under the aegis of a new hegemony, that of the Philistines.

That latter assumption is contradicted first of all by the fact that there is practically no Philistine pottery whatever in Megiddo VI.[44] But more than this: it seems that such an unfounded theory has seldom been put forward by such a serious scholar. I am not aware of any real evidence, either in the sources or in archaeological investigations, regarding Philistine penetration into the Jezreel Valley prior to the reign of Saul. The Pax Philistaea that Alt and others speak of[45] is based on general assumptions for which no concrete proof has been offered. The affair of Shamgar Ben-anath remains the only witness to Philistine presence in the north. I am unable to find any support whatever for the conjecture by Alt and others that "Sisera of Harosheth Ha-goyim" and the "kings of Canaan" in the Song of Deborah pertain to the Sea Peoples. The Philistines were called in by scholars to explain the political and occupational gap in the plain after the Canaanite factor disappears from the stage during the second half of the 12th century, because they agreed that the Canaanite cities, including Megiddo, did not fall into Israelite hands until the reign of David.

Megiddo VI is no longer a Canaanite city. It contains no evidence for Philistine domination. It is an unwalled settlement in which the ceramic tradition continues in large measure that of the local Canaanite culture in company with an abundance of collared-rim jars so typical of Israelite occupation. Its buildings are entirely different, and Megiddo's venerable sacral tradition is unequivocally terminated. Does all this not indicate that Megiddo VI was the first Israelite settlement founded there? The newly discovered occupational gap at Taanach fits this assumption very well.

Evidently the second half of the twelfth century saw the end of the Canaanite cities in the central valley. Clans from Menasseh began to occupy the empty spaces, even though their progress and the firm establishment of their settlements were not achieved without further crises and occasional recessions.

FOOTNOTES

1. Cf. provisionally Y. Aharoni, *IEJ*, 17 (1967), pp. 247 ff.; *BA*, 31 (1968), pp. 18 ff.

2. B. Mazar, "The Sanctuary of Arad and the Family of Hobab the Kenite," *JNES*, 24 (1965), pp. 297–303.

3. B. Maisler (Mazar), *PEFQS* (1934), pp. 192–94.

4. A. Van Selms, *VT*, 14 (1964), pp. 294–309.

5. W. F. Albright, *JPOS*, 1 (1920–22), p. 55; A. Alt, *ZAW*, 19 (1944), p. 73 (=*Kleine Schriften*, I, p. 262); J. Bright, *A History of Israel* (1959), p. 157.

6. J. T. Milik, *BASOR*, No. 143 (1956), pp. 5 f.; F. Ch. Fensham, *JNES*, 20 (1961), pp. 197 f.

7. Milik, *op. cit.*, pp. 3–6.

8. S. Yeivin, *RB*, 65 (1958), pp. 585–88.

9. Concerning the location of Allon in Zaanannim, cf. Y. Aharoni, *The Settlement of the Israelite Tribes in Upper Galilee* (1957), pp. 79, 99–100 (Hebrew).

10. W. F. Albright, *JPOS*, 1 (1921), pp. 54 ff.; A. Alt, *ZAW*, 19 (1944), pp. 67 ff. (=*Kleine Schriften* I, pp. 256 ff.).

11. L. H. Vincent, *RB*, 32 (1923), pp. 435 ff.

12. For a summary and references cf. Trude Dothan, "Philistine Civilization in the Light of Archaeological Finds in Palestine and Egypt," *Eretz-Israel*, 5 (1958), pp. 55 ff. (Hebrew).

13. W. F. Albright, *AJA*, 36 (1932), pp. 295 ff.

14. Summarized by Albright, *loc. cit.*

15. But see now V. Hankey, *AJA*, 70 (1966), pp. 169–71, concerning the Mycenean stirrup vases of type III C:1b that were found in the 1931 season and seem to conform to those described by the excavators as having been retrieved from the anthropoid burials. I have also been informed by personal communication from Dr. T. Dothan and Mr. E. Oren, who is preparing this material for publication, that the burials also contained Mycenean vessels of type III B.

16. Dr. Dothan points out an apparent Philistine bowl (*op. cit.* [above, n. 12], p. 56, fig. 1:13), but granted the similarity it would be unsound to base the date of the coffins on one isolated vessel in burials, the majority of which have been disturbed.

17. T. Dothan, *loc. cit.* (above, n. 12).

18. However, it must be remembered that the *ṭ-k-r* and the *d-n-n* are depicted in a similar manner on the reliefs of Ramses III.

19. T. Dothan, *op. cit.* (above, n. 12), p. 65, fig. 8.

20. The skeleton of a woman was found in one of the coffins, but T. Dothan's assumption that all of this type were female burials, which determined the difference in style, is hard to accept.

21. Albright had already gained the impression that this type, found partly in the excavations of 1926, was the older; cf. *op. cit.* (above, n. 13), p. 298.

22. Y. Aharoni, *The Land of the Bible* (1967, henceforth *LB*), pp. 168–69.

23. It is possible that some of the anthropoid burials (the "Philistine type") are from the twelfth century (Level VI), and the question arises as to whether Shamgar Ben-anath may have destroyed the settlement represented in that stratum.

However, a date so late is hardly reasonable in the light of the other data, and it is contradicted by the biblical tradition: Beth-shan appears in the list of unconquered Canaanite towns (Judges 1:27) which pertained to the period after the battle of Deborah, and this can only be Level VI, the last Canaanite-Egyptian city at the site. About Judges 1 see below and p. 260 ff.

24. P. W. Lapp, *BASOR*, No. 173 (1964), p. 8; No. 185 (1967), pp. 3, 25 f. (See now Lapp in *BASOR*, No. 195 [1969], pp. 2-49—Ed.)

25. *BA*, 30 (1967), pp. 8 f.

26. W. F. Albright, *BASOR*, No. 62 (1936), p. 27.

27. A. Alt, *Sellin Festschrift* (1927), pp. 17 ff. (=*Kleine Schriften*, I, pp. 197 f.).

28. *LB*, pp. 232 f.

29. Cf. especially M. Noth, *ZDPV*, 58 (1935), pp. 185 ff.; *idem, Das Buch Josua* (1953), pp. 85 ff.

30. B. Maisler (Mazar), *BJPES*, 12 (1946), pp. 91 ff., (Hebrew); *LB*, pp. 68 f. The various suggestions to interpret these borders in any situation during the Israelite period (cf. K. Elliger, *PJB*, 32 [1936], pp. 34–73; M. Noth, *PJB* 33 [1937], pp. 36–51) stand in striking contrast to the exclusion of Gilead.

31. *LB*, pp. 215 ff. Cf. also Joshua 11:3; only "the Emorite" to "Jebusite" looks like a gloss, since the Jebusites obviously do not belong to the north. The victorious Israelites pursue the Canaanites to the Valley of Mizpeh (below Hermon!) and to Great Sidon; these are the borders of "the land which remains."

32. Only Sidon is beyond the borders of the tribal areas. Since this city is missing in the parallel passage of Joshua 19:29–30 it seems doubtful that it was included in the original list; cf. *LB*, p. 214.

33. Cf. A. Alt, *PJB*, 20 (1924), pp. 34 ff. (=*Kleine Schriften*, III, pp. 169 ff.); *LB*, p. 175.

34. On the possible location of Gideon's Ophrah in the vicinity of the Jezreel Valley, cf. *LB*, pp. 240 f.

35. W. F. Albright, *BASOR*, No. 68 (1937), p. 25, and cf. especially his remark in *BASOR*, No. 74 (1939), p. 23, note 49: "That Megiddo VI was an Israelite settlement seems practically certain, in view of the astonishingly close similarity of its coarse pottery to that of the Israelite hinterland and the equally striking disparity in details between it and the contemporary ware of Tell Abū Huwam in the Plain of Acre."

36. W. F. Albright. *BASOR*, No. 78 (1940), p. 8. Since the pottery published in *Megiddo*, II, is only a small typological selection, the general impression may be very irritating. According to Albright (*loc. cit.*) the collared-rim jars were "apparently more abundant on the site of Megiddo, as at Bethel and Beth-zur, than all other pottery together." They are typical of Stratum VI, and already appear sporadically in Stratum VII A.

37. Aharoni, *op. cit.* (above, n. 9), pp. 17 ff.; *idem, Antiquity and Survival*, 2 (1957), pp. 146 ff.

38. Trude Dothan, *The Philistines and their Material Culture* (1967), pp. 41 f. (Hebrew).

39. *Megiddo*, II, pp. 5, 45.

40. *Megiddo*, II, pp. 33 f.: bricks of reddish clay, partially baked, porous and friable; and cf. *Megiddo*, I, p. 7.

41. *Hazor*, III–IV, in print.

42. Aharoni, *op. cit.* (*supra*, n. 9), pp. 20 ff.; *LB*, p. 207.

43. A. Alt, "Megiddo im Übergang vom kanaanäischen zum israelitischen Zeitalter," *ZAW*, 19 (1944), pp. 67 ff. (=*Kleine Schriften*, I, pp. 256 ff.).

44. Trude Dothan, *op. cit.* (above, n. 38), p. 56 (Hebrew).

45. Alt, *op. cit.* (above, n. 43), p. 82 (=*Kleine Schriften*, I, p. 271).

THE MEGIDDO STABLES:
A REASSESSMENT

James B. Pritchard

THE tangible character of archaeological evidence often gives to the history into which it is woven a ring of authority. A building can be measured, drawn, photographed, described in detail, and its relation to strata below and above can be recorded with precision in well-drawn sections. In a sense, archaeology is a science that demands credibility.

Yet the use made of even the most scrupulously recorded archaeological data in reconstructing the past from which it comes is a step in which probability is involved. And the attempt to link archaeological evidence with biblical traditions about events and persons is a process in which opinion plays an even larger role. A careful assessment of probability over the scale of doubtful–possible–probable–certain is even more imperative in this synthesis. While archaeological data may be certain, a credibility gap arises from an uncritical assessment of its value in the reconstructing of the past and its supposed relevance for a particular history written in the Bible.

Equally imperative is a reassessment of conclusions. In the euphoria of discovery, interpretations have sometimes been given which, upon further study, have had to be retracted—but not until after the earlier hypothesis had hardened into certainty and had been widely quoted.[1] Other cherished interpretations have dissolved with the reexcavation of a site by improved methods and more extensive sampling.[2]

Prominent among the examples frequently cited of how archaeological and biblical data can be fitted together is that of the "stables of Solomon" at Megiddo.[3] A reexamination of the published evidence for the so-called stables at Megiddo raises some questions about the function attributed to these buildings by the excavators and repeated without qualification ever since.

This paradigm of biblical archaeology was first suggested in 1931 by P. L. O. Guy. In the second provisional report on the excavations at

Megiddo[4] Guy interpreted two unique complexes of buildings in Stratum IV as the stables of Solomon by reference to the traditions in Kings and Chronicles to (a) Solomon's building operation at Megiddo (I Kings 9:15), (b) Solomon's chariot cities (I Kings 9:19) and (c) Solomon's trade in chariots and horses (I Kings 10:26–29 and II Chron. 1:14–17). Without considering the variant readings and the critical problems in the passages, Guy took these traditions at their face value as trustworthy historical sources and built upon them detailed explanations of many features of the buildings at Megiddo.[5]

Guy's dating of Stratum IV to the time of Solomon was not uncontested. As early as 1940, J. W. Crowfoot assigned the "chariot city" of Stratum IV to the time of Ahab rather than to the period of Solomon, on the basis of architectural features that were similar to those at Samaria.[6] K. M. Kenyon, who did not question the interpretation of the buildings as stables, took a similar position and dated the building of Stratum IV at about 850–750 BC.[7]

In January of 1960, Yigael Yadin made some excavations at Megiddo and concluded that "city IV proper (IVA) with its solid city wall of the 'offsets and insets' type (built in part on a filling of the older casemate wall), and the two complexes of stables . . . is *not* Solomonic but was built after the destruction of the Solomonic city by Pharaoh Shishak. . . . The work was that of a later sovereign, most probably King Ahab. . . ."[8] Yadin's case for the lowering of the date for the Stratum IV buildings is clear and the reasons are compelling. Yet having demolished the Solomonic date in a few days of digging, he did not reopen the question of the identification of the buildings as stables made by Guy some thirty years earlier. Mentioning the boast of Shalmaneser III that he had defeated the forces of a coalition of 12 kings, among whose forces were two thousand chariots of Ahab,[9] he hastened to assign the impressive complex of buildings "most probably" to King Ahab. The link with the Bible had been broken but another connection, he ventured, could be forged with an Assyrian inscription mentioning a biblical character. And, lest the reassignment of date should be too much of a shock, Yadin added: "This does not exclude the possibility that Solomon's city had stables too, but these were not the excavated ones. . . ."[10]

If the more recent argument for the removal of the Megiddo IV buildings from the period of Solomon is valid—as it seems to be—then one of the strong reasons for the identification of the buildings as stables has disappeared. It may therefore be profitable to reappraise the archaeological evidence published by the excavators of Megiddo solely on its own merits, without any recourse to the biblical traditions about Solomon, to whom they were first thought to belong. Is it still possible to call these buildings stables?

The evidence published for the fourteen partly preserved pillared buildings consists of two plans, one of the northern and one of the southern complex,[11] some cross-sections of architectural remains,[12] selected photographs, and descriptive texts written by P. L. O. Guy,[13] and by R. S. Lamon and G. M. Shipton.[14]

The principal arguments adduced for identifying the pillared buildings as stables for horses are based upon the following features: (1) holes cut in some of the pillars, (2) stone basins or troughs called "mangers," (3) the unique plan not unlike that of a modern Western barn or stable, (4) paving in areas assumed to be stalls for the horses and (5) mudbrick structure thought to be a watering tank in the center of an open court in front of the southern complex. Let us consider briefly each of these elements.

(1) Holes in Pillars

One argument for calling the buildings stables is the presence of holes in the corners of the pillars that had supported the roof.[15] Lamon and Shipton summed up the argument thus: "Holes, through which the halters could be tied, were cut in the corners of the pillars and were conveniently situated just above the top of the mangers and almost invariably on the side toward the central passage."[16] A careful examination of the plans and sections reveals that this feature was not universal. The plan for the southern complex shows no "halter-holes" in the columns, even though a column in Locus 1612 is standing above the level of the top of the "manger."[17] The northern complex, however, had fifty-four columns, of which twenty were pierced with holes through a corner. It is not always possible to tell how high these columns stood, but in Locus 351 it is apparent from the section given[18] that only two out of the eight columns that were standing to a height above the mangers were pierced with holes. It is also interesting to note that in Locus 367 two of the columns were pierced with holes on the "stall" side as well as on the side of the aisle between the "stalls." Thus, it would seem that according to the published plans and sections the evidence for this feature of the construction is not consistent and, as we shall suggest below, may be interpreted differently.

(2) *"Mangers"*

In the southern compound the excavators reported that they found fifteen "mangers," although about half of them had been displaced from their original positions between the stone columns.[19] Nine of these are actually shown in the plan,[20] but not a single detailed drawing of a "manger" is given. Fortunately, however, the measurements of one example from Locus 1483 are given as 1.20 by 0.60 and 0.70 meters high, with a trough 90 by 30 centimeters cut in the top.[21] The depth of the trough is given as from 12 to 15 centimeters. The stone mason had cut the block to a depth of only about one-fifth of the thickness of the stone. It is obvious that such a shallow trough—only six inches—would scarcely be the most practical container for grain or other food for a horse. For the northern and larger complex, only five basins are shown on the plans and in the section.[22]

(3) *Plan of the Buildings*

In his preliminary report written in 1931,[23] P. L. O. Guy noted the obvious similarity between the Megiddo buildings and the plan of the three pillared buildings of the Fifth City at Tell el-Hesi,[24] which Bliss cautiously suggested might have been a bazaar or barracks.[25] Guy also cited as possible parallels the row of pillars found by Macalister at Gezer[26] and the double row of standing stones discovered at Taanach.[27]

The closest parallel to the Megiddo buildings of Stratum IV is the pillared building (71) of Strata VIII–VII excavated by Yadin at Hazor.[28] The rectangular building has as its characteristic feature two rows of stone pillars, with nine in one and ten in the other, that separated the building into three sections or halls. Between the pillars were evidences of "shelves (cells)" built of two rows of rubble stones.[29] Although the position of these inter-pillar constructions was identical with the so-called mangers at Megiddo, the excavators assert that "there is no similarity whatever to the stables at Megiddo, and the characteristic features of stables are entirely wanting."[30]

Later in the report they exclude the interpretation of the building as a stable on the grounds of the position of the entrance to the building at the corner,[31] and conclude that the pillared building was "nothing less than a royal storehouse."

More recent evidence for the building with bins between the columns has appeared in the eighth-century complex of standard houses at Tell es-Sa'idiyeh. In the spans between the four mudbrick columns and the two pilasters that supported the roof of House 6 are basins constructed of rows of rubble stone and plastered with mud.[32] These basins are identical in plan and structure with those of the pillared building at Hazor.[33] Thus it would appear that the eighth-century feature of inter-column bins is clearly in a tradition that reaches back to the ninth century at Hazor and at Megiddo, where a similar purpose was served by well-cut stone basins or shelves in a building of greater elegance and more costly construction. It is obvious that the later poorly constructed basins could not have served as mangers for horses.

(4) Plastered and Paved Areas

In one feature, the buildings were remarkably uniform. The central of the three sections into which each building was divided by the two rows of pillars was invariably plastered with a fine lime plaster, while the two outside sections were paved with rough stones.[34] It was assumed that the paving with rough stones in the "stall" areas was for the purpose of preventing horses' hoofs from slipping. What was not taken into account was the adverse effect of rough stones on the hoofs and the second thought that a lime-plastered surface might have been much better suited to the care of horses.

(5) "Water Tank" 1672

In the center of the courtyard before the southern complex of buildings was a sunken structure built of sun-dried mudbricks, measuring approximately 2.30 meters square and 2 meters deep.[35] The inside was plastered with a layer of mud about 2 centimeters thick. This structure was interpreted as "probably" a water tank for the horses. Anyone who has ever seen the effect of a few heavy rains on mudbrick is aware that this tank, even though coated with 2 centimeters of mud, would have dissolved quickly if filled with water. Even though the floor of the courtyard had been paved with lime plaster, no evidence of the use of the available impermeable material was noted or reported for the mudbrick bin which was interpreted as a tank.

One of the difficulties in the interpretation of the buildings as stables was freely admitted by the excavators: among the artifacts found in the area there was not the slightest suggestion of anything that might be associated with horses or chariots.[36]

Checking through the catalogue of objects found in loci of the so-called stables, one finds listed in the Megiddo publication no less than fifty-two objects,[37] an assemblage which suggests the remains of human rather than animal occupation. The largest single category is twenty-two bowls, followed by ten storage jars, six jugs, a flask, a lamp, a pottery basket. Incidental artifacts such as two scaraboids, three amulets, a bronze chisel, two beads, three spindle whorls, a hair pin, an animal horn, a bronze weight, a glass inlay, a figurine, and a limestone roller complete the inventory of objects found. When one considers the ornate fittings depicted on the reliefs of Assyrian cavalry[38] of the ninth century, it would be reasonable to expect something in the way of these trappings in an area given over to the housing of horses. Rather one finds the ordinary components of the remains of human beings in the buildings of Stratum IV at Megiddo.

The excavators saw one additional difficulty with their interpretation of the buildings. From the plan it was apparent that the standard building had only one doorway, and this was in the center of the main aisle.[39] If there was indeed a "manger" between each pair of pillars, then access to the "stalls" could only have been by a passageway at the end of the row, so that "to have led out any particular horse must have necessitated the removal first of all the horses between it and the door, wherever the opening was located."[40]

After this survey of the principal arguments based on the archaeological evidence that have been used to support the hypothesis that the buildings were stables, it must be admitted that the two features of the structures most difficult to explain differently are the holes in some of the pillars and the stone blocks with basins. But were they tethering-posts and mangers? Without the biblical support for Solomon's stables, it is rash indeed to construct a theory upon the presence of twenty holes pierced in columns, particularly when these apertures could have been made for securing drag ropes by which these heavy roof supports were transported from the quarry to the site or for some other purpose. Furthermore, the stone basins, too shallow to have been used for feeding horses, could have served some household purpose that as yet eludes us, as indeed similar facilities in stone and clay are known to have served an unexplained function in the pillared building at Hazor and the house of columns at Tell es-Sa'idiyeh.

As for the plan of the buildings, all one can say is that it has analogies
in structures at Hazor and at Tell el-Hesi. Nothing found in the buildings,
as the excavators took pains to point out, suggest that they had been
used as stables. The interpretation of the mudbrick bin within the courtyard of the southern complex as a water tank is impossible, and the explanation of the differentiation between the floors of rubble stones for
"stalls" and plaster floors for the grooms is far from decisive.[41]

Finally, our concern with specific details, important as they are, must
not obscure a larger question. Is there evidence that horses were kept in
stables and not in open enclosures? As far as I know, there is no evidence in the ancient Near East for stables, especially buildings that resemble in plan those in use in the contemporary West.

A generation ago the excavators of Megiddo described the findings in
Stratum IV by the use of such romantic terms as "paddock," "parade
ground," "cavalry horses," "squadrons," "a veterinary establishment," "a
harness store," "officers' horses," and sought to tie up the remains there
with the equally romantic account of the grandeur of the Solomonic empire. If the link of this stratum with Solomon has been broken—as it
seems to have been—then the remains recorded deserve a reassessment
as to function.

Without the suggestion which was so readily available from the traditions in Kings which the excavators sought to apply to the two complexes
of buildings at Megiddo, the possibility of their having served such a
highly specialized function as stables for horses is greatly diminished. In
the light of our lack of evidence for the use to which these pillared
buildings were put, it is more credible to venture a more general explanation of their having been possibly storehouses or barracks.

FOOTNOTES

1. An admirable example of willingness to reassess evidence, even at the cost of abandoning an earlier position, is Nelson Glueck's recent conclusions about Tell el-Kheleifeh. The apertures found in the walls of a building at Tell el-Kheleifeh during 1938–40 interpreted as "flue-holes" for a "smelter" of Solomon at Ezion-geber, were some twenty-five years later considered to have been apertures resulting from "the decay and/or burning of wooden beams laid across the width of the walls for bonding or anchoring purposes." See *BA*, 28 (1965), pp. 70 ff.

2. How the walls of the Fourth City (1400–1385 BC) fell at Jericho is described by J. and J. B. E. Garstang, *The Story of Jericho* (rev. ed. 1948), pp. 136 ff. According to K. Kenyon, the later excavator of Jericho, these walls actually belonged to the Early Bronze Age (*Archaeology in the Holy Land* [2d ed., 1965], p. 210). The "Tower of David," excavated by Macalister in 1923–25, has recently been re-dated to the 2d century BC by K. M. Kenyon, *Jerusalem: Excavating 3000 Years of History* (1967), pp. 23, 115, Pls. 7 and 8.

3. M. Burrows, *What Mean These Stones* (1941), pp. 127–28. C. C. McCown, *The Ladder of Progress in Palestine* (1943), pp. 179–81. W. F. Albright, *The Archaeology of Palestine* (1949), pp. 124–25. G. E. Wright, *Biblical Archaeology* (1957), p. 132. J. B. Pritchard, *Archaeology and the Old Testament* (1958), pp. 31–34. Gus W. Van Beek, *The Interpreter's Dictionary of the Bible* (1962), Vol. K–Q, p. 340, who assigns the southern complex of stables "almost certainly" to Solomon. J. Bright, *A History of Israel* (1959), p. 192. M. Noth, *Die Welt des Alten Testaments,* (2d ed., 1953), p. 103. B. W. Anderson, *Understanding the Old Testament* (2d ed., 1966), p. 153.

4. *New Light from Armageddon, OIC* No. 9 (1931), pp. 37 ff.

5. *OIC* No. 9, p. 46.

6. *PEQ* (1940), pp. 146–47.

7. *Archaeology in the Holy Land* (1960), pp. 269–70.

8. *BA*, 23 (1960), p. 68. See *IEJ*, 16 (1966), p. 142; 17 (1967), pp. 119–21; *RB*, 75 (1968), pp. 396–401 for summaries of the 1966 and 1967 campaigns at Megiddo.

9. *ANET*, p. 279.

10. *BA*, 23 (1960), p. 68.

11. *Megiddo*, I, figs. 34 and 49; subsequently the plan of Locus 5082 was re-covered and published *Megiddo*, II, fig. 414.

12. *Megiddo*, I, fig. 35.

13. *OIC* No. 9, pp. 37–48, which is more an explanation of his theory of identification than a description of the discoveries.

14. *Megiddo*, I, pp. 32–47.

15. *OIC* No. 9, p. 38.

16. *Megiddo*, I, p. 35.

17. *Megiddo*, I, fig. 35.

18. *Megiddo*, I, fig. 35, C–D.

19. *Megiddo*, I, p. 38.

20. *Megiddo*, I, fig. 34.

21. *Megiddo*, ɪ, p. 35.

22. *Megiddo*, ɪ, fig. 49; *Megiddo*, ɪɪ, fig. 414, and section of Locus 351 in *Megiddo*, ɪ, fig. 35.

23. *OIC* No. 9, pp. 42–43.

24. F. J. Bliss, *A Mound of Many Cities* (1894), pp. 90–97 and plan on p. 91.

25. *Ibid.*, p. 96.

26. *Gezer*, ɪɪ, pp. 406 ff.; ɪɪɪ, Pl. 223.

27. E. Sellin, *Tell Ta'annek* (1904), pp. 18, 104, fig. 10.

28. *Hazor*, ɪ, pp. 11–14, Pls. 8, 9, 172; ɪɪ, pp. 6–9, Pl. 200.

29. *Hazor*, ɪ, p. 12.

30. *Hazor*, ɪ, p. 13.

31. *Hazor*, ɪɪ, p. 9.

32. *Expedition*, 6 (1964), No. 4, p. 7, upper left.

33. In the post-exilic building in R.16 at Lachish, where rooms 11 and 12 are separated by a row of monoliths (*Lachish*, ɪɪɪ, pp. 146–48) it appears that there is a similar bin (*Lachish*, ɪɪɪ, Pl. 24:5 and 6).

34. *OIC* No. 9, pp. 37–38.

35. *Megiddo*, ɪ, p. 34.

36. *Megiddo*, ɪ, p. 47.

37. Loci 1575, 1611, 1698, 1576, 1612, 1483, 1541, 399, 361, 351, 362, 363, 364, 365, 366, 367, 375, 378, 379, 380, 404, 403, 407.

38. *ANEP*, Nos. 356–61 and 365.

39. The evidence consists of door jambs for Loci 351, 364, 367 and 403, *Megiddo*, ɪ, fig. 49. However, the later excavations of the buildings at the northwest of the north complex did not reveal a doorway in the expected place. Both ends of the central passageway are closed by walls (*Megiddo*, ɪɪ, fig. 414).

40. *Megiddo*, ɪ, p. 37.

41. The excavators are careful to point out that since lime floors were used in open courts, a similar treatment of the "passageways" might indicate that they, too, were not roofed (*Megiddo*, ɪ, p. 39).

THE SCRIPTS IN PALESTINE
AND TRANSJORDAN IN THE
IRON AGE

Joseph Naveh

THREE alphabetic scripts developed in Syria-Palestine in the Iron Age
—Phoenician, Hebrew and Aramaic. Their common ancestor, the Proto-
Canaanite script, was born in Palestine presumably at the end of the
Middle Bronze Age and existed throughout the Late Bronze Age and the
early part of the Iron Age. In the eleventh century BC, with the development of the linear forms, the stabilization of the right-to-left direction,
and the reduction of the number of letters to twenty-two consonants, the
Proto-Canaanite developed into the Phoenician script.[1] The Hebrews
adopted this script together with other cultural values from the Canaanites
in the twelfth or eleventh century BC. They followed the current Phoenician until the ninth century, when they began to develop their own national script. The Aramaic script began its independent development a
century later; it seems likely that the Aramaeans borrowed the Phoenician
script in the eleventh or tenth century BC.[2]

It is, therefore, difficult to decide whether a tenth- or a ninth-century
script is Phoenician, Hebrew, or Aramaic. Other data, such as origin,
language, contents and even historical data, should be taken into consideration in order to define the nationality of a tenth- or ninth-century inscription. This is the situation concerning the Gezer Calendar, which has
no specific Hebrew linguistic features, and could be considered also as a
Phoenician inscription. However, if we fix the Gezer Calendar in the late
tenth century,[3] when Gezer was an Israelite city (I Kings 9:16), we
thereby determine it as a Hebrew inscription.

The nationality of some minor ninth-century inscriptions found in Galilee
can be determined as Aramaic only according to their language: *lšqy'*—
"belonging to the butlers" ('En-Gev);[4] *ltb[ḥ]y'*—"belonging to the
butchers" (Tel Dan)[5] and a fragment from Hazor inscribed *]š' zy l[*.[6]

A sherd bearing the inscription *byt š['n?*] found in Tel Beth Shan[7] poses a problem: does the uncontracted diphthong in Northern Palestine indicate an Aramaic inscription, or a Hebrew one in which the historical orthography survived?

We encounter such problems in short inscriptions even later. At Tel Zeror a sherd was found bearing the letters]'.*l'lsmk*.[8] The *mem* and *kaf* are not Hebrew, but it is difficult to decide whether this late eighth-century inscription is Phoenician or Aramaic. This site is situated on the Via Maris, where the Wadi 'Ara road comes out into the Plain of Sharon. It seems thus more likely that in the late eighth century we should find an Aramaic inscription left behind by the Assyrians, rather than a Phoenician one. This is in accordance with the form of the *alef* which shows some characteristics toward the Aramaic development.

A similar case is that of another late eighth-century sherd inscribed *lmlkrm* which was found at Samaria.[9] The stance of the *kaf* and *mem* and mainly the head of the *kaf* show that it is not Hebrew but Phoenician–Aramaic. As the script has no specific Phoenician or Aramaic features, it is impossible to decide whether the writer was writing in Phoenician— as the name is more Phoenician[10]—or in Aramaic; for the latter possibility the historical and geographical data should be taken into consideration.

By the seventh century the various sister-scripts were developing independently, so that the problem of distinguishing between them does not arise. Thus the late seventh-century jar inscription from Azor, near Jaffa, could be determined as Phoenician script,[11] although it bears only an indication of the ownership—*lšmly*—which is a common Semitic proper name.

The above listed inscriptions show that all three scripts were used in Palestine in the Iron Age. Though Hebrew was the most common, inscriptions in the other two scripts were found, mainly at the border sites, and presumably were written by non-Israelites.

From the eighth century onwards, Aramaic was spoken and written by people other than the Aramaeans, as the Assyrians introduced it as a common means of communication among the various nations living in the Assyrian empire. Moreover, it became a *lingua franca* and was used as a diplomatic and commercial language. An Aramaic papyrus of the late seventh century BC was found at Saqqarah in Egypt; it is a letter sent to the Pharaoh, probably from Ashkelon, requesting military help against the Babylonians.[12]

The Saqqarah letter is contemporary with the Hebrew ostraca from Arad, Stratum VI;[13] a comparison between these two scripts and with the Phoenician of the same time is most instructive.[14] In the late seventh century the Hebrew script had undergone some two hundred and fifty years of independent development, and was widely used in Palestine. The independent Aramaic script went back some one hundred and fifty years, while the Phoenician continued to develop independently from the other two sister-scripts. Nevertheless, the comparison of the various letters shows clearly that the Aramaic script was much more developed than the Hebrew, while the Phoenician script took an intermediate course between the two. The Aramaic script omits various bars and looks like shorthand in comparison with the Phoenician and especially with the Hebrew script. This phenomenon can be explained through differing geopolitical and cultural factors prevailing among the respective peoples who used the various scripts.

As Aramaic turned into a *lingua franca,* it was used and developed by scribes and merchants who introduced abbreviated letter-forms in order to produce a quick, and efficient script. People writing in Aramaic were generally not Aramaeans and were therefore less sensitive to a national scribal tradition.

On the other hand, while the Hebrew script was used at first by both kingdoms, it was restricted from the late eighth century onwards to Judah alone, and was written by a nation dwelling in a mountainous land, away from international highways and tending to preserve their traditional values.

The Phoenicians wrote in their national script, but it was a relatively widespread commercial means of communication used by this people trading throughout the ancient world. It is therefore understandable that the Phoenician script should seem to take a middle course, in comparison with the free development of the Aramaic on the one hand and the conservatism of Hebrew on the other.

The conservatism of the Hebrew script at the end of the seventh and in the early sixth century is remarkable, since at that time writing spread beyond scribal circles. There is some evidence that not only the educated highest social classes could write, but also members of the lower classes. It seems likely that the Hebrew script developed along one line, i.e., from early lapidary forms toward later cursiveness. From the eighth century onwards the sway of the cursive style was so strong that even stone inscriptions and seals were engraved in cursive letters which emphasized the shading, a natural by-product of pen-and-ink writing.[15] To be sure, the Hebrew inscriptions are mainly in a formal cursive, but in the late seventh century we can trace two other sub-styles of the cursive, i.e., free and vulgar, which seem to bear witness to the existence of a literate society.[16]

In addition to the Israelites, the Philistines lived in Palestine and the Ammonites, Moabites and Edomites in Transjordan. There is almost no epigraphic material which enables us to describe the script of the Philistines in the Iron Age,[17] but the inscriptions found in various sites in Transjordan provide a clear picture of the scripts used by the peoples living there.

The most famous inscription found in Transjordan is the Mesha stele, also called the Moabite Stone; in addition, two other fragmentary stelae of the same period were found in Moab.[18] Though almost no ninth-century Hebrew inscriptions are known at present, several letter-forms of these Moabite stelae (*waw, kaf, mem, nun, pe, ṣade and taw*) display definite Hebrew characteristics; in the eighth-century and later Hebrew inscriptions, further development of these features can be followed. In later Moabite inscriptions, mainly seals from the seventh and sixth centuries,[19] we see clear Aramaic letters written side by side with letters of Hebrew form or of specific local character. It is important to note that the inscriptions bearing Edomite theophoric names found in Elath[20] and recently in Umm el-Biyara near Petra[21] exhibit a similar or even identical script. It seems likely, therefore, that the writing of the Moabites and the Edomites in the ninth century BC did not differ from that of the Hebrews, while in the late seventh and sixth centuries we already find clear signs of the intrusion of Aramaic elements into these two scripts. This intrusion began probably in the last third of the eighth century BC when the political influence of Israel and Judah came to an end, and the Assyrians appeared on the King's Highway south of Damascus.[22]

Besides the Edomites and Moabites, the Ammonites also lived along this highway, but closer to Damascus. Though it seems likely that the language of the Ammonites—as that of the Moabites and the Edomites —was somewhat similar to Hebrew, they did not adopt the Hebrew script. The seventh-century Ammonite seals were written in the contemporary lapidary Aramaic.[23] This phenomenon may indicate that the Ammonites adopted the Aramaic script sometime in the ninth century from the Aramaeans who lived in Damascus; later on they followed the Aramaic scribal tradition common in the Assyrian empire.

Recently some most interesting epigraphic material was found in Gilead; it consists of numerous inscribed plaster fragments from Tell Deir 'Alla on the eastern bank of the Jordan.[24] Though the texts have not yet been deciphered, the general impression is that the language is neither standard Aramaic nor Hebrew, but some dialect spoken in Gilead. The script, however, seems to be identical with the current Aramaic. If this assumption is correct, as the writer suggests, these inscriptions are to be fixed *circa* the mid-eighth century BC, bearing the earliest Aramaic cursive known till now.[25] On the other hand, if this is considered to be a local script retarded in development, it cannot be later than the seventh century BC.[26] However, in a local script we would expect some clear peculiarities which do not occur in the Aramaic script.

The few Egyptian hieroglyphic inscriptions and the Assyrian and Babylonian cuneiform inscriptions left behind by the conquerors and found on some Iron Age sites in Palestine have been omitted from the above discussion because its purpose was to describe the North-West Semitic scripts from a comparative point of view. This short essay dedicated to Professor Nelson Glueck is an attempt to show how the twenty-two letters reflect the cultures of the various peoples who lived in Palestine and Transjordan.

FOOTNOTES

1. Cf. F. M. Cross, Jr., *Eretz-Israel*, 8 (1967), pp. 8*-24*; see also B. Mazar, *IEJ*, 18 (1968), pp. 94–96, and Mazar, *Proceedings of the Israel Academy of Sciences and Humanities*, I, No. 7 (1964), p. 7.

2. W. F. Albright, *BASOR*, No. 90 (1943), p. 32; F. M. Cross, Jr. and D. N. Freedman, *Early Hebrew Orthography* (1952), pp. 31–32; Cross, *op. cit.* (n. 1), p. 12*.

3. F. M. Cross, Jr., *BASOR*, No. 168 (1962), p. 15.

4. B. Mazar *et al.*, *IEJ*, 14 (1964), pp. 27–28, Pl. 13.

5. N. Avigad, *PEQ* (1968), pp. 42–44, Pl. XVIII.

6. Y. Yadin *et al.*, *Hazor*, III–IV (1961), Pl. 357:1. However, other fragmentary inscribed sherds from Hazor show either tenth-century Phoenician scribal tradition, i.e. a *bet* with a rightward base, which occurs in the Byblos inscriptions (see *Hazor*, II, p. 71, Pl. 169:3), or its development in the ninth century (*ibid.*, Pl. 169:1—the *waw*, and Pl. 169:4—the *taw*). Such key-letters are generally exceptional in small fragments.

7. N. Tsori, *BIES*, 25 (1961), pp. 145–46, Pl. VI:3 (Hebrew).

8. Still unpublished; my thanks are due to Dr. M. Kochavi for showing me the sherd and supplying me with a photograph of it.

9. G. A. Reisner *et al.*, *Harvard Excavations at Samaria* (1924), p. 238, Pl. 55a.

10. Cf. Z. S. Harris, *A Grammar of the Phoenician Language* (1936), pp. 119 and 145.

11. B. Peckham, *IEJ*, 16 (1966), p. 11, n. 2; M. Dothan, *'Atiqot*, English Series 3 (1961), pp. 181–84, Pl. XXVIII:4–5.

12. A. Dupont-Sommer, *Sem*, 1 (1948), pp. 43–68; J. A. Fitzmyer, *Bib*, 46 (1965), pp. 41–55. J. T. Milik in *Bib*, 48 (1967), pp. 561–63 suggests that the papyrus was sent from Tyre.

13. Y. Aharoni, *IEJ*, 16 (1966), pp. 1–7, Pl. 1; *idem*, *BA*, 31 (1968), pp. 13–17, figs. 1, 9, 11.

14. No lengthy Phoenician ink-inscription from the seventh century has been found up till now, but the Phoenician cursive of this time can be reconstructed on the basis of two jar inscriptions written in ink (see Ch. Clermont-Ganneau, *Recueil d'Archéologie Orientale*, III (1900), pp. 74–75, Pl. II C–F) and a sixth-century papyrus from Saqqarah (N. Aimé-Giron, *ASAE* 40 [1941], pp. 433–60, Pl. XL). The early sixth-century graffiti of Ipsambul (*CIS* I, 111–13) may also be helpful. Apart from the Arad Stratum VI ostraca, the late seventh-century Meṣad Ḥashavyahu ostracon (Naveh, *IEJ*, 10 [1960], pp. 129–39, Pl. 17) and the early sixth-century Lachish letters (H. Torczyner [Tur-Sinai], *Lachish* I [1938]) can be included for the study of the Hebrew cursive of this period. For the Aramaic cursive see also the Assur ostracon (M. Lidzbarski, *Altaramäische Urkunden aus Assur* [1921], pp. 5–15, Pl. I) and the clay tablet from 571/70 BC published by J. Starcky in *Syr*, 37 (1960), pp. 99–115.

15. However, one cannot explain the absence of the lapidary style in the development of the Hebrew script merely by the strong sway of the cursive. It seems likely

that the widespread custom of erecting stelae and votive inscriptions did not prevail either in Israel or in Judah. Thus there was no opportunity of preserving the specific elements for cutting in stone.

16. Cf. J. Naveh, *HTR*, 61 (1968), pp. 68–74.

17. It is presumed that in the twelfth century BC the Philistines wrote in a Cypro-Mycenaean type of writing (see the views of R. de Vaux, W. F. Albright and F. M. Cross, Jr., on the Deir 'Alla tablets given by G. E. Wright in *BA*, 29 [1966], pp. 73–74). However, it is reasonable that in the eighth and seventh centuries, when the Philistine kings bore names like Ḥanun, Ṣidqa and Mitinti, they spoke a Semitic language and wrote in a script similar to those current in this region. The sherd inscribed -]*pḥr* from Ashdod (M. Dothan and D. N. Freedman, *'Atiqot*, English Series 7 [1967], pp. 84–85, Pl. XV:8) does not feature any local characteristics, but the seal *l'bd'l'b/bn šb't/'bd mtt bn/ṣdq'* (see A. Bergman [Biran], *JBL*, 55 [1936], pp. 224–26 and H. Tadmor, *BA*, 29 [1966], p. 98; for a clear facsimile drawing see G. A. Cooke, *A Text Book of North Semitic Inscriptions* [1903]. Pl. XL:6) may perhaps indicate that the Philistine script absorbed, in addition to Hebrew, some Phoenician or Aramaic features.

18. R. E. Murphy, *BASOR*, No. 125 (1952), pp. 20–23; W. L. Reed and F. V. Winnett, *BASOR*, No. 172 (1963), pp. 1–9.

19. These are the seals *lkmšṣdq, lkmšyhy, lkmš'm / kmš'l / hspr, 'mṣ hspr* and *lmnšh bn / hmlk* from the seventh century, and two *mš'* seals from the sixth century BC. The latter bear clear Aramaic *'ayin* and *shin*. A common feature of all these seals is the large-headed *mem*. Cf. J. Naveh, *BASOR*, No. 183 (1966), pp. 28–30 and the bibliography there. Since the publication of this paper I have been able to examine in the Palestine Archaeological Museum in East Jerusalem the Barley Letter found in Samaria: it appears that no example of *mem* is similar to the Moabite-Edomite type as suggested in *BASOR*, No. 183 (1966), pp. 29–30, n. 24.

20. N. Glueck and W. F. Albright, *BASOR*, No. 71 (1938), pp. 17–18; Glueck, *BASOR*, No. 72 (1938), pp. 9–13; *idem, BASOR*, No. 82 (1941), pp. 3–6; Albright, *ibid.*, pp. 11–15; Glueck, *BASOR*, No. 188 (1967), pp. 8–10.

21. C. M. Bennett, *RB*, 73 (1966), pp. 398–401, Pl. XXIIb. The ostracon illustrated on Pl. XXIIa seems also to have a large-headed *mem*, but the state of preservation of the letters is not sufficient for a detailed examination of this script; nevertheless, it seems likely that it is earlier than ostracon 6043 (*BASOR*, No. 82) from Elath.

22. See Naveh, *loc. cit.* (n. 19).

23. N. Avigad, *IEJ*, 15 (1965), p. 227.

24. H. J. Franken, *VT*, 17 (1967), pp. 480–81; cf. *ILN* of July 20, 1968, pp. 30–31—Franken dated these inscriptions in the Persian Period.

25. J. Naveh, *IEJ*, 17 (1967), pp. 256–58.

26. Professor W. F. Albright, in a letter of August 9, 1968, wrote to me about the Deir 'Alla material: "My own date for the specimen characters would be in the seventh century rather than in the eighth. A date in the mid-eighth century is almost incredible since at that time the site was almost certainly inside Israel, and one would expect contemporary Hebrew forms. In the middle of the seventh century Israel had long ceased to exist so that the characters are perfectly in line with both date and location." (Professor Naveh notes that he completed his article in December 1968.—Ed.)

AMMONITE AND MOABITE SEALS*

N. Avigad

THE cultural history of Ammon and Moab in biblical times is still shrouded
to a great extent in obscurity, owing to the meager archaeological evidence which has come to light in these two countries. Surface exploration,
sporadic archaeological excavations, and casual discoveries have, however,
yielded valuable material for reconstruction of a skeletal framework of
their past.[1] Among the smaller finds which contribute their modest share
to this aim may be counted the inscribed Ammonite and Moabite seals
that are the subject of this article. Outstanding among scholars who devoted
themselves to the exploration of the lands of Ammon and Moab is
Professor Nelson Glueck. It is, therefore, most satisfying to contribute
this paper to a Festschrift volume in his honor.

A. Ammonite Seals

The number of known Ammonite seals is steadily increasing, and their
importance for the study of the Ammonites and their culture cannot be
overestimated given the scanty epigraphic material which has so far
turned up in ancient Ammon.[2] Our knowledge of the Ammonite script,
language and onomasticon is greatly dependent upon the inscribed seals.[3]

It is remarkable how relatively many seals of importance the small
land of Ammon yielded. They comprise, *inter alia,* two official seals of
the *'ebed*-class; at least one of the *na'ar* class; two seals belonging to
female functionaries (the only ones of their kind so far known among
West-semitic seals); and the seal of an Ammonite priest (?). They
evidently manifest the rise of Ammon as an important state of Transjordan in the seventh century BC.[4]

So far, we are unable to trace the beginnings of Ammonite glyptic art.
The main group of seals belongs probably to the seventh century BC,
a date based on palaeographic comparison with two well-dated seals

*This article is based on a chapter to be included in a Corpus of Northwest
Semitic Seals being prepared by the writer.

belonging to royal officials of an Ammonite king, i.e. "Adonipelet, servant of Amminadab"[5] and "Adoninur, servant of Amminadab."[6] This Amminadab is known to have been king of Ammon at the time of Ashurbanipal (*circa* 661 BC) and to have paid tribute to the Assyrian king.

In the same tomb with the seal of Adoninur were found two other seals, of "Menaḥem, son of Yenaḥem"[7] and of a certain "Shuba'el."[8] Closely related to this group are two parallel seals from Ammon belonging to "'Alyah, maid-servant of Ḥanan'el"[9] and to "'NMWT, maid-servant of DBLBS."[10] One seal is identified as Ammonite by the name of the Ammonite deity mentioned in its inscription: "Seal of Mannu-Ki-Inurta, blessed by Milcom."[11] Among other seals which should be included in the same category for palaeographical reasons, mention should be made of those of "Abyaḥaz, son of Yenaḥem,"[12] "Menaḥem, son of Shôḥer"[13] and "'W', son of MR'L."[14]

This selected group of seals shows a remarkably homogeneous script. In the main it represents the current lapidary Aramaic script of the seventh and sixth centuries BC, with some palaeographic peculiarities of its own. The main characteristics of the Ammonite script are its pronounced vertical stance and the forms of the following letters: the *he* with only two horizontal bars; *waw* with a horizontal (or oblique) short stroke below the tip of the vertical shaft; the *ḥet* with only one bar; *mem* with a horizontally stretched w-shaped head; *ṭet* with a single cross-line; a zigzag-shaped *samekh;* a square *'ayin* (which is not typical Aramaic; the open *'ayin,* which is the regular Aramaic form, is rare) and a tall, cross-like *taw.*

The Ammonites of the seventh century BC adopted the Aramaic script[15] but not the language, as is evident by the use of *ben, bat, na'ar* and *'amat* instead of their Aramaic equivalents. The native Ammonite language and script seem to have been kindred to Hebrew, as Moabite was. The personal proper names are for the most part of common Northwest Semitic repertory. The iconography of the seals shows strong Assyrian and lesser Egyptian affinities, but most seals are undecorated.

In what follows, a number of as yet unpublished seals will be discussed which are palaeographically identified as being Ammonite of the seventh century BC. They enrich the known corpus of Ammonite seals and add new features of glyptic and epigraphic interest. These seals were purchased in Jerusalem during the last few years, and are said to have come from Jordan (Pl. 30, 1–5).[16]

1. A seal in the shape of a duck, with its head and beak turned

and facing back over its body. It is made of red jasper and is of superior workmanship. It has a suspension hole, and is 21 millimeters long, 8 millimeters wide and 15 millimeters high.

On its flat sole-shaped bottom is incised an inscription in two lines which are separated by two parallel lines and flanked on each side by a vertical line. The inscription is well done and reads:

L'MR'L | BN YNḤM "Belonging to Amar'el, son of Yenaḥem"
The seal is sculptured in imitation of the well-known Mesopotamian duck-shaped weights which are, however, much larger[17]. Duck-shaped stamp-seals, corresponding in size to our seal, are known from Mesopotamia in the Late-Assyrian and Neo-Babylonian periods. They are regularly made of chalcedony and have conventionalized human or animal figures incised on their bottom.[18] Since they never bear inscriptions and, seemingly, no impressions of this kind have ever been found, their use as stamp-seals rather than weights remained open to discussion.[19] Ours is the first inscribed seal of this kind so far known. The inscription points to its Ammonite origin. Noteworthy forms of letters are the *mem*, *yod* and *ḥet*. They should be compared with the corresponding letters on the seal of the maid-servant 'Alyah mentioned above.[20]

The personal proper name Amar'el "God has spoken, commanded" finds its closest parallel in the El'amar seal from Megiddo.[21] Theophorous names with the verb *'mr* are found on two other Hebrew seals: Aḥi'amar[22] and Amaryahu.[23] The latter appears also in the Gibeon inscriptions[24] and in the Bible.

The name *ynḥm* "He (god) will console" has been found on two other Ammonite seals,[25] and our present example shows that it was a favorite name among the Ammonites. It is an imperfect form from the same root as the common name *mnḥm*, and is a hypocoristicon of *ynḥmyhw* "Yahu will console" recently found on a Hebrew ostracon from Arad.[26]

2. A scaraboid of red limestone with black spots, perforated lengthwise, 15 by 14 by 9 millimeters. The flat bottom is divided into three registers. In the center register a four-winged beetle is engraved in a very crude manner. It is flanked by two devices which seem to represent some kind of scepter or staff. The left one is a stylized lotus stalk, and to the right is a hooked staff reminiscent of the Egyptian *was* scepter. A close parallel to this assemblage and its crude execution is provided by another Ammonite seal.[27]

In the upper and lower registers are two lines of inscription, each followed by a short dividing stroke. The inscription reads:

LŠWḤR | HNSS

PLATE 35. Tribute procession of the Lydians from Persepolis, Apadana, eastern
stairway

PLATE 36. Cover for incense burner in Pl. 37 (cf. *AJA*, 71 [1967] Pl. 59, fig. 20)

PLATE 37. Incense burner from Usak tumulus (cf. *AJA*, 71 [1967] Pl. 59, fig. 20)

PLATE 38. Pyramid Tomb, Sardis, north steps

PLATE 39. Pasargadae, the 'B' Staircase (cf. *Iran,* 1, Pl. IIIa)

PLATE 40. Head of young man (god?) bordered by dolphins, from the Treasure of the Oxus

PLATE 41. Sardonyx gem showing eagle and serpent, possibly symbol of lunar god Nasrum

PLATE 42. Petra. View of southern colonnade of paved street, after 1956 excavations, showing Portico Wall and Byzantine shop walls

PLATE 43. Petra. General view of Trench III from north, showing Portico Wall and Wall K behind

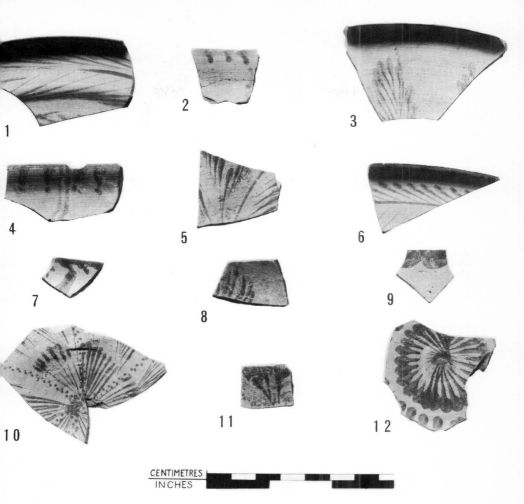

CENTIMETRES
INCHES

PLATE 44. Painted-ware sherds from Petra

PLATE 45. Painted-ware sherds from Petra

Šwḥr is a rare name which appears once on another Ammonite seal *mnḥm bn šwḥr.*[28] It represents the participle of the root *šḥr* meaning "to look for, to seek" (Prov. 11:27). The proper name *šḥr,* on the other hand, occurs on Hebrew seal-impressions and is regarded as a hypocoristicon of biblical *šḥryhw* where the first element is usually interpreted "dawn." In the light of our seal it may perhaps be the perfect of the verb *šḥr.* For participle forms of proper names see biblical Obed, Oded and Shomer. For plene writing of similar names see the seals: *ḥwnn bn y'znyh*[29] (Aramaic script) and *ḥwrṣ bn pqll*[30] (Hebrew script), both of approximately the early sixth century BC. The *waw* as internal *mater lectionis* appears earlier in the world *'rwr* in the Royal-steward epitaph of the eighth to seventh century BC.[31]

Hnss is a new and problematic word in seal inscriptions. The first letter *he* is obviously the definite article, and the remaining letters *nss* should thus designate a title, profession or nickname.[32] The root *nss* seems to derive from Hebrew *nês* "standard, pole, flag" meaning "to lift up or to raise a standard."[33] Hence we should read and translate our inscription as follows: *Le-Shawḥer ha-nassâs* "belonging to Shôḥer the Standard-bearer."

Standards are known to have been widely used in antiquity for military and cultic purposes. In the Bible they are frequently mentioned. If our interpretation is correct, the owner of the seal may have been a functionary in charge of such symbols at the Ammonite court, army or temple. Admittedly, one would expect the seal of such a man to be of a higher artistic quality. Linguistically however, it is most satisfying to have new evidence for the use of the Hebrew vocabulary by the Ammonites. It seems to be sheer coincidence that the seal is decorated with devices reminiscent of scepters and staffs. Somewhat similar devices occur on other seals.

The palaeography of the seal is of special interest, showing a number of Aramaic forms: *waw, ḥet, he* and *samekh.* The most interesting feature is the *he* with its middle stroke touching the corner. It is characteristic of the cursive hand of the Persian period, but it makes its first appearance in Aramaic documents from Assur of the seventh century BC.[34] In the same documents occur also our cursive *samekh,* which appears on one of the Ammonite *'amah*-seals mentioned above.[35]

3. A dark-brown limestone scaraboid, perforated, 16 by 12 by 9 millimeters. It has two lines of inscription which are separated by two parallel lines. At the end of the first line there is a star which serves as space filler. The inscription reads:

L'L' BN / ḤṬŠ "Belonging to Ela', son of Ḥattush"

The script is rather crude and vulgar. The *alefs* are peculiar, in that the two strokes at the right do not continue to meet at the left of the vertical shaft. The ḥet has the form of an H; the ṭeṭ is an irregular, pointed oval with a single cross-bar.

Both names are new in the onomasticon of the seals, but they are known from the Bible. Ela' is mentioned in I Kings 4:18 as the father of one of Solomon's purveyors. The same name occurs in Samaria ostracon No. 38. It is probably a hypocoristicon containing the theophorous *El* and the final *alef*. *Ḥṭš* is probably the biblical Ḥattush; which is mentioned as the name of a descendant of Zerubbabel (I Chr. 3:22) and of several other notables who returned from Babylon (Ezra 8:2; Neh. 3:10, 10:4, 12:2). Its etymology is unknown and it is apparently not Hebrew. It should be compared with Akkadian *Ḥanṭûšû*.[36]

4. A conical seal of brown limestone with black spots, round perforated top, 15 millimeters in height, oval base of 12 by 10 millimeters. Two lines of inscription are separated by a double line:

LNDB'L | BN 'L'ZR "Belonging to Nadab'el, son of El'azar"

The Z-shaped zayin is the only distinct Aramaic (or Phoenician) character. The name Nadab'el—"God has shown his generosity"—occurs on several other seals, and seems to have been very popular among the Ammonites. Biblical proper names compounding the very *ndb* are: Abinadab, Aḥinadab and Yehonadab. El'azar "God has helped" is a common biblical name. In another Ammonite(?) seal it appears in reverse composition 'Azar'el.[37]

5. A scaraboid of hard, ivory-colored limestone, polished, with finely cracked surface; not perforated, 15 by 12.5 by 6 millimeters. The oval bottom has a borderline and two horizontal lines dividing the inscription which reads:

LMNḤM | BN TNḤM "Belonging to Menaḥem, son of Tanḥûm"

Menaḥem, meaning "consoler," is a common Semitic name and occurs on several Ammonite seals. Tanḥûm, however, has been found so far only in Hebrew seal-impressions.[38] It is a well known name from post-biblical literature. In the Bible the feminine form Tanḥûmet is a masculine proper name.

The most typical letter is the tall, cross-shaped *taw* which is characteristic to all Ammonite seals. The first *mem* is also typical, but the second is of a different type. The *mem* at the end of the second line combines both forms and shows the inconsistency of the engraver in writing this letter. The ḥet differs from the other ḥets on Ammonite seals in that it has two horizontal bars. The same ḥet, however, occurs also in the Ammonite statue-inscription. Possibly this letter points to an earlier, transitional phase of the Ammonite script.

B. Moabite Seals

Unlike Ammon, Moab yielded a monumental inscription with the famous Mesha stele; this provided important data on the script and language of the Moabites in the ninth century BC, which are closely akin to Hebrew. We have no contemporary Moabite seals. The extant seal-inscriptions continue in general the scribal tradition of the Mesha inscription, but they develop some new palaeographic characteristics. Considering these developments, the main group of Moabite seals may be assigned to the eighth and seventh centuries BC. The most characteristic letter in this respect is the *mem* which, unlike the W-headed Mesha-inscription *mem*, has a large head, sometimes almost half of the height of the letter, with two short vertical strokes which do not cross the horizontal line,[39] and a strongly curved main downstroke. The *ḥet* has two horizontal bars as in the Mesha-inscription, but each of the two vertical strokes extends upward or downward respectively. The *'ayin* is sometimes square. The *taw* preserves the X-shaped Hebrew form. These forms of letters can be observed in a number of seals bearing the name Kemosh which are undoubtedly Moabite, i.e. *Kmšṣdq*,[40] *Kmšyḥy*[41] *Kmš'm/Kmš'l/hspr*,[42] and the seals *Kmšntn* and *Kmsm'š* which will be discussed below.

It follows that at a time when Ammonite seals used the Aramaic script, the seals of the neighboring Moab retained the tradition of Moabite-Hebrew writing. But two seals bearing the name *mš'* show an open *'ayin* and *shin* with three strokes joining at the round bottom.[43] These are developed Aramaic forms of letters which are still missing in the main group of the seventh-century Ammonite seals. Hence they seem to indicate an adaptation of the Aramaic script on Moabite seals at a later date, say the sixth century BC.[44]

It is noteworthy that the Moabite group, too, yielded several seals of dignitaries such as those of the scribes *Kmš'm/Kms'l/hspr*[45] and *'mṣ hspr*,[46] and that of the royal minister *mnšh bn hmlk*.[47] The latter two seals reveal the use in Moab of explicit Hebrew names and of similar titles in the royal administration.

Some new seals, which will be discussed below, represent both types, early and late. They add new names to the Moabite onomasticon, and confirm the established palaeographic characteristics of the Moabite seal-inscriptions (Pl. 30, 6–8).

6. This seal, which is now in the British Museum (BM 116598), was discovered in the Ur excavations conducted in the twenties by Sir Leonard Woolley. It comes from the Neo-Babylonian E-nun-maḫ Temple, and was found above a shell-floor dating to the Persian period. In the catalogue of the excavation-report[48] the seal (U526) is described as being a lapis-lazuli ring bezel, circular domed above, one centimeter in diameter (0.6 centimeter thick). It is further described as having on its flat face an Aramaic-inscription. Elsewhere[49] the same inscription is termed Pehlevi. No reproduction of the seal has been published.[50]

The seal has a round border line surrounding an inscription of two lines:

KMŠ/NTN "Kemosh-natan"

This is a new name in the series of known personal names which are composed with the name of the national Moabite god, Kemosh. In the use of the verb *ntn* it compares with other theophorous names as: Yeho-natan, Elnatan, Ba'alnatan etc. The letters reveal the characteristics of the Moabite script outlines above.

The dating of the seal is made difficult by its reported provenance above a Persian floor level. Such a late date seems to be inconceivable for palaeographic reasons. One should rather regard it as intrusive in the upper disturbed level, and relate the seal to the Neo-Babylonian phase of the Temple, possibly to the end of the seventh century. The seal probably belonged to a Moabite exile, businessman, or the like, who resided in Ur. It was undoubtedly engraved by a Moabite engraver who produced a seal which is unconventional in form and composition.

7. A scaraboid seal[51] of brown agate, perforated, 17 by 15 by 10 millimeters. The seal is divided by double lines into three registers. In the upper register is represented a crescent with a horizontal bar under-neath; a star on its left; and an unidentified device on its right. Astral symbols seem to have been common on Moabite seals,[52] whereas on Ammonite seals they are apparently absent.

In the two lower registers is engraved in two lines the somewhat worn, but easily legible inscription:

LKMŠM/'Š "Belonging to Kemosh -*m'š*"

This is another unknown name of the Kemosh-class. The second element *m'š* is new and problematic, and requires scrutiny. The only known word spelled *m'š* appears in Punic and Neo-Punic votive inscriptions[53] meaning "statue" (suzerain, divine, and votive). The earliest among them is the recently discovered inscription from Pyrgi (Italy), which is dated to the early fifth century BC.[45] *M'Š* is the plene spelling of the defective *mš* which occurs both in Phoenician and Punic inscriptions.[55]

Albright[56] has pointed out the semantic transition from Ugaritic (and Proto-Sinaitic) *mt*, a title of a son born to Ba'al, meaning "lord" and *mtt* "lady," to Phoenician *mš* meaning "statue." Y. Yadin[57] has recognized the same appellation in obscure biblical and extra-biblical names like *mš'm*, *'nmš*, *ddymš*, etc., and has interpreted it as a theophorous element.

Following this line of thinking I would suggest that the second element *m'š* in the name of our seal be regarded as the full version of *mš*, and interpreted "Lord." Thus *Kmš-m'š* may be a syncretistic name corresponding to *Kmš-'l* mentioned above, or more likely it should be compared with similar compounds of names such as Hebrew *Adoniyahu*, or Phoenician *'šmn-'dn*, *'dn-b'l*, and the like. As to the early use of *alef* in the *m'š* of our seal (eighth to seventh century BC), reference should be made to *z't* in line 3 of the still earlier Mesha inscription.

8. A conical seal of dark green stone, perforated near the top; 20 millimeters in height; oval bottom of 16 by 12 millimeters. The seal is divided by two double lines into three registers. In the upper register are three letters and in the second are two letters which give the reading:

LMŠ/PṬ "Belonging to *mšpṭ*"

In the second line two oval devices serve as space fillers. In the bottom register is represented a winged and tailed sun-disc, but the disc itself is left unfinished. The body of the seal is well shaped, but the engraving is of inferior workmanship.

The inscription shows vulgar forms and reveals some palaeographic anomalies. The *lamed* turns to the left instead of to the right. The second letter is a reversed W-shaped *mem* with a short tail. The *shin* has three strokes which meet at a rounded bottom. The *pe* at the beginning of the second line is crude but clear. The last letter is a misdrawn reversed and upside-down cursive *ṭet*.

For the misshaped *mem* and the three-stroke *shin* we have close parallels in two Moabite seals bearing the name *mš'*, which probably date to the sixth century BC.[58] For the curious form of the *ṭet* compare a similar, but upright, cursive *ṭet* in a Phoenician-inscription of the fourth century BC.[59] The latter inscription also shows similar forms of *pe* and *shin*. A sixth century date for our seal seems to be permissible.

The name *mšpṭ* is new and should be vocalized *Mishpaṭ*, "Judgment." Similar noun-forms with preformative *mem* in personal names are frequently found in the Bible, e.g. Mibsam and Mishma', sons of Ishma'el (Gen. 25:13, 14); Mibsar, an Edomite chieftain (Gen. 36:42); Mibhar the Hagrite, one of David's heroes of foreign descendance (I Chr.

11:38); Mispar, one of those who returned from the Exile (Ez. 2:2), etc. It is remarkable how this otherwise rare form of personal name is to be found among Ishmaelites, Edomites, Hagrites and, to judge from our seal, also among Moabites.

Mšpṭ is apparently a hypocoristicon of theophorous proper names such as **mšpṭmlk* or **mšpṭyhw*, comparable in construction to Phoenician *mqnmlk* and Hebrew *mqnyhw*. In Elephantine both patterns occur: *mbṭḥ* and *mbṭḥyh*.[60]

FOOTNOTES

1. See G. M. Landes, "The Material Civilization of the Ammonites," in *The Biblical Archaeologist Reader*, 2 (1964), pp. 69–88; A. H. van Zyn, *The Moabites* (1960).

2. The *Yeraḥ'azar* statue-inscription from Amman (R. D. Barnett, *ADAJ*, 1 [1951], pp. 34 ff., Pl. XIII) has not yet been satisfactorily deciphered. A longer inscription, said to have been discovered in Amman in 1962, has remained unpublished to date (following G. M. Landes, *ibid.*, p. 83, n. 36).

3. For first summary treatments of the Ammonite seals by the writer see: *IEJ*, 2 (1952), pp. 163 f., and *Tur-Sinai Jubilee Volume* (1960), p. 323 (in Hebrew). The significance of the seals for Ammonite studies has been demonstrated by W. F. Albright in his "Notes on Ammonite History" in *Miscellanea Biblica B. Urbach* (1954), pp. 131–36.

4. Albright, *ibid.*, p. 133.

5. C. C. Torrey, *AASOR*, 2–3 (1923), p. 104.

6. L. Harding, *PEFA*, 6 (1953), p. 51, Pl. VI:1.

7. N. Avigad, *IEJ*, 2 (1952), p. 163 f.

8. *Op. cit.* (above, n. 6), p. 52, Pl. VI:3.

9. N. Avigad, *PEQ*, 1946, pp. 125–31.

10. A. Reifenberg, *Ancient Hebrew Seals* (1950), No. 36. Albright, *op. cit.* (above, n. 3), p. 134, n. 19, is certainly right in correcting Reifenberg by reading the first letter *d* and the last *s*, but it seems to me that the fourth letter is *b* and not *k* as suggested by him.

11. N. Avigad, *IEJ*, 15 (1963), pp. 222 ff., Pl. 40:B–D.

12. D. Diringer, *Le iscrizioni antico-ebraiche palestinesi* (1934), Sig. No. 103. N. Avigad, *BASOR*, No. 189 (1968), p. 49.

13. *Tur-Sinai Jubilee Volume* (see n. 3), p. 321.

14. P. Hammond, *BASOR*, No. 160 (1960), pp. 38 ff.

15. See J. Naveh's article above, pp. 277 ff.

16. Seals Nos. 1–4 were in the possession of Mr. Joab Sasson and later acquired by the Israel Museum; No. 5 is in the possession of Mr. S. Moussaieff. The writer wishes to thank them for permission to publish the seals.

17. Cf. J. B. Pritchard, *ANEP*, No. 120.

18. H. H. von der Osten, *Ancient Oriental Seals in the Collection of Mr. Edward T. Newell* (1934), Pl. XXXII, Nos. 500–12. One such engraved duck-shaped chalcedony seal made its appearance recently in Israel as a surface find at Ḥurvat Uzza in the Negeb (Dept. of Antiquities No. R. 3999). I owe this information to Mr. L. Y. Rahmani.

19. *Ibid.* p. 9.

20. *Loc. cit.* (above, n. 9).

21. S. Moscati, *L'epigrafia ebraica antica 1935–1950* (1951), p. 56:14.

22. *Ibid.*, p. 77:13.

23. N. Avigad, *IEJ*, 13 (1963), p. 324.

24. J. B. Pritchard, *Hebrew Inscriptions and Stamps from Gibeon* (1954), p. 8.

25. Avigad, *op. cit.* (above, n. 7) with discussion on the name; Diringer, *op. cit.* (above, n. 12).

26. Y. Aharoni, *BA*, 31 (1968), p. 11.

27. *Loc ćit.*, (above, n. 7).

28. *Loc. cit.*, (above, n. 13).

29. Diringer, *op. cit.* (above, n. 12), Sig. No. 21.

30. *Ibid.*, No. 22.

31. N. Avigad, *IEJ*, 3 (1953), p. 143.

32. Three such designations with the definite article have appeared so far on seals: *hspr* "the scribe" on two Moabite seals (see below, notes 42, 46); *hṣrp* "the goldsmith" on another Moabite seal (Diringer, Sig. No. 102); and *hghb* "the locust" on a Hebrew seal (Avigad, *IEJ*, 16 [1966], p. 50). Another instance, *hmlk*, is not relevant to our discussion.

33. The participle *nôses* occurs in a difficult passage of the Bible (Isa. 10:18), where the commentators vary widely in their interpretations. The AV, interestingly translates "Standard-bearer," which, however, does not seem to be in place there. Similarly, see *nôsesah* in Isa. 59:19.

34. F. Rosenthal, *Die aramäistische Forschungen, etc.*, (1939) Schrifttafel 1, col. 13.

35. Reifenberg, *loc. cit.* (above, no. 10).

36. K. L. Tallqvist, *Assyrian Personal Names* (1914), p. 86.

37. N. Avigad, *BIES*, 18 (1954), p. 150 (in Hebrew).

38. In Beth-Shemesh, Lachish and Gibeon. See Pritchard, *op. cit.* (above, n. 24), p. 28, with bibliographical references.

39. J. Naveh, *BASOR*, No. 183 (1966), p. 29.

40. M. Lidzbarski, *Ephemeris für semitische Epigraphik* (1902), p. 136.

41. *Ibid.*, p. 140.

42. A. Reifenberg, *BJPES*, 12 (1945/6), p. 45, Pl. II:3 (Hebrew); *idem, op. cit.*, (above, n. 10), No. 28.

43. *Ibid.*, *BJPES*, Pl. II:4; N. Avigad, *Eretz-Israel, 1* (1951), pp. 33–34 (Hebrew).

44. Naveh, *loc. cit.* (above, n. 39).

45. *Loc. cit.* (above, n. 42).

46. Diringer, *op. cit.* (above, n. 12), No. 74.

47. Avigad, *IEJ*, 13 (1963), p. 134. On the suggested Moabite character of the last two seals cf. J. Naveh, *op. cit.* (above, n. 39), p. 29, n. 24.

48. Sir Leonard Woolley, *Ur Excavations*, IX, *The Neo-Babylonian and Persian Periods* (1962), p. 109.

49. *Ibid.*, p. 32.

50. My thanks are due to Dr. R. D. Barnett, who enabled me to check the seal at the British Museum, and to Professor Jonas Greenfield, who independently identified the seal and kindly transferred to me the right of publication, which had been granted to him by Dr. Barnett.

51. The seal is in the possession of Mr. S. Harari, Tel Aviv, who has kindly permitted the writer to publish it.

52. Compare the seal *mnšh bn hmlk* (above, n. 47) with star, crescent and under-stroke; and the *yr'* seal (*BIES*, 18, [1954], Pl. 4:7) with all three devices of our seal. On reconsideration these two seals now seem to be Moabite.

53. For bibliography see Charles F. Jean-Jacob Hoftijzer, *Dictionnaire des Inscriptions Sémitiques de l'Ouest* (1965), pp. 168 f.

54. G. Garbini, *Archeologia Classica*, 16 (1964), pp. 66–76; A. Dupont-Sommer, *Journal Asiatique*, 152 (1964), p. 290, fig. 1, 1.9.

55. For bibliography see above, n. 53.

56. *BASOR*, No. 110 (1948), p. 17, n. 54; *idem.* "The Proto-Sinaitic Inscriptions and their Decipherment," *HTS*, 22 (1966), pp. 41 f.

57. *Eretz-Israel*, 6 (1961), pp. 53 f.

58. *Loc. cit.* (above, n. 43).

59. J. Friedrich, *Phönizisch-Punische Grammatik* (1951), Schrifttafel I, cols. 18–19.

60. A. Cowley, *Aramaic Papyri of the Fifth century B.C.* (1923), No. 22:2, 25.

Addendum. Additional note to n. 2: After this paper went to press the said Ammonite inscription has been published. It throws important light on the history of the Ammonite language and script. See: S. H. Horn, "The Ammān Citadel Inscription," *BASOR*, No. 193 (1969), pp. 2–13; F. M. Cross, "Epigraphic Notes on the Ammān Citadel Inscription," *ibid.*, pp. 13–19.

IV
The Persian Period
and Beyond

THE CAVE INSCRIPTIONS FROM KHIRBET BEIT LEI

Frank Moore Cross, Jr.

I

IN 1963 Dr. Joseph Naveh published a group of important inscriptions, graffiti scratched on the antechamber wall of a tomb of bench-type cut in the eastern slope of Khirbet Beit Lei (Bayt Layy), a site some eight kilometers east of ancient Lachish.[1] The inscriptions of the west and south walls are of unique interest in view of their content, but difficult to decipher.

The hindrances to decipherment are several. The surface of the soft limestone wall is covered with pickmarks and is uneven. Scratches cover the wall in various patterns, and are often difficult to distinguish from the lines forming letters made by a crude stylus. Moreover, the wall surface has suffered some damage either by weathering or by gouge, as we can determine in areas where the decipherment is certain. As Naveh has remarked, certain letters are blurred, others incomplete. A few are missing, apparently, owing to scraping and/or deterioration of the surface. Unfortunately, the character of the surface and the texture of lines made by the engraver's stylus are not always obvious in photographs. Advances in decipherment require work upon the original now in the Israel Museum in Jerusalem[2] (see fig. 1).

In the main our decipherment differs little from the pioneer readings of Naveh, whose excellent eye for form is well known. However, the readings proposed here are far-reaching in significance for the interpretation of the texts.

1. Inscription A (West Wall)

The inscription is bounded on the right and left by deep lines, probably drawn at the time when the inscription was made. The text consists of two lines, separated from Inscription B (probably written by the same

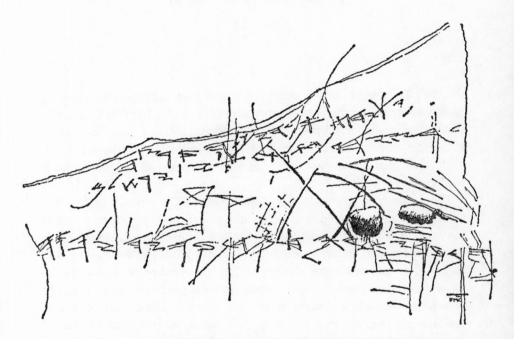

Figure 1. Inscriptions A and B from a cave near Khirbet Beit Lei. The drawing is traced from a photograph and checked against the original now in the Israel Museum. Lines adjacent to the letters have been included in the drawing and a few more distant to suggest the character of limestone surface. However, most of the distant lines and scratches have been ignored.

scribe) by the letters *'alef reš,* for *'ar[ūr]* scrawled several times elsewhere in the tomb.

Naveh read:

1. yhwh 'lhy kl h'rṣ h
2. ry yhd lw l'lhy yršlm

1. "Yahveh (is) the God of the whole earth; the moun-
2. tains of Judah [Yĕhūd!] belong to him, to the God of Jerusalem."

There are a number of difficulties. Line 1 begins well to the left of line 2 and line 1 of Inscription B, as well as the margin line. Moreover, traces of the letters *yod* and *nun* (or perhaps *kaf*) appear to the right of Naveh's first word *yhwh*. Finally, there is evidence of erosion on the right at the beginning of both lines 1 and 2.

The *lamed* of *kl* in line 1 is impossible. It is scratched deeper than the scribe's usual ductus; it is too short, too much on the vertical, and its hook at this period is utterly anomalous. Finally, it is too small and too crowded to be taken as a letter.

The use of the article *he* is odd in a poetic or semipoetic context (see below). *He* at the end of the line is expected to be the end of a word; there is no word divider before it, and there is ample space for letters after it.

There are a number of problems in the second line as well. Most glaring are: the reading *yhd,* an Aramaic form; the tortured syntax of the sentence; and, above all, the reading *lw* for *lô.* The last-mentioned reading we regard as impossible. *Waw* does not become a vowel letter for *ô* before the fourth century in Hebrew.[3] The suffix is always written with *-h* (i.e., *lh*).

We wish to decipher the text as follows:

1. [']'n'ŷ[5]. yhwh[.] 'lhykh.[6] 'rṣh
2. [7]rŷ. yhdḥ[8] wĝ'lty.[9] yršlm

'ănî[10] yahwê 'ĕlōhêkā[11]
'erṣē 'ārê yĕhūdā
wĕgā'altî yĕrūšālēm

I am Yahweh thy God:
I will accept the cities of Judah,
And will redeem Jerusalem.

The text is obviously poetic, a rubric and a parallelistic bicolon symmetrically balanced in syllable count: 8/7/8. The formulaic pair 'ārê yĕhūdā / yĕrūšālēm is familiar.[12] Parallels to this use of the roots *rṣy* and *g'l* are frequent. For example, compare Psalm 85:2 *rṣyt yhwh 'rṣk,* "Thou hast accepted, O Yahweh, thy land," and Isa 52:9: *kynḥm yhwh 'mw g'l yršlm,* "For Yahweh has comforted his people; he has redeemed Jerusalem."

We shall return to questions of interpretation of Inscription A after dealing with the other major texts.

2. Inscription B (West Wall)

As we have noted, the inscription appears to be in the same hand as inscription A. Naveh reads:

> hmwryh 'th ḥnṅt nwh yh yhwh
> "The (mount of) Moriah thou hast favored,
> the dwelling of Yah, Yahveh."

This decipherment also has a number of difficulties. I do not believe that the initial *he* of the line exists. It stands outside the margin; it is not a normal form; the horizontals do not narrow in triangular fashion as is the case with all other *hês* in all three major texts, and is characteristic of sixth-century forms; *ḥnnt* is anomalous, and the entire phrase *hmwryh 'th ḥnnt* is awkward if not bad Hebrew. The phrase *nwh yh yhwh* is also very strange. Most serious of all in Dr. Naveh's decipherment, however, is the reading *waw* for a sign quite unlike *waw,* but virtually identical with late, Palaeo-Hebrew *qof.* Hence both *mwryh* and *nwh* disappear.

The key to the decipherment, I believe, is in recognizing repetition of the sequence *nqh yh.* We should read:

> [12a]nqh yh 'l ḥnn.[13,14,15] nqh[16] yh yhwḥ
> Absolve (us) O[17] merciful God!
> Absolve (us) O Yahweh!

3. Inscription C (South Wall)

Naveh correctly reads this short inscription, written, we believe, by the scribe of Inscriptions A and B.

> hwš'[18] [y]hwh
> Deliver (us) O Lord

It is evident that Inscription C and Inscription B are closely related in character, and both, indeed, are in context with Inscription A.

II

The script of the Cave Inscriptions is a characteristic vulgar semiformal hand closely akin to the script of the Gibeon jar-handles of the sixth century BC, and not far separated from the archetype of the Palaeo-Hebrew scripts of the fourth to the second centuries BC.

'Alef is a developed form of the cursive *'alef* first identified by Professor N. Avigad. As we have shown elsewhere,[19] this *'alef* flourishes in the interval between the early eighth and the sixth centuries. The developed (or degenerate) type of this *'alef* found in our inscriptions is latest in the series, comparable to the Gibeon type of the sixth century BC.

Hê has a relatively long leg, a secondary lengthening clearly, and a tendency for the horizontals, especially the lower two, to narrow toward a point, giving a triangular effect. This tendency reaches its climax in post-Exilic Palaeo-Hebrew scripts. The Beit Lei form can scarcely be earlier than the sixth century BC.

Waw evolves little between the late eighth century BC and the sixth. The form of the *waw* in these inscriptions is developed, having a short leg.

Yod is broad and squat, a form typical of the late seventh and sixth centuries, persisting into the Palaeo-Hebrew of the fourth century BC.

Kaf is most interesting. The lower arm has moved away from the right vertical, meeting the upper arm quite close to its tip. This is quite different from the seventh-sixth century cursive in which the upper arm moved leftward away from the vertical (in the manner of Aramaic *kaf*). The form of Inscription A, however, is the prototype of the Palaeo-Hebrew *kaf* of certain of the Maccabaean coin scripts, and survives in more developed form at Qumran (e.g., 1Q palaeo-Lev.). A similar form of *kaf* is used in Phoenician beginning as early as the eighth century BC and appearing sporadically in the seventh and sixth centuries. There is no reason to think, however, that Palaeo-Hebrew took over a Phoenician style.[20]

Lamed in our texts reveals the "L" form which developed first in the seventh century BC.[21] It persists into the sixth century and survives in the Palaeo-Hebrew scripts.

Mêm in the word *Jerusalem* has a sharply reduced shoulder, a trait which marks forms of the seventh century and later.[22]

The single, obscure *'ayin* appears to be triangular, a form frequent in the sixth century and in the post-Exilic Palaeo-Hebrew scripts.[23]

We have referred above to the late, cursive form of *qof* which has been confused with *waw*. It is a regular Palaeo-Hebrew form. The greatly elongated leg, like the lengthened leg of *dalet* and *he*, is a late element.

Of the remaining letters, none requires comment. Typologically, they are without great interest, their forms evolving slowly in our period.

Śin does not show the rounding at the bottom of its double "v" which marks the latest pre-Exilic cursive and the Palaeo-Hebrew scripts.

To summarize: the Cave Inscriptions have a number of features characteristic of the sixth-century Hebrew script and a few otherwise found only in the Palaeo-Hebrew script of the fourth to first centuries BC. It dates from no earlier than the sixth century BC; certain letters, notably *'alef, dalet, waw, mêm, ṣade* and *šin* are probably no later than the sixth century BC.[24] In conclusion, the Beit Lei inscriptions A–C are safely dated to the sixth century BC.

III

These three inscriptions obviously are not ordinary tomb inscriptions. Indeed their content is such that I believe we can assert positively that they are not funerary inscriptions and have no reference to the dead.[25] Moreover, the drawings in the cave, human figures and ships, and what we can best label as "doodling" are inappropriate tomb decorations and hardly come from the hand of mourners or near kin of the deceased. If we add to this the singular absence of pottery dating from the age of the tomb, and note that Persian pottery was found in the tomb shaft, we are led to the conclusion that the tomb was opened (and robbed presumably) in antiquity. We are inclined, therefore, to attribute the inscriptions and sketches to chance visitors, or to refugees or travelers who took shelter in the cave.

One inscription is a petition for deliverance; another a plea to be spared from guilt or punishment. The third (A) takes the form of a prophetic oracle in which Yahweh speaks in the first person, and in poetic form. The couplet affirms God's acceptance and redemption of Jerusalem and Judah in language reminiscent of Jeremiah and Second Isaiah. It is very difficult to avoid the speculation that Inscription A is the citation of a lost prophecy, and that it and its companion inscriptions were written by a refugee fleeing the Chaldeans who conquered Judah and destroyed the holy city in 587 BC. Most documents, especially manuscripts and papyri, found in Palestinian caves were left behind by men in such circumstances. The same may be true of these graffiti. Perhaps such speculations are built on too flimsy a foundation of facts; at all events we shall suppress the temptation to suggest that the oracle and the petitions may have been the work of a prophet or his amanuensis fleeing Jerusalem.

FOOTNOTES

1. J. Naveh, "Old Hebrew Inscriptions in a Burial Cave," *IEJ*, 13 (1963), pp. 74–96. The site of the cave is at map co-ordinates 1437×1078 on the 1:100,000 map.

2. Through the kindness of Dr. Naveh the writer was able to study the inscriptions in various lightings in 1964, and to prepare drawings and tracings checked against the original (see fig. 1).

3. See Cross and Freedman, *Early Hebrew Orthography* (1952), Chapter IV, esp. pp. 46 f. It has become increasingly clear that the Judean 3 masc. sing. pronominal suffix was originally -*ū*>-*ō* (derived from -*uhu*). We also can state with confidence that the -*w* of *yrḥw* of the Gezer Calendar stands for -*êw* (*yarḥêw*) the articular suffix added to a plural or dual noun. Professor Dean McBride and the writer plan a more detailed study of the articular (or deictic) suffix in Hebrew and Phoenician. A recent example of the former is *byth 'lyšb* "*the* house of 'Elyašîb," in the 'Arad Letter published by Y. Aharoni, *BASOR*, No. 184 (1966), pp. 14 f. For Phoenician examples, see Donner-Röllig, *Kanaanäische und aramäische Inschriften*, II (1964), pp. 20 f. and the literature cited. On the usage *wrḥhw* (Sabaean) or *wrḫśw* (Minaean) before month names in South Arabic, see provisionally S. Smith, *VT*, 2 (1952), p. 287.

4. Only the top of *yod* is visible on the stone (see fig. 1), and a trace of the bottom of *nūn* or perhaps *kaf* (in which case read *'ānōkî*). It is clear, however, from the margin and the traces that several letters are missing.

5. Following the head of *yod* is a word-divider before the *yod* of *yhwh*.

6. Following *hê* is a clear word-divider below the lower left arm of the letter.

7. The traces of *'ayin* show a typical triangular form of sixth-century style. Cf. F. M. Cross, ". . . The Inscribed Jar Handles from Gibeon," *BASOR*, No. 168 (1962), p. 22.

8. The two lower strokes of the head of *hê* form a triangle, a characteristic sixth-century form. Only a trace of the upper stroke is extant. The right downstroke is faint but clear enough. Apparently the following word-divider is missing.

9. In the space between a clear *waw* and a clear *'alef*, there is ample room for a letter. Part of a vertical slanting down to the right appears on the stone, and a trace of a horizontal. The faint lines fit well with a late *gimel*.

10. As noted in n. 4, *'ānōkî* is a possible but much less likely reading. *'ănî* used of the deity is frequent in sixth-century prophecy, especially in Ezekiel. Cf. also such phrases as *'ny 'l* in Isa 43:12 and 45:22.

11. Note the writing of the pronominal suffix: -*kh*. This is, of course, the expected writing of the literary form -*kā* (versus the vulgar form -*k*, -*ak*). See *Early Hebrew Orthography*, p. 43, and excursus, pp. 65 ff.

12. For example, Isa. 44:26: *h'mr lyrwšlm twšb wl'ry yhwdh tbnynh*. One may also compare the pairs *'ry yhwdh/ /yšby/'š yršlm* especially in Jeremiah (11:12; 6:8; etc.). Cf. also Isa. 5:3.

12a. Naveh reads *mêm*. However, the broad shoulder is *very* strange, fitting better certain broad-headed *nūns* (Gibeon Jar-handles). Happily, the sequence *nqh yh* in the second part of the line permits us to read *nūn*. Apparently the scribe made the first movement of the head of *nūn*, then, after lifting his stylus, completed a rather broad-headed form.

13. A clear *lamed* is written below what appears to be the false start of *hê*, the following letter of *'lhm*.

14. We should read *ḥêt*, not *hê*, although *ḥêt* does not have the top horizontal break through to the right normally as does *hê*, nor is the triangular head characteristic of *ḥêt* as it is of *hê*.

15. The head of *nūn* may be doubly ticked and read *mêm*. The alternate is to read *'lhm*, "God." Note that a word divider stands after *nūn*.

16. On this meaning of *nqy* in the piel, cf. Psalm 19:3, Joel 4:21, etc. The sense can as easily be "spare from punishment"; cf. Jer 30:11; 46:28 etc.

17. *yh* is to be taken probably as the particle of entreaty known in Ugaritic, in Aramaic, and in New Hebrew (as well as in Arabic). In Aḥiqar 127, 129, it is written *yh* as is expected in the orthography of this period. Evidently the particle is dialectal in Canaanite. Cf. in Ugaritic *ya 'ili-mi*, "O El!" In classical Hebrew it may be hidden behind the late, short form of the Divine name *yah*, e.g., in such a context as Psalm 130:3.

18. This is the expected spelling; the *waw* represents the diphthong: *hawša'*. Cf. *Early Hebrew Orthography*, p. 53.

19. "Epigraphical Notes on Hebrew Documents of the Eighth–Sixth Centuries B.C.: III. The Inscribed Jar Handles from Gibeon" [hereafter *EN III*], *BASOR*, No. 168 (1962), pp. 18 f.

20. Attempts to show mixing of script styles (after the final separation of Hebrew and Aramaic scripts from their Phoenician ancestral script) have regularly failed as more data have accumulated. Methodologically, resort to explanation of letter forms by "borrowings" from neighboring national scripts may be used only after all other explanations have been exhausted, and even then remain dubious.

21. See the discussion in "Epigraphic Notes on Hebrew Documents of the Eighth–Sixth Centuries BC: II. The Murabba'ât Papyrus and the Letter found Near Yabneh-Yam" (hereafter *EN II*), *BASOR*, No. 165 (1962), p. 40, and *EN III*, pp. 21 f.

22. Cf. *EN II*, p. 40; *EN III*, p. 22.

23. The *'ayin* of Yabneh-yam anticipates the triangular form. Cf. *EN II*, p. 40.

24. It should be noted that the fifth century is a blank in the history of the Hebrew scripts. I am inclined to date a few seals to this period, but no certainly fixed material is extant. We presume that Palaeo-Hebrew (as distinct from the old Hebrew script) arose in the fifth century. Seals of fixed date, coins, jar stamps, and manuscripts now fill out the Palaeo-Hebrew series from the fourth century BC to the Age of Bar Kokhba.

25. The curse formulae in the tomb are probably older, and may be funerary imprecations.

NEW EXCAVATIONS AT SARDIS
AND SOME PROBLEMS
OF WESTERN
ANATOLIAN ARCHAEOLOGY

George M. A. Hanfmann and Jane C. Waldbaum

I. Introduction

FOR many decades, Nelson Glueck has been a shining example of a scholar who on the one hand has pioneered new methods and approaches in archaeology, and on the other, has advanced the cause of archaeology by carrying to the general public, especially in America, something of the adventure, excitement, and joy of archaeological discovery.

In this volume, which seeks to do justice to Nelson Glueck's broad horizons by unfolding a panorama of Near Eastern archaeology, we should like to present some comments on western Anatolian archaeology, with particular reference to recent discoveries at Sardis. Some of these observations bear on questions to which Nelson Glueck has made masterly contributions; e.g. the elucidation of distinctive native cultures.[1]

In contrast to past eras, when archaeology in western Turkey was considered a branch of Classical archaeology, the main object of which was to uncover Ionian Greek monuments, modern archaeology in this area is turning towards clarification of the indigenous Anatolian cultures. Lydia, Phrygia, Caria, the "Syro-Hittites" in the Iron Age, the Hittites, Trojans, and Yortan cultures in the Bronze Age, more and more claim the attention of excavators.[2] A definite shift has taken place in the past thirty years toward a unitarian conception of Anatolia, ever since the publication of Bossert's *Altanatolien*,[3] and this view is well reflected in the publications of the Turkish Historical Society,[4] in the writings of K. Bittel[5] and E. Akurgal,[6] and in M. Mellink's eminently informed summaries.[7]

The importance of Anatolia as a crossroads between Near Eastern and Aegean civilizations through the ages is also of prime concern to present investigators. Both literary and historical sources and excavated evidence lead time and again to Anatolia as the key area in the understanding of some of the major problems of eastern Mediterranean archaeology.

In the following pages we shall note some discoveries and problems of western Anatolia which have bearing on the meeting of eastern, western, and native Anatolian cultural elements in this area, from the "Dark Ages," which began when the civilizations of the second millennium BC collapsed, to the third century BC, when much of the area under the Hellenistic rulers was transformed into Greek city states.

II. Achaeans and Assyrians: Western Anatolian
Contacts with East and West

In 1924 E. Forrer published the first of his famous articles in which he identified a number of Greek place names and legendary figures in the Hittite archives and equated Ahhiyawa with the Achaeans.[8] His theories and the rebuttals by F. Sommer[9] raised the question of who the Ahhiyawa were, and whether their Bronze Age center was in Anatolia, Greece, or the islands off the Anatolian coast.

The most recent proposal, by J. Mellaart, would even equate Troy, Bulgaria, Macedonia, and parts of Thrace north of the sea of Marmara with Ahhiyawa, and see this kingdom as the guardian of a tin route to the Balkans.[10] New fuel has also been added to the fires of controversy by the inscriptions of Amenophis III (*circa* 1380 BC) which seem to mention various Cretan place names together with Mycenae and Troy.[11]

In 1966, about 250 sherds, some late Mycenaean, many "Submycenaean," a number Protogeometric in style, were excavated at Sardis from an area about 11 by 11 meters and about 12.6 meters deep in its deepest part (E5-W6/S98-S109; lowest level 89.9).[12] Two major strata were involved, but only a skimpy wall and the skeleton of an equid indicated that this was probably in some way a built up area (Pls. 31 and 32). Other interesting associated finds were a couple of pieces of iron, including a curved knife, a curious seal with a cervid or equid, probably Protogeometric in date, and an unusual fibula, also Protogeometric.[13] The excavator, G. Swift, Jr., pointed out that though numerous, these painted sherds were in a minority of perhaps two to five percent; he also observed that a number of the Aegean-style painted fragments seemed to be of local clay and make. They have not yet been published in detail, and scholars specializing in Mycenaean ware have had little opportunity to comment. Still the preliminary assessment, enhanced by some earlier finds,[14] would range the Mycenaean affiliates from III B (thirteenth century) into III C:2 (late twelfth to eleventh century). What is important is that the Protogeometric stratum was followed without major interruption by a stratum with Greek geometric sherds. This in turn was succeeded by a stratum which seemed to have been terminated by a devastating conflagration attributed to the invasion of the Kimmerians in the early seventh century BC.[15]

There has been much controversy as to whether the Hittites or the Mycenaeans had drawn prehistoric Lydia (possibly to be equated with Assuwa of the Hittites) into their ambient. We did not think the material from Sardis sufficient for a decision in 1962. Since then, however, our finds favored the theory that the date given by Herodotus for the beginning of the dynasty of "Herakleidai," 505 years before the accession of Gyges (*circa* 1185 BC?), must be connected with the arrival of conquering Aegean warriors, rather than with Hittites or with the emergence of a native dynasty. Mycenaean chieftains may have seized the rule; some similar event is thought to have set the House of Moksos (Mopsus) as a ruling dynasty over the Danuna, whose existence has been revealed by the Luvian-Phoenician bilingual of Karatepe in Cilicia.[16] Like the dynasty of Mopsos, the Herakleidai at Sardis would have given up their Mycenaean Greek tongue to adopt a native language.[17]

The situation may have been similar in Ephesus. A tantalizing find, made under odds of at least 1000:1, revealed a disturbed Mycenaean tomb containing a beautiful set of Mycenaean vases of the fourteenth to thirteenth century (Myc. III A:2) under the parking space in front of the Gate of Persecution on the Byzantine Citadel[18] (Pl. 33). Scholarly opinion has been inclining toward acceptance of Ephesus as Apasas, capital of the famous kingdom of Arzawa, mentioned in the Hittite records.[19] This find, and the find of a figurine of a Hittite priest on the flank of the original citadel of Ephesus[20] reopen the question "Hittite or Achaean" (or "Arzawan or Mycenaean") rulers of Ephesus in the Bronze Age.[21]

The observation of cultural continuity through the so-called "Dark Ages" made at the "Lydian Market" in Sardis, bears on one of the most important problems of ancient history. At present, finds at Sardis favor the idea of a "native" (Lydian? speaking) culture surviving from *circa* 1200–680 BC and absorbing invaders, while maintaining some sort of contact with areas using Greek types of pottery. At Gordion in Phrygia too, recent finds have established a sequence reaching from Late Bronze Age to historic Phrygian.[22] Contrary to the theories of Akurgal, Carpenter, and others,[23] neither western nor central Anatolia became "menschenleer" after the collapse of Hittite power.

States using "Late Hittite" writing (Luvian Hieroglyphic) were able to maintain themselves in eastern, southern, and central Anatolia. From the 12th century on Assyrians repeatedly penetrated large areas of the south (Cilician Tarsus was captured 696 BC) and the east. Some historical traditions intimate that western Anatolian states did try to turn eastward in the eighth and early seventh centuries BC. Assyrian sources maintain that Gyges sent a delegation to Assurbanipal, forming an alliance with him early in the seventh century BC.[24] There are also good arguments for contacts between Lydia and Mesopotamia to be derived from Lydian coinage, as it seems to be based on the Babylonian weight system.[25] A couple of fragments of Assyrian glazed alabastra have been found in the House of Bronzes sector at Sardis,[26] and at least one Neo-Babylonian seal was found among the first Sardis excavation material.[27] On the whole, however, archaeological material from western Anatolia has so far failed to yield any evidence as conclusive as the vessels of Assyrian type found in a royal tomb at Gordion[28] or the Assyrian tablets from Tarsus.[29]

III. Gold Production at Sardis and the Wealth of Croesus

For classical antiquity, Anatolia was the great land of metallurgy, famous especially for the gold sands of the Pactolus[30] and as the birthplace of iron.[31] This information has been utilized in such accounts of natural resources of western Anatolia as T. R. S. Broughton's "Roman Asia Minor," in T. Frank's *An Economic Survey of Ancient Rome*,[32] and for a specific region in Cadoux's *Ancient Smyrna*.[33] C. Roebuck's chapter on "Search for Metals" in *Ionian Trade and Colonization*[34] is also well informed on archaeological material. Modern Turkey is still rich in metals, and most of the country has been systematically surveyed for mineral resources by scientists sent out by the Mineral Researches Institute, Ankara (M.T.A.)[35] and other organizations.[36] Some of the explorative techniques used were geared to identifying large areas of deposits, but much information collected in these reports should be of value to the problems of identifying ancient mines, open workings, and other metallurgical installations.[37] In eastern Anatolia, outside the borders of Turkey, recent Soviet excavations at Metsamor, west of Erivan in the Ararat Plain, have revealed a metallurgical center for refining copper and tin ores, and blast furnaces for the production of bronze dating to the second millennium.[38]

In western Turkey, one of the critical problems has been to establish the truth of the many ancient references to Pactolus gold and the source of the wealth of Croesus. In 1924, T. L. Shear published an article in which he denied the existence of gold in exploitable quantities in the Pactolus, at least in modern times.[39] Unpublished reports to the M.T.A., however, made by S. Birgi in 1944 and N. Saydamer in 1963, proved that most of the torrents coming from Tmolus still have varying concentrations of gold in their alluvia.[40] Nevertheless, the accidental discovery of installations for the purification of gold dating to the time of Croesus came as a surprise to the Sardis Expedition.

The discovery was made in 1968 by archaeologist A. Ramage and conservators R. E. Stone and S. M. Goldstein[41] (Pl. 34, fig. 1). Dated by pottery finds to the second quarter of the sixth century (Croesus: 560–547 BC), the metallurgical facilities consisted of two areas of clay-lined hollows (usually 0.15 to 0.20 meter in diameter and 0.09 to 0.10 meter deep) interpreted as "cupels" used for "cupellation," a method for purifying either gold or silver of base metal impurities.[42] There were perhaps three hundred of these clay basins in at least two superposed layers. Used ones typically consist of rings of dark gray clay, with quantities of slag and vitrified matter adhering to the inner surface. Before firing, the inner surface was lined with light ash to absorb the slag. Bits of light and dark gold foil, and tiny droplets of gold exhibiting traces of processing and working were found in a dump near the "cupels" and at least one in a "cupel." Fragments of clay vessels (crucibles?) with gold which had penetrated into cracks prove that gold was the metal treated here.[43]

It is assumed that a "button" of gold was heated in a "cupel" of highly porous material, together with a quantity of lead; a strong current of air was blown over the surface of molten metal, probably by using bellows and tuyeres, and the oxidized lead extracted other base metals and passed off as lead oxide (litharge).[44] Lead oxide was indeed observed in the "cupels" and some forty pounds of PbO (or "litharge") from the two cupellation areas and a dump of waste material were also found. Several terracotta fragments appeared as possible tuyeres

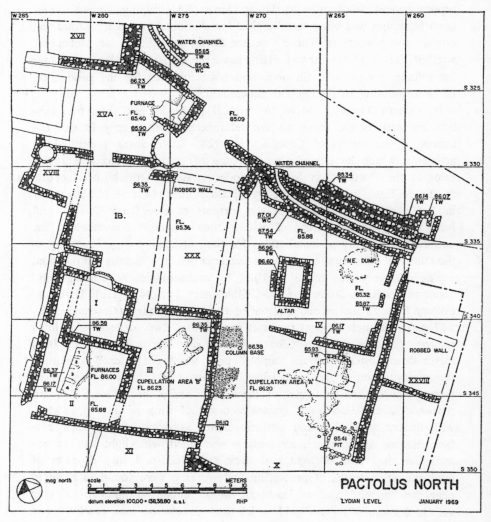

PN 71a

Figure 1. Plan of the gold processing area. Sardis, Pactolus North.

(blowpipe or bellows nozzles) used to maintain fire at high temperatures, and an iron pipe may have also been used for blowing. A series of five small furnaces (0.50 to 0.70 meter wide, 0.50 meter deep) are considered possible devices for heating containers needed in "cementation," a process to separate or "part" silver from gold either before or after cupellation was performed.[45] In a tentative reconstruction of this process, nuggets or grains of gold ore, or even old electrum coins, would be melted down to cakes or lumps and then pounded into foil. The foil would then be packed in layers into pots with the cementation mixture (crushed brick or pottery, salt, and alum). Foil was used in order to expose the greatest possible surface of electrum to the cementation mixture. The pots would then be sealed and heated to a dull red heat for perhaps several days, during which time the cementation mixture would form a chloride with the silver and leave the gold. The remaining gold would be expected to have a grainy or spongy texture due to removal of the silver, and in fact some samples of gold foil found at Pactolus North did show this characteristic texture.

The silver content of early Lydian coinage is a burning question both for historians of the invention of early coinage and for economic theoreticians. In 1958, the Swedish scholar Sture Bolin published a study accusing earlier students of numismatics and economics of undue optimism concerning the origins of coinage. Pointing out the discrepancies between the remarkably precise weights and strikingly variable fineness of the earliest series of Lydian electrum coins (gold content from 55 to 31 percent, silver from 45 to 69 percent), Bolin argued that far from giving full gold value by weight, or anything like it, the Lydian state cheated its customers from the beginning by deliberately raising the silver content of the electrum beyond that found in natural ore.[46]

Bolin's Achilles' heel was lack of data on the natural silver content of Lydian gold, a defect which statistics of possible, widely varying silver contents of gold ores from other areas would not obviate.[47] One of the purposes of research on the Sardis gold finds is, therefore, to determine the composition of Pactolus gold ore and the Lydian capability of separating gold from silver and adjusting at will the ratio of processed gold/silver alloy. Work is only beginning on the numerous but tiny samples of gold found at Sardis, and any results which we cite must be understood as possibly subject to later corrections.

Very few samples of natural ore have been tested. It is possible, however, to make some tentative comparisons between the silver content of the Pactolus ore and that of samples of worked gold. From the report made by S. Birgi to the Mineral Research Institute in Ankara in 1944, we understand that the silver content of at least one sample of gold from the Pactolus was determined as 14.5 percent. A neutron activation test, made on a grain of ore considered to be highly gold-rich by Dr. Sevim Okar, at the Çekmece Center for Nuclear Research in Istanbul under Professor M. Talat-Erben showed results of about 24.9±1.5 percent silver. Two samples of gold from the Pactolus North installations were also tested in this way, resulting in averages of 17.5±0.95 percent silver for light gold foil and 22.2±1.8 percent silver for dark gold foil. These results were not very conclusive, except to suggest a rather high silver content for natural Pactolus gold. According to Professor Talat-Erben, this test provides no evidence for possible separation of silver from gold.

The next series of analyses, however, seemed more significant. In September 1968, three samples of gold were submitted to Drs. N. Bayçin and A. Uluocak of the Mineral Research Institute, Ankara, for spectrographic analysis, with the following results: the first sample, a "bead" or globule of gold, proved to have a silver content of 10 to 30 percent and is thought to represent the natural electrum alloy; the second was a piece of light gold foil containing 1 to 10 percent silver; the third was a piece of dark gold foil with a pitted or spongy surface, which was found to have only 0.1 to 1.0 percent silver and is therefore a probable product of cementation.

The results of Birgi's analysis, the neutron activation tests on natural ore, and the spectrographic analysis of the gold "bead" provide tentative indications that the usual range of silver and impurities in gold ore from the Pactolus may vary between 10 and 30 percent. As Clarence A. Wendel, Minerals Attaché, U. S. Embassy, Ankara, noted, this is below or just within the range of "electrum" as defined by modern standards.[48] It is too early to say with assurance that higher percentages of silver may not have occurred.

The results of spectrographic analysis also give some indication that the Lydians were able to separate gold from silver. Furthermore, without anticipating detailed test evaluations, we may say that the Lydian attempts to purify base metals from gold had some success as well. Two samples of light gold foil from the gold installation tested by X-ray diffraction showed no more than 1.0 percent lead or copper. The sample of dark gold foil tested spectrographically had only traces of lead, and low copper (0.01 to 0.1 percent). The sample of light gold foil had 0.1 to 1.0 percent copper, 0.01 to 0.10 percent lead, and the gold "bead" had 1 to 10 percent copper, 0.01 to 0.10 percent lead. This seems to show that the "bead" with high silver and copper was not yet treated; the light foil with high silver, low copper and lead was a product of cupellation; while the dark (pitted) foil had been cupelled and cemented. It is probable, therefore, that both the removal of "base metals" (cupellation) and the parting of silver from gold (cementation) had been carried out at the Pactolus North installations, although more tests on a greater number of samples will be needed to assure these conclusions.

It was under Croesus that the distinction between "white gold," as Herodotus calls the modern electrum[49] and purified or "cooked" (*apephthos*) gold was established. Thus the base of the lion monument of Delphi was known to contain four bricks or ingots of purified gold weighing 2½ talents each and 113 bricks of "white gold" weighing two talents each.[50] It was Croesus, too, who first struck a "purified" gold series and a silver series of coins, as opposed to the old electrum series,[51] and gold and silver coins of Croesus have been found in the treasury of Persepolis and in Darius' foundation deposit under the apadana.[52]

We do not know where, in terms of "fineness" of gold content, the line between "pure" and "white" gold was drawn at the time. The touchstone method was probably known, but how precise a determination was made is one of the questions which continuing work at Sardis may help to answer.[53]

Were the earliest Lydian coins intentionally adulterated with silver by Croesus' father or grandfather? Preliminary findings favor Bolin's pessimistic view. So far, the silver content of 14.5–25.0 percent for known gold ore from Sardis does lie below the range of 45 to 69 percent silver observed in analysis of early Lydian coins. The analytical foundation, however, is still very narrow and partly uncertain, but we hope that continued investigations with modern techniques may answer this question.

IV. The Persian Era at Sardis

The Persian era is perhaps the least known, certainly the least understood phase of Anatolian archaeology, yet this is the period *par excellence* for the intermingling of eastern (Persian), native (Lydian) and western (Greek) styles in art and architecture.

In 547 BC the Persians captured the kingdom and city of Croesus and made it into the major western satrapy of the Persian empire.[54] In stark contrast to the remarkable homogeneity of the Achaemenid court style in the Iranian capitals, the Persians abroad did not seek to impose uniformity on the major arts of subject regions. Even at satrapal courts the Achaemenid court style appeared primarily in articles of personal use (armor) and adornment.

At Sardis, this kind of object is exemplified by beautiful Achaemenid jewelry identified as Lydian by C. D. Curtis[55] but recognized as Achaemenid by H. T. Bossert,[56] G. M. A. Hanfmann,[57] E. Akurgal,[58] and W. S. Smith.[59]

Spectacular finds of silver objects, some of them identical with objects shown in the reliefs of Persepolis, (Pls. 36 and 37) and silver phialae stamped with double bull figures à la Persepolis, have recently been made in a chamber tomb of Lydian type at Ikiztepe near Güre in the upper Hermus valley, along with a Greek (?) graffito and Lydian pottery.[60]

Research on these and other objects of the Achaemenid period, such as silver bowls, horse trappings, and bronze mirrors, is in progress and may eventually prove the existence of an Irano-Anatolian style in bronzes and silver vessels.[61] Tribute carried by the "Lydians" on the apadana reliefs of Xerxes (486–465 BC) appears to include objects of this kind[62] (Pl. 35).

Whether Persia or Anatolia was the giving partner in architecture is the question which has arisen in connection with two unusual architectural monuments at Sardis, and the answer is of importance for the formative stages of Achaemenian architecture. The so-called "Pyramid Tomb" had either a sarcophagus or a small monument on top of a six-stepped platform (Pl. 38). The monument and its masonry was compared by H. C. Butler with the Tomb of Cyrus the Elder at Pasargadae.[63] Recent reexcavation by C. H. Greenewalt, Jr., and C. Reagan has revived interest in the Sardis monument.[64] Greenewalt has pointed out comparisons with masonry known from Daskylion and Pasargadae[65] (Pl. 39). The writer (Hanfmann) has suggested that this may indeed be the monument of a noble Persian who fell in the battle for Sardis, and which Xenophon on his visit to Sardis took to be that of "Abradatas and Pantheia high above the Pactolus."[66]

The other "Persian" monument at Sardis is an impressive wall of hard, yellow limestone with traces of staircases bonded in with a wall of green sandstone, which was discovered in 1960 on the north side of the acropolis of Sardis (AcN).[67] David Stronach, the excavator of Pasargadae, has pointed out the striking resemblance to staircases in the palace of Pasargadae.[68] On the other hand, the technique and tooling in this "Acropolis North" wall are clearly the same as those of Lydian royal graves at Bin Tepe, earlier than the capture of Sardis by Cyrus.[69] As large scale masonry construction was new to Iran, Stronach proposes that Cyrus may have carried off Lydian architects and masons to build his palace at Pasargadae.[70] It has long been known that Lydian and Ionian masons worked on the palace of Darius at Susa.[71]

With more precise observation of the use of tools as exemplified in studies made by Nylander, research on masonry architecture of the Persian Period in Anatolia will be a rewarding task. Studies of relevant material are being carried forward by A. Kasper, who has reinvestigated the chamber tombs of Belevi near Ephesus[72] and of Elaia on the road to Pergamon. Together with C. H. Greenewalt he will make a detailed study of the "Pyramid Tomb" at Sardis.

How far the Persians contributed concepts or forms to sculpture has been a moot question. For a long time several reliefs with Persian themes in a "Greco-Persian" provincial style have been known from the region of Daskylion in northwest Anatolia. They have been strikingly added to by several funerary stelae found in a Byzantine tomb on the Acropolis of Daskylion, one of which bears an Aramaic inscription.[73]

Even if one does not subscribe to H. Möbius' ingenious thought that these stelae originally adorned a sepulchral precinct of a satrap, they emphasize the existence of a style which went along the same "Royal Roads" as the spread of the Aramaic language. The resemblance, for instance, of the funerary cart on a Daskylion stele to a cart on Persian coins of Sidon is very striking.[74]

V. The Synagogue and the Jewish Community at Sardis

The question of the spread both of Achaemenid provincial iconography and Aramaic official language in western Anatolia is certainly worth pursuing in future research. It will be recalled that such a document as the great Lydian-Aramaic bilingual found at Sardis does not seem to have received from Semitologists the same attention as that received by the Lydian text from specialists in Anatolian linguistics.[75]

We have no idea how many people could speak Aramaic at Sardis during the Persian era (547–334 BC). The owner of the sepulchre protected by the stele with the Lydian-Aramaic bilingual thought it necessary to write protective curses in Aramaic and date the monument by regnal years of Artaxerxes. Many higher Persian officials and probably some of middle station would have been required to speak and to write Semitic Aramaic. Such background makes it less strange that Sepharad, so famous in the history of Judaism, really was Sardis. In a persuasive article, Professor I. Rabinowitz has pointed out that the Persian form *Sfard,* derived from Lydian *Sfard,* constitutes a powerful linguistic argument for this identification.[76] Obadiah clearly considers "the exiles of Jerusalem who are in Sepharad" not only a symbol of great dispersal to a far-away place, but also an important Jewish community.[77]

The assumption that a large Hebrew population existed at Sardis under the Persian rule no longer rests on an isolated notice of early diaspora. Ever since the Sardis Expedition in 1962 discovered the gigantic Synagogue of Sardis, which presupposes a Jewish congregation of several thousand people settled at Sardis in the second century AD, it has become necessary to reexamine both the literary tradition about the Jews of Sardis and the archaeological data available.[78]

In comparing the importance of information from the Synagogue of Dura Europos, the Qumran caves, and the Synagogue of Sardis, A. T. Kraabel has stated: "Nothing in the remoteness of Qumran or at Dura can compare to the procession of empires at Sardis . . . If the Jews are in Sardis as early as Obadiah, then any convincing explanation of the phenomena of the prosperity of the Jewish community at Sardis will include the hypothesis that the Jews were so powerful and integrated because they had been in the city and had been important to the city for a long period of time."[79]

Excavations at Sardis have brought forth evidence that the city was fiercely destroyed and then replanned on a Hellenistic regular plan sometime during the Early Hellenistic era.[80] The fateful events were explained by a strange chance find. Emerging again out of the Synagogue, where they were reused as parts of the piers of the Main Hall, were found a series of inscriptions originally inscribed on the *parastades* (pilasters in the porch) of the temple of the Mother of the Gods (Metroon).[81]

Datable between March and July of 213 BC, the inscriptions are partly letters from Antiochus III to the people of Sardis, and partly decrees of the city of Sardis. It was known that Antiochus beseiged his relative Achaios for two years, that he captured him by treachery and had him cruelly dismembered.[82] It now appears that the king in his fury had ordered at least partial destruction of the city and imposed various measures of punishment. Upon the intercession of Queen Laodike, he relented and permitted a restoration described as a new *synoikismos.* The powerful Zeuxis, virtually the king's viceroy in Asia Minor, was to supervise the reconstruction.

This information bears on the tradition concerning the Jewish community at Sardis. According to Josephus[83] it was this very Zeuxis to whom the king wrote: "Learning that the people in Lydia and Phrygia are rebelling . . . I determined to transport two thousand Jewish families . . . from Mesopotamia and Babylonia to the fortresses and most important (necessary) places (*anankaiotatous topous*)." Antiochus goes on to say that the Jewish settlers may use their own laws, bring their own belongings; they are to be given houses and land for fields and vineyards and pay no taxes on their produce for ten years.

Josephus does not name Sardis, and some scholars used to think that the Jews were settled only in military colonies, for one might understand "the most necessary places" in this sense, rather than in the general sense of "important." The new inscriptions from Sardis put the matter in a different light. Here is a city with an impregnable citadel from which all western Asia was commanded, a city now largely destroyed, which was to be rebuilt and resettled—and preferably *not* with the natives who had put up such a desperate resistance and whom the king distrusted. Here is Zeuxis bringing large numbers of Jewish settlers from Mesopotamia. It seems an inescapable conclusion that Sardis would have drawn a large share, and that the importance of the Jewish community at Sardis may well go back to the *synoikismos* of 213 BC. By the time of Caesar and Augustus the Jews of Sardis were wealthy enough to tempt the city to stop payment of the temple tax to Jerusalem,[84] and influential enough not only to rebut this attempt, but also to secure an official plot of land for the Synagogue and special consideration of Jewish dietary needs from city officials.

At the moment, there is still a gap in our archaeological documentation between the account by Josephus of the events of 213 BC, the huge Synagogue complex which was built as part of the "urban renewal" after AD 17 and so richly decorated between AD 200 and 400, and the literary evidence for the Persian and Hellenistic eras. Yet here, as at other Hellenistic sites of western Anatolia, we may well hope that attentive search will result in more complete archaeological documentation of the emergence of Anatolian Diaspora. This emergence, and its importance for early Christianity, is one of the most significant of the many elements which will continue to make western Anatolia a major challenge for archaeological efforts in the twentieth century.

VI. Conclusions

The problems which we have considered have led us from the times of the Trojan War to the late Roman Empire. At the time with which our sketch began, western Anatolia was largely a prehistoric backwater and a bone of contention between Hittites and westerners. The collapse of its existing states created a power vacuum which Aegean marauders sought to fill. In this sense, the deep inland penetration of "Submycenaeans" revealed at Sardis is perhaps a forerunner of the post-Bronze Age so-called "Aeolic" and "Ionian migrations" to the western shores of Asia Minor, an advance of the West which was, however, stopped by the rise of such inland powers as Lydia and Phrygia.

In the improvement of gold refining technology, indispensable for an effective bimetallic coinage, we caught a glimpse of one of the major developments which made possible Lydia's meteoric ascent to fantastic affluence, to domination over all western Anatolia, and to the position of a world power. For once, primacy was with the "Anatolian" component.

With Persia, the East acceded to the political and economic resources of western Anatolia, but we have seen how a great interchange of artistic and cultural ideas took place—with Lydian architects working for Persian kings and regal Persian silver being imitated for Anatolian chiefs and nobles.

A new, primarily spiritual and religious element entered the picture with Judaism. Jewish communities in western Anatolia were able to adjust to the successive empires of Persia, Greece, and Rome. The process gives us an important insight into the cultural and religious complexities of this region.

During the millennium encompassed by the finds at Sardis, western Anatolia was transformed from a marginal prehistoric province to perhaps the most populous, certainly one of the most prosperous areas of the ancient world. There is still much to be learned both in the field and by systematic scholarly research about this critical area. If the vigorous pace of archaeological activity during the last two decades is continued, new discoveries will soon add to and alter our knowledge of the problems of western Anatolian archaeology.

FOOTNOTES

1. E.g., his recent study, *Deities and Dolphins: The Story of the Nabataeans* (1965).

Abbreviations and short title forms used in this article and not commonly found in journals of Near Eastern archaeology are:

Belleten: Türk Tarih Kurumu Belleten

Dana: C. Palache, H. Berman, and C. Frondel, *Dana's System of Mineralogy* 7th ed., I, III (1944, 1962).

Dergi: Türk Arkeoloji Dergisi. Department of Antiquities, Ankara.

Kunst Anatoliens: E. Akurgal, *Die Kunst Anatoliens von Homer bis Alexander* (1961).

Rayonnement: Le Rayonnement des Civilisations Grecque et Romaine sur les Cultures Périphériques, Huitième Congrès International d'Archéologie Classique (1963).

"Sardis und Lydien": G. M. A. Hanfmann, "Sardis und Lydien," *Akademie der Wissenschaft und der Literatur. Abhandlungen der Geistes- und sozialwissenschaftlichen Klasse* 1960 nr. 6, (1960).

2. See S. Lloyd, *Early Anatolia* (1956), pp. 213–19; O. R. Gurney, *The Hittites* (1961), pp. 220 f., 228; A. Goetze, "Hittite and Anatolian Studies," in *BANE* (1965), pp. 421–37; R. D. Barnett, "Phrygia and the Peoples of Anatolia in the Iron Age," *CAH[2]*, II, fasc. 56 (1967), pp. 28 ff. for bibliography on these sites.

3. H. T. Bossert, *Altanatolien: Kunst und Handwerk in Kleinasien von den Anfängen bis zum völligen Aufgehen in der griechischen Kultur* (1942).

4. *Belleten* (1937 to present).

5. K. Bittel, *Grundzüge der Vor- und Frühgeschichte Kleinasiens* (1945, 1950).

6. *Kunst Anatoliens; Orient und Okzident: Die Geburt der griechischen Kunst* (1966); "Urartäische und altiranische Kunstzentren," *Türk Tarih Kurumu Yayinlarindan,* 6, Seri 9 (1968).

7. M. Mellink, "Archaeology in Asia Minor," *AJA,* 59 (1955) to present.

8. E. Forrer, "Vorhomerische Griechen in den Keilschrifttexten von Bogazköi," *MDOG,* 63 (1924), pp. 1–22; "Die Griechen in den Bogazköi Texten," *OLZ,* 27 (1924), pp. 113–18.

9. F. Sommer, "Die Ahhiyawa-Urkunden," *Abhandlungen der Bayerischen Akademie der Wissenschaften,* Phil-Hist. Abt., Neue Folge 6 (1932); "Ahhijava-Frage und Sprachwissenschaft," *ibid.* Neue Folge 9 (1934); "Ahhijava und kein Ende?" *Indogermanische Forschungen,* 55 (1937), pp. 169–297. See also O. R. Gurney, *The Hittites* (1961), pp. 46 ff. and bibliography for summary of the controversy.

10. J. Mellaart, "Anatolian Trade with Europe and Anatolian Geography and Culture Provinces in the Late Bronze Age," *AnSt,* 18 (1968), pp. 189 ff., especially pp. 192 f., 196. Cf. A. Goetze, *Kleinasien[2]* (1957), p. 183, n. 5, who suggests that Ahhiyawa may have been a kingdom in the vicinity of Troy, led by Achaeans but composed of natives with Anatolian names.

11. E. Edel, "Die Ortsnamenlisten aus dem Totentempel Amenophis III," *BBB,* 25 (1966), pp. 37 ff.

12. G. F. Swift, Jr., "'Lydian Trench' Area: The Deep Pit," in "The Ninth

Campaign at Sardis (1966)," *BASOR*, No. 186 (1967), pp. 31 f., figs. 9–15; *Nestor* (1 Jan. 1967), p. 473.

13. O. Muscarella in a letter of January 29, 1969, informs us that the fibula best fits Blinkenberg's Type IV: C. Blinkenberg, *Fibules Grecques et Orientales* (1926), pp. 87–106.

14. *BASOR*, No. 154 (1959), pp. 29 f., fig. 13, Protogeometric and Geometric, Trench "S"; *BASOR*, No. 162 (1961), pp. 14 ff., fig. 5, Mycenaean and Submycenaean, House of Bronzes, Deep Sounding; *BASOR*, No. 173 (1963), pp. 6 ff., Mycenaean, Submycenaean, Protogeometric, Geometric, House of Bronzes, Deep Sounding.

15. Cf. *BASOR*, No. 182 (1966), p. 10. On the Kimmerians see M. Mellink, ed., *Dark Ages and Nomads c. 1000 B.C.: Studies in Iranian and Anatolian Archaeology* (1964); T. Sulimirski, "The Cimmerian Problem," *BInstArch*, 1 (1959), pp. 45–64.

16. R. D. Barnett, "Mopsos," *JHS*, 73 (1953), pp. 140 ff.; "Phrygia and the Peoples of Anatolia in the Iron Age," *CAH²*, II, fasc. 56 (1967), p. 27.

17. This is different from the penetration of trade goods and souvenirs into inland Anatolia, as indicated by occasional finds of individual pots at such places as Çerkes Sultaniye in the Hermus valley. See G. M. A. Hanfmann and J. C. Waldbaum, "Two Submycenaean Vases and a Tablet from Stratonikeia in Caria," *AJA*, 72 (1968), pp. 52 f. and n. 13 for this and other examples of Mycenaean and Submycenaean pottery from coastal and inland Asia Minor.

18. H. Gültekin and M. Baran, "The Mycenaean Grave Found at the Hill of Ayasuluk," *Dergi*, 13 (1964), pp. 125–33; M. Mellink, "Archaeology in Asia Minor," *AJA*, 68 (1964), pp. 157 f. Pl. 50, figs. 10–13. We are greatly indebted to H. Gültekin and M. Baran for their kindness in sending us the negative of the crater Pl. 33).

19. G. M. A. Hanfmann, "A 'Hittite' Priest From Ephesus," *AJA*, 66 (1962), pp. 1 ff., 4; J. Garstang and O. R. Gurney, *The Geography of the Hittite Empire* (1959), pp. 83 ff., 88.

20. Hanfmann, *AJA*, 66 (1962), pp. 1 ff.

21. The Mycenaean stronghold at Miletus and its identification with Achaean Millawanda has long been recognized. See V. Desborough, *The Last Mycenaeans and Their Successors* (1964), pp. 161 ff., 219; F. Stubbings, "Recession of Mycenaean Civilization," *CAH²*, II, fasc. 39 (1965), p. 5.

22. R. S. Young, "The Gordion Campaign of 1965," *AJA*, 70 (1966), pp. 276 f.

23. E. Akurgal, *Kunst Anatoliens*, pp. 6 f., 72 f.; R. Carpenter, *Discontinuity in Greek Civilization* (1966), pp. 65, 80.

24. P. Naster, *L'Asie Mineure et l'Assyrie aux VIIIe et VIIe Siècles av. J.C.*, Bibliothèque de Mouseon VIII (1938), pp. 88, n. 17, 93 ff., 105; J. G. Pedley, *Sardis in the Age of Croesus* (1968), pp. 44 f.

25. B. V. Head, *A Catalogue of the Greek Coins of Lydia*, XXII (1901), pp. 5, 7 f.

26. *BASOR*, No. 162 (1961), p. 12.

27. C. D. Curtis, *Sardis*, XIII, Part 1, *Jewelry and Gold Work* (1925) Pl. XI. 8, No. 120, identified as Neo-Babylonian by E. Porada (letter, Feb. 1946) and found in the same tomb as an Achaemenid seal, No. 115, Pl. XI. 30; cf. a similar one, E. P. Warren Collection, Boston Museum of Fine Arts, inv. No. 27.652.

28. R. S. Young, "The Gordion Campaign of 1957: Preliminary Report," *AJA*, 62 (1958), p. 152 and frontispiece; "Bronzes from Gordion's Royal Tomb," *Arch*, 11 (1958), pp. 227–31.

29. H. Goldman, *Excavations at Gözlü Kule Tarsus* III, *The Iron Age* (1963), pp. 8, 10, 20, 130, 132; A. Goetze, "Cuneiform Inscriptions from Tarsus." *JAOS*, 59 (1939), pp. 1–16.

30. E.g. Herodotus I.93; Strabo 13.4.5; Euripides, *Bacchae* 152. According to Strabo, the gold in the Pactolus had given out by his time.

31. The Chalybes: Xenophon, *Anabasis* V.5.1; Strabo, 12.3.19,; and the Dactyloi, Strabo 10.3.22, were peoples associated in antiquity with Anatolian iron working.

32. Vol. IV (1938), pp. 620 ff. Cf. also R. J. Forbes, *Study of Ancient Technology*, VIII and IX; S. Przeworski, "Die Metallindustrie Anatoliens in der Zeit von 1500–700 vor Chr.," *Internationales Archiv für Ethnographie*, Suppl. 36 (1939).

33. 1938, p. 20.

34. 1959, pp. 87 ff.

35. Maden Tetkik ve Arama Enstitüsü, abbr. M.T.A.

36. E.g., Mining Assistance Commission (Maden Yardim Komisyonu). Cf. also C. W. Ryan, *A Guide to Known Minerals of Turkey* (1957), M.T.A. and U. S. Operations Missions in Turkey; H. Kromer, "Turkish Mineral Potential Expands," *Engineering and Mining Journal*, 157 (January 1956), pp. 88–90.

37. Dr. Glueck's work in the Wadi Arabah, e.g. "Explorations in Eastern Palestine II," *AASOR*, 15 (1935), pp. 20 ff.; "The Recently Discovered Ore Deposits in Eastern Palestine," *BASOR*, No. 63 (1936), pp. 4 ff.; supplemented more recently by B. Rothenberg ("Ancient Copper Industries in the Western Arabah," *PEQ*, 94 [1962], pp. 5–69), has opened the way to archaeological research of this sort in the Near East. Interdisciplinary cooperation with geology, geophysics, chemistry, physics, and the rapidly developing study of the history of metallurgy and technology by metallurgists such as C. S. Smith, as well as archaeologists, should form the overall objective of future research, as, e.g., Smith's participation in the excavations at Tal-i-Iblis, Iran, where evidence was found for early copper smelting (*Iran, 5* [1967], p. 147). T. A. Wertime, "A Metallurgical Expedition Through the Persian Desert," *Science*, 159 (1 March 1968), pp. 927–35; and "Man's First Encounters with Metallurgy," *Science*, 146 (4 Dec. 1964), pp. 1257–65, are other examples of this type of investigation from the standpoint of the natural scientist.

38. B. Mkrtiachan, "The Mystery of Metsamor," *New Orient*, 8 (1967), pp. 76–78.

39. "The Gold Sands of the Pactolus," *ClassW*, 17 (1924), pp. 186 ff.

40. M. Saydamer, "Report on Gold Found in the Alluvium of the Pactolus" (1963); S. Birgi, "Gold Deposits in the Region of Sardis (Salihli)" (1944). (Both in Turkish.)

41. Toward the end of the campaign, L. J. Majewski, chief conservator, and G. M. A. Hanfmann also took part in the research. Much effective help was given by Clarence A. Wendel, Minerals Attaché, U. S. Embassy, Ankara, and Mrs. Inez Pulver, Consul, Izmir. The laboratory of Geology, Science Faculty, Ege University, Bornova-Izmir under Professor E. Izdar and Dr. M. Ardos permitted the use of their facilities for microphotography. Arrangements for analysis were made with Director General Dr. S. Alpan of M.T.A., and with the Director of the Çekmece Center for Nuclear Research in Istanbul, Dr. S. Akpinar. The latter institute has published the results in their annual report. We are grateful to Dr. Nilüfer Baygin, head of the Research Laboratory, M.T.A. and A. Uluocak, and to M. Talat-Erben and S. Okar for their collaboration and prompt communication of their results. The authors would like to thank Sidney Goldstein for his helpful comments and criticism of this section of the manuscript.

42. R. J. Forbes, *Studies in Ancient Technology*, VIII (1964), pp. 172 ff. Cupellation of silver may have been known to Early Bronze Age metalworkers in the Aegean (see K. Branigan, "Silver and Lead in Prepalatial Crete," *AJA*, 72 [1968], p. 225). H. Wulff, *The Traditional Crafts of Persia* (1966, pp. 13 f.), refers to ancient and modern cupellation of gold and silver in Persia.

43. Examination of a "crucible" showed dendrites of gold adhering to fracture surfaces; the largest dendrite was about one millimeter long. Microscopic examination showed smaller dendrite crystals adhering to all three sides of the fragment. These crystals conformed to the lamination in the fracture surface, tending to collect in the fracture surfaces (air pits). From an unpublished report by R. E. Stone, August 6, 1968.

44. Detailed reports will appear in *Dergi* and *BASOR* for 1969. Preliminary notices appeared in *The New York Times,* Oct. 20, 1968 (Science page); *Newsweek,* Nov. 4, 1968, pp. 98 f.; *Time,* Nov. 8, 1968, p. 85.

45. The question of whether cementation was, in fact, carried out here, in what order the processes of cupellation and cementation were performed, and whether or not purified silver was also treated at this installation will be examined and hopefully answered in future seasons at Sardis.

46. Dr. J. H. Kroll, Junior Fellow, Harvard, first referred us to S. Bolin, *State and Currency in the Roman Empire to 300* A.D. (1958), pp. 23 ff.; Table 1, p. 17, shows known weights of the so-called "Lion-Head" series (half-stater weights vary from 4.38 to 4.76 grams), to which now a considerable hoard from Gordion must be added. Cf. A. R. Bellinger, "Electrum Coins from Gordion," in C. M. Kraay and G. K. Jenkins, eds., *Essays in Greek Coinage presented to Stanley Robinson* (1968), pp. 10–15. Bolin's Table 2, p. 24, showing the variations in fineness of the "Lion's-Head" series, is based primarily on the specific gravity analyses of J. Hammer, "Der Feingehalt der griechischen und römischen Munzen," *ZfN,* 26 (1908), pp. 22 ff. and B. V. Head, *op. cit.,* pp. 1 ff.

47. *Dana,* I (1944), p. 91; gold ores show a range of from 0.09 to 20.0 percent silver, ordinarily up to 10 to 15 percent silver.

48. *Dana,* I, p. 91; electrum (argentian gold) is defined as gold having a silver content of 20 percent or higher.

49. Herodotus I:50–52.

50. Curiously, commentators disregard the fact, mentioned by Herodotus in the first part of the chapter, that Croesus had melted down couches covered with gold and silver, golden goblets, and other precious items. It seems probable that the metal from the pyre was part of the "uncountable gold" used for the lion, in which case it was gold previously worked and remelted, not "natural" gold.

51. Herodotus, I:94.

52. A. Olmstead, *History of the Persian Empire* (1948), p. 188; E. Schmidt, *The Treasury of Persepolis and Other Discoveries in the Homeland of the Achaemenians* (*OIC* No. 21, 1939), pp. 76 f., fig. 56.

53. The touchstone, mentioned by Theognis of Megara *circa* 500 BC (I:450), was apparently considered a Lydian invention; Theophrastus (*Peri Lithon* 47) said that "touchstones are only found in Tmolus in Lydia," and Pliny the Elder (*Nat. Hist.* 33:126) called it "Lydian Stone." The technique of using it is discussed by Theophrastus, *op. cit.,* 45–46; cf. E. R. Caley and J. F. C. Richards, *Theophrastus on Stones: Introduction, Text, English Translation, and Commentary* (1956); C. Frondel, *Dana,* III (1962), p. 225, says "Lydian-stone, also called touchstone or basanite, is a velvety black jasper . . . used in testing the color of the streak of gold alloys as a measure of the gold content. Fine grained black igneous rocks and slate also were used. . . . A skilled person can by this method obtain under favorable circumstances a precision of about 1 part in 100 in estimating the gold content of a gold-silver alloy."

54. Olmstead, *op. cit.,* p. 41; R. Frye, *The Heritage of Persia* (1963) pp. 77 f.

55. C. D. Curtis, *Sardis,* XIII, *Jewelry and Goldwork,* Part I 1910–1914 (1925), pp. 11 ff. Pl. I.1a–f.

56. *Altanatolien,* figs. 168–79.

57. "Sardis und Lydien," p. 30 and n. 2: jewelry in graves 836 and 27A; coins of Artaxerxes II found in grave 836.

58. *Kunst Anatoliens,* fig. 118.

59. *Interconnections in the Ancient Near East* (1965), p. 58; cf. also H. J. Kantor, "Achaemenid Jewelry in the Oriental Institute," *JNES,* 16 (1957), pp. 4 ff.; P. Amandry, "Orfèvrerie Achémenide," *Antike Kunst,* 1 (1958), p. 9.

60. M. J. Mellink, "Archaeology in Asia Minor," *AJA,* 71 (1967), p. 172, Pl. 59, compares a Persian incense burner from this tomb with those on reliefs at Persepolis; cf. E. F. Schmidt, *Persepolis,* I, *OIP* 68 (1953), Pls. 96–98, 121–22; *Persepolis,* II, *OIP* 69 (1957), Pl. 69 F., p. 94. We are greatly beholden to Burhan Tezcan for his generous permission to reproduce the silver incense burner and to M. J. Mellink for the kind loan of photographs.

61. E. Porada, *The Art of Ancient Iran: Pre-Islamic Cultures* (1965), p. 166, Pl. 49; E. Akurgal, *Orient und Okzident* (1966), p. 217, fig. 67; D. P. Hansen, "An Archaic Bronze Boar from Sardis," *BASOR,* No. 168 (1962), pp. 27–36, figs 1–3. A. Oliver has recently grouped a number of bronze mirrors with horse protomai around an example found at Sardis: "A Group of Anatolian Bronze Mirrors," abstract, *AJA,* 72 (1968), p. 169; and cf. H. C. Butler, *Sardis,* I, *The Excavations* (1922), fig. 82.

62. E. Schmidt, *Persepolis,* I, Pl. 32; *Persepolis,* II, frontispiece: E. Porada, *op. cit.,* p. 152, Pl. 43, "vessels with handles of winged bulls; metal bowls, rings decorated with griffins." The identification of the Lydians was proposed by R. D. Barnett, "Persepolis," *Iraq,* 19 (1957), p. 69. A well-defined body of material in a Greek-like style which illustrates the interests of Persian satrapal courts is provided by the "Graeco-Persian gems"; a monograph by Miranda Marvin may at long last present us with a coherent picture of this important material.

63. Butler, *Sardis,* I, p. 170, figs. 174, 185–88. Cf. D. Stronach, "Excavations at Pasargadae: First Preliminary Report," *Iran* 1 (1963), pp. 28 f., Pl. Ia; "Excavations at Pasargadae: Second Preliminary Report," *Iran,* 2 (1964), pp. 23 ff., figs. 1, 2, Pl. Ia, b.

64. *BASOR,* No. 162 (1961), p. 31; *BASOR,* No. 166 (1962), p. 28, fig. 24.

65. We are very grateful to the excavator, David Stronach, for kindly providing us with pictures of the Pasargadae staircases.

66. Xenophon, *Cyropaedaea,* 7:3.2–16; *BASOR,* No. 162 (1961), p. 31, n. 45.

67. *BASOR,* No. 162 (1961), p. 37, figs. 1, 21, 22, misdated to Hellenistic times. The correct dating was first proposed by Mr. Norbert Schimmel of the Fogg Museum Visiting Committee, Subcommittee on Sardis, who pointed out that the drafting of the masonry was the same as in Lydian sepulchral architecture at Bin Tepe. Cf. *BASOR,* No. 177 (1965), p. 33; No. 182 (1966), p. 27, fig. 22.

68. D. Stronach, personal communication: cf. "Urartian and Achaemenian Tower Temples," *JNES,* 26 (1967), p. 284, n. 49. Cf. also E. Porada, *op. cit.,* pp. 146 ff., fig. 80 (Tomb of Cyrus). The use of masonry of two colors she notes in Pasargadae and Ionia; it is also paralleled in Sardis AcN and in the Lydo-Persian twin grave at Ikiztepe (red roof, yellow tomb structure), as observed by G. M. A. Hanfmann on a visit in 1967.

69. C. Nylander, "Clamps and Chronology," *IrAnt,* 6 (1966), p. 146; "Old Persian and Greek Stonecutting and the Chronology of Achaemenian Monuments," *AJA,* 69 (1965), pp. 49–55.

70. Stronach, oral communication.

71. Porada, *op. cit.,* p. 156, after R. G. Kent, "Old Persian Grammar, Texts, Lexicon," *AOS* 33 (1950) p. 144.

72. G. Perrot and C. Chipiez, *Histoire de l'Art dans l'Antiquité,* v (1890), pp. 280 ff., figs. 180 ff.

73. E. Akurgal, "Griechish-persische Reliefs aus Daskyleion," *IrAnt*, 6 (1966), pp. 147 ff.; A. Dupont-Sommer, "Une Inscription araméenne inédite d'époque perse trouvée à Daskyleion (Turquie)," *CRAI* (1966), pp. 44 ff.; F. M. Cross, Jr., "An Aramaic Inscription from Daskyleion," *BASOR*, No. 184 (1966), pp. 7 ff; G. M. A. Hanfmann, "The New Stelae from Daskyleion," *BASOR*, No. 184 (1966), pp. 10 ff. There has been a general disposition to allow influences of the Persian way of life for such sculptures as the classical monuments of Lycia, e.g., P. Demargne, "La Sculpture en Lycie et les formes du classique grec," *Rayonnement*, pp. 500 ff. Persians themselves were of course often superbly represented by Greek artists.

74. H. Seyrig, "Antiquités Syriennes," *Syr*, 36 (1959), pp. 52 ff., Pl. XI, 1–2; Hanfmann, *BASOR*, No. 184 (1966), p. 12, n. 19.

75. W. H. Buckler, *Sardis: Lydian Inscriptions*, VI, Part 2 (1924), pp. 1 ff., n. 1, Pl. 1; A. Thumb, "Lydian Inscriptions from Sardis," *AJA*, 15 (1911), pp. 149 ff. S. A. Cook, "A Lydian Aramaic Bilingual," *JHS*, 37 (1917), pp. 77 ff., 219 ff. P. Kahle and F. Sommer, "Die Lydisch-Aramäische Bilingue," *Kleinasiatische Forschungen*, 1 (1927), pp. 18 ff. R. Gusmani, *Lydisches Wörterbuch* (1964), No. 1.

76. I. Rabinowitz, "Sepharad," *Encyclopaedia Biblica* (Hebrew, 1967).

77. Obadiah 20.

78. The Synagogue of Sardis, built in the second century AD, renovated *circa* AD 400, and destroyed in AD 616, is the largest early synagogue preserved. It contained fine mosaics on the floors of the Main Hall and Forecourt and marble *skoutlosis* revetments on the walls. Menorahs of bronze and marble, shrines, and inscriptions, some of which were in Hebrew, insure the identification of the building. See D. G. Mitten, "The Synagogue," *BASOR*, No. 170 (1963), pp. 38 ff; No. 174 (1964), pp. 30 ff.; No. 177 (1965), pp. 17 ff.; No. 182 (1966), pp. 34 ff.; *The Ancient Synagogue of Sardis* (pamphlet, 1965); G. M. A. Hanfmann, *BASOR*, No. 187 (1967), pp. 9 ff.; L. J. Majewski, "Evidence for the Interior Decoration of the Synagogue," *BASOR*, No. 187 (1967), pp. 32 ff.; G. M. A. Hanfmann, "The Ancient Synagogue of Sardis," Fourth World Congress of Jewish Studies, *Papers*, 1 (1967) pp. 37–42; "Sardis," *Encyclopaedia Judaica*, forthcoming; Y. Shiloh, "The Torah Scrolls and Menorah Slab from Sardis," *Yediot*, 30 (1966), p. 245.

79. A. T. Kraabel, *Judaism in Western Asia Minor Under the Roman Empire with a Preliminary Study of the Jewish Community of Sardis, Lydia* (unpubl. Th.D. Thesis, Harvard, 1967), pp. 241 f.

80. *BASOR*, No. 182 (1966), pp. 24 f.

81. D. G. Mitten, "The Synagogue," *BASOR*, No. 174 (1964), p. 34, discovery of IN 63.118–21; L. Robert, *Nouvelles Inscriptions de Sardis* (Paris, 1964), pp. 9 ff., on Zeuxis.

82. Polybius, 7:15–18.

83. Josephus, *Jewish Antiquities*, 12:147–53, English translation by R. Marcus, Loeb Classical Library, VII, pp. 76–79. Literature on the letter, L. Robert, *op. cit.*, p. 12, who considers it authentic.

84. Josephus, *op. cit.*, 16:171. Gaius Norbanus Flaccus, proconsul of Asia between 31 and 27 BC, to the magistrates and council of Sardis: "Caesar (Augustus) has written . . . that the Jews shall not be prevented from collecting sums of money, however great they may be, in accordance with their ancestral custom, and sending them up to Jerusalem."

Addendum. Since this article was submitted, the results of the neutron activation studies have been published by S. Okar and A. Aydin, *Sart Hafriyatinda Bulunan Altin Numunelerinin Notrön Aktivasyon Analizi*, Çekmece Nükleer Araştirma Merkezi, CNAEM 66, Istanbul (May 1969).

ANOTHER DEITY WITH DOLPHINS?

R. D. Barnett

Professor Nelson Glueck's impressive and beautifully illustrated publication on his excavations at Khirbet et-Tannur, *Deities and Dolphins,*[1] is an invaluable contribution to the history of the Nabataeans. In its tenth chapter Professor Glueck studies the somewhat unexpected association of the Goddess Atargatis of Tannur and other deities with dolphins (see his Pl. 10 on p. 24). Indeed, that the goddess of an Arab people, the Nabataeans, living far inland, should be so associated is strange enough. Except for the many prominent merchants and travelers among them, few Nabataeans could have ever seen a dolphin. As Glueck says, "Meeting her, as we did, practically in the middle of the desert, flaunting dolphins on top of her head, seemed at first almost as strange as it would have been to have encountered a camel swimming far out at sea!" He then points out that this is not the only example of dolphins in Nabataean art, and he collects a remarkable number of examples of representations of deities associated with dolphins in the Orient at Parthian Hatra, at Aphrodisias in Caria, at Olbia and in the Mediterranean at Aquileia, Puteoli and elsewhere, down to a date as late as that of the Mildenhall Treasure in England (sixth–seventh century AD). Some of these deities (Aquileia, Puteoli, Lixus, Mildenhall) are male.

There is one more example, however, in the Treasure of the Oxus, which Professor Glueck has pardonably overlooked. The reason it escaped his eagle eye was simple enough: in common with some other interesting pieces of the Treasure, it was for some obscure reason not illustrated in the second (1926) edition of O. M. Dalton's otherwise admirable Catalogue of that Treasure.[2] In 1964 the Trustees of the British Museum reissued the work in a third edition, when the present writer, in providing an entirely new set of photographs for the plates, took the opportunity of illustrating some omitted by Dalton. One of these was Dalton's No. 41 (on Pl. XII of the new edition) (Pl. 40; fig. 1). It is described as "head

Figure 1. Head of young man (god?) bordered by dolphins from the Treasure
of the Oxus (enlarged)

of a beardless man. The hair is curly, the face and nose long, and the
cheeks full. Border of dolphins. At back a wire as in preceding number." (Of this last is said that it is "probably for fastening a garment, but
more adapted for attachment to straps or bands on harness or accouter-
ments than to garments.") "D. 1.64 in 4.15 cm. Weight 197 grains.
The border has been clipped. The dolphins may indicate Greek influence." Dalton appears to have overlooked two points: first, that the
youthful face has apparently small horns (or are they small locks of hair?)
pointing upward at each side of his forehead; second, that the human
face is sternly frontal—a feature hardly found in classic Greek or
Oriental art, except for ridicule, and therefore not normally to be expected
here before the Parthian period, i.e., before the middle of the second
century BC. The implications of this observation for the dating of the
Oxus Treasure are discussed elsewhere.[3]

What, however, are we to make of this sullen-faced youth, with his
hair in thick locks and tiny horns(?), surrounded by a whole school of
plunging dolphins? I can only make the weak suggestion that if these are
horns, then as the horns in the East indicate divinity, this is some half-

Grecized Oriental deity of the Parthian period; or if we look for any Greek parallel, it will stand for a river god, such as Achelöus in Sicily, often represented as bearded but bullheaded. Perhaps we have here the river god of the Oxus himself? The dolphins suggest water, fertility, and safe homecoming to the merchants with their wares.

It is perhaps not inopportune to comment on another Nabataean motif discussed in judicious fashion by Professor Glueck (his pp. 480–83). This is the eagle struggling with a serpent, which is found carved almost in the round at Khirbet Tannur, and occurring also at Zaharet-el Bedd in Northern Gilead and scratched in a graffito at Dura Europos (his p. 481 and Pl. 141c).[4]

Into their company, Professor Glueck rightly draws a sculptured panel showing the same subject of eagle and serpent from Ausan in South Arabia (his pp. 488–89 and Pl. 142) and noted as "in a private collection in Aden." It seems to me we may go further to see in this eagle with snake an actual South Arabian lunar deity, known by the name of Nasrum (the eagle) and associated with the moon god 'Amm. The subject is in fact illustrated on a brown and bluish sardonyx gem in the British Museum (BM. 120304), with the name Na'dim inscribed in Himyaritic letters and an invocation of later date in Kufic characters, perhaps of the eighth century AD (Pl. 41; fig. 2).

Figure 2. Sardonyx gem showing eagle and serpent, symbol of lunar god Nasrum.

This gem has been published several times, and was recognized by my late colleague John Walker as representing the South Arabian god Nasrum.[5] The same theme of an eagle fighting with a serpent, in this case two-headed, was met in the Yemen on an alabaster stele by Ahmed Fakhry, who also refers to a stele in Istanbul Museum.[6]

FOOTNOTES

1. Nelson Glueck, *Deities and Dolphins: The Story of the Nabataeans* (1965).

2. O. M. Dalton, *The Treasure of the Oxus and Other Examples of Early Oriental Metalwork in the British Museum* (1926).

3. See my article "The Treasure of the Oxus," *IrAnt* (in press).

4. Professor Glueck shows (p. 473) that the eagle alone was regarded by the Nabataeans as symbol of Zeus-Hadad or Ba'al-shamin.

5. J. Walker, "A South Arabian Gem with Sabaean and Kufic Legends," *Le Muséon*, 75 (1962). *Idem*, "A New Type of Arab Coinage," *NumChron*, 17 (1937), pp. 271–79, fig. 4.

6. A. Fakhry, *An Archaeological Journey to the Yemen* (1952), Part I, pp. 128 f., fig. 82, and Part III, Pl. XLVII (quoted by Walker).

ARCHAEOLOGY AND BABYLONIAN JEWRY

Jacob Neusner

I

THE archaeological investigations of Professor Nelson Glueck, his disciples and colleagues, into the history of Israelite religion before 450 BC and of Judaism afterward, have no parallel across the Euphrates. The sites of the major Jewish academies and settlements remain unexamined. Peripheral areas, such as Dura-Europos, have shown that one may hope for important discoveries. Central Babylonia has, moreover, yielded significant finds of Parthian and Sasanian material. One might expect, therefore, that purposeful examination of the regions in which large numbers of Jews were settled might produce commensurate results. But that examination has yet to take place. In part, the reason was the neglect by archaeologists, until the 1930s, of Parthian and Sasanian strata in favor of older ones in Babylonian projects. While much has been done since to remedy that situation, the potential Jewish sites are not even catalogued, and surface examination has yet to take place. Strikingly, when Jacob Obermeyer wrote his *Die Landschaft Babylonien im Zeitalter des Talmuds und des Gaonats* (1929), he added the subtitle, "Geographie und Geschichte *nach Talmudischen, Arabischen, und Anderen Quellen*" (italics supplied). His stress lay primarily on literary materials, and this despite his own extensive travels in the region as teacher in the house of the Persian refugee-Prince, Abbas-Mirza-Naïb-aṣṣalṭanah. Obermeyer by no means stood alone in his attitude toward the artifacts of material culture. More recently, in commenting upon a passage in the Talmud (T.B. Berakhot 35b) relating to the agricultural calendar in Babylonia, the distinguished Talmudic historian Moshe Dov Beer provided extensive discussions of literary evidence on the climate of the Jordan valley. This, he supposed, is similar to that of the part of Babylonia between the Tigris and Euphrates along the Royal Canal where Jews lived. At no point did he turn to the various climatological or other studies readily available to explain the literary passage at hand.[1] Rather than speculation based upon literary evidence from another country, one might easily consult K. Mason, ed., *Iraq and the Persian Gulf* (1944), pp. 166 ff., 447–57, for a full account of normal meteorological patterns and consequent agricultural practices of the region.

How shall we account for the fundamentally anti-archaeological bias of past scholarship on Babylonian Jewry? First, "Talmudic history" is fundamentally a category of literary studies. Its purpose is not to illumine the life of the Babylonian Jewish community, but rather to investigate the sequence of generations of the Talmudic academies of the region.[2] The interest of Talmudic historians, to begin with, focused upon what happened in the rabbinical schools and among the sages. Further, since the life of the streets and the affairs of the schools were supposed to be pretty much identical, Talmudic historians saw little purpose in going beyond the pages of the Babylonian Talmud and later commentaries. One could find out not only whatever was important, but also whatever one wanted to know, in literary accounts. This bias depends upon the theological conviction that in the rabbinical schools, the "whole Torah" revealed at Sinai was preserved, both the written text as we now have it, as well as the oral traditions supposedly handed on alongside. No rational argument about the nature of the Babylonian Talmud as a *historical* source was ever thought necessary, for a fundamentally sacred text obviously contained whatever was so. The text did not merely yield history —it *was* history. What is noteworthy is the persistence of the effects of that conviction long after the belief itself has been set outside the realm of scholarly discourse. If, therefore, "Talmudic history" has on the whole neglected even the available results of archaeological studies, the primary reason was that, with the noteworthy exceptions of S. Krauss and S. Lieberman, the earlier scholars were really not interested in the kind of materials made available by archaeology or in the sort of broader questions that might be answered upon that basis. I do not suggest that where archaeological results could prove useful in the explication of one or another discrete text, for instance to explain the meaning or reference of a particular word or practice, Talmudists, including "Talmudic historians," proved disinterested. On the contrary, a work such as Joshua Brand, *Klei HaḤeres beSifrut HaTalmud* (1953), was welcomed by Talmudists. But "Talmudic history" was fundamentally a branch of literary studies, and not a very important one at that. In such a setting archaeology was likely to attract little sustained interest, so that even as eminent a geographer as Obermeyer could stress his use of Talmudic,

Arabic, and other sources to the exclusion of his own observations, in the title of his book.

The late Professor Erwin Goodenough frequently pointed out, moreover, that "philological method" generally predominated in Jewish scholarship. The appreciation of archaeological data was limited by almost exclusive concentration on texts as the source of all information, and upon the explication of texts—after they were critically edited—as the sole legitimate, authentic, scholarly task. Since modern Jewish scholarship followed the model of nineteenth-century German university science, it is quite natural that the methods and orientation decisive at the outset should prevail. What is not natural is that matters should have changed so little later on. Biblical studies constitute a striking contrast. There archaeological results are consulted by everyone, and both in the State of Israel and in Jewish centers of higher learning elsewhere literary studies constitute only one, though an important, aspect of biblical scholarship. The reasons for this exceptional situation are complicated. One of them is certainly the constructive influence of Professor Nelson Glueck and others of his generation, particularly Professor W. F. Albright, upon the study of the Bible under Jewish auspices. A second, applicable in the State of Israel, is the emotional attachment of Israelis to archaeology as the route by which their own roots in the country are uncovered. Hence the popularity—it has been called mania—of biblical archaeology. No similarly fruitful influence has yet affected archaeological studies of later Judaism, and no equivalent motive has led to equivalent researches in other lands where Jews have lived. Once again we see that the sociology of learning, as much as the inner momentum of research or the state of the evidence, shapes both our results *and* our methodology.

A third relevant factor should be briefly mentioned. Since 1948 it has not been possible for scholars of Jewish origin to pursue researches, whether archaeological or of any other kind, in 'Iraq. Hence, the field is closed to those who would be most interested in working in it.

To be receptive to the importance of archaeology one must first of all be willing to face the broader issues, answers to which are made more readily available by archaeological researches than otherwise. One must begin, I think, by supposing that literary evidence is important as one testimony, but only one among many, to the way things were. That evidence cannot be seen as an end in itself, still less as the measure by which archaeological data are to be evaluated and interpreted. (Editor's note: see above, pp. 64–80, for the same view from another perspective.) The disputed interpretation of the synagogue murals at Dura-Europos provides an excellent example of the dubious use of literary sources as a court of higher appeal for the interpretation of archaeological data, as I have suggested in *History of Religions* (4 [1964], pp. 81–102). Since I am not qualified to offer an interpretation of the iconography or symbolism of the Dura synagogue, it suffices merely to note that we have no scholar's handbook of ancient Judaism, only what various groups later on chose to preserve and hand on for our use. These groups, especially the Christian monasteries and the Rabbinical schools, had their particular purposes; to serve those purposes they selected some traditions, sayings, and stories, or whole documents in the former case, and ignored or suppressed others. If, as in the case of Dura, archaeology provides us with a new corpus of data which otherwise we should not have had, then to begin with we cannot suppose that those data are to be interpreted according to the literary evidence transmitted for particular theological reasons among wholly unrelated groups or parties. I cannot enter into the discussions of whether the Talmud, or Philo, or any other literary materials offer the key to the Dura synagogue and the philosophy of the designer of its murals. Professor Morton Smith has admirably summarized the state of current thought—and, I think, greatly improved upon it—in his "Goodenough's *Jewish Symbols* in Retrospect," *Journal of Biblical Literature*, 86 (1967), pp. 53–68. It is fruitless to debate matters in generalities, and the time has come for specialists to take over, concentrating first of all on the history of Dura-synagogue art as it is revealed in relationship to other archaeological evidences.

II

Having introduced the knotty problem of the relationship of literary to archaeological evidence concerning the history of Babylonian Judaism, I may cite one example of the complex difficulties yet to be considered. The seventh-century AD magical bowls of Nippur, a town just east of Sura, where the rabbinical school founded by Rav was located, contain a number of references to a rabbi also mentioned in rabbinic traditions, Joshua b. Peraḥiah. What is striking is that in these references the rabbi appears as a magician. We shall review first the exempla provided by Montgomery[3] and then the rabbinic traditions. Finally we shall see how the two kinds of materials relate to one another.

The rabbi appears in bowls Nos. 8, 9, 17, 32 (=33), as follows:

No. 8: [That there flee from the house of this Geyônài bar Mâmâi the evil Lilith . . . And again, you shall not appear to them in his house nor in their dwelling . . . because it is announced to you, whose father is named Palḥas and whose mother Pelaḥdad—because it is announced to you] that Rabbi Joshua bar Peraḥia [sic] has sent against you the ban. . . . Thou Lilith, male Lilis and female Lilith, Hag and Ghul, be in the ban . . . [of Rabbi] Joshua b. Peraḥia, and thus has spoken to us Rabbi Joshua bar Peraḥia, A divorce writ has come to you from across the sea, and there is found written in it [against you] whose father is named Palḥas and whose mother Pelaḥ-dad . . . they hear from the firmament . . . Hear and obey and go from the house . . . And again, you shall not appear to them either in dream by night nor in slumber by day, because you are sealed with the signet of El Shaddai and with the signet of the house of Joshua b. Peraḥia and by the Seven which are before him . . .

There follow adjurations by the Strong One of Abraham, etc. On the divorce issued to Lilith from her victim, Montgomery comments, "This was a happy thought of the magicians, who thus applied the powers of binding and loosing claimed by the rabbis to the disgusting unions of demons and mortals. . . . The magical writ affects the same forms and formalism as that of the divorce court . . . The names of both parties are exactly given, hence the parents of the liliths are here specifically named."[4] In addition, the terms of the divorce are properly given, and properly served on the divorcée. Divine authority is invoked. The writ has come down from heaven, and so, like writs from abroad, special forms are included. The commissioners and witnesses are angels. The rabbi seals the divine decree.

Further references to R. Joshua are as follows:

No. 9: The bowl I deposit and sink down, and the work I operate, and it is in [the fashion of] Rabbi Joshua bar Peraḥia. I write for them divorces, for all the Liliths who appear to them . . .

No. 17: This day above any day, years, and generations of the world, I Kômêš bath Maḥlaphta have divorced, separated, dismissed thee, thou Lilith, Lilith of the Desert, Hag and Ghul . . . I have fenced you out by the ban which Joshua bar Peraḥia sent against you. I adjure you by the honor of your father and by the honor of your mother, and take your divorces and separations, thy divorce and thy separation, in the ban which is sent against you by Joshua b. Peraḥia, for so has spoken to thee Joshua b.P.: A divorce has come to thee from across the sea. There is found, you whose mother is Palḥas and whose father Pelaḥdad, you Liliths: And now flee and go forth and do not trouble Kômêš b.M., in her house and her dwelling. I bind and I seal with the seal of El Shaddai and with the seal of Joshua b. Peraḥia the healer . . .[5]

No. 32: . . . The bowl I deposit and sink down, a work which has been made like that of Rav Jesu bar Peraḥia sat and wrote against them—a ban writ against all the Demons and Devils and Satans and Liliths . . . Again he wrote against them a ban-writ which is for all time . . .

To the Jews in sixth and seventh century AD Nippur, therefore, the figure of R. Joshua b. Peraḥiah was associated with two anti-demonic prophylaxes, first, the ability to issue a legal bill of divorce against female demons, second, the pronouncement of a ban against demons. The divorce and the ban seem confused; in No. 8, the ban is announced, and then the proper formula for a divorce delivered from abroad is introduced, together with the necessary witnesses, signatures, and sealing, the last-named with the signet of God and Joshua's house. In Nos. 9, 17, and 32 the divorce is more clearly explicated, again in proper legal language. Lilith is adjured to receive the divorce, as is legally necessary.

III

Three questions require answers.

First, is the procedure of issuing a bill of divorce against demons to be located elsewhere in the Nippur bowls published by Montgomery? And if so, what authorities are associated with the procedure? Of the forty-two exempla, the figure of divorce appears in eight. Of these, Joshua occurs in all but three. Strikingly, in the exempla where Joshua is absent, the language includes an *explanation* of the divorce procedure, which we do not find in the Joshua-bowls:

No. 11: Behold I have written for thee (i.e., a divorce), and behold I have separated thee . . . *[like the demons] who write divorces for their wives and do not return to them.* Take thy divorce from . . . [Italics supplied]

No. 26: Again, bound and held art thou, evil Spirit and mighty Lilith. . . . But flee from their presence and take thy divorce and thy separation and thy writ of dismissal.

Similar language occurs in No. 18. Montgomery comments, "The additional thought appears here (No. 11) that inasmuch as demons divorce their spouses, divorce-writs must be as effective on them as among human kind."[6]

Yamauchi[7] provides Mandaean instances of the appearances of the word *GYṬ* in text 21, lines 10, 11:

> . . . *as the demons write a bill of divorce for their wives* in truth, *and may not return again* . . . Behold, take your bill of divorce and receive your oath . . . [Italics supplied]

PṬR appears in 21:9. *ŠBYQT* occurs in the meanings of "dismiss," "divorce," "forsake," and "leave" nineteen times, though not all usages signify the language of divorce-writs so far as I am able to tell. This brief survey shows that the use of divorce-magic was not unique to the Jews who invoked the name, ban, sealing, and magic of R. Joshua b. Peraḥiah. But it is equally clear that R. Joshua was associated only with such a technique, appearing in the context of ban and divorce alone. J. Z. Smith provides below further discussion of the scholarly literature.[8]

Second, do we find in rabbinic literature the use of a divorce, writ, or the language of a divorce, as an anti-demonic prophylaxis? I am not able to offer a definitive answer. I find no reference whatever to the use of a document of divorce as a means of protection from demons in Trachtenberg[9] or Ginzberg.[10] Since the Joshua-bowls refer consistently to Lilith, one might suppose that the use of a divorce to banish her was based upon her mating with Adam:

> She remained with him only a short time because she insisted upon enjoying full equality with her husband. She derived her rights from their identical origin. With the help of the Ineffable Name, which she pronounced, Lilith flew away from Adam, and vanished in the air. Adam complained before God . . . who sent three angels to capture her . . . The only way to ward off the evil [she does to babies] is to attach an amulet bearing the names of her three angel captors to the children . . .[11]

No reference to writing a bill of divorce is given by Ginzberg. While that fact cannot be offered as definitive, I think it highly suggestive. Similarly, Kohut makes no mention of such a prophylaxis in connection with Lilith.[12] We do have some instances in which rabbis drove off 'Igrath (=Lilith),[13] in particular b. Pesaḥim 112b. In both instances there, heavenly respect for the rabbi's learning (Torah) led to her being forced to accept his commands. Abaye thereupon said, "I order you never to pass through settled regions." Finally, we may note that Ludwig Blau[14] and Gideon Brecher[15] provide no reference whatever to divorcing Lilith. It is far easier to say what *is* in the Talmud and cognate rabbinic literature than what is *not* to be found there.[16] I can only tentatively suggest that while rabbinic literature knows Lilith well, at no point does a rabbi refer to *divorcing* her in the manner described by the magical bowls or in any other way.

One may suppose that the general, universal view that demons divorce their wives produced the specific, Jewish practice attributed to R. Joshua b. Peraḥiah of casting various spells, but especially, a legal bill of divorce, against the demon. One may, alternatively, interpret the explanatory clause, "like the demons who write divorces for their wives and do not return to them," as evidence that the exorcist supposed it to be an exceptional or strange practice, requiring an explanation (for the demon? for the Mandaean client?). The absence of a similar explanation in the Joshua-bowls may mean that the practice of divorcing demons was sufficiently well-known among Jews not to demand further comment. The absence—if it is absence—of attestation in Talmudic literature merely signifies that the rabbis did not recognize, approve, or care to preserve evidence about, such a practice. It does not tell us anything about the practice or knowledge of ordinary Jews.

Third, what other traditions about R. Joshua b. Peraḥiah existed in Palestinian and Babylonian rabbinical schools? First of all, as has already been noted, no passage suggests that R. Joshua b. Peraḥiah composed bills of divorce against demons. The extant traditions should be divided according to time and place. In the Tannaitic Midrashim, we find no reference whatever to R. Joshua. In the Mishnah, R. Joshua is cited twice, in Ḥagigah 2:2, on the ordination controversy, and in Pirqei Avot 1:6, which contains his saying in the chain of tradition, that one should provide himself with a teacher and a fellow-disciple, and judge people favorably. Nothing in the Mishnah of R. Judah the Prince suggests that R. Joshua was a magician. The Tosefta reveals a saying of his on purity laws (Makhshirin 3:4). The references in the two Talmuds deal with only two matters. First, in TB Menaḥot 109b, we find a *beraita,* citing R. Joshua b. Peraḥiah, that it is just as hard to accept high office as it is to leave it.

The other matter, however, is more important. (It occurs in TB Sanhedrin 109b, with a parallel in TB Sotah 47a. (The incident is further echoed in TJ Ḥagigah 2:2 and Sanhedrin 6:9, but there the rabbi in question is Judah b. Tabbai.) The *locus classicus* is fully discussed by Herford.[17] It is attached to a *beraita* that one should not too harshly repel penitents or potential converts to Judaism. R. Joshua b. Peraḥiah's treatment of Jesus is cited. When Yannai the King killed the rabbis, Joshua and his disciple Jesus fled to Alexandria. Šimeʻon b. Sheṭaḥ called them back when times proved more favorable. On route home they found a certain inn, where R. Joshua praised the hostess. Jesus disagreed, saying she had narrow eyes. Joshua then excommunicated him for looking too closely at the woman, saying, "Wretch, do you thus busy yourself?!" Jesus tried without success to repent. Finally, being repulsed, Jesus went and hung up a tile and worshiped it. At that time Joshua called on him to repent, without result. "So a teacher has said, 'Jesus the Nazarene practised magic and led astray and deceived Israel.'" Herford suggests that the story is based upon a Palestinian tradition. In any case, we may be sure that the legend of Joshua as a visitor to Egypt was known in the schools of both countries.[18]

IV

On the relationship between Joshua b. Peraḥiah in the magical bowls and the Talmudic passage, Montgomery comments:

> We find then in these magical bowls an independent tradition concerning an early hero of the Law, who appears as endowed with magic powers, and who furthermore was able to make the ascent of the soul to heaven. He was accordingly one of the earliest to attain that spiritual privilege . . . Joshua was possibly one of the good company of apocalyptists and our magic tradition may preserve a true reminiscence of his personality and claims.[19]

To this I may add another viewpoint, derived from my study of the social and religious role of the rabbi within Babylonian Jewry.[20] We must, first of all, regard the Joshua of the bowls as an authentic portrait of what some people, presumably Jews though not necessarily so, thought about the rabbi. They regarded him as both lawyer and magician. As a lawyer, he was expected to know the precise formula for a bill of divorce and to be able to issue a ban. Thus we noted in No. 9, Joshua b. Peraḥiah's divorces for all the Liliths who appear to them; in No. 17, both the ban spoken by Joshua and the divorce spoken (read) to Lilith by Joshua, in the appropriate legal language; in No. 32, a ban-writ against the demons. Now what we should not find unusual is that rabbis, whose effective legal jurisdiction extended mostly to matters of exchanges of property and personal status,[21] should be consulted on drawing up bills of divorce. What is surprising is that those legal documents were presumed effective, as in the Mandaean magical bowls, against demons. Here the second religious role of the rabbi becomes important, namely, his capacity, because of his mastery of Torah and his ability on that basis to exercise, independent of the wishes of heaven, the supernatural powers inherent in the Torah, to do works of magic against demons (among other miracles).

We noted above that Abaye, among others, was believed to be able to overcome demons because "in heaven his Torah was highly regarded." I have elsewhere cited considerable evidence that knowledge of Torah produced the capacity to do supernatural actions.[22] In the magical bowls, the two predominant roles of the rabbi are united in the figure of Joshua b. Peraḥiah. The law is effective—against demons. The rabbi carries out the law—for supernatural purposes. We find, however, little direct evidence that in the rabbinical schools of either Babylonia or Palestine such supernatural powers were attributed to R. Joshua. One can hardly argue that everyone who went to Alexandria came home a magician, despite the general reputation of the place.

What I find difficult to account for is the attribution of so central a magical role to R. Joshua b. Peraḥiah, who, as we have seen, played a relatively minor, and generally not-supernatural, role in rabbinic traditions of both Palestine and Babylonia. I may, with much hesitation, conjecture on why those who made the bowls selected R. Joshua above all other rabbis. Perhaps, as Montgomery suggests, his relationship to Jesus, believed by many Jews to be an expert magician, and by the rabbis to be R. Joshua's disciple, was sufficient also to distinguish R. Joshua as a magician. If the disciple was so puissant, how much more should the Jews, disciples of the rabbis and under their effective control by the seventh century, turn to his rabbinical master?

v

The R. Joshua of the magical bowls and the R. Joshua of the schools were not wholly unrelated, but they were also not closely correlated. The figure of the lawyer-magician is well-known to us in the Babylonian Talmud, but R. Joshua b. Peraḥiah was not singularly noted as such a figure. On the other hand, the bowls contain one important perspective on R. Joshua, that of the ordinary people who used them. Whether or not rabbis and those under their immediate influence and control also used magical bowls is not entirely clear. We know, of course, that the rabbis had other means of driving away demons. But those in no way exclude the use of the prophylaxes held in common among the various peoples of Babylonia, including other Jews. At any rate, we do know precisely what traditions on R. Joshua the rabbinical schools chose to preserve and to hand on as authentic and correct. For the most part, these are inconsequential. The striking tradition about the flight to Egypt brings us closest of all to the Joshua of the bowls, and provides at least a hint on why Joshua was otherwise so neglected. He was, to be sure, included *per force* in the sayings of Avot and in related sayings (cf. Ḥagigah 2:2 already cited), but otherwise almost wholly excluded. Only in the environment of the Amoraic schools in Babylonia was the apparently very old story of the trip to Egypt preserved, possibly for polemical purposes in a time marked by conversions of significant numbers of Jews to Christianity,[23] and now perhaps made useful by the more hospitable reception of magic in the later rabbinical schools, including that near Nippur itself.[24]

FOOTNOTES

1. Moshe Dov Beer, *Ma'amadam HaHevrati veHakalkali shel Amora'ei Bavel* (1962), pp. 52–53. An even more striking illustration is J. Newman, *The Agricultural Life of the Jews in Babylonia* (1932), who seems not to have read a single current archaeological report, including work done in the 1920s on Ctesiphon, a city near which large numbers of Jewish farmers were situated, not to mention the studies of Assyriologists on earlier agricultural conditions. The single archaeological title in his brief bibliography is S. Kraus, *Talmudische Archaeologie.* Likewise S. Funk, *Juden in Babylonien* (1903), makes no mention of Nippur, near the town of Sura.

2. Yet, though one would suppose we should now have extensive histories of the Babylonian Talmudical academies, the opposite is the case. See my *History of the Jews in Babylonia.* III. *From Shapur I to Shapur II* (1968), p. 213, n. 1.

3. James A. Montgomery, *Aramaic Incantation Texts from Nippur* (1913).

4. *Ibid.,* p. 159.

5. Montgomery notes that No. 17 is a replica of No. 8, often incorrect, however.

6. *Ibid.,* p. 172.

7. Edwin M. Yamauchi, *Mandaic Incantation Texts* (1967).

8. Below, pp. 344–47.

9. Joshua Trachtenberg, *Jewish Magic and Superstition* (1961).

10. Louis Ginzberg, *Legends of the Jews* (1946). Since Lilith occurs in the magical bowls, one might surmise that a similar bill of divorce of Lilith might be referred to in Talmudic literature. Ginzberg refers to no such phenomenon. He does note in Vol. I, p. 66, that she was warded off by an amulet.

11. *Ibid.,* pp. 66–67.

12. Alexander Kohut, *Über die jüdische Angelologie und Dämonologie in ihrer Abhängigkeit vom Parsismus* (1866), pp. 86–89.

13. I here refer to Kohut's identification of 'Igrath with Lilith, but it was in fact rejected by both Ginzberg and Blau, with good reason.

14. *JE,* VIII, pp. 87–88.

15. Gideon Brecher, *Transcendentale, Magie, und Magische Heilarten im Talmud* (1850), pp. 47, 50, 54.

16. Nor do I find anything relevant in M. Margalioth's *Sefer HaRazim* (1967).

17. R. Travers Herford, *Christianity in Talmud and Midrash* (1966), pp. 51 ff.

18. See also J. Z. Lauterbach, *JE,* VII, p. 295, and A. Hyman, *Toledot Tannaim veAmoraim* (1910), II, pp. 647–48. Hyman notes that the Tosefta saying has to do with the ritual purity of Alexandrian wheat (perhaps the kernel of the legend of his flight from Palestine?). No tradition concerning R. Joshua b. Perahiah is found in Bereshit Rabbah.

19. *Op. cit.,* pp. 227–28.

20. I refer to my *History of the Jews in Babylonia* I (1965), II (1966), III (1968), IV (1969) and V (1970).

21. See II, pp. 251–87, III, pp. 195–338, for a review of the cases and evidence.

22. For further discussion of the rabbi as a holy man, see II, pp. 126–50, and III, pp. 95–191.

23. See III, pp. 8–29.

24. Further discussion of the rabbi as lawyer-magician will be found in IV, Chapter Five. My thanks are due to Professors Yohanan Muffs, Jewish Theological Seminary of America, and Morton Smith, Columbia University, for helpful comments.

ADDENDUM

Jonathan Z. Smith

THE earliest publication I know of is text No. 1 in A. H. Layard, *Discoveries in the Ruins of Nineveh and Babylon* (1853) in the translation of T. Ellis (pp. 512–13—Montgomery No. 11):

> This is a bill of divorce to the Devil, and to . . . and to Satan, and to Nerig, and to Zachiah, and to Abitur of the mountain, and to . . . and to the night monsters, commanding them to cease from Beheran in Batnaiun, and from the country of the north, and from all who are tormented by them therein. Behold I make the counsels of these devils of no effect, and annul the power of the ruler of the night-monsters. I conjure you all, monsters, . . . both male and female, to go forth. I conjure you and . . . by the sceptre of the powerful one, who has power over the devils, and over the night monsters, to quit these habitations. Behold I now make you cease from troubling them, and make the influence of your presence cease in Beheran of Batnaiun, and in their fields. In the same manner as the devils write bills of divorce and give them to their wives, and return not to them again, receive ye your bills of divorce, and take this written authority, and go forth, leave quickly, flee, and depart from Beheran in Batnaiun, in the name of the living . . . , by the seal of the powerful one, and by this signet of authority. Then will there flow rivers of water in that land, and there the parched ground will be watered. Amen, Amen, Amen, Selah.

Layard conjectures that this is the oldest of the seven inscriptions he has, dating it the third to second century BC (p. 525). Ellis gives the following commentary: ". . . there is one thing to which I wish to call the attention of Oriental scholars, namely the subject of the inscription of No. 1. It is a *letter of dismissal,* or *bill of divorce* to Satan and other evil spirits. The word here used to express this is *GYṬ*', the very word found in the Talmud to express the same thing. . . . The ancient Jews supposed that the devils or evil spirits were propagated like mankind; that they eat, and drank, married, and it would seem quarreled with their wives, and divorced them."

Layard No. 1 is commented upon and re-translated by M. A. Levy, "Uber die von Layard aufgefundenen chaldäischen Inschriften auf Topfgefässen. Ein Beitrag zur Hebräischen Paläographie und zur Religionsgeschichte," *ZDMG,* 9, (1857), pp. 465–91; and D. Chwolson, *Corpus inscriptionum hebraicarum* (1882), I, pp. 103–20. M. Schwab, "Les coups magiques et l'hydromancie dans l'antiquité orientale," *Proceedings of the Society of Biblical Archæology,* 9 (1889–90), p. 300, reprints the text and translation of Levy and offers no interpretation, in his full notes which follow (pp. 301–6), of the divorce, only noting (p. 300) that "un acte de divorce" is "en signe de répulsion." Although in the course of this article (pp. 292–342) he discusses a number of other magical bowls and inscriptions, no others have "divorce" of demons as a motif.

There is no mention of the divorce motif in the text or the discussion of R. Stübe, *Jüdisch-Babylonische Zaubertexte* (1895).

This exhausts the material prior to Montgomery known to me. Post-Montgomery, there are a few references to divorce in the texts published by C. H. Gordon—though none which contain reference to R. Joshua b. Peraḥiah in this practice. I believe the following references constitute a complete list:

(a) C. H. Gordon, "Aramaic Incantation Bowls," *Or,* 10 (1941), pp. 116–41 (pt. I):

Bowl No. 5 (p. 123 Louvre AO 1915): "Dismissed and divorced are all . . . ; bound by Zarḥiṣi'el the star . . . (lines 1–2)—*ŠBYQT* is the term. Gordon has no comment.

(b) *Ibid.,* pp. 339–60 (Pt. III) Bowl, Iraq Museum No. 11113 a text with lacunae. Gordon translated (p. 351), "Lo I have written for thee thy bill of divorcement and I have dismissed, abandoned and banished (thee) . . . they do not return again; take thy bill of divorcement and re(ceive) thine adjuration."

(c) C. H. Gordon, "An Aramaic Exorcism," *ArOr,* 6 (1934), pp. 466–74 and Pls. XXII–XXV from a jar in the Iraq Museum No. 5497. The text is also printed in W. H. Rossell, *A Handbook of Aramaic Magical Inscriptions* (1953), pp. 107–9, No. 28. Gordon introduces his translation (p. 466) by noting, "The exorcism is intended to expel a harmful lilith named Hablas from the home of one Mazdewai and the latter's husband. The praxis here, to wit, that of banishing a lilith by serving a bill of divorcement on her, is already known from previously published texts . . ." The text of Gordon's translation follows:

(I.=Immā; I.S.=Immā Salmā)

p. 470 (1) In Thy name! Mazdewai, the daughter of Immā Salmā (and) Beryl, the son of Immā, her husband. (2) In Thy name do I act! Salvation from the heavens! Mazdewai, the daughter of I.S.; Beryl, the son of I., her husband—that there may live and be preserved for her, sons and daughters (!) and that nothing bad whatsoever may injure them. In the name of the L(ord) and 'I am that I am.' For the binding of Bagdānā (!) (3) who is the king; (to wit), the king of demons and devil(s) and the great ruler of the liliths—I adjure thee, O Lilith Ḥablas, the granddaughter of Lilith Zarnai, who dwells on the threshold of this Mazdewai, the daughter of I.S., and of this Beryl, the son of I. Amen. (4) (O thou) who fillest this habitation (?), smitest, strikest and castest down and stranglest and killest and castest down (?) both boy(s) and girl(s). *WMLR MṢY WMR MYṢYT'.* I adjure thee that thou be smitten in the membrane of thy heart and with the lance of Qatros, the mighty. And mayest thou be uprooted. And again (5) mayest thou cease and be distant from this Mazdewai, the daughter of I.S., from this Beryl, the son of I., her husband—amen—from their sons and daughters, that they have or will have, and from their house, from all their yard and from all their threshold. *Lo I have written (a divorce) for thee, lo I have dismissed thee (6) and lo I have abandoned thee and lo I have banished thee with a bill of divorcement Amen??? as demons and devil(s) write and serve divorces on their wives and again they do not return to them in their residence (?)*; so, thou wicked lilith—(7) (be thou) male lili (or) female lili(th)—and strangler and daughter (of demons) and ghost (?) and? and profane one—*take (thy) divorce and thy document of dismissal and thy letter of banishment and flee and take flight and go out and depart* from this Mazdewai, the daughter of I.S. (and) from her husband Beryl (8) the son of I.

p. 471

—amen—from his sons and daughters and from all his yard. And appear to them neither in visions of the day nor in impure fancies of the night, in the shape of neither man nor woman, nor any??. and do not approach them and do not molest (9) them and do not devour their sons (!) and their daughters, that they have or will have. Sealed with the great seal of the Holy One. *It is sealed on thy divorce.* The Holy One, YH, holy is He, Hosts is His name, *YHYHYHYH,* I am that I am, awful and holy, Amen, (10) amen, amen, selah. *TL' KBL' TL'* in them *TL'.* "Even as the mountains encircle Jerusalem, so the Lord encircles his people, from henceforth and forever." "Beloved, cherished art thou (?), O Israel. Thy amulet (?)—also (?) I shall bring thee up into the ark. Meat with ? I shall feed thee, and wine (11) with ? I shall make thee drink." Again (?) salvation from the heavens for this Mazdewai, the daughter of I.S. Healed? in the name of the L(ord). I adjure thee, O Lilith Ḥablas the granddaughter of Lilith Zarnai, who smitest and strikest and killest—I adjure thee (that thou be smitten) in the membrane of thy heart with the lance of Qatros, the mighty. *Lo I have written (a divorce) for thee, lo I have dismissed thee as the demons write and serve divorces upon their wives and again they do not return to them. Now take thy divorce and receive thine adjuration and fly* (12) and flee and get out of the house, out of the yard, out of the threshold, out of the four (walls), (out of) the midst of the house, out of the body of Mazdewai, the daughter of I. Amen, amen, selah.

Gordon compares this text with Layard Bowl No. 1, Montgomery Nos. 11, 18 and with text No. 5 in M. Lidzbarski, "Mandäische Zaubertexte," *Ephemeris für semitische Epigraphik,* ɪ (1902), pp. 102 f. (=Yamauchi No. 21, quoted above).

(d) *GYṬ'* occurs in a bill of divorce for demons on a bowl from the Iraq Museum No. 9737 published by Gordon, "An Aramaic Incantation," *AASOR,* 14 (1934), pp.411 f., lines 5–7:

Lo I have written [a divorce] (6) for thee and lo I have expelled thee, as the demons write divorce[s] to their wives and again they do not return. Take (7) thy divorce and receive thine oath and flee and take flight . . .

(e) In a bowl in the Jewish Theological Seminary, No. 950 in Gordon, "Aramaic and Mandaic Magical Bowls," *ArOr,* 9 (1937), p. 87, line 5, the demons are given a "bill of divorcement."

This, to my knowledge, exhausts the explicit references to divorce of demons in Aramaic materials outside Montgomery.

A SEQUENCE OF POTTERY
FROM PETRA

Peter J. Parr

Introduction

NO ASPECT of the ancient Near East has occupied the attention of Professor Nelson Glueck more than has the civilization of the Nabataeans, and no single scholar has contributed more to our knowledge and true understanding of that civilization than has he. With the beginning of his archaeological exploration of Transjordan in 1932, a new and totally unexpected chapter opened in the history of Nabataean studies. During the immediately preceding years a number of books on Nabataean history and culture had appeared, from the pens of Kennedy,[1] Kammerer[2] and Cantineau,[3] and these had seemingly told the story once and for all. These works of synthesis were the culmination of two and a half decades of extensive exploration by scholars of the highest caliber, to say nothing of courage, such as Brünnow and Domaszewski, Butler, Jaussen and Savignac, Bachmann, Wiegand and Dalman. The amount of architectural and epigraphic data recovered and recorded by them from the Hauran, Transjordan, and the Hejaz was so immense that the confidence displayed by the synthetists is readily understood. Kammerer's book, in particular, seemed definitive. Its picture of the Nabataeans as entirely and perpetually nomadic, eschewing industry and agriculture, applying themselves solely to trading across the desert, and employing what artistic talents they had only on the carving of rupestrian funerary monuments at a few religious centers, was convincing enough, since it fitted the observed facts, even though it contradicted the testimony of one of the best ancient authorities on Nabataea, Strabo. Today Kammerer's account is judged to be largely inaccurate, but its readers in 1930 can hardly be blamed for having failed to recognize its uneven and unsatisfactory nature, when it was based on so solid and so learned a foundation of fieldwork. Forty years later, it is easy to see how uneven and unsatisfactory that fieldwork itself really was, despite the great contributions it made to the study of certain aspects of Nabataean civilization; but, if it is so easy, this is only because our eyes have been opened by Nelson Glueck.

The fact that within a few years of its publication Kammerer's book was already obsolete was almost entirely due to Glueck's own researches. Before long his discoveries in Transjordan had shown that the Nabataeans were, for the most significant part of their history, as much an urban and peasant people as a nomadic tribe. Settlement after settlement belonging to them was plotted on the archaeological map, and the agricultural basis of their civilization at its peak was revealed. When Glueck's explorations were extended in later years to the Negev, the evidence became even more clear. The achievements of the Nabataeans were seen to amount to far more than the commercial successes of energetic traders; they were the achievements of a settled and sophisticated community, practicing the science of irrigation farming, building towns, temples and fortresses throughout their lands, and as skilled in the civilized arts and crafts as any of their Levantine neighbors. In short, Glueck's work resulted in an almost entire reversal of the traditional picture, and added to the appreciation of Nabataean culture all those dimensions which the work of his predecessors had so conspicuously lacked.[4]

The secret of Glueck's successful investigations was, of course, the use he made of the relatively new technique of sherd identification; the key he employed to unlock the door of Nabataean history was their distinctive painted pottery. This pottery had first been identified by the Horsfields at Petra in 1929,[5] but it was Glueck who most energetically and productively applied the new knowledge to Nabataean research, and by so doing opened the new chapter of which we have spoken. It might almost be said that for the next thirty years or so pottery was to occupy the rôle in Nabataean studies that architecture and texts had occupied in the preceding thirty. At a time when Glueck was finding Nabataean ware on hundreds of sites in Transjordan, first the Horsfields and then Margaret Murray were excavating it in quantity at Petra, while Colt and Baly at Sbaita and Glueck himself at Tannur were adding to the haul. The process has continued until the present time; as a result of American expeditions to Dhiban, of Israeli activities in the Negev, and of renewed Jordanian and British work at Petra, there is today an enormous body of Nabataean material available for study. There was, however, one important respect in which the excavators of Nabataean pottery differed from their predecessors, the explorers of Nabataean architecture. Whereas Brünnow and Domaszewski, Jaussen and Savignac, Bachmann, and the rest, did not hesitate immediately to publish analytical, typological and chronological studies of the monuments, not one of the excavators did likewise for the pottery. The reasons for this surprising omission need not be discussed here; it is enough to record that it was not until 1959, exactly thirty years after the Horsfields' first campaign at Petra, that Philip Hammond published the first general study of Nabataean painted pottery.[6] This paper, together with the one which followed it three years later,[7] was a praiseworthy attempt to analyze the forms, decorative motifs, and techniques of the Nabataean ware, but it was (as the author recognized) woefully inadequate on the chronological side, simply because of the complete absence of stratified material on which to base such a study. To all intents and purposes we are in the same position today, another ten years later; for although there is promise of stratified material from Dhiban, Avdat and Petra, none of this is as yet generally available in usable form, while the comprehensive study by Avram Negev, based on the Avdat material and so eagerly awaited, remains unpublished.[8] For the delay in publishing the Petra evidence the present writer is much to blame; and it is in partial, and most inadequate, retribution that he intends to devote the following pages to a preliminary survey of some of that evidence. In view of the dominant rôle played by pottery studies in the work of Professor Glueck, it is hoped that such a survey will not appear inappropriate as a contribution to this birthday *florilegium*.

Excavations at Petra, 1958–64

The establishment of a closely dated sequence of Nabataean and Roman pottery from Petra was, from the first, one of the principal aims of the excavations which began there in 1958 under the auspices of the British School in Jerusalem. Other objectives were to uncover remains of the earliest Nabataean occupation of the site, and to investigate in detail the architectural development of a restricted part of the city.[9] The area where these aims were most successfully achieved was in the center of the city, alongside the paved and colonnaded street which flanks the southern bank of the wadi Musa as it cuts from east to west across the Petra basin. Since the clearance of the street by the Jordanian authorities in 1956–57, the final layout of this part of Petra had been obvious in its outlines.[10] On the northern side of the street, between its colonnade and the wadi, was a range of rooms, part of which was excavated, while on the opposite side the rear wall of the southern colonnade (which was some five meters deep) was pierced at intervals by doorways leading to still unexcavated buildings. (Pl. 42). This wall (called in the following pages the Portico Wall) formed the limit of the 1956–57 clearance, but a further five meters south of it, and running parallel to it, there was visible on the surface the line of another wall (here called Wall K).[11] The 1956 campaign had also shown that at a late period in the history of the area rough walls had been erected within the colonnades, reusing earlier building stones, including drums from the original columns. These are presumably the remains of shops, and they testify to a decline in municipal standards at this time.

Unfortunately, no precise evidence was adduced in the publication of the work for the chronology of the various structures. The latest coins found in the levels overlying the street and colonnades were of the sixth century AD, but two thirds of the total coins were of the fourth century, and Miss Kirkbride's suggestion that the shops were built about this time seems reasonable. That they were not built much before the end of the third century is proved by the discovery of an inscribed statue or altar base, dated to *circa* AD 283, built into one of the walls.[12] As for the street itself, the only pertinent evidence was part of a monumental Greek inscription found in the débris of the southern colonnade, and apparently coming from a free-standing arch flanking the street on that side. The dedication, to Trajan, can be precisely dated to AD 114 and although it is not certain that the building and the street are contemporary, indications observed by Miss Kirkbride pointed this way; it seemed probable to her that the street also should be assigned to the early years of Roman rule in Petra.[13] It was partly on this assumption, and in the hope that the street and its colonnades might effectively seal underlying levels and structures of the independent Nabataean period, that several small areas adjacent to the street were among those chosen for investigation in 1958.

Trench III, the particular area to be discussed in part in the following pages, lay some ninety meters east of the monumental gateway at the western end of the street. Originally restricted to the northern side of the paving, the trench was later extended to the south, so that eventually a complete cross-section was excavated from the wadi on the north to beyond Wall K on the south, with the exception of the area immediately beneath the street itself, where the paving was left intact (Pl. 43). The northern part of the trench was very much complicated by the presence of massive masonry foundations, some of them relatively late, and will not concern us here; the southern part, with which we shall deal, was more straightforward (though not without its problems) and provided a stratigraphic picture which included the street, the Portico Wall and Wall K, as well as earlier structures. In the pages which follow attention will be concentrated upon the sequence of events in this part of Trench III as they are revealed in the main North-South cross-section running south from the paved street (fig. 1).

This includes only a portion of the total evidence from the excavations in this area, and it is to be expected that when all the material is eventually analyzed various modifications will have to be made in the interpretation offered here. That these will be modifications, and not major alterations, can be taken as certain, however, since the stratification with which we are dealing on this occasion was among the most distinct and incontrovertible of any revealed in Petra, and was dug with exceptional care and skill.[14] For this reason it is felt that the present review of the evidence, though not complete or final, is much more than tentative and can be accepted as giving a reliable picture of the structural and ceramic development; it is this alone, in the writer's opinion, which justifies its publication prior to the final report. Our main concern will be with the relative chronology of the structures uncovered, and the evidence will be presented in a series of phases, beginning with the earliest. Representative pottery from certain of these phases, judged to be the most significant groups, will also be published, though it should be noted that this will account for only an infinitesimal proportion of the total pottery recovered, even from this one area of excavation. As for absolute chronology, no attempt will be made at an exhaustive discussion since to do so with only part of the evidence available might be misleading. However, the evidence of the coins found will be included, and some suggestions as to dating will be put forward.[15]

The Sequence

PHASE I

Throughout the entire length of the section under review, the lowest level reached consisted of natural wadi deposits, and there was no trace of the sandstone which forms the dominant element in the geology of Petra. It is thus clear that in early times the width of the wadi Musa was at this point considerably greater than it is at present, the original settlers finding a broad expanse of riverine gravels and clays on which

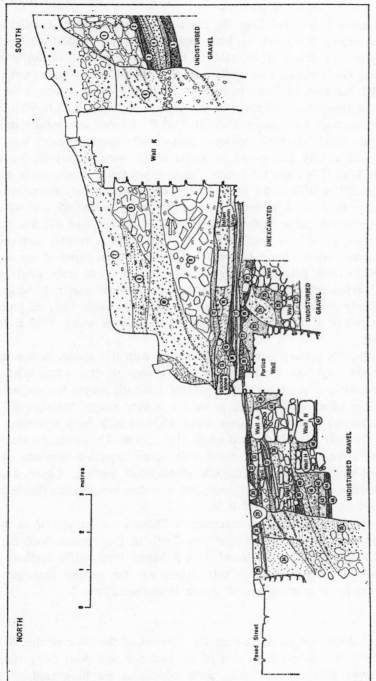

Figure 1. Section of Trench III

they erected their buildings. In the area excavated, these buildings had been largely destroyed by later activity, and no reconstructable plan survives; all that can be said is that they consisted of fairly small rectangular rooms. The walls which survived were quite well preserved, however, in places to a height of about a meter, although the only wall of this phase to appear in the present section (fig. 1), Wall H, is no more than 0.80 meter high. It, and its fellows, are solidly built of medium sized limestone boulders packed with smaller stones and clay, and with a clay facing—all materials which were readily available locally. Wall H is some 0.65 meter thick; other walls of this phase ranged from 0.30 to 0.70 meter in thickness. The contemporary floors are also of clay; they are represented in the section by layers 45 and 47. The original stratification to the south of Wall H, above floor 47, was largely destroyed by a later wall, but north of Wall H a reliable sequence is preserved. Above floor 45 (which has itself been repaired on several occasions with patches of clay) a few centimeters of gray, sandy earth (44) represent the earliest surviving occupational material, while immediately above this a layer of stony and ashy earth (43) is probably the result of a partial destruction of the building of which Wall H forms a part.

Very little pottery was found associated with this phase. A few sherds from the clay floor (45) were of hard orange or gray ware, often with a thin white slip on the outside. Their most distinctive feature was the presence of many fine grits, producing a very rough, "sandpaper" surface. Similar sherds came from layer 43, and it is from this layer also that the only published sherd came (fig. 2, No. 1). Layer 43 also produced a fragment of what could well be an imported amphora of fine orange-buff ware with a smooth creamy-buff surface. Layer 44, the occupation debris, had no sherds; but a bronze coin, which disintegrated upon discovery, was found in it.

It should be noted that structures of Phase I do not appear elsewhere in the area covered by this section. South of the Portico Wall the top of the undisturbed wadi gravel is at a higher level, while further south again, beyond Wall K, it is still higher, and the earliest structures uncovered in these areas are of phases later than Phase I.

PHASE II

This designates no more than the renewal of the floor of the Wall H building. On the northern side of the wall the new floor (42) rests on the layer of stony and ashy earth which, as we have said, is most

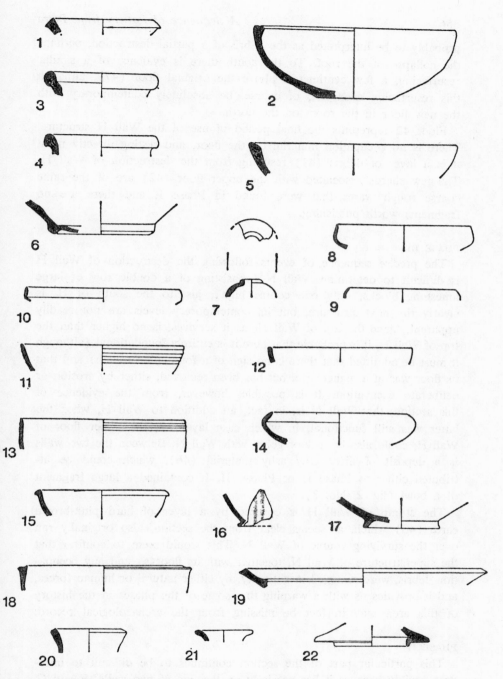

Figure 2. Pottery from Phases I (No. 1), II/III (No. 2), IV (Nos. 3–6),
and V (Nos. 7–22).
(Scale 1:4)

probably to be interpreted as the débris of a partial destruction, perhaps the collapse of the roof. To the south there is evidence of a similar resurfacing, a few centimeters above the original floor (47), although this resurfacing need not, of course, be absolutely contemporary with the new floor in the room on the north.

Floor 42 represents the final period of use of the Wall H structure. There is no occupation material on the floor, and resting directly upon it is a layer of débris (41) resulting from the destruction of Wall H. The few sherds associated with the upper floor (42) are of the same coarse rough wares that were found in Phase I, and there are no fragments worth publishing.

PHASE III

The precise sequence of events following the destruction of Wall H is difficult to determine. Wall N (consisting of a double row of large limestone blocks, only one course high), just to the south of H, is clearly the next structure, but its contemporary levels are not readily apparent. Since the top of Wall N, as it survives, is no higher than the top of Wall H, it is probable that here it is entirely foundational (although it must be admitted that there is no sign of a foundation trench) and that its floor was at a higher level but has been removed, either by erosion or deliberate excavation. It is possible, however, from the evidence of this section, that Wall N is, in fact, an addition to Wall H, when the latter was still functional, in which case layer 42, the upper floor of Wall H, could also be a floor going with Wall N. Between the two walls is a deposit of dirty gray ashy material (46), which could be attributed either to Phase II or Phase III. It contained a large fragment of a bowl (fig. 2, No. 2).

The stump of Wall H is covered by a layer of hard pink-brown earth (40) which, as seems clear from the section, also originally ran over the surviving course of Wall N. This would seem to confirm that the superstructure of Wall N, together with its floor(s) and any occupation debris, were removed in antiquity, by either natural or human forces, and it provides us with a warning that some of the phases in the history of this area may in fact be missing from the archaeological record.

PHASE IV

This particular part of the section continues to be difficult to interpret, mainly because it lies precisely on the line of two walls, E and C, which obscure the sequence of occupation levels. The earlier of the walls, E, was noted at the time of excavation as being bonded with another wall, A, which overlies Wall N and is on the same axis. Although this bonding is not seen on the section, where the relevant spot (below the number 38) is an undifferentiated deposit of loose sand and stones (perhaps a disturbance in Wall E), it seems best to accept that Walls E and A are contemporary. If this is so, there is a phase (Phase IV) earlier than their construction, represented by a series of thin gray occupation levels alternating with harder layers and floor surfaces, which appear in this section only as a small pocket (39) beneath Wall E, but which are well preserved elsewhere. These levels produced a fair amount of pottery (fig. 2, Nos. 3–6), mostly fairly coarse and gritty, though well fired and hard.

PHASE V

Wall A is the major feature of this phase, and is part of a complex of rooms revealed throughout the area excavated. Approximately 0.85 meter wide, it is constructed of irregularly shaped limestone boulders, packed with smaller stones and clay; its faces are finished with a clay rendering. It thus follows the same tradition of building established in Phase I, and differs from Wall H only by reason of its greater thickness. It is significant that the only sandstone block found in Wall A belongs to a later repair associated with other sandstone walls (see below). The builders at Petra are thus still in this phase dependent upon locally available materials, and there is no suggestion of the quarrying of sandstone blocks. Wall E is, as has been said, most probably contemporary with Wall A, and is also of limestone, though the boulders are smaller and the construction apparently less robust. South of Wall A, and clearly bonded with it, another wall, D (not visible in the section) forms a right-angled return, and in the corner so formed there is preserved a small area of limestone paving (in the section, the horizontal stone below layer 48). The immediate continuation of this paving and of Wall D to the south is destroyed by the foundation trench of the Portico Wall, but south of this again similar structures appear (Walls Q and R) which, by reason of their absolute level and orientation can certainly be taken as part of the same phase of construction. These, it should be noted, are the earliest structures surviving south of the Portico Wall. (The area excavated here, however, was very small and was largely taken up with these walls; the stratification is therefore not too clear and cannot be altogether relied upon.)

There was very little pottery clearly associated with the actual construction of the buildings of this phase, and this was of the hard gritty wares found in Phase IV, but a large amount was recovered from a long series of layers of gray occupational débris, gravelly and sandy deposits, and floor surfaces (one of which had the disintegrated remains of a stone paving) in use with Walls A and E, although not appearing on the main section. This pottery (figs. 2–3, Nos. 7–25) looks reasonably homogeneous, although since the deposits here were very soft and friable, especially near the walls themselves (where a few disturbances and stratigraphic discontinuities may well be the result of minor seismic movements) the possibility of intrusions from later phases cannot be ruled out. Side by side with the gritty wares, this pottery included, for the first time, fine wares (e.g. fig. 2, Nos. 10–12), and one fragment of a bowl with linear painted decoration (fig. 2, No. 16).

A *terminus post quem* for the construction of the buildings of this phase is provided by a coin of Aretas II (*circa* 100 BC) found in a layer immediately underlying the paving in the corner of Walls A and D. A comparable coin, as well as a much earlier one (minted at Aradus in the third century BC) came from the occupation layers referred to.

PHASE VI

According to the main north-south section, Wall E seems to have gone out of use, and its remains are buried beneath a succession of occupation surfaces and débris (37). Elsewhere in the same area, however, the layers of the next phase, VII, lie immediately above those of the preceding phase, V, and it is possible that the main section is here deceptive; if Wall E is not absolutely vertical, layer 37 could still be the upper part of the occupation material contemporary with it, and in which case it should be assigned to Phase V. The pottery from Phase VI seems very similar to that from V, although there is much more Nabataean painted ware present (fig. 3, Nos. 26–34; and Plate 44, Nos. 4, 9, and 11). One small fragment of a black-glazed vessel, with a thin glaze on an orange-red body, also came from a layer of this phase.

PHASE VII

Walls A and (presumably) Q and R remain in use, but minor alterations are effected. Wall A itself is thickened by the addition of a single line of small regularly dressed sandstone blocks along its northern face (Wall B, not visible in the section), while another wall, C, more roughly built of sandstone, runs at right angles to this, exactly on the line of the earlier Wall E. These are the earliest sandstone structures

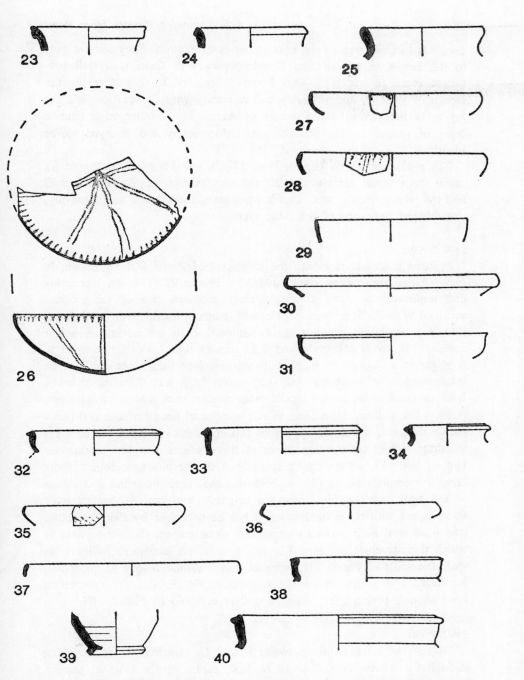

Figure 3. Pottery from Phases V (Nos. 23–25), V/VI (No. 26), VI (Nos. 27–34), and VII (Nos. 35–40).
(Scale 1:4)

uncovered in this part of the area under consideration. They survive only
to the height of one course. Contemporary with them is a well preserved stone paving. (Pl. 43). From a layer of earth just below the
stones of Wall B, and probably contemporary with its erection and the
laying of the paving, came a coin of Aretas II. Another coin, from a
layer of gravel on the paving, was unfortunately too decayed to be
identified.

The published sherds (fig. 3, Nos. 35–40, and Pl. 44, Nos. 2 and 8)
come from levels associated with the construction of Walls B and C
and the paving. A few other sherds from occupation débris on the paving,
unpublished here, are of the same types.

PHASE VIIA

Perhaps contemporary with the structures of Phase VII (although, in
view of the uncertainty, designated here Phase VIIa) is an interesting
and important structure at the extreme southern end of the section,
south of Wall K. This consists of a wall, running north-south (and therefore not appearing on the main section), built of sandstone ashlar
masonry; it is one course (about 0.35 meter) thick, and is preserved to
a height of 1.50 meters. Against its western face runs what can best be
interpreted as a water conduit, 0.55 meter high and 0.30 meter wide,
built of smaller sandstone blocks, with a slab roof and a paved floor.
Against the wall on the eastern side is a series of floor surfaces and occupation deposits, which do appear in the main section (layers 2 and 3);
standing upright on the uppermost of these was a complete storage jar
(fig. 4, No. 41), while many fragments of similar jars were found in the
layer immediately above (1), representing the débris from the destruction
of the wall and conduit. Since the original stratigraphic connection of
these layers with those further south has been broken by the foundation
trench of Wall K, it is clearly impossible to be certain about the phase to
which this structure belongs. The fact that it is a sandstone building, as
were the walls of Phase VII, suggests that it should belong at this point,
however. The pottery from the occupation débris and the destruction
level should, perhaps, be more accurately assigned to Phase VIII.

PHASE VIII

Wall A, with its additional walls B and C, remained in service long
enough for a new clay floor to be laid, replacing the original paving.
No pottery was associated with this re-flooring. Resting immediately
upon the clay floor, a thin deposit of fallen stones and sand represented

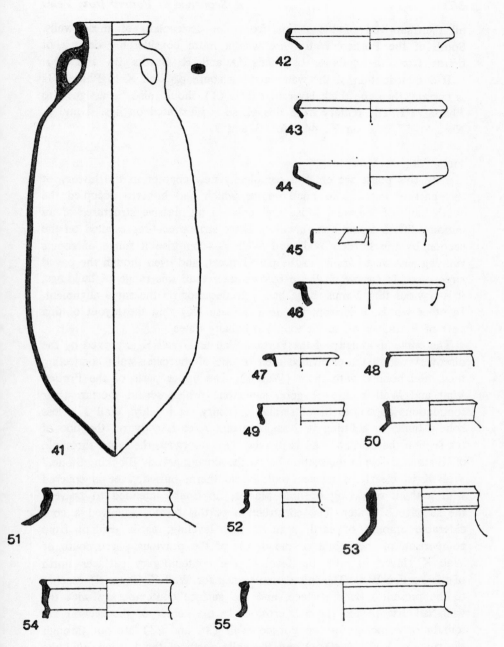

Figure 4. Pottery from Phase VIII.
(Scale 1:4; No. 41 Scale 1:8)

all that survived of the débris from the destruction of these walls. South of the Portico Wall there was a more considerable deposit of débris from the collapse of Walls Q and R (layers 24 and 25).

If our attribution of the water conduit south of Wall K to Phase VII is correct, then the thick layer of debris (1) should also be assigned to Phase VIII. The pottery from this phase is illustrated on figs. 4 and 5, Nos. 41–57, and on Pl. 44, Nos. 3 and 7.

PHASE IX

With this phase we enter a completely new chapter in the history of this part of Petra. The small houses which had hitherto occupied the south bank of the wadi Musa are replaced by massive structures of an entirely different plan and function. These structures—represented on the section by the Portico Wall and Wall K—comprise a range of rooms running east-west parallel to the paved street, and even though the paved street itself is (as we shall see below) later than this range of buildings, it is obvious that it must have had a predecessor on the same alignment. In other words, it is from this time (Phase IX) that the layout of this part of Petra, as we see it today, originally dates.

The contemporaneity of the Portico Wall and Wall K is proved by the discovery within the excavated area of one of the cross-walls connecting them and bonded with them (Wall J). The upper parts of the Portico Wall and Wall K are of good sandstone ashlar set in mortar; their foundations appear to be of smaller masonry set in clay. Wall J is less solidly built, as befitting its less important rôle. Exactly on the line of the section the Portico Wall is pierced by a doorway, the worn threshold of which is visible in the section below the stone marked "Blocking Stone." Wall K is, clearly, a terrace wall; its southern, buried, face is covered with a thick rendering of lime plaster, no doubt intended to prevent the seepage of water. The construction of this terrace involved a considerable amount of earth removal and leveling, as is evident from comparison of the height of the débris of the previous phase south of Wall K (layer 1) with the level of the contemporary surfaces north of the Portico Wall. The foundation trench for Wall K (layer 6) reaches to the present ground surface, and the surface contemporary with the wall had disappeared through erosion. In the center of the section the foundation trenches for the Portico Wall (36 and 23) are cut through the ruins of Walls A, D, Q and R, while north of the Portico Wall the foundation trench is sealed by a layer of hard stony material (33) which seems to be a packing beneath the floor surfaces going with the

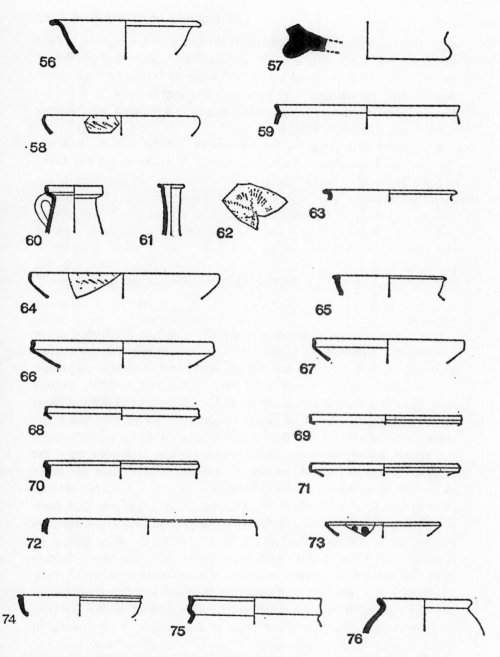

Figure 5. Pottery from Phases VIII (Nos. 56–57), IX (Nos. 58–63), X (Nos. 64–65), and XI (Nos. 66–76). (Scale 1:4)

wall. This same packing level also seals the filling of a deep trench (35) at the extreme northern end of the section. This trench runs parallel to, and beneath, the later paved street, and while its satisfactory interpretation involves the discussion of evidence additional to what is presented here, it might tentatively be suggested that it is associated with another terrace wall, similar to Wall K.

A *terminus post quem* for the construction of the Portico Wall and its associates is provided by a coin of Aretas IV (8 BC to AD 40) found in layer 33; another coin of the same date was found in the filling of the deep trench, layer 35. In the deposits associated with this building activity, especially in the foundation trenches, a great quantity of pottery was found. Theoretically this need not constitute a homogeneous group, and until more detailed studies are made only a small selection is published here (fig. 5, Nos. 58–63 and Pl. 44, Nos. 5 and 10. On this plate, Nos. 1 and 12 are also most probably of this phase).

PHASE X

It is not at all easy to specify which layers if any in the section under consideration represent the original floor surfaces in use with the Portico Wall and Wall K. North of the Portico Wall a series of layers (31 and 32), comprising surfaces and occupation débris, run over the packing layer (33) and the foundation trench (36). The correct phasing of these is, however, made difficult by two facts: first, they were very much disturbed by later pits, so that their actual excavation was complicated and not always entirely accurate; and, second, since it is known from the previous excavations of Miss Kirkbride (above, p. 351) that the floors of the Byzantine rooms in the colonnade were only a little higher than the absolute level with which we are dealing, it is obvious that there is here a great compression of the archaeological deposits. It cannot by any means be assumed that all of the stages in the long history of occupation of this part of Petra between the construction of the Portico Wall and that of the Byzantine shops are represented in the section, and there is the very real possibility that continual and intensive occupation has resulted in the removal from time to time of earlier deposits; in other words, that there has been a denudation of archaeological layers rather than an accumulation. (This is particularly likely as a site such as Petra, where all of the layers are basically of sand, and hence soft and easily eroded). In short, it is impossible to say, from the stratigraphic evidence, whether the layers marked 31 and 32 on the section date from the earliest or from a later period of utilization of the Portico Wall.

The situation south of the Portico Wall, within the room bounded by this wall and Wall K, is similar, though here there is a little positive evidence for the denudation process just described. Immediately above the foundation trench (23), a remnant of occupation débris on a floor surface (22) may represent the original utilization of the room. It is cut to north and south by pits (18 and 19), which themselves contain stratified layers suggesting, perhaps, the repairing and patching of sub-sidences and similar damage to the original floors. This phase of disturb-ances is followed by a series of horizontal layers (17) running up to the footings of Wall K and to the threshold of the doorway in the Portico Wall, near which, however, they have been partly worn away by use. The fact that these horizontal surfaces run to what are clearly the footings of Wall K might lead one to suppose that they are the original occupation surfaces with this wall. The other evidence just cited, however, and the probability which has been mentioned of the denudation of layers and the consequent lowering in absolute level, suggests to the present writer that this is not the case. It is postulated, therefore, that the sequence of phases following the construction of the Portico Wall and Wall K is as follows:

PHASE X: earliest *surviving* occupation (layer 22)

PHASE XI: Disturbances, subsidences, repairs (18, 19, 21)

PHASE XII: later floors and occupation (17)

To which of these phases the layers north of the Portico Wall (31 and 32) should be assigned is uncertain; probably to more than one. It is much to be regretted that there is no stratigraphic record of the work carried out in this area in 1956; a section through the Byzantine shops and the immediately preceding levels would probably have clinched the inter-pretation of this all-important stage in the history of the architectural development of Petra. In its absence we have no way of correlating the stratigraphy north of the Portico Wall with that to the south, except by comparison of the pottery, and this cannot usefully be attempted until all the evidence from the total area of excavation has been analyzed. For the time being, therefore, we must be content with the general equation of layers 31 and 32 with Phases X–XIII. Three identifiable coins came from these layers; two were of the reign of Aretas IV (8 BC to AD 40) and the other was of that of Rabbel II and Gamilath (*circa* AD 76–106).

The pottery from these three phases is illustrated on figs. 5–7, Nos. 64–105; Pl. 44, No. 6; and Pl. 45, Nos. 3–7.

PHASE XIII

Layers 31–32 are cut by the upper part of the trench dug for the foundations of the paved street (layer 28), which must therefore be attributed to a later phase than the Portico Wall. In view of the uncertainties, already explained, in the correlation of the stratigraphy north of the Portico Wall with that to the south, it is impossible to establish the precise relative chronology of the street in terms of our present sequence of phases. Phase XIII—the construction of the street—need not necessarily be as late as the Phase XII utilization of the room behind the Portico Wall, and in fact a preliminary study of the pottery from layer 28 (fig. 7, Nos. 106–10 and Pl. 45, Nos. 1–2) suggests that it might more reasonably be equated with Phase XI.

PHASE XIV

With the possible exception of a few pits, the paved street is the latest feature represented on the section north of the Portico Wall, and for the rest of our sequence we are restricted to the area of the room between the Portico Wall and Wall K. Here, another series of floors and occupation material (layers 16 and 15) succeeds the Phase XII occupation, and with these new floors is associated additional building activity, including the erection of stone benches along some of the walls of the room. These do not appear in the section, and only a small remnant of the surfaces going with them are in fact preserved there.

PHASE XV

The room now seems to have gone out of use, layers 16 and 15 representing the latest surviving occupation. Resting immediately upon them is a layer of destruction débris (14), which includes some large ashlar blocks and a broken column drum.

PHASES XVI–XVIII

This fallen débris must eventually have begun to spill out through the doorway in the Portico Wall onto the colonnade, and to have proved an inconvenience, for the doorway was blocked. This presumably happened

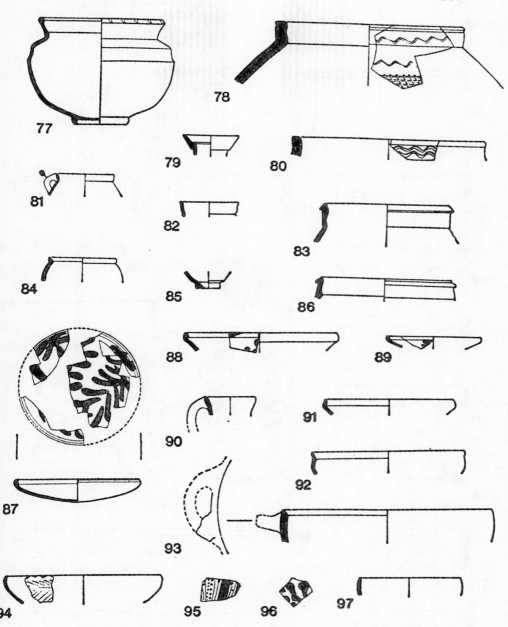

Figure 6. Pottery from Phases XI (Nos. 77–86), XII (Nos. 87–93), and X/XII (Nos. 94–97). (Scale 1:4)

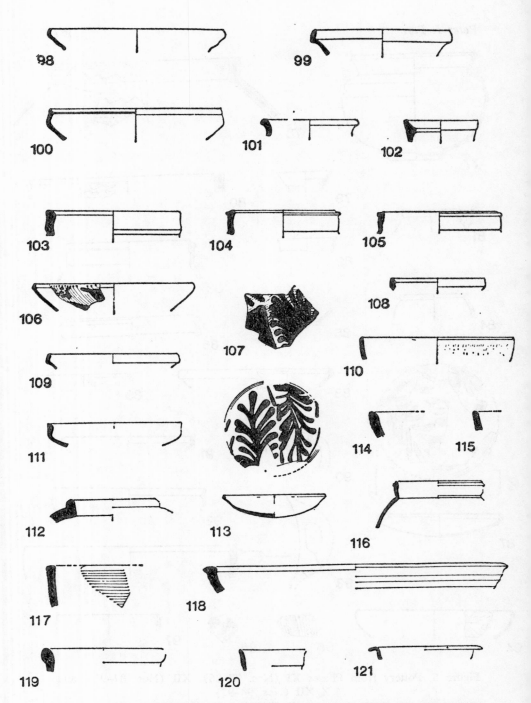

Figure 7. Pottery from Phases X/XII (Nos. 98–105), XIII (Nos. 106–10), XIV (Nos. 111–15), and XV (Nos. 116–21).
(Scale 1:4)

at a time when the colonnade was occupied by the small shops excavated in 1956, although the precise chronology cannot, of course, be determined. Although only one course of the blocking remains, it is perhaps reasonable to suppose that it originally reached to the full height of the doorway. If this is so, then it must have collapsed and been removed before the deposition of the next layer (12), which is an accumulation of clean water-laid silt representing a phase (Phase XVII) when the site was abandoned and neglected. This silt runs over the surviving stone of the blocking in the doorway and presumably, therefore, over the Byzantine shops; these latter, then, must also have been deserted by this time. The silt contained a coin of Constantinus II (AD 337–400). Finally, a thick layer of stone débris and rubble (11) indicates the first of several stages in the history of the collapse of Wall K, and with this phase (Phase XVIII) we may bring our sequence to a close.

Summary and Conclusions

If, in the foregoing pages, the writer has devoted most of his words to a discussion not of pottery but of stratigraphy, it is because he is convinced that the primary duty of an excavator lies in the presentation, as fully and as honestly as possible, of that stratigraphic evidence upon which all else depends. The illustrations of the pottery can be left, for the time being, to speak for themselves, although one or two general remarks may be made. Before doing so, however, we must stress that although the interpretation of the section we have been considering is by no means devoid of problems, the picture which emerges from the discussion is, in outline at least, clearcut and acceptable. Three main stages can be discerned in the architectural development of this part of Petra: an initial stage of small buildings of unpretentious design and construction (Phases I–VIII); a second stage, of monumental structures belonging to an ambitious civic plan (Phase IX); and a third stage, when the paved street was constructed, perhaps superseding an earlier thoroughfare (Phase XIII). A final stage of degeneration and abandonment may be added (Phases XIV–XVIII).

As for chronology, the earliest coins found throughout the area excavated (though not always in secure stratigraphic contexts) are of a type minted in Aradus in the mid-third century BC, and this suggests that the earliest building activity in this central part of Petra is to be dated to somewhere about, or perhaps a little later than, that time. The presence of fragments of imported amphorae as early as Phase I (page 354, above) would prove that this phase was indeed not much earlier than the third century. The other pottery from the earliest phases is coarse and undistinguished, and it is not until Phase V that the first examples of fine bowls and, most important, a fragment of a vessel with painted decoration (fig. 2, No. 16), appear. This ceramic development would seem to date to somewhere after about 100 BC, since a coin of Aretas II antedates the construction of the Phase V buildings (page 358, above). From then on painted Nabataean ware is common. Initially the decoration is of a flowing, naturalistic style, executed in bright orange or light red paint, with a delicate brush technique (cf. Pl. 44). This style lasts until at least Phase IX, when the Portico Wall and Wall K were built, at a date which, judging from the coin evidence (page 364, above), must have been later than the beginning of the reign of Aretas IV in 8 BC. The first clear evidence for the existence of another style of painting, heavier and more formal, in a solid purplish-red pigment (Pl. 45, Nos. 1–5), occurs in Phase XI, although there are many examples of this type of decoration in the layers north of the Portico Wall which we cannot assign more closely than to Phases X–XII (page 365, above). The coins from these same layers suggest that they span the greater part of the first century AD, and the construction of the paved street, assigned to Phase XIII, is clearly later than *circa* AD 76, when Rabbel II and Gamilath began to reign. It is to be regretted that a closer date for this important stage in the history of Petra is not deducible from the evidence so far reviewed.

As for the later phases, the previous removal of the shops which came to occupy the colonnade seriously impairs our understanding of the sequence of events, as we have already mentioned. The almost complete painted bowl, fig. 7, No. 113, comes from Phase XIV, but there is no way of dating this, except from the pottery itself. That it precedes the blocking of the doorway through the Portico Wall (Phase XVI) is clear, and that this blocking is to some degree contemporary with the late shops has been postulated (page 369, above); but it is unsafe to go beyond this. Painted sherds continue to occur in the latest phases, and some of them are of a type which appears debased and remote from the true Nabataean painted styles (e.g. fig. 8, No. 124); but these upper phases are represented only by layers of débris and silt, and the pottery from them cannot be considered necessarily homogeneous. For the time being, the later history of the development of Nabataean painted pottery remains obscure.

Also obscure, for the time being, is the history of other significant

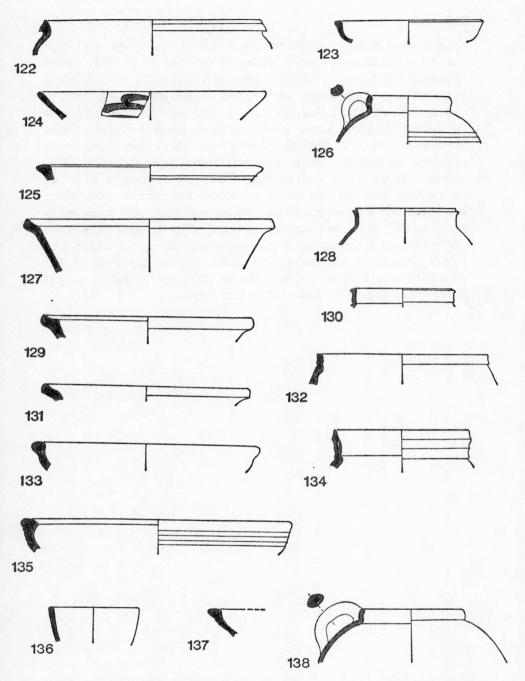

Figure 8. Pottery from Phases XVI (No. 122), XVII (Nos. 123–27), and XVIII (Nos. 128–38).
(Scale 1:4)

ceramic types from Petra, particularly lamps, *terra sigillata*, and lead-glazed ware. Although a great number of examples of all these classes of pottery was found in the excavations as a whole, the few specimens published here (the lamps from Phases X–XII on Pl. 45, Nos. 6 and 7; the lead-glazed base from Phase VIII on fig. 5, No. 57; and the sigillata bowl from Phases X–XII on fig. 6, No. 97) cannot be used as evidence either to date the phases from which they come or to illuminate the problems surrounding these pottery types themselves. This is indeed disappointing, and we must await an exhaustive study of all the evidence from the excavations to retrieve the situation. Meanwhile, it is hoped that the selection of the evidence which has been presented in the preceding pages will already have helped to bring a little more clarity into our understanding of pottery typology during the centuries of Petra's existence, and in particular to have advanced the study of that remarkable and beautiful painted ceramic which has figured so largely in the archaeological researches of Nelson Glueck.

FOOTNOTES

1. Sir Alexander Kennedy, *Petra, Its History and Monuments* (1925).

2. A. Kammerer, *Pétra et la Nabatène*, 2 vols. (1929–30).

3. J. Cantineau, *Le nabatéen*, 2 vols. (1930–32).

4. For the most recent statement of Glueck's reconstruction of Nabataean civilization, see his *Deities and Dolphins* (1965). The relevant chapters in *The Other Side of the Jordan* (1940) and *Rivers in the Desert* (1959) are also still extremely valuable.

5. G. Horsfield and A. Conway, "Historical and Topographical Notes on Edom," *Geographical Journal*, 66 (1930), pp. 375, 386.

6. P. C. Hammond, Jr., "Pattern Families in Nabataean Painted Ware," *AJA*, 63 (1959), pp. 371–82.

7. "A Classification of Nabataean Fine Ware," *AJA*, 66 (1962), pp. 169–180.

8. Since these words were written, a short study of Nabataean pottery has been published by Karl Schmitt-Korte in *Archäologischer Anzeiger* (1968), pp. 496–519. Interesting though this is, it is still almost entirely a typological study and adds nothing to our knowledge of the chronology.

9. Cf. P. J. Parr, "Excavations at Petra, 1958–59," *PEQ*, 92 (1960), pp. 125–26.

10. This Jordanian work was directed by Miss Diana Kirkbride. Cf. *ADAJ*, 4–5 (1960), pp. 117–22.

11. Both these walls had been traced along a part of their course by the German expedition of 1916 and are shown on its plan as part of the Large Temple and the adjacent Lower Market. Cf. W. Bachmann *et al.*, *Petra* (1921), Pl. I.

12. Cf. D. Kirkbride, *ADAJ*, 4–5 (1960), p. 119.

13. *Ibid.*, pp. 119–20. Apart from this reference, this inscription, the most complete and important of its kind yet found in Petra, has most unfortunately not yet been published. It should be remarked that the Abbé Jean Starcky does not accept this evidence for a Roman date for the colonnaded street, and has argued that it belongs to the time of the independent Nabataean kingdom (cf. *SDB*, 7 [1964], col. 948).

14. This exacting task was carried out very largely by Miss Kay Wright (now Mrs. John Prag), without whose expertise this study could not have been written, and to whom I am consequently greatly indebted. Many other people naturally helped to make the work at Petra possible, but full acknowledgment of their contributions must await the final report.

15. For the identification of these coins, and of the many hundreds found elsewhere during the excavations, I am much indebted to Fr. Aug. Spijkerman, O.F.M., of the Studium Biblicum Franciscarum in Jerusalem. If the present study has any value, it is entirely because of the learned and amiable assistance he has unstintingly afforded me.

DESCRIPTION OF POTTERY ON FIGURES 2–8

Phase	No.	Description	Excavation Registration No.
PHASE I	1	Hard yellow-buff ware, slightly paler core. Very few grits. Traces of white wash on surfaces.	107.127: 1
PHASE II OR III	2	Hard orange ware, with some small grits. Brown wash on outside of vessel.	107.149: 1
PHASE IV	3	Orange ware, light gray core. Fine dark grits.	107.112: 1
	4	Pink-buff ware, light gray core. Fine grits. Inner surface of vessel very rough; outer surface has buff slip.	107.111: 1
	5	Hard orange ware, with fine grits.	107.102: 1
	6	Hard gray ware. Some medium grits.	107.105: 1
PHASE V	7	Very fine dark gray ware. Hand made.	107. 90: 1
	8	Hard, very fine, thin pink ware.	107. 72: 1
	9	Thin gray ware, fired red near surfaces. Dark gray slip outside.	107. 65: 5
	10	Very fine pink ware. Band of white paint on outside of rim.	107. 73: 1
	11	Hard, fine light gray wave, fired red near surfaces. Red-brown paint over rim.	107. 65: 6
	12	Very fine orange ware, with deeper slip on outside of vessel.	107. 67: 1
	13	Close to No. 6	107. 65: 8
	14	Hard light gray ware, fired red near surfaces. Gritty, and surfaces rough.	107. 65: 9
	15	Gray-brown ware, gritty. Traces of brown slip on inside and outside surfaces.	107. 65:13
	16	Hard, fine orange-brown ware. Outer surface smooth and creamy. Decoration in bright orange paint.	107. 65:11
	17	Gray-buff ware, some grits. Outer surface smoothed.	107. 67: 3
	18	Orange-brown ware, some grits. Brown slip on both surfaces.	107. 65:10
	19	Hard pink ware, some grits. Thick white slip on both inner and outer surfaces.	107. 65: 3

Phase	No.	Description	Excavation Registration No.
PHASE V (CONT'D)	20	Reddish ware, gritty and rough. Surfaces black.	107. 65: 2
	21	Fine orange-brown ware. Darker orange slip inside and outside.	107. 66: 2
	22	Hard dark pink ware, rather sandy. Reddish-brown slip inside and outside.	107. 72: 2
	23	Hard gray ware, fine grits. Surfaces gray.	107. 67: 2
	24	Hard brown-buff ware, gritty.	107. 71: 1
	25	Hard gray-buff ware, gritty. Surfaces rough and uneven.	107. 72: 3
PHASE V/ VI	26	Fine pink ware. Decoration in orange paint.	107.140:(2255)
PHASE VI	27	Very fine orange ware. Pale pink slip outside. Decoration in reddish-orange.	107. 97: 1
	28	Fine dull brown-red ware. Darker red slip outside. Decoration in same color. (cf. Pl. 44, No. 4)	107. 98: 2
	29	Fine, hard orange ware. Darker red slip outside.	107. 96: 6
	30	Very fine light gray ware, fired red near surfaces. Band of white paint outside rim.	107. 95: 3
	31	Light gray ware, fired dull red at surfaces. Very fine grits. Traces of thick white slip outside.	107. 96: 1
	32	Hard pink bricky ware, some small grits. White slip outside.	107. 95: 1
	33	Similar to No. 32.	107.101: 1
	34	Fine red ware, with light gray core. Some grits, giving rough surface. Brown slip outside.	107.101: 1
PHASE VII	35	Fine red ware. Decoration in light purplish-red.	107. 29: 3
	36	Fine gray ware, fired dull brown near surfaces. Band of dark gray slip outside rim.	107. 29: 2
	37	Fine orange ware. Band of white paint over rim outside.	107. 29: 6
	38	Dull orange ware, some fine grits giving a rough surface. Whitish slip outside.	107. 29: 1
	39	Heavy pink-buff ware with light gray core. Many fine gray grits and mica inclusions. Surfaces smoothed.	107. 60: 2

Phase	No.	Description	Excavation Registration No.
PHASE VII (CONT'D)	40	Heavy brick-red ware, very gritty, with rough surfaces. Creamy slip outside.	107. 29: 4
PHASE VIII	41	(No description available)	111. 6
	42	Dull brown ware with gray core.	109. 44: 2
	43	Light brown ware. Band of white paint over outside of rim.	109. 44: 1
	44	Fine dull orange-red ware with light gray core. Dark gray slip on outside.	107. 26: 4
	45	Fine orange ware. Decoration and band over rim outside.	107. 26: 8
	46	Fine dark gray ware.	109. 44: 3
	47	Fine orange ware. Darker orange slip on outside surface.	107. 26:10
	48	Very fine orange ware, with dark brown slip on outside surface.	107. 26: 5
	49	Reddish ware, with thin light gray core. Darker red slip over inner & outer surfaces.	107. 27: 3
	50	Dull red ware with light gray core. Many fine grits, and surfaces rough. Cream slip outside.	107. 26: 1
	51	Bright orange-red ware, a few grits. Thick creamy-buff slip outside.	111. 6: 2
	52	Dull light red ware, gray near surfaces. Gray-brown slip outside.	111. 6: 5
	53	Bricky red ware with gray core. Gray slip outside.	111. 6: 3
	54	Bright orange-red ware, very fine grits. Deeper brown-red slip inside and outside.	111. 6: 1
	55	Dark gray ware, fired dull red near outer surface. Medium white grits.	111. 6: 6
	56	Soft bright orange ware, flaking. Deeper orange slip inside and outside.	111. 6: 8
	57	Yellow-buff ware. Dark green glaze, inside and outside, very worn and devitrified.	111. 6: 4
PHASE IX	58	Fine orange ware. Band of white paint on outside of rim. Other decoration in orange-red paint.	109. 41: 6
	59	Fine red-brown ware. Orange-red slip outside.	107. 33: 4
	60	Orange-red ware, rather gritty. Whitish slip outside.	109. 45: 7

Phase	No.	Description	Excavation Registration No.
PHASE IX (CONT'D)	61	Very fine dull orange-brown ware. Paler slip outside.	109. 45: 6
	62	Close to No. 58	109. 41: 7
	63	Buff-brown ware, with lighter buff slip on both surfaces.	107. 33: 2
PHASE X	64	Very fine orange-pink ware. Band of light red paint on outside of rim, and decoration inside in same color.	109. 40: 4
	65	Hard, fine bricky red ware. Pale buff slip on both surfaces.	109. 40: 3
PHASE XI	66	Hard dark gray ware, fired red near surfaces. Gritty, with surfaces rough and uneven. Band of whitish paint on rim outside.	109. 29: 1
	67	Very fine orange-red ware. Band of white paint on outside of rim.	109. 28: 3
	68	Fine dull red ware. Band of white paint on outside of rim.	109. 30: 1
	69	Very fine red ware, with traces of darker red slip outside.	109. 29: 7
	70	Orange-brown bricky ware, with fine white grits.	109. 30: 5
	71	Close to No. 68	109. 30: 2
	72	Fine dull orange ware.	109. 28: 4
	73	Red ware, with some very small white grits. Surfaces rough. Decoration in very dark gray-brown paint.	109. 28:15
	74	Dull orange ware with paler core. Gray slip outside.	109. 28: 5
	75	Hard red-brown ware. Fired brighter red near surfaces. Gritty. Fawn slip on both surfaces.	109. 31: 3
	76	Fine pale yellow-buff ware.	109. 29: 5
	77	Fine pink ware. Surfaces burnished.	109. 29: (2282)
	78	Greenish-buff ware with some very fine grits. Surfaces very smooth.	109. 31: 1
	79	Fine red ware. Whitish slip inside and outside.	109. 28:10
	80	Pale greenish-buff ware. Surfaces very smooth.	109. 29: 4
	81	Very fine orange-red ware.	109. 30: 3
	82	Very fine red ware. Buff slip on both surfaces.	109. 28: 9
	83	Dull red ware, some small grits. Gray slip on surfaces.	109. 31: 2

			Excavation
Phase	*No.*	*Description*	*Registration No.*

PHASE XI (CONT'D)

84 Pale buff ware. Fired cream near surfaces. Surfaces smoothed. — 109. 31: 8

85 Dull bricky red ware. — 109. 28:12

86 Orange-red bricky ware. Light buff slip outside. — 109. 29: 2

PHASE XII

87 Very fine metallic pink ware. Decoration in very dark gray paint. — 109. 22:(2276)

88 Fine red ware with thin gray core. Some grits. Decoration in heavy black paint. — 109. 16: 1

89 Fine red ware. Decoration in deep red paint. Light red slip outside. — 109. 27: 4

90 Dull light brown ware, light buff slip on both surfaces. Some grits, with surfaces rough. — 109. 16: 4

91 Gray ware, fired red near surfaces. Gritty. Band of white paint on outside of rim. — 109. 27: 3

92 Very fine medium gray ware. Purplish-brown slip inside, light brown wash outside. Band of gray slip on outside of rim. — 109. 27: 1

93 Dull red ware, gritty. Whitish slip outside. — 109. 16: 5

PHASE X/ XII

94 Fine orange ware. Band of light purplish-red paint on outside of rim, and decoration inside in same color. — 107. 10: 2

95 Fine orange-red ware. Decoration in purple paint. (Cf. Pl. 45, No. 5.) — 107. 3: 9

96 Very fine dark gray ware, fired red near surfaces. Decoration in light red paint. — 107. 3:11

97 *Terra Sigillata.* Pale creamy ware, not micaceous. Dull red glaze. — 107. 3:12

98 Fine orange ware. Band of white paint on outside of rim. — 107. 3: 4

99 Dull pink ware, with a paler core. A few fine grits. Band of white paint on outside of rim. — 107. 11: 4

100 Fine gray ware, fired red at surface. Light brown slip inside and out, except for band of white paint on outside of rim. — 107. 10: 4

Phase	No.	Description	*Excavation* *Registration No.*
PHASE XI/ XII (CONT'D)	101	Orange-brown ware, with some grits. Light gray slip outside, buff slip inside.	107. 3: 7
	102	Orange ware, with some medium and fine grits. Darker orange slip inside and outside.	107. 12: 4
	103	Gray ware, fired brown-red at surface. Gritty. Gray-brown slip on both surfaces.	107. 11: 6
	104	Dull orange ware, with a few very fine grits. Band of white paint on outside of rim.	107. 12: 1
	105	Bright orange ware with some fine grits. Whitish slip outside.	107. 3: 5
PHASE XIII	106	Fine orange ware. Band of white paint just over rim outside. Decoration in heavy purplish-brown paint. (Cf. Pl. 45, No. 2.)	107. 5: 4
	107	Close to No. 106 (Pl. 45, No. 1).	107. 5: 2–3
	108	Light gray ware, with very fine grits.	107. 5a: 1
	109	Orange-brown ware. White painted band on outside of rim.	107. 5a: 3
	110	Fine orange ware. Darker orange slip inside, and thin white slip outside.	107. 5: 1
PHASE XIV	111	Light gray ware, fired red at surfaces. Fine white grits.	109. 14: 3
	112	Thick flaky brown ware, sandy and with fine grits.	109. 14: 1
	113	Dull red ware. Band of white paint on outside of rim; rest of decoration in dark purplish-red.	109. 23:(2251)
	114	Dull red bricky ware, with fine grits. Surfaces dark gray.	109. 14: 4
	115	Close to No. 114.	109. 14: 5
PHASE XV	116	Fine red ware, micaceous, with very fine grits. Outer surface dark gray.	109. 13: 1
	117	Orange-red ware, some medium-sized grits.	109. 13: 9
	118	Heavy dull brown-red ware, with many medium grits and rough surfaces. Whitish slip outside and on top of rim.	109. 13: 3
	119	Light gray-brown ware, fired pink at surface. Gritty. Buff slip outside.	109. 13: 6

Phase	No.	Description	Excavation Registration No.
PHASE XV (CONT'D)	120	Fine black ware, fired red at surfaces. Gray-brown slip outside and inside.	109. 13: 7
	121	Fine pink ware, with a few very fine grits.	109. 13: 2
PHASE XVI	122	Red ware, with many medium and fine grits. Whitish-buff slip inside and outside.	109. 17: 1
PHASE XVII	123	Red ware, with some small grits.	109. 11: 3
	124	Bricky red ware with light gray core. Thick white slip outside. Decoration in black paint.	109. 11: 2
	125	Bricky red ware, with medium grits. Gray slip outside.	109. 10: 1
	126	Fine buff ware.	109. 11: 1
	127	Dark brown-gray ware, fired red at surfaces. Fine white grits. Surfaces have streaky slip of dull red and brown.	109. 12: 2
PHASE XVIII	128	Yellow-buff ware, with fine grits. Gray slip outside.	109. 9:11
	129	Dull brick red ware, with very fine grits. Buff slip outside.	109. 9: 1
	130	Gray ware.	109. 9: 5
	131	Close to No. 129.	109. 9:13
	132	Close to No. 129.	109. 9: 2
	133	Bricky red ware with very thin gray core. Fine white grits. Gray slip inside and outside.	109. 9:10
	134	Yellowish-buff ware with fine grits.	109. 9:11
	135	Close to No. 129.	109. 9:12
	136	Fine gray ware, fired red at surfaces. Buff slip inside and outside.	109. 9:17
	137	Red ware, with paler red slip.	109. 9:14
	138	Brick red ware, medium grits. Gray slip on outside and inside.	109. 9: 6

PHASES OF SHERDS SHOWN IN PL.44

No.	1	Reg. No.	107.22:18	Phase ?IX
	2		107.78: 1	VII
	3		111. 5	VIII
	4		107.92: 2	VI
	5		107.14:10	IX
	6		109.40: 4	X
	7		109.46: 3	VIII
	8		107.76:13	VII
	9		107.96: 4	VI
	10		109.41: 7	IX
	11		107.95: 6	VI
	12		107.22:19	?IX

PHASES OF SHERDS SHOWN ON PL.45

No.	1	Reg. No.	107. 5: 2–3	Phase XIII
	2		107. 5: 4	XIII
	3		107. 6: 6	
	4		107. 6: 5	
	5		107. 3: 9	X–XII
	6		107. 3:13	
	7		107. 3:14	

BIBLIOGRAPHY OF NELSON GLUECK

Compiled by Eleanor K. Vogel

1920 Review of Gotthard Deutsch, *Jew and Gentile,* in *Hebrew Union College Monthly* (Dec. 1920), pp. 5–10

1921 Review of Israel Zangwill, *The Voice of Jerusalem,* in *Hebrew Union College Monthly* (Dec. 1921), pp. 46–51

1927 *Das Wort ḥesed im alttestamentlichen Sprachgebrauche als menschliche Verhaltungsweise in profaner und religiöser Bedeutung,* Thüringischen Landesuniversität, Jena (1927), pp. 1–36
Das Wort ḥesed im alttestamentlichen Sprachgebrauche als menschliche und göttliche gemeinschaftgemässe Verhaltungsweise, ZAW, 47 (1927) pp. 1–68

1929 "Recent Archaeological Work in Palestine," *Central Conference of American Rabbis Yearbook,* xxxix (1929), pp. 265–92

1930 "Buried Treasures in Palestine," *Asia,* 30 (1930), pp. 690–97

1932 Review of W. F. Albright, *The Archaeology of Palestine and the Bible,* in *The Jewish Quarterly Review,* 24 (1932), pp. 233–35

1933 "The Archaeological Exploration of el-Ḥammeh on the Yarmuk," *BASOR,* No. 49 (1933), pp. 22–23
"Palestinian and Syrian Archaeology in 1932," *AJA,* 37 (1933), pp. 160–72
"From Dr. Glueck's Report on his Explorations in Eastern Palestine," *BASOR,* No. 50 (1933), pp. 8–11
"Stone Age Carvings in Transjordan," *The New York Times* (May 28, 1933), sec. 9, p. 8
"A Note to Genesis 4:11," *JPOS,* 13 (1933), pp. 101–2
"Further Explorations in Eastern Palestine," *BASOR,* No. 51 (1933), pp. 9–19
"Prehistoric Rock-Drawings in Transjordan" (with George and Agnes Horsfield), *AJA,* 37 (1933), pp. 381–86
"Report of the Director of the School in Jerusalem," *BASOR,* No. 52 (1933), pp. 28–35
"Recent Excavations of Jewish Interest in Palestine," *Judaean Addresses,* IV (New York: Bloch, 1933), pp. 212–25

1934 *Explorations in Eastern Palestine, I* (*Annual of the American Schools of Oriental Research*, xiv [1934]), pp. 1–113
"Jerash in the Spring of 1933," *BASOR*, No. 53 (1934), pp. 2–13
"The Civilization of the Moabites," *AJA*, 38 (1934), pp. 212–18
"King Solomon's Copper Mines," *ILN* (July 7, 1934), pp. 26, 36
"Explorations in Eastern Palestine and the Negeb," *BASOR*, No. 55 (1934), pp. 3–21
"Exploration of Edom and Moab," *Hebrew Assn. for the Exploration of Eretz Israel and Its Antiquities*, 2 (1934), pp. 33–38 (Hebrew)

1935 *Explorations in Eastern Palestine, II* (*Annual of the American Schools of Oriental Research*, xv), 1935
"Tell el-Hammeh," *AJA*, 39 (1935), pp. 321–30

1936 "Solomon's Copper Mines," *Ha-Meassef Chorev* (March 3, 1936), pp. 107–8 (Hebrew)
"The Boundaries of Edom," *Hebrew Union College Annual*, xi (1936), pp. 141–57
"Christian Kilwa," *JPOS*, 16 (1936), pp. 9–16
"The Recently Discovered Ore Deposits in Eastern Palestine," *BASOR*, No. 63 (1936), pp. 4–6
"The Theophany of the God of Sinai," *JAOS*, 56 (1936), pp. 462–71
"Explorations in Eastern Palestine, III," *BASOR*, No. 64 (1936), pp. 9–10

1937 "Explorations in Eastern Palestine, III (continued)," *BASOR*, No. 65 (1937), pp. 8–29
"Archaeological Exploration and Excavation in Palestine, Transjordan and Syria during 1936" (with W. F. Albright), *AJA*, 41 (1937), pp. 146–53
"An Aerial Reconnaissance in Southern Transjordan," *BASOR*, No. 66 (1937), pp. 27–28
"Mining in Ancient Palestine," *Palestine and Middle East Economic Magazine*, ix:6 (June 1937), pp. 302–4
"A Newly Discovered Nabataean Temple of Atargatis and Hadad at Khirbet et-Tannûr, Transjordania," *AJA*, 41 (1937), pp. 361–76
Review of Elihu Grant, *Rumeileh* (Ain Shems), and W. F. Badè, *A Manual of Excavation in the Near East*, in *The Jewish Quarterly Review*, 28 (1937), pp. 87–90
"Syrian Gods in a Nabataean Temple," *ILN* (August 21, 1937), pp. 298–300
"Copper and Iron Mines in Ancient Edom," *Trade, Industry and Crafts in Ancient Palestine*, Library of Palestinology, ix–x (1937), pp. 51–60 (Hebrew)
"The Nabataean Temple of Khirbet et-Tannûr," *BASOR*, No. 67 (1937), pp. 6–16
"An Aerial Reconnaissance in Southern Transjordan (continued)," *BASOR*, No. 67 (1937), pp. 19–26
"Explorations in the Land of Ammon," *BASOR*, No. 68 (1937), pp. 13–21
"Report of the Director of the School in Jerusalem," *BASOR*, No. 68 (1937), pp. 32–39

1938 "Archaeological Exploration and Excavation in Palestine, Transjordan and Syria during 1937," *AJA*, 42 (1938), pp. 165–76
"The Early History of a Nabataean Temple" (Khirbet et-Tannûr), *BASOR*, No. 69 (1938), pp. 7–18
"January News-Letter from the School in Jerusalem," *BASOR*, No. 69 (1938), pp. 28–29
"February News-Letter from the School in Jerusalem," *BASOR*, No. 70 (1938), pp. 27–28
"King Solomon's Naval Base at Ezion-geber, *ILN* (July 30, 1938), p. 212
"Digging Up the Facts," *B'nai B'rith National Jewish Monthly*, 53 (1938), pp. 10–11, 28
"Ezion-geber: Solomon's Naval Base on the Red Sea," *BA*, 1 (1938), pp. 13–16
"Ezion-geber," *Antiquity* (Sept. 1938), pp. 345–49
"King Solomon Appears in a New Role," *The New York Times Magazine* (Sept. 18, 1938), pp. 14–15, 19
"King Solomon's Naval Base on the Red Sea," *British Weekly* (Sept. 22, 1938), p. 461
"Nabataean Syria and Nabataean Transjordan," *JPOS*, 18 (1938), pp. 1–6
"The First Campaign at Tell el-Kheleifeh (Ezion-geber)," *BASOR*, No. 71 (1938), pp. 3–17
"Newsletter from Jerusalem," *BASOR*, No. 71 (1938), pp. 44–46
"Solomon Made a Fleet of Ships," *Hadassah Newsletter* (October 1938), pp. 13–14
"Solomon's Seaport: Ezion-geber," *Asia*, 38 (1938), pp. 591–95
"The Topography and History of Ezion-geber and Elath," *BASOR*, No. 72 (1938), pp. 2–13
"Newsletter from Jerusalem," *BASOR*, No. 72 (1938), pp. 20–21
"Report of the Director of the School in Jerusalem," *BASOR*, No. 72 (1938), pp. 28–34

1939 "Abomination," *The Universal Jewish Encyclopedia*, I (1939), pp. 31–32
"Archaeological Exploration and Excavation in Palestine, Transjordan and Syria during 1938," *AJA*, 43 (1939), pp. 146–57
"On the Occasion of the Centenary of Edward Robinson's First Journey to Palestine in 1838," *BASOR*, No. 74 (1939), pp. 2–4
"King Solomon's Seaport of Ezion-geber," *ILN* (Aug. 5, 1939), pp. 246–47
Review of M. A. Murray, *Petra, the Rock City of Edom*, in *Journal of the Royal Geographic Society* (August 1939), pp. 171–72
"Gateway to Arabia: Ezion-geber," *Asia*, 39 (1939), pp. 528–32
"The Second Campaign at Tell el-Kheleifeh (Ezion-geber:Elath)," *BASOR*, No. 75 (1939), pp. 8–22
"The Earliest History of Jerash," *BASOR*, No. 75 (1939), pp. 22–30
"Surface Finds in Edom and Moab," *PEQ*, 71 (1939), pp. 188–92
Review of B. Maisler, *History of Palestine*, in *Qiriath Sefer*, 16 (1939), pp. 37–40 (Hebrew)

Explorations in Eastern Palestine, III (Annual of the American Schools of Oriental Research, XVIII–XIX), 1939

"The Nabataean Temple of Qaṣr Rabbah," *AJA,* 43 (1939), pp. 381–87

"Ezion-geber: Elath, the Gateway to Arabia," *BA,* 2 (1939), pp. 37–41

"Report of the Director of the School in Jerusalem," *BASOR,* No. 76 (1939), pp. 27–32

Review of Hans Rhotert (ed.), *Transjordanien Vorgeschichtliche Forschungen,* in *Antiquity* (Dec. 1939), pp. 416–24

1940 "Archaeological Exploration and Excavation in Palestine and Transjordan during 1939," *AJA,* 44 (1940), pp. 139–44

"The Pittsburgh of Old Palestine," *Scientific American* (Jan. 1940), pp. 22–24

The Other Side of the Jordan, New Haven: American Schools of Oriental Research, 1940

"Kenites and Kenizzites," *PEQ,* 72 (1940), pp. 22–24

"King Solomon's Pittsburgh," *New Haven Register,* Sept. 22, 1940

"The Third Season of Excavation at Tell el-Kheleifeh," *BASOR,* No. 79 (1940), pp. 2–18

"Ezion-geber: Singapore of Solomon," *Asia,* 40 (1940), pp. 663–69

"Ezion-geber: Elath, City of Bricks with Straw," *BA,* 3 (1940), pp. 51–55

"Ostraca from Elath," *BASOR,* No. 80 (1940), pp. 3–10

"Report of the Director of the School in Jerusalem," *BASOR,* No. 80 (1940), pp. 37–43

"Reports from Recipients of Grants from the Penrose Fund" (with Millar Burrows), *Yearbook, American Philosophical Society* (1940), pp. 132–33

1941 "Chosen People," *The Universal Jewish Encyclopedia,* III (1941), pp. 164–66

"Egypt," *The Universal Jewish Encyclopedia,* IV (1941), pp. 5–11

"The Nabataean Temple of Khirbet Tannur, Transjordan," *Bulletin of the Cincinnati Art Museum,* 12:1 (Jan. 1941), pp. 3–11

"The Excavations of Solomon's Seaport: Ezion-geber," *The Smithsonian Report for 1941,* pp. 453–78

"How Archaeology Has Contributed to Our Knowledge of the Bible and the Jew," *Central Conference of American Rabbis Yearbook,* (1941), pp. 299–327

"Ezion-geber: Solomon's Naval Base on the Red Sea," *Butrava,* 5 (Feb. 1941), pp. 15–18

Review of W. F. Albright, *From the Stone Age to Christianity,* in *Jewish Social Studies,* 3 (1941), pp. 329–30

"Excavations in Palestine and Transjordan in 1940," *AJA,* 45 (1941), pp. 116–17

"Ostraca from Elath (continued)," *BASOR,* No. 82 (1941), pp. 3–11

"Clarence Stanley Fisher in Memoriam," *BASOR,* No. 83 (1941), pp. 2–4

1942 "Tell el-Kheleifeh," *QDAP,* 9 (1942), pp. 215–16

"Nabataean Syria," BASOR, No. 85 (1942), pp. 3–8

"Further Explorations in Eastern Palestine," *BASOR,* No. 86 (1942), pp. 14–24

"Sir W. M. Flinders Petrie," *BASOR*, No. 87 (1942), pp. 6–7

Review of C. H. Gordon, *The Living Past*, in *The Jewish Quarterly Review*, 32 (1942), pp. 449–50

"Report of the School in Jerusalem," *BASOR*, No. 88 (1942), pp. 6–7

1943 "A Letter from the East," *Hebrew Union College Bulletin*, II:2 (1943), pp. 1–3

"Jabesh-Gilead," *BASOR*, No. 89 (1943), pp. 2–6

"Three Israelite Towns in the Jordan Valley: Zarethan, Succoth, Zaphon," *BASOR*, No. 90 (1943), pp. 2–23

"Archaeological Activity in Palestine and Transjordan in 1941–1942," *AJA*, 47 (1943), pp. 125–31

"Some Ancient Towns in the Plains of Moab," *BASOR*, No. 91 (1943), pp. 7–26

"The Jordan," *BA*, 6 (1943), pp. 62–67

"Report of the Director of the School in Jerusalem," *BASOR*, No. 92 (1943), pp. 4–6

"Ramoth-Gilead," *BASOR*, No. 92 (1943), pp. 10–16

"On the Site of Asophon in the Jordan Valley," *BASOR*, No. 92 (1943), pp. 26–27

1944 "On the Trail of King Solomon's Mines," *The National Geographic Magazine* (Feb. 1944), pp. 233–56

"This is the Land," *Hebrew Union College Bulletin*, IV:1 (1944), pp. 1–2

"The Geography of the Jordan," *The National Geographic Magazine* (Dec. 1944), pp. 719–44

"Report of the Director of the School in Jerusalem," *BASOR*, No. 96 (1944), pp. 3–4

"Wadi Sirhan in North Arabia," *BASOR*, No. 96 (1944), pp. 7–17

1945 "A Chalcolithic Settlement in the Jordan Valley," *BASOR*, No. 97 (1945), pp. 10–22

"Report of the Director of the School in Jerusalem," *BASOR*, No. 100 (1945), pp. 3–5

"A Settlement of Middle Bronze I in the Jordan Valley," *BASOR*, No. 100 (1945), pp. 7–16

"What Is Biblical Archaeology," *Kohelet* (1945), pp. 1–32 (Hebrew)

The Other Side of the Jordan, New Haven: American Schools of Oriental Research (lithoprint), 1945

The Other Side of the Jordan, Bialik Foundation, 1945 (Hebrew)

1946 "Adding Link to Link," *Liberal Judaism*, 13:10 (1946), pp. 9–15, 39

"Band-Slip Ware in the Jordan Valley and Northern Gilead," *BASOR*, No. 101 (1946), pp. 3–20

"The Holy Land," *Hebrew Union College Bulletin*, V:3 (1946), p. 14

"The Jordan Valley," *Land and Life*, 113 (1946), pp. 13–18

The River Jordan, Philadelphia: The Westminster Press, Lutterworth Press, Jewish Publication Society of America, 1946

The River Jordan, Bialik Foundation, 1946 (Hebrew)

"Transjordan," *BA*, 9 (1946), pp. 45–61
"Report of the Director of the School in Jerusalem," *BASOR*, No. 104 (1946), pp. 3–5
"Some Chalcolithic Sites in Northern Gilead," *BASOR*, No. 104 (1946), pp. 12–20

1947 "A Word of Tribute," *Hebrew Union College Bulletin*, vi:4 (1947), p. 3
"New Year's Message from President Glueck," *Hebrew Union College Bulletin*, vii:1 (1947), p. 1
"Opening Day Message," *Hebrew Union College* (Oct. 4, 1947), pp. 1–11
"The Civilization of the Edomites," *BA*, 10 (1947), pp. 77–84
"An Archaeologist Looks at Palestine," *The National Geographic Magazine* (Dec. 1947), pp. 739–52
"Report of the Director of the School in Jerusalem," *BASOR*, No. 108 (1947), pp. 2–5

1948 *The Inaugural Address of Nelson Glueck as Fourth President of the Hebrew Union College* (March 13, 1948), pp. 1–11
Founder's Day Address at Jewish Institute of Religion (March 21, 1948), pp. 1–5
Review of Seton Lloyd, *Foundations in the Dust*, in *Middle East Journal*, 2 (1948), pp. 488–90
Review of C. C. McCown, *Tell en-Nasbeh*, in *Union Seminary Quarterly Review*, 3 (1948), pp. 41–42
"Rosh Hashonah Sermon," Temple Israel, Boston (Oct. 3, 1948), pp. 1–6

1949 "Judah Leon Magnes," *BASOR*, No. 114 (1949), p. 3
"Stephen Samuel Wise" (with Shalom Spiegel), *American Academy for Jewish Research, Proceedings*, xviii (1949), pp. xxiii–xxv
"Yom Kippur Address," Temple Beth Elohim, Charleston, S.C., Oct. 1, 1949
"A Message from Dr. Nelson Glueck," *Chicago Sinai Congregation Bulletin*, vii:10 (1949), p. 1

1950 Review of B. S. Vester, *Our Jerusalem, An American Family in the Holy City 1881–1949*, in *Middle East Journal*, 4 (1950), pp. 259–60
The Spirit and Purpose of Free Synagogue, Sermon of Dedication of Stephen Wise Free Synagogue (Jan. 21, 1950), pp. 1–8
"How Can Organized Religion Advance American Democracy?" *Liberal Judaism*, 18:1 (June 1950), pp. 4–5

1951 *Explorations in Eastern Palestine, IV* (*Annual of the American Schools of Oriental Research*, xxv–xxviii) Parts 1–2, 1951
"Go, View the Land," *BASOR*, No. 122 (1951), pp. 14–18
"No Compromise with Principle," *Central Conference of American Rabbis Yearbook*, lxi (1951), pp. 393–96
Review of L. A. Mayer, J. Pinkerfeld, J. W. Hirschberg, *Some Principal Muslim Religious Buildings in Israel*, in *Middle Eastern Affairs*, 2 (1951), pp. 106–7
"Some Biblical Sites in the Jordan Valley," *Hebrew Union College Annual*, xxiii, Part I (1951), pp. 105–29

1952 "The American Law and Tradition Concerning State and Church,
       Religion in the Public Schools," *Jewish Education,* 23:3 (1952), pp. 17–18
"Come Let Us Reason Together," *Central Conference of American Rabbis
       Yearbook,* LXII (1952), pp. 332–39
Review of C. S. Coon, *Caravan: The Story of the Middle East,* in *Middle
       Eastern Affairs,* 3 (1952), pp. 118–19
"Note by Nelson Glueck," *Year Presents a Picture History of Bible and
       Christianity* (1952), p. 7
"The Zodiac of Khirbet et-Tannûr," *BASOR,* No. 126 (1952), pp. 5–10
"Biblical Settlements in the Jordan Valley," *Bulletin of the Israel Exploration
       Society,* 2 (1952), pp. 102–7 (Hebrew)
"Discovery in a Thunderstorm," *This I Believe,* Edward R. Murrow, comp.,
       (1952), pp. 59–60

1953 "Israel's Hidden Treasures," *Hadassah Newsletter,* 33 (1953), pp. 8–9
"Religious Leaders Helped Ohio Grow and Prosper," *Cincinnati Times-Star*
       (Feb. 28, 1953), pp. 8, 18
"Archaeology and History," *Israel Life and Letters* (May–June 1953),
       pp. 12–13
"Deuteronomy 23:8, 9," *Mordecai M. Kaplan Jubilee Volume* (1953), pp.
       261–62
"The Present and Future of the Hebrew Union College–Jewish Institute of
       Religion," *Central Conference of American Rabbis Yearbook,* LXIII (1953),
       pp. 310–18
"In the Footsteps of the Former Dwellers of the Negev," *Ba-Machaneh* (Aug.
       20, 1953), pp. 2–5 (Hebrew)
"Exploring the Negev," *The Jerusalem Post,* Sept. 4, 1953
"Wells and Waterholes, a Testimony of Prior Habitation," *Ba-Machaneh*
       (Sept. 9, 1953) pp. 1–2, 19 (Hebrew)
"In the Negev 5000 Years Ago," *Ba-Machaneh* (Sept. 22, 1953), pp. 1–2
       (Hebrew)
"Mineral Finds in Southern Negev," *The Jerusalem Post* (Sept. 28, 1953), p. 4
"Archaeology in Israel," *Israel Life and Letters* (Oct.–Nov. 1953), pp. 2–4
"Explorations in Western Palestine," *BASOR,* No. 131 (1953), pp. 6–15
"Nabataeans Were More than Rich Traders," *The Jerusalem Post* (Dec. 18,
       1953), p. 6

1954 "The Araba," *Encyclopedia of Islam,* I (1954), p. 558
"From the President of the Hebrew Union College, Cincinnati," *The Synagogue
       Review,* 28:7 (London, March 1954), p. 204
"An Archaeologist Looks at the Near East," *Land Reborn,* 5:2 (1954), p. 6
"The Bible in the Light of Modern Archaeological Discoveries," *Journal of
       Educational Sociology,* 27 (1954), pp. 360–68
"Biblical Archaeology and Progressive Judaism," *Aspects of Progressive Jewish
       Thought,* World Union for Progressive Judaism (1954), pp. 154–58
"Chalcolithic Settlements in the Negeb Discovered," *The Explorers Journal,*
       32 (1954), pp. 7–9
"The Early Nabataean Kingdom," *Ba-Machaneh* (April 22, 1954), p. 20
       (Hebrew)

"Two Hundred Ancient Cities in the Negev," *Davar* (Aug. 13, 1954), pp. 2, 6 (Hebrew)

"The Age of Abraham in the Negev," *Davar*, Aug. 20, 1954 (Hebrew)

"In the Footsteps of Abraham our Father, He Continued to Travel Toward the Negev," *Davar* (Aug. 26, 1954), pp. 7–9 (Hebrew)

"The Negev 4000 Years Ago," *Davar* (Aug. 27, 1954), p. 3 (Hebrew)

"Along an Ancient Highway, from Machtesh Ramon Southward," *Davar* (Sept. 3, 1954), p. 3 (Hebrew)

"The Negev Was Not Desolate," *Davar*, Sept. 17, 1954 (Hebrew)

"The City of Abraham in the Negev," *Israel Life and Letters* (Sept.–Oct. 1954), p. 4

"Digging for Buried Treasure" (filmstrip), *Union of American Hebrew Congregations* (1954), pp. 5–12

The Other Side of the Jordan, Bialik Foundation, 1954 (Hebrew)

1955 "He Continued to Travel Toward the Negev," *Sheluchot* (Jan. 1955), pp. 9–12 (Hebrew)

"The Search for Antiquities of the Negev," *La-Merchav*, Jan. 21, 1955 (Hebrew)

"The Negev Will Flower Again," *Hadassah Newsletter* (Sept. 1955), pp. 3, 15

"The Age of Abraham in the Negeb," *BA*, 18 (1955), pp. 2–9

"Further Explorations in the Negeb," *BASOR*, No. 137 (1955), pp. 10–22

Review of Wendell Phillips, *Qataban and Sheba*, in *The New York Times Book Review* (March 6, 1955), p. 3

"The Negev in the Days of Abraham," *La-Merchav* (April 6, 1955), p. 4 (Hebrew)

"The Third Season of Explorations in the Negeb," *BASOR*, No. 138 (1955), pp. 7–29

"Convocation Sermon, April, 1955," *Hebrew Union College Bulletin*, VII:4 (1955), pp. 2–5

"Journey to Abraham's Times," *Israel Life and Letters* (April–May 1955), pp. 6–8

"New Frontiers—In the Jerusalem School," *American Annual Manual, The World Union for Progressive Judaism* (May 1955), pp. 9–11

"Early Settlement in the Southern Negev," *La-Merchav* (July 22, 1955), p. 3 (Hebrew)

"Past Civilizations of the Negev, Part I," *Ba-Machaneh* (Aug. 17, 1955), p. 9 (Hebrew)

"Part II: The Nabataeans," *Ba-Machaneh* (Aug. 31, 1955), p. 7 (Hebrew)

"Sydlandet," *Statens Historiska Museum from Bibelns Land* (Stockholm, Aug. 26, 1955), pp. 19–20

"Filling in the Empty Spaces of the Negev," *The Jerusalem Post* (Sept. 2, 1955), p. 5

"The Site of the Copper Smelters from the Days of Solomon," *Ba-Machaneh* (Sept. 5, 1955), p. 9 (Hebrew)

"Settlement in the South: The Nabataeans," *The Jerusalem Post*, Sept. 9, 1955

"Solomon's Copper Mines in the Arava," *The Jerusalem Post* (Sept. 16, 1955), p. 5

"The Negev in Antiquity," *La-Merchav* (Sept. 16, 1955), p. 3 (Hebrew)

"Settlements in the Time of the Patriarchs in the Negev," *Ba-Machaneh* (Sept. 28, 1955), p. 12 (Hebrew)

"They Knew How to Preserve the Soil," *La-Merchav* (Sept. 30, 1955), p. 3 (Hebrew)

"Was There Water in Wadi Bekarah?" *La-Merchav* (Oct. 7, 1955), p. 4 (Hebrew)

"Strategic Roads," *Ba-Machaneh* (Oct. 12, 1955), p. 8 (Hebrew)

"The Negeb in the Frame of History," Hebrew Union College–Jewish Institute of Religion (Oct. 1955), pp. 1–15

"On the Way to the Sinai Desert," *La-Merchav* (Oct. 21, 1955), p. 3 (Hebrew)

"Uncovering the History of the Negev," *La-Merchav* (Nov. 4, 1955), p. 3 (Hebrew)

Review of Millar Burrows, *The Dead Sea Scrolls*, and E. L. Sukenik (ed.), *The Dead Sea Scrolls of the Hebrew University*, in *The New York Times Book Review* (Nov. 20, 1955), p. 54

1956 "The Area between Beersheba and Kurnub," *La-Merchav* (Jan. 6, 1956), p. 3 (Hebrew)

"A Nabataean Painting," *BASOR*, No. 141 (1956), pp. 13–23

"Filling in the Empty Spaces of the Negev," *Bibliotheca Orientalis*, 13 (1956), pp. 85–86

"The Fourth Season of Exploration in the Negeb," *BASOR*, No. 142 (1956), pp. 17–35

"Ancient Highways in the Wilderness of Zin," *Proceedings of the American Philosophical Society*, 100 (1956), pp. 150–55

"The Negev: Immense Past, Immense Promise," *The New York Times Magazine* (May 6, 1956), pp. 1, 10, 11, 60, 62, 64

Review of Leonard Cottrell, *The Mountains of Pharaoh*, in *The New York Times Book Review* (May 6, 1956), pp. 6, 31

"The New Old Negev," *Midstream*, 2:3 (1956), pp. 2–4, 99

"The First Settlers of the Negev," *La-Merchav*, Aug. 3, 1956 (Hebrew)

"What We Found between Tel Yeruham and Kurnub," *La-Merchav* (Aug. 17, 1954), p. 4 (Hebrew)

"O Novo Velho Neguev," *Aonde Vamos?* 15:688 (Aug. 30, 1956), pp. 2, 26–27 (Portuguese)

"Settlements in the Negev in the Bronze Age," *Eretz-Israel*, 4 (*Ben Zvi Jubilee*, 1956), pp. 34–36

"The Nabataeans of the Negev," *Hadassah Newsletter* (Sept. 1956), pp. 3, 10

"Judaean Kingdom Fortresses in the Negev," *La-Merchav* (Sept. 19, 1956), p. 3 (Hebrew)

"The Holy Mountain in the Negev," *La-Merchav* (Oct. 5, 1956), p. 3 (Hebrew)

Review of Werner Keller, *The Bible as History*, in *The New York Times Book Review* (Oct. 28, 1956), pp. 1, 38

1957 "Memorial Tribute," *In Memoriam, Leo Baeck* (1957), pp. 12–20

"Fifth Season of Exploration in the Negeb," *BASOR*, No. 145 (1957), pp. 11–25

Herbert R. Bloch, Feb. 3, 1889–Mar. 20, 1957, pp. 1–7

"Five Years of Archaeological Exploration in the Negev," *Antiquity and Survival*, 2 (1957), pp. 273–86

"Five Years of Archaeological Exploration in the Negev," *World Congress of Jewish Studies*, 2 (1957), English, pp. 11–12, Hebrew, pp. 8–9

"In the Footsteps of Abraham Our Father," *Hadoar*, 37:28 (1957), pp. 44–46 (Hebrew)

"A New Boundary of the Negev," *Ba-Machaneh* (Aug. 7, 1957), pp. 11–13 (Hebrew)

"Education Is Spur to Life of Thinking," *Cincinnati Post-Times-Star*, Nov. 8, 1957

1958 "Sixth Season of Archaeological Exploration in the Negeb," *BASOR*, No. 149 (1958), pp. 8–17

"Bible in the Desert," *The Day I Was Proudest to Be an American*, D. B. Robinson, ed. (New York: Doubleday, 1958), pp. 203–5

Review of Millar Burrows, *More Light on the Dead Sea Scrolls*, in *The New York Times Book Review* (May 11, 1958), p. 6

"Foreword to Lecture by Dr. Nelson Glueck at Wayne State University," May 6, 1958

"His Wisdom Which Was Great," *Frank L. Weil, 1894–1957, In Memoriam* (1958), pp. 9–12

"Studies in Negev Archaeology," *Ma'ariv* (Sept. 14, 1958), pp. 22–23 (Hebrew)

The Lion of Judah. Judah Leon Magnes, 1877–1948 (Nov. 6, 1958), pp. 1–16

Review of James B. Pritchard, *Archaeology and the Old Testament* and *The Ancient Near East: An Anthology of Texts and Pictures*, in *Saturday Review* (Nov. 15, 1958), pp. 23, 32

"Following Signposts of the Bible," *The New York Times Magazine* (Dec. 7, 1958), pp. 31–33, 36, 38

"Exploring the World of the Bible," *World Over* (Dec. 26, 1958), p. 11

"The Seventh Season of Archaeological Exploration in the Negeb," *BASOR*, No. 152 (1958), pp. 18–38

"Fifth Season of Archaeological Exploration in the Negev," *Eretz-Israel*, 5 (*Mazar Jubilee*, 1958), pp. 41–46

"Archaeology and the Bible," *National Educational Television Center*, ten kinescopes, 1958

1959 *Rivers in the Desert: A History of the Negev*, New York: Farrar, Strauss, Jewish Publication Society of America; London: Weidenfeld, 1959

"Victory in the Desert," *Central Conference of American Rabbis Journal*, (Jan. 1959), pp. 3–9

"A Seal Weight from Nebi Rubin," *BASOR*, No. 153 (1959), pp. 35–38

"Ninth Annual Testimonial Dinner Address," National Conference of Christians and Jews (May 18, 1959), pp. 9–14

"A Big Day in the Desert," *Cincinnati Enquirer*, Aug. 30, 1959

"Rivers in the Desert," *Technion Yearbook*, 16 (1959), pp. 56–60, 143–49

"Message from the Negev," *Jewish Exponent*, Oct. 2, 1959

"An Aerial Reconnaissance of the Negev," *BASOR*, No. 155 (1959), pp. 2–13

"The Bible as Divining Rod," *Horizon*, 2:2 (1959), pp. 4–19
"The Negev," *BA*, 22 (1959), pp. 82–97
"The Untold Story of Christ's World," *Look* (Dec. 22, 1959), pp. 25–27

1960   "Book of Faith and of History, New Discoveries Do Not Undermine
the Essential Truth of the Bible," *The New York Times Magazine* (Sept.
25, 1960), pp. 29, 76, 77
"Archaeological Exploration of the Negev in 1959," *BASOR*, No. 159 (1960),
pp. 3–14
"Authority and Freedom," *Central Conference of American Rabbis Yearbook*,
LXX, 1960, pp. 162–70
"The Bible and Archaeology," *Five Essays on the Bible* (1960), pp. 60–80
"Factors Influencing the Rise of Civilization in the Upland: Illustrated by the
Negev," *City Invincible*, Carl H. Kraeling, ed. A Symposium on Urbaniza-
tion and Cultural Development in the Ancient Near East (Oriental Insti-
tute of the University of Chicago, 1960), pp. 46–60
"Signposts of the Bible," *The Jewish Digest* (Dec. 1960), pp. 59–66
Rivers in the Desert: A History of the Negev, Tel Aviv: Hakibbutz Ha-
meuchad, 1960 (Hebrew)
Rivers in the Desert: A History of the Negev, New York: Grove Press, Inc.,
1960
Explorations in Eastern Palestine, IV, Part I, Tel Aviv: Hakibbutz Hameuchad,
1960 (Hebrew)

1961   *Das Wort ḥesed im alttestamentlichen Sprachgebrauche als menschliche
und göttliche gemeinschaftgemässe Verhaltungsweise* (Berlin: Alfred
Töpelmann, 1961)—reprint of *ZAW*, 47 (1927)
"Inaugural Benediction," *Congressional Record*, CVII, p. 971
"Inaugural Benediction," *Prayers for All Occasions*, pp. 18–19
Letter to the Editor, *The Christian Century* (March 29, 1961), pp. 399–400
"Invoking the Blessing for the President," *Hebrew Union College Bulletin*,
(March 1961), pp. 14–15
"Tribute to William Foxwell Albright" (with G. E. Wright), *BASOR*, No. 162
(1961), pp. 1–2
"Archaeological Exploration of the Negev," *ILN*, Part I (May 27, 1961),
pp. 880–83, Part II (June 3, 1961), pp. 934–37
"The Archaeological History of the Negev," *Hebrew Union College Annual*,
XXXII (1961), pp. 11–18
"The Effect of Modern Discoveries on Judaism," *Aspects of Progressive
Judaism and Human Responsibility* (1961), pp. 83–98
"Exploring Southern Palestine (The Negev)," *The Biblical Archaeologist
Reader*, I (New York: Doubleday Anchor, 1961), pp. 1–11
"Following Signposts of the Bible," *Fields of Learning*, H. J. Gottlieb and
E. Knowles, eds. (New York: Harper, 1961), pp. 72–80
"King Solomon's Pittsburgh," *The Treasures of Time*, Leo Deuel, ed. (Cleve-
land: World, 1961), pp. 191–206
"The Nabataean Temple at Khirbet Tannur," *Third World Congress of
Jewish Studies* (1961), p. 1

"Rosh Hashonah Message," *The Southwest Jewish Chronicle,* 35:3 (1961)

1962 "Albright, William Foxwell," *Encyclopaedia Britannica* (1962), s.v.
"Edom," *Encyclopaedia Britannica* (1962), s.v.
Review of Roland de Vaux, *Ancient Israel,* in *The New York Times Book Review* (Feb. 11, 1962), pp. 3, 30
"Archaeology in the Negev," *Jewish Frontier,* 29:2 (1962), pp. 28–29
"The Bible and Archaeology," *Beth Mikra,* I (1962), pp. 19–33 (Hebrew)
"Nabataean Torques," *BA,* 25 (1962), pp. 57–64
"Champion of Man's Brotherhood" (Stephen Wise Used His Talents for Israel and the Jews), *The Jerusalem Post,* July 6, 1962
"Nelson Glueck, Archaeologist," *Is My Job for You?* R. M. Gardner, ed. (New York: Day, 1962), pp. 96–101
Rivieren in de wildernis, Kampen: J. H. Kok, 1962 (Dutch)

1963 Review of Paul W. Lapp, *Palestinian Ceramic Chronology 200 B.C.– A.D. 70, AJA,* 67 (1963), pp. 104–5
"Biblical Archaeology and Reform Judaism," *In the Time of Harvest,* D. J. Silver, ed. (New York: Macmillan, 1963), pp. 194–99
Review of E. Anati, *Palestine Before the Hebrews,* in *The New York Times Book Review* (June 2, 1963), p. 6
"The Role of the Hebrew Union College in Jerusalem," *Central Conference of American Rabbis Journal,* (Oct. 1963), pp. 10–14
"Elath and Ezion-geber," *Elath: The Eighteenth Archaeological Convention* (1963), pp. 9–20 (Hebrew)
"Jews Mourn the Death of Kennedy," *B'nai B'rith Messenger,* Nov. 26, 1963
"Nabataean Dolphins," *Eretz-Israel,* 7 (*L. A. Mayer Memorial Volume,* 1963), pp. 40–43
"Solomon's Mines," *The World of the Past,* J. H. Hawkes, ed. (New York: Knopf, 1963), pp. 438–40

1964 "The Civilization of the Edomites," *The Biblical Archaeologist Reader,* II (New York: Doubleday Anchor, 1964), pp. 51–58
"The College-Institute and Jewish Life as It Confronts the Challenges of Today," *The Observer,* Feb. 21, 1964
"History and Miracle in the Negev," *Essays in Honor of Solomon B. Freehof* (1964), pp. 195–201
Letter to *U. S. Catholic,* 30:5 (1964), p. 59
"The Archaeological History of the Negev," *Jewish Heritage,* 7:2 (1964), pp. 32–36
"Lessons from the Past," University of Southern California (1964), pp. 9–20
"Conclusions of the Archaeological Exploration in the Negev," *Az le-David, Jubilee Book in honor of David Ben Gurion* (1964), pp. 165–73 (Hebrew)
"Dead Sea Scrolls," *The World Book Encyclopedia* (1964), s.v.

1965 "Ezion-geber," *The Bible Today,* 16 (1965), pp. 1042–50
Review of E. A. Speiser (ed.), *At the Dawn of Civilization: The World History of the Jewish People,* I, in *The New York Times Book Review* (May 23, 1965), pp. 6, 7

Deities and Dolphins: The Story of the Nabataeans, New York: Farrar, Strauss, 1965
"Ezion-geber," *BA*, 28 (1965), pp. 70–87
"Further Explorations in the Negev," *BASOR*, No. 179 (1965), pp. 6–29

1966 *Deities and Dolphins: The Story of the Nabataeans*, London: Cassell, 1966
"Solomon's Foundries," *Hands on the Past*, K. W. Marek [C. W. Ceram], ed. (New York: Knopf, 1966), pp. 307–11
"Introduction," *Journal of the Palestine Oriental Society* (1966)—reprint of Vols. I–XX
Explorations in Eastern Palestine, IV, Parts 1–2, *Annual of American Schools of Oriental Research,* XXV–XXVIII, University Microfilms, 1966

1967 "Albright, William Foxwell," *Encyclopaedia Britannica* (1967), s.v.
"Edom," *Encyclopaedia Britannica* (1967), s.v.
"Nabataean Symbols of Immortality," *Eretz-Israel*, 8 (*Sukenik Memorial Volume*, 1967), pp. 37–41
Ḥesed in the Bible (Cincinnati: Hebrew Union College Press, 1967), pp. 35–107
"From an Archaeologist's Diary," *The Voice*, 2:1 (1967), p. 7
"Some Edomite Pottery from Tell el-Kheleifeh," *BASOR*, No. 188 (1967), pp. 8–38
"Transjordan," *Archaeology and Old Testament Study* (1967), pp. 428–53
"Iron II Pottery from Tell el-Kheleifeh," *Yediot*, 31:1–4 (1967), pp. 124–27 (Hebrew)

1968 *The River Jordan* (revised), New York: McGraw-Hill, 1968
Rivers in the Desert: A History of the Negev (with corrections), New York: Norton, 1968
"Tell el-Kheleifeh, Elath, Eçyôn-Gébèr," *Bible et Terre Sainte*, 102 (1968), pp. 1–2, 6–16, 21 (French)
"Why I Am a Biblical Archaeologist," *Cincinnati*, 1:9 (1968), pp. 51–59
"Jews of North and South America," *Diaspora Jewry and Eretz Yisrael* (1968), pp. 11–15 (Hebrew)
"The Dawn of Conscience," *Rosh Hashanah Annual*, IV (South Africa, 1968), pp. 33–34
Dateline: Jerusalem, Cincinnati: Hebrew Union College Press, 1968

1969 Review of Abba Eban, *My People: The Story of the Jews*, in *The New York Times Book Review* (January 12, 1969), p. 10
"Some Ezion-geber:Elath Iron II Pottery," *Eretz-Israel*, 9 (*W. F. Albright Volume*, 1969), pp. 51–59
"The Bible in the Light of Modern Archaeological Discoveries," Uriel Simri, ed. *Proceedings of the First International Seminar on the History of Physical Education and Sport* (1969), pp. 7–13
Preface in *Israel: The Reality*, Cornell Capa, ed., Cleveland: World, 1969

INDEX

G. means Nelson Glueck

M